D0652845

WIT

THEMES

ISSUES

and

DEBATES

in

PSYCHOLOGY

RICHARD GROSS

Hodder & Stoughton

A MEMBER OF THE HODDER HEADLINE GROUP

Dedication

To all those psychologists, philosophers, scientists and other academics, past and present, whose intellectual efforts I have tried to distill into this single, relatively short, book. I hope that I have represented their ideas with a reasonable degree of accuracy, and I apologise for any inaccuracies that may not have been filtered out.

To Jan, for her continuing – and seemingly endless – love and support, without which the completion of this project, while providing me with intellectual challenge and satisfaction, would not have assumed the overall meaning that it has.

To all those who care about me and understand the importance for me of my academic pursuits, with love.

British Library Cataloguing in Publication Data

Gross, Richard D.
 Psychology: Themes, Issues and Debates
 I. Title
 150

ISBN 0 340 62031 5

First published 1995
Impression number   10   9   8   7   6   5   4   3   2   1
Year   1999   1998   1997   1996   1995

Typeset by Wearset, Boldon, Tyne and Wear
Printed in Great Britain for Hodder & Stoughton Educational, a division of Hodder Headline Plc, 338 Euston Road, London NW1 3BH by Bath Press Ltd, Avon

Contents

Introduction

The idea for *Themes, Issues and Debates in Psychology*, I now realise, was incubating for a long time, although it seemed to come in a sudden flash of inspiration (which doesn't happen too often to this author!).

It grew from two main and related sources; firstly, an awareness of the many and important interconnections between different topics/theories/ areas of research, and secondly, being asked to give talks at student conferences.

I have taught psychology for more than twenty years, and A level for about eighteen of those. As that time has elapsed, the more I have come to regard the traditional way of carving up the discipline into distinct sections/topics/areas etc. as artificial and almost a distortion of psychology 'as it really is'.

As a way of trying to help my own students, and those attending the conferences at which I speak, cope with the huge amount of material that has to be absorbed, I more and more adopted a *thematic* approach: if we can find links and connections between topics/sections of the syllabus, which are 'officially' separate and distinct, that mass of material may seem less daunting. Just as importantly, thinking about how, say, ethical issues, methodology, and culture and gender, are always relevant when evaluating or critically discussing any theory, no matter which section of the syllabus/area of psychology it 'belongs to', should help you to write better essays, seminar papers or practical reports.

When having to 'do' attribution, say, or attachment, in a 35-minute talk, what's likely to be the most productive way of approaching the task? Instead of seeing it as a 'topic' to be covered in a tiny fraction of the time I would normally have to teach it in, I assume that at least most of the audience will already be familiar with most of the material (at least in outline), and then I proceed to point out how attribution (or whatever it is I'm supposed to be talking about) can be found under many different headings, in relation to many different topic areas, including some that may come as a surprise.

This, in essence, is the approach that I have adopted in this book. I am assuming at least some degree of familiarity with many of the theories, concepts, ideas and studies that are used to illustrate a particular theme, issue or debate, although sometimes I have chosen to describe these in detail.

The point here is that *Themes, Issues and Debtes in Psychology* is meant to *complement* other textbooks that you will need to use to provide the basic material in the degree of detail required. The topic-based approach of traditional textbooks, and the thematic approach of this one, can sit side by side quite happily at various points in your course. If it is truly complementary, it can help 'set the scene' for a new topic by pointing out some of the critical questions that need to be asked, make connections across topics and different sections of the syllabus, as well as summarize some of the major theories, studies and so on. This should make it easier for you to digest the larger, topic-based textbook.

Themes, Issues and Debates is not meant to be used *after* you have absorbed all the material from the main textbook, but rather as a way of synthesizing, integrating, as well as revising (some of) that material *as you go along*.

Because it isn't written for any syllabus in particular, I have enjoyed the luxury of being free to explore certain themes, issues and debates (such as feminist psychology and cross-cultural psychology) which are often neglected or which get submerged under the ocean of topic-based material. Instead of just touching on these in passing, I have been able to devote a whole chapter to each one; this means that there will be material that isn't familiar to most readers from other textbooks, but this is often related to other material that is.

At the same time, most chapters 'spill over' into each other, which illustrates the point I made earlier about the difficulty of breaking psychology up into discrete 'chunks'. For example, sexism, heterosexism (the focus of Chapter 6, *Psychology, Women and Feminism*) and ethnocentrism (the focus of Chapter 8, *Cross-Cultural Psychology*) are all discussed in Chapter 7, *Normality and Abnormality*. Similarly, while Chapter 11 is devoted to *Psychology as Science*, this is a recurrent theme throughout the book.

The end-of-chapter summaries are longer, and more detailed, than is usual in textbooks. I feel that this is important, firstly because of the complexity of the ideas and issues being discussed, and secondly because, in my opinion, the summaries that appear in many textbooks are too brief to be of any real value. I hope that they will represent a genuine aid to your learning and understanding.

Acknowledgements

I would like to thank Hugh Coolican and Paul Humphreys for their constructive comments and criticisms regarding the original proposal for this book, Rob McIlveen for his helpful comments on the proofs, Tim Gregson-Williams for supporting the proposal of a somewhat 'unorthodox' academic textbook, and Louise Tooms for her editorial support and cheerful, light-hearted manner. I would also like to thank Caroline Stephenson for tracking down pictorial material, and the important 'behind-the-scenes' people whom I didn't get to meet but whose efforts are essential for the production of a book such as this.

The person as psychologist

Introduction

Instead of starting this opening chapter with the customary definition of psychology as the scientific study of behaviour and mental processes, I would like to propose that a more useful way of thinking about the discipline of psychology is to see it as part of the sum total of what people do. Like other scientific disciplines, *psychology is a human activity*, although a rather special one (as we shall see below).

Similarly, psychologists (again like other scientists) are, first and foremost, *people* – they are people long before they ever become psychologists and being a psychologist is only a part of their total activity as a person. It follows from this, that if we are to properly understand what psychology is, and how it has changed during its history, as well as its achievements and limitations, we need to understand (among other things) *psychologists as people*.

But (you are probably saying to yourself), this is what *psychologists* do – how can we understand psychologists as people before we have looked at what psychologists say about people (as people)? We seem to be facing a conundrum – are psychologists in some sense studying themselves? Exactly! One of the things that makes psychology unique among scientific activities is that the investigator and the subject matter are, in all essential details, the same: instead of having physicists studying gravity or light (which are definitely not human), or astronomers studying the stars and solar system (which are also definitely not human), we have a small number of human beings (psychologists) studying a much larger number of human beings (people) – but apart from these labels, there is no difference!

If that is so, surely we could learn something about psychologists as people by turning things around and looking at *people as psychologists*. In other words, if we are to understand psychologists as people before we can properly appreciate what they do as scientists, why not begin by looking for ways in which we are *all* scientists, as part of our everyday social activity? This way of looking at 'ordinary' people (non-psychologists or lay people) is one which psychologists themselves have found very useful, and can be seen in two major areas: (i) that part of social psychology concerned with how we form impressions of other people's personality and how we explain the causes of their – and our own – behaviour (*person perception*), and (ii) that part of individual differences concerned with personality, specifically, Kelly's *personal construct theory*.

The lay person as psychologist: people as scientists

According to Gahagan (1984),

> *It has at times been observed that had the physical sciences not been developed to their contemporary level the world would be a very different place, one in which we would have little control over communications, disease, food production, and so forth. If, however, psychology as a scientific activity had not emerged, less difference between the contemporary world and the past would be detectable.*

This is not meant as a criticism of psychology, but rather as a way of drawing attention to a fundamental point, namely that 'human beings have the capacity to reflect on their own behaviour and reflect on its causes; the human being is essentially a psychologist and always has been' (Gahagan, 1984).

To the extent that we, as ordinary people, can already do the kinds of things that psychologists, as scientists, are trying to do (that is, reflect on the causes of behaviour), we are bound to be less affected than we are by sciences which, by definition, are the domain of people with special training and expertise. However, the examples given by Gahagan of the ways in which science has changed the world are all applications of scientific knowledge (namely, technology). What we should perhaps be asking, therefore, is whether there is an equivalent technology of psychology which has changed people's lives.

But is there another sense in which psychology could change our lives, namely by influencing the way we do psychology in our everyday lives – the way we think about ourselves and others, the kinds of explanations we propose of behaviour, the theories we construct about 'what makes people tick'? This is what Gahagan seems to be getting at when she states that 'the infant science of psychology (it is only about a hundred years old) has as yet had little effect on the existing heritage of lay people's psychology'. This leads very neatly to the views of another psychologist, Fritz Heider, who introduced the notion of *commonsense psychology*.

Commonsense psychology – looking for hidden causes of behaviour

Heider, a European who emigrated to the USA, was very much influenced by Gestalt psychology (see Chapter 2) and he wanted to apply this theory of object perception to the perception of people (*social or person perception*). His *The Psychology of Interpersonal Relations* (1958) marked a new era in social psychology (Leyens & Codol, 1988).

For Heider, the starting point for studying how people understand their social world is 'ordinary' people. How do people usually think about and infer meaning from what goes on around them? How do they make sense of their own and other people's behaviour? These questions relate to what Heider called commonsense psychology; he saw the 'ordinary' person (the lay person or 'person in the street') as a *naive scientist*, linking observable behaviour to unobservable causes (much as the professional scientist does):

Figure 1.1 Fritz Heider (1896–1989) introduced the notion of commonsense psychology

> *The causal structure of the environment, both as the scientist describes it and as the naive person apprehends it, is such that we are usually in contact only with what may be called the offshoots or manifestations of underlying core processes or core structures . . . Man is usually not content simply to register the observables that surround him . . . The underlying causes of events, especially the motives of other persons, are invariances of the environment that are relevant to him; they give meaning to what he experiences and it is these meanings that are recorded in his life space and are precipitated as the reality of the environment to which he then reacts.*

(Heider, 1958)

So, a fundamental feature of commonsense psychology is the belief that underlying people's overt behaviour are causes, and it is these causes, rather than the observable behaviour itself, which provide the meaning of what people do. Such basic assumptions about behaviour need to be shared by members of a culture, for without them, social interaction would be chaotic; indeed, commonsense psychology may be regarded as part of the belief system which forms part of the culture as a whole and which distinguishes one culture from another.

> *What interested him [Heider] was the fact that within our culture we all subscribe to essentially the same version of everyday psychology – for example, that human behaviour often reflects inner determinants such as abilities, wants, emotions, personalities, etc., rather than, say, witchcraft or the spirit forces of our ancestors . . .*

Of course, it is important that we do subscribe to a common psychology, since doing this provides an orientating context in which we can understand, and be understood by, others. Imagine a world in which your version of everyday psychology was fundamentally at odds with that of your friends – without a shared 'code' for making sense of behaviour, social life would hardly be possible . . .

(Bennett, 1993)

Of course, commonsense psychology (at least that shared by members of Western culture) does not involve the belief that internal, unobservable causes are the only causes of behaviour. Indeed, Heider identified two basic, potential sources or causes of behaviour, namely *personal* or *dispositional* (internal) and *situational* or *environmental* (external), and this distinction lies at the heart of *attribution theory*, which deals with the general principles that govern how the social perceiver selects and uses information to arrive at causal explanations (Fiske & Taylor, 1991). In other words, one of the major 'tasks' that we all face in our daily interactions with others is to decide whether their behaviour can be explained in terms of internal causes (such as abilities, emotions, personality, motivation and attitudes) or external causes (such as the behaviour of other people, the demands of the situation and physical aspects of the environment). This decision is the *attribution process* and it is what theories of attribution are trying to explain.

Understanding which set of factors should be used to interpret another person's behaviour will make the perceiver's world more predictable and give him or her greater control over it. These basic insights of Heider's provided the blueprint for the theories of attribution that followed (Hewstone & Antaki, 1988); these are discussed in Chapter 2.

According to Antaki (1984), attribution theory promises to 'uncover the way in which we, as ordinary men and women, act as scientists in tracking down the causes of behaviour; it promises to treat ordinary people, in fact, as if they were psychologists'. So, if we are all already psychologists, it is not surprising that the science of psychology should have had as little impact as Gahagan, for one, thinks it has; in other words, there already exists a body of 'knowledge' (a set of beliefs or assumptions is a more accurate term) that we all use for interpreting and predicting people's behaviour (commonsense or *folk* psychology), that forms part of our culture and so is highly resistant to change and which is deeply ingrained in our everyday interactions with others.

However, it may be possible to find examples of psychological theories which have proved so powerful that they could be seen as having become part of commonsense psychology. By being absorbed into the culture, they may well become detached from the identity of the psychologist(s) responsible for them, becoming part of

Oedipus, Schmoedipus– as long as he loves his Mother!

Figure 1.2

what we take for granted about the causes of behaviour. Popular beliefs such as 'male homosexuals had too close a relationship with their mothers as children', 'the child's first few years are critical' and 'boys need a father' can all be traced, more or less directly (and more or less accurately) to the psychoanalytic theory of Sigmund Freud. It is not the truth or falsity of this theory which is relevant here but the impact that these ideas have had on the thinking of ordinary people and non-psychologists in general.

There is no doubting the tremendous impact that Freud has had, both within psychology and without. According to Clift (1984):

> *He [Freud] has provided us with a set of ideas and concepts which, both in literature and everyday conversation have helped us to formulate questions about ourselves, our inner experience and our social conditioning. He helped to explode the myth of 'rational Man' and has brought us face to face with our irrational selves, a new image of ourselves at least as valid as any other major image-of-man that Social Science has offered and perhaps as challenging and disturbing as any it is ever likely to offer.*

Similarly, Thomas (1990) argues that:

> *Sigmund Freud is probably the most famous of all psychologists. His work has had an important influence on the development of psychology and, perhaps, an even more fundamental impact on Western culture . . . His ideas and development of them by other people have influenced our conception of morality, family life and childhood and thus perhaps the structure of our society; and they have changed our attitudes to mental illness. Freudian assumptions are now part of the fabric of literature and the arts.*

Freud's psychoanalytic theory is discussed in Chapters 12 and 13.

The conceptual tools of the everyday psychologist

In making sense of human action, the everyday psychologist draws upon a considerable range of constructs and conceptual 'tools', which can be seen as falling into two broad categories:

1 *psychological* (or *mentalistic*), which may be seen as properties of the individual (desires, emotions, personality, etc.); and
2 *social*, which refer to the properties of the group(s) and society to which we belong (social rules, norms, roles, etc.), that is, the sources of behaviour that lie outside the individual.

These two categories correspond very closely to the internal (dispositional) and external (situational) causes which Heider identified (see above).

EVERYDAY MENTALISTIC PSYCHOLOGY

According to Wellman (1990, cited by Bennett, 1993), at the heart of everyday thinking about action lie two vital constructs: desire and belief.

What people do results from their *believing* that certain actions will bring about ends that they *desire*; almost every time we ask someone why they did something, we will be trying to find out about their desire or belief – or both.

In everyday psychology, these are accepted as the causes of what we do: 'Beliefs and desires provide . . . the internal mental causes for overt actions' (Wellman, 1990, cited by Bennett, 1993). However, everyday psychology goes much further than this. The everyday psychologist also has some idea ('theory') about the causes of desires and beliefs; specifically, beliefs arise from perception, while desires result from basic emotions and physiological causes. Also, action is seen as producing certain *re*actions, typically, *emotional* ones: other people's emotions provide important cues about how to behave towards them (for instance, try to comfort them, or avoid them), and they provide insights into the strengths of their desires and beliefs.

Although emotion is clearly a basic construct of everyday psychology, there is more to the lay person's conceptual 'tool bag'. Other central constructs, perhaps the most important of all, are *thinking* and *intention*.

Thinking is an active process, in which the mind is engaged in a variety of directive processes, such as attention, interpretation, and storing information and recalling it. This means that beliefs, for example, can arise in the absence of direct perception and may result from inference (which *is* based on direct perception).

Intentions mediate between desire and action; they 'function to actualize (some but not all) desires' – they translate our wants into strategic courses of action that will help us to satisfy those wants, and this translation involves planning and other cognitive activity and information processing.

But does this elaborated version of everyday psychology need to be elaborated even further if it is to approximate the average adult's version? Wellman thinks so. For example, what about our attempts to understand recurrent patterns of behaviour (as distinct from specific acts)? We commonly identify *personality traits* in our attempt to explain and predict people's behaviour and, having done so, we are then in a position to predict all kinds of desires and beliefs that the person might have. Particular actions can now be understood in a broader psychological context than desires and beliefs on their own can provide – we may now see them as part of an overall, coherent picture, rather than as disconnected, discrete elements (see Chapter 4).

EVERYDAY SOCIAL PSYCHOLOGY

This is generally much more implicit than everyday mentalistic psychology and Wellman has much less to say about it. As most social psychologists would agree, action is to a considerable degree constrained by forces outside the individual, in the form of norms and social rules and conventions (see Chapter 4). According to Wegner and Vallacher (1977, quoted in Bennett, 1993), people are 'implicit situation theorists' who subscribe to 'a set of expectations concerning the rules of behaviour in

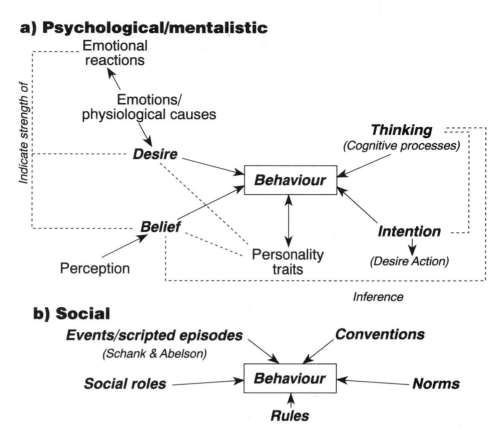

Figure 1.3 A schematized summary of Wellman's (1990) everyday psychology

various settings'. Expectations also apply to the behaviour (social roles) of people occupying particular positions in particular situations. Everyday social psychology also includes our understanding of *event episodes*, which are *scripted* episodes, 'a predetermined stereotyped sequence of actions' (Schank & Abelson, 1977; see Fig. 1.3), such as eating at a restaurant.

Implicit and explicit theories – some similarities between formal and informal psychology

We have seen that a crucial respect in which ordinary people can be regarded as scientists is their assumption that behaviour is caused either by internal or external factors, and the search for those causes (the attribution process). This can be seen as part of the process by which we form impressions of other people; only if we attribute internal causes to a person's behaviour can we use that behaviour as an indication of what the person is like, since external causes, by definition, refer to influences on behaviour other than the actor him- or herself.

However, there is much more involved in forming impressions of others than simply the attribution of causes.

> *When we form impressions of others we are making guesses or*
> *inferences based both on whatever selection of data, derived from our*
> *observation of them, are at hand and the theories that we already*
> *have about them. The study of person perception is the study of how*
> *the lay person uses theory and data in understanding other people.*
>
> (Gahagan, 1984)

FORMING IMPRESSIONS

The kind of theories that the lay person uses when forming impressions of others are commonly referred to as *intuitive theories* (see, for example, Nisbett & Ross, 1980) or, more commonly, *implicit personality theories*, the most investigated (and arguably the most important) kind being *stereotypes* and the related process of *stereotyping*, which Oakes et al. (1994) define as 'the process of ascribing characteristics to people on the basis of their group memberships'. For example, we observe a man wearing a grey, pinstripe suit and carrying a copy of the *Financial Times* and a briefcase (the data), label him as a 'businessman' and then infer that, like other business men, he votes Conservative (the theory). We already have an implicit theory of businessmen, a generalized belief about the characteristics shared by this particular group of human beings, so that when we observe a member of this group, without knowing anything at all about him as an individual, we immediately 'know' what he is like – the very limited data is supplemented by the theory, which then allows us to predict what this complete stranger is like and how he is likely to behave.

Being able to make such predictions at least gives us a sense of being in control, even if they are not actually put to the test and, within limits, even if they are not confirmed when they are. As a kind of *person schema*, stereotypes illustrate the general cognitive tendency to store knowledge and experience in the form of simplified, generalized representations – it would be impossible (as well as completely unnecessary) to store the details of each individual chair, cat or person we encounter. As Atkinson et al. (1990) say, 'Without schemata and schematic processing, we would simply be overwhelmed by the information that inundates us. We would be very poor information processors.'

The importance of schemas and other implicit theories lies not in their accuracy, but in their capacity for making the world a more manageable place in which to live. If psychologists are to understand human behaviour, they must look not at *how good* people are at explaining and predicting the world (especially the world of human behaviour), but rather at *how they go about* doing it.

> *We act and choose on the basis of what we see, feel and believe . . .*
> *When we are mistaken about things, we act in terms of our erroneous*
> *notions, not in terms of things as they are. To understand human*
> *action it is therefore essential to understand the conscious mode in*
> *which things appear to us.*
>
> (Asch, 1952)

An early advocate of the view that it is essential to understand people's constructions of the world was Schutz, a sociologist, according to whom:

> *All our knowledge . . . in common-sense as in scientific thinking, involves constructions . . . strictly speaking, there are no such things as facts, pure and simple. All facts are from the outset facts selected from a universal context by the activities of our minds . . . This does not mean that, in daily life or in science, we are unable to grasp the reality of the world. It just means that we grasp merely certain aspects of it, namely those which are relevant to us.*
>
> (Schutz, 1932, quoted in Bennett, 1993)

This highlights the 'conceptually driven' nature of our everyday understanding; it is guided not by the intrinsic properties of the world, but by our prior ideas and beliefs about it. This does not mean, however, that the data provided by the external environment is irrelevant (as the example of the businessman illustrates), only that the data is 'filtered' through our schemas and implicit theories, so that we are incapable of seeing things 'as they really are'.

If we accept this basic *constructionist* argument, then it is not very surprising that people disagree about 'the way the world is' in their everyday dealings with each other. When applied to science, the constructionist viewpoint raises some very important – and awkward – questions concerning the very nature of scientific activity.

As we shall discuss in detail in Chapter 11 (and to some extent in Chapters 6, 7 and 8 as well), the *positivist* view of science (including psychology) maintains that the distinguishing characteristic of science is its *objectivity*, whereby the scientist, equipped with appropriate empirical methods, has access to the world 'as it really is'. This assumes that the observations, measurements, experiments, etc. that the scientist performs are unbiased, that data can be collected without any kind of preconception or expectation influencing their collection.

However, by analogy with the lay person's use of theory and data to understand other people, the scientist (including the scientific psychologist) also collects data through the 'lens' of theory – there is simply no way of avoiding it. According to Popper (1972), for example, observation is always pre-structured and directed, and this is as true of physics as it is of psychology. Similarly, Deese (1972) argues that, despite the essential reliance of science on observation, data plays a more modest role than is usually believed. The function of empirical observation is not to find out what causes what or how things work in some ultimate sense, but simply to provide justification for some particular way of looking at the world. In other words, observation justifies (or not) a theory which the scientist already holds (just as the lay person already has his or her stereotype of particular social groups), and it is theories which determine what kinds of data are collected.

The interdependence between theory and data is shown in Deese's belief that (i) theory in the absence of data is not science, and (ii) data alone do not make a science. Both theory *and* data are necessary for science, and so-called facts do not exist independently of a theoretical interpretation of the data:

Fact = Data plus **Theory**

Having seen the crucial role of theory in science, plus the use of data and theory in both science and everyday psychology, it is important to ask if the implicit/intuitive theory of the lay person meets the criteria of a theory as defined by philosophers of science and psychologists.

According to Wellman (1990), three essential features of a theory are that it (i) has *coherence* (the different concepts making up the theory should be interconnected, so that it becomes impossible to consider a single concept in isolation, i.e. the meaning of any given concept is determined by its role in the theory as a whole); (ii) should make *ontological distinctions* (it 'carves' up phenomena into different kinds of entities and processes, i.e. it makes fundamental distinctions between different classes of things); (iii) provides a *causal explanatory framework* (it accounts for the phenomena it deals with by identifying their causes). Wellman believes that, in terms of all three criteria, everyday psychology can reasonably be considered to constitute a theory.

Implicit and explicit theories – some differences between formal and informal psychology

Even if we agree with Wellman that the implicit theories of the everyday psychologist share with scientific theories the three features described above, it is difficult to deny that the scope of everyday theories is nothing like as broad as that of academic psychology (Bennett, 1993). There are other important differences of which we should be aware.

APPLYING SCIENTIFIC METHOD

The lay person may be only dimly aware, or completely unaware, of the reasoning he or she has followed when making inferences about others, and this reasoning may change from situation to situation. Scientists are obliged to follow a set of rules governing the use of theory – the scientific method – such as *falsification*, i.e. being able to show that the theory is false, rather than merely finding data to support it (Popper, 1959). Everyday psychologists, on the other hand, tend to look for evidence which supports their position (i.e. *verification*,) but, of course, they are not obliged to follow the rules of scientific method.

THE PURPOSE OF PSYCHOLOGICAL THEORIES

Similarly, ordinary people are not obliged, unlike the professional psychologist, to spell out or articulate their theories (i.e. to make them explicit) because they formulate and use them for very different purposes. While the *psychologist as scientist* is trying to construct scientific laws of human behaviour and psychological processes (i.e. to understand and predict these as an end in itself), the *lay person as psychologist* is using theories as 'guidelines for their everyday transactions with others' (Gahagan, 1991).

For example, whereas you or I might steer clear of someone who looks very aggressive or whom we believe to be very short-tempered, the psychologist studying aggression may be interested in finding out what cues people use to judge others as aggressive-looking or why some people are, in fact, more aggressive than others. In other words, the theories of the informal psychologist 'guide his daily behaviour, and make the behaviour of others appear more intelligible and predictable than it would otherwise. We have to make sense of others' behaviour in order to act at all ourselves' (Gahagan, 1984).

So the major purpose served by intuitive or implicit theories is a practical or pragmatic one; they are used by people as psychologists in their ordinary, day-to-day life. By contrast, the formal psychologist (the psychologist as scientist) is interested in the theories themselves, testing them, trying to establish their validity, modifying them in the light of new or conflicting evidence, sometimes testing rival theories, etc. These are some of the basic features of formal scientific activity in general.

Berger and Luckmann (1966) talk about 'recipe knowledge', knowledge that gets results, as the primary purpose of lay theories. By contrast, scientists are interested in 'truth' (rather than usefulness); they want to construct as full an account as possible of the structures, processes, and contents associated with a particular phenomenon.

In short, everyday psychologists draw on their theories in an unselfconscious way ('theories as lived'), while scientists use theories *as theories*: whereas the former may use constructs about, say, what causes people to act as they do (the attribution process), the latter produces *constructs about constructs*, an explanation of everyday explanation (a 'second level' explanation) (theories of attribution).

While it may be true that professional psychologists are primarily concerned with establishing knowledge about psychological processes and only secondarily concerned with the uses to which it will be put (Gahagan, 1984), we should not forget that research is sometimes aimed at trying to solve essentially practical problems (e.g. blind mobility, design of machinery, shape and size of coins), that is, as *applied research*. Also, and perhaps more importantly, the majority of psychologists are actually employed in one or other applied fields of clinical, educational or occupational/industrial psychology, where psychological knowledge and principles are implemented in practical settings.

However, no hard-and-fast distinction should be drawn between applied and 'pure' research or between applied and 'academic' fields of psychology; they clearly overlap quite considerably in various ways.

The relationship between formal and informal psychology

Professionals and ordinary people have in common the task of trying to understand other people's motives and their personalities. The professional 'spies' on the lay person as he or she undertakes the task of 'being' a psychologist.

Person perception is the term given (by professional psychologists) to the study of the lay person as psychologist; hence, it represents the convergence of professional and lay, formal and informal, psychology (Gahagan, 1991).

According to Harré et al. (1985),

> *the task of scientific psychology consists of making the implicit psychologies of everyday life explicit, and then, in the light of that understanding, applying the techniques of theory-guided empirical research to develop, refine and extend that body of knowledge and practices.*

They cite Freud's theory of dreams as an obvious extension of our commonsense or folk beliefs about the source of dream contents. Commonsense forms 'part of the literature', i.e. a proper part of the body of knowledge available in the science of psychology; it is the platform from which the enterprise of psychology must start (Harré et al., 1985).

Man-the-scientist: Kelly's psychology of personal constructs

Three years before the publication of Heider's book in which he proposed the notions of commonsense psychology and the naive scientist, George Kelly wrote a book called *A Theory of Personality: The Psychology of Personal Constructs* (1955).

According to Kelly, not only are scientists human, but humans can also be thought of as scientists. Personal construct theory (PCT) is a theory about the personal theories of each one of us and one of its distinctive features is that applies as much to Kelly himself – as the originator of the theory – as it does to everyone else. If science is first and foremost a human activity, a form of behaviour, then any valid psychological theory must be able to account for that activity or behaviour which, of course, includes the construction of psychological (in the case of scientific psychology) theories. PCT can do this very easily (which is not true of most psychological theories) and so is said to be *reflexive*.

According to Weiner (1992),

> *It is puzzling that while psychologists try to explain the behaviour of their clients, or people in general, the theories they have formulated cannot account for their own scientific activity . . .*

Kelly's theory . . . can explain scientific endeavours, for Kelly considered the average person an intuitive scientist, having the goal of predicting and understanding behaviour. To accomplish this aim, the naive person formulates hypotheses about the world and the self, collects data that confirm or disconfirm these hypotheses, and then alters personal theories to account for the new data. Hence the average person operates in the same manner as the professional scientist, although the professional scientist may be more accurate and more self-conscious in their attempts to achieve cognitive clarity and understanding.

Our hypotheses about the world take the form of *constructs*; they represent our attempt to interpret events (including the behaviour of other people and ourselves) and these are continually being put to the test, every time we act.

Kelly's training was originally in physics and mathematics and he worked for a time as an engineer; in the light of this, it is not surprising that he should choose the psychological model of *man-the-scientist*. He wondered why it was that only those with university degrees should be privileged to feel the excitement and reap the rewards of scientific activity (Fransella, 1980): 'When we speak of *man-the-scientist* we are speaking of all mankind and not merely a particular class of men who have publicly attained the stature of "scientists". We are speaking of all mankind in its scientist-like aspects' (Kelly, 1955).

Figure 1.4   Frankenstein is a symbol of the scientist's ultimate aim to predict and control

This model of human beings not only seems intuitively valid (i.e. people really are like what the model says they are like), but it has quite fundamental implications for how we make sense of (construe) what is going on in psychological research and how it needs to be conducted if anything meaningful is to come out of it.

In Kelly's own words,

It is customary to say that the scientist's ultimate aim is to predict and control. This is a summary statement that psychologists frequently like to quote in characterizing their own aspirations. Yet, curiously enough, psychologists rarely credit the human subjects in their experiments with having similar aspirations. It is as though the psychologist were saying to himself, 'I, being a psychologist, and therefore a scientist, am performing this experiment in order to improve the prediction and control of certain human phenomena; but my subject, being merely a human organism, is obviously propelled by inexorable drives welling up within him, or else he is in gluttonous pursuit of sustenance and shelter'.

In other words, in their role as scientists, psychologists perceive people as something less than whole persons, certainly as something very different from themselves; people are 'reduced' to the status of *subject*, implying that the psychologist is in control and dictates what will happen in the experimental situation, while the other merely responds to events in a passive and unthinking way. Quite apart from the dehumanizing nature of the term (Heather, 1976; and see Chapter 10), there is a fundamental methodological issue involved. One of the many other psychologists who implicitly accepts the view of people as intuitive scientists is Orne (1962), who introduced the term *demand characteristics* to refer to all the cues which convey to a subject the experimental hypothesis and which, accordingly, represent important determinants of the subject's behaviour. The very fact that experimental psychologists do all they can to prevent the subject from inferring the true purpose of the experiment (i.e. the experimental hypothesis) and thus consciously or unconsciously complying with it, demonstrates that the former believe that the latter, like themselves, 'search for meaning in their environment, formulate hypotheses, and act on the basis of these belief systems' (Weiner, 1992). In other words, if ordinary people did not engage in essentially the same kind of intellectual activities as scientists do, it would not be necessary to use the often elaborate controls and deceptions which are an almost inevitable feature of traditional experimental research, (see Chapter 11).

A contradiction seems to have emerged: how can people be both 'subjects' (very different from the psychologist) and, simultaneously, capable of working out (or at least of puzzling about) what is going on in the mind of the psychologist (very similar to what the psychologist is doing in his or her role as scientist)?

Using Kelly's concept of constructs, 'we might see the subject as one who is desperately trying to construe the constructions processes of the psychologist' (Fransella, 1980). Clearly, from this perspective, we cannot justify the use of the term 'subject'; not only are people themselves scientists, but psychologists can only hope to understand and predict the behaviour of others to the extent that they are aware of the constructs that those others place upon events. A piece of behaviour may appear extraordinary to the observer but be totally meaningful in the context of the person's own world view: 'To understand the behaviour of others, we have to know what construct predictions are being put to the test' (Fransella, 1980).

As a consequence of the 'human-as-scientist' model, the psychologist and the client ('subject') are now equal partners; the former is no longer of higher status and 'in charge' (Weiner, 1992).

> *Construct theory sees each man as trying to make sense out of himself and his world. It sees psychology as a meta-discipline, an attempt to make sense out of the ways in which men make sense out of their worlds. This not only puts the psychologist in the same interpretive business as his so-called subject – it makes them partners in the business, for on no other basis can one man understand another.*
>
> (Bannister & Fransella, 1980)

While, as we have seen, 'subject' reduces the person to something less than a whole person, for PCT the person is the irreducible unit: 'Traditional psychology is not, in the main, about persons. By making the person the central subject matter of psychology, construct theory changes the boundaries and the content of the existing science' (Bannister & Fransella, 1980).

Research within a PCT framework would look very different from its present form. It would be about 'the process whereby people come to make sense of things' and would involve working *with* and not *on* subjects. The constructions of the researcher would be explicitly stated and the results obtained

> *will be seen as less important, in the end, than the whole progress of the research itself – which, after all, represents one version of the process it is investigating. The crucial question, about any research project, would then be how far, as a process, it illuminated our understanding of the whole human endeavour to make sense of our lives, and how fruitful it proved in suggesting new exploratory ventures.*
>
> (Salmon, 1978, quoted in Bannister & Fransella, 1980)

These views regarding the nature of psychological research are echoed in feminist psychology (see Chapter 6) and in collaborative/new paradigm research (see Chapter 11).

Homo psychologicus: human beings as natural psychologists

According to Humphrey (1986), 'The minds of human beings are part of nature. We should ask: What are minds for? Why have they evolved in this way rather than another? Why have they evolved at all, instead of remaining quite unchanged?'

What answers does he provide to these intriguing questions?

While we possess language, creativity and self-awareness which (as far as we know) no other animal possesses, and while human societies are infinitely richer, more stable and more psychologically demanding than anything which exists elsewhere in nature, nowhere on earth can human beings survive outside society; consequently, nowhere on earth can we survive without a deep sensitivity to, and understanding of, our fellow creatures.

> *Did people . . . then evolve to be psychologists by nature? Is that what makes our families and commitments work? Has that been the prime mover behind the evolution of our brains and our intelligence? If so, it would mean that almost all the earlier theories of human evolution had got it upside down. Fifteen years ago, nothing in the textbooks about evolution referred to man's need to do psychology: the talk was all of tool-making, spear-throwing and fire-lighting – practical rather than social intelligence.*

It has been argued that the mark of the first man-like ape was the ability to walk on hind legs, to eat and digest a wider range of grassland food, and to relate his fingers to his thumb. However, as important as these were, 'Not fingers to thumb, but person to person. The real mark of a man-like ape would have been his ability to manipulate and relate himself – in human ways – to the other apes around him.'

Humphrey argues that there is sufficient archaelogical evidence to suggest that by two million years ago the fundamental pattern of human social living had already been laid down. While the Kalahari Bushmen may be biologically modern, in many respects their lifestyle has not changed in the last million years; by observing them, we can still see just how far the success of a hunter–gatherer community depends on the psychological skills of its individual members. Their social system works but only because they, like all human beings,

> are . . . supremely good at understanding one another. They come of a long, long line of natural psychologists whose brains and minds have been slowly shaped by evolution . . .
>
> . . . Small wonder human beings have evolved to be such remarkable psychological survivors, when for the last six million years their heavy task has been to read the minds of other human beings.

Figure 1.5 Self-awareness/consciousness and the ability to understand and predict the behaviour and responses of others may be the essential characteristics of human beings which make them distinctive from all other species

But how do we do it? Essentially, says Humphrey, as intelligent social beings, we use our knowledge of our *own* thoughts and feelings (through 'introspection') as a guide for understanding how others are likely to think and feel and, therefore, behave. Indeed, he goes further and argues that we are conscious (i.e. we have self-awareness) precisely because this is so useful to us in this process of understanding others and thus having a successful social existence. Consciousness is a biological adaptation which has evolved to enable us to perform this introspective psychology.

Consistent with Humphrey's discussion of the evolution of human beings as nature's psychologists (*phylogenesis*) is the recent interest among developmental psychologists in how an understanding of other people's minds develops in the individual child (*ontogenesis*). Harris (1989), for example, believes that it is children's awareness of their own mental states which allows them to project mental states onto others. There is considerable evidence that children can understand others' beliefs, desires and emotions by age three or four, with the beginnings of this appearing as early as two years old (Smith & Cowie, 1991). (Further discussion of Humphrey's theory of consciousness, plus some discussion of the development of the child's 'theory of mind', will be found in Chapter 13.)

Conclusion

To begin a book about psychology by looking at people as psychologists seems, in some ways, the only logical way to begin. Since most of us are, by definition, neither psychologists nor any other kind of scientist in a literal sense, the person-as-psychologist is a metaphor: let's 'pretend' that everyone is a psychologist/scientist and see where that takes us, how it might help us to understand human beings. Compared with other metaphors (for example, people-as-information-processors, which denotes the cognitive approach – see Chapters 12 and 13), it seems highly appropriate; after all, science (including psychology) is done by people, scientists are people and, as far as we know, science is a uniquely human form of behaviour. By contrast, information-processing machines are designed by people and it seems rather odd to liken people to something which they design for a particular purpose. However valid the metaphor may be, we are unique among information processors, since we design and make them as part of scientific activity, something which only human beings 'naturally' do. We are clearly much more than mere organisms, however complex we may be biologically; if nothing else, we are organisms that do science, making us unique within the biological world.

Evolutionary theory (Humphrey's theory of consciousness), a major theory of personality (Kelly's PCT) and a major theory of social perception (attribution theory) all converge on the same way of trying to grasp the nature of human beings: if trying to make sense of our experience, to predict how people are likely to behave, and inferring the causes of people's behaviour (and not being able to avoid doing these things) are characteristics of human thought, then we are, indeed, all psychologists.

Summary

- Psychology is part of the sum total of what people do, a (rather special) human activity.
- One of the things that makes psychology unique as a science is that the investigator and the subject matter are, essentially, the same.
- A useful way of trying to understand 'ordinary' (lay) people is to regard them as psychologists/scientists, as in *person perception* (in particular, the attribution process) and Kelly's PCT.
- Ordinary people can already do the kinds of things that psychologists as scientists are trying to do (such as reflecting on the causes of behaviour).
- Heider was interested in *commonsense* (or folk) *psychology*, i.e. how the lay person acts as a *naive scientist*, by linking observable behaviour to unobservable causes.
- The causes of behaviour are what give meaning to what people do.

- Social life requires that members of a particular culture share the same basic version of everyday psychology.
- Heider distinguished between *personal* or *dispositional* (internal) and *situational* or *environmental* (external) causes, which is the central feature of *attribution theory*. Assigning internal or external causes to behaviour is called the *attribution process*.
- Influential psychological theories, notably Freud's psychoanalytic theory, may become part of our taken-for-granted beliefs about the causes of behaviour.
- The everyday psychologist uses two broad categories of constructs/conceptual tools: *psychological/mentalistic* and *social*.
- According to Wellman, *desire* and *belief* are two crucial constructs involved in everyday psychology; these are major causes of behaviour but they too are seen as being caused, by *perception* and *emotions* respectively.
- Thinking and intention are also central constructs which form part of everyday mentalistic psychology, and we commonly identify personality traits in our attempt to explain/predict people's behaviour.
- Everyday social psychology refers to social norms, rules and conventions, and social roles, and also includes understanding of event/scripted episodes.
- The study of person perception is the study of how the lay person uses theory and data in understanding other people.
- The lay person's theories are called *intuitive/implicit* personality theories, an important example being *stereotypes* (and the related process of *stereotyping*). Stereotypes are a kind of *person schema*.
- Schemas and other implicit theories make the world more manageable, through making it more predictable; this is more important than their accuracy.
- Many sociologists, psychologists and philosophers of science argue that our knowledge of the world is *constructed* by us; this challenges the *positivist* view of science, according to which science is *objective*.
- Scientific observation is always prestructured and directed; data are always collected in the light of a particular theory and 'facts' do not exist independently of theory.
- Implicit theories seem to display the three criteria of explicit, scientific, theories, namely *coherence, ontological distinctions*, and *causal explanatory framework*.
- Scientists, but not everyday psychologists, are obliged to follow the rules of *scientific method*, including *falsification*, (as opposed to mere *verification*); the former are also obliged to articulate their theories, i.e. to make them *explicit*.

- Psychologists as scientists are trying to construct laws of behaviour/psychological processes as an end in itself, while the lay person's theories serve a *practical/pragmatic* purpose ('recipe knowledge').
- Many psychologists are involved in *applied research* and work in applied fields, suggesting that no hard-and-fast distinction can be drawn between formal and informal psychology.
- The task of scientific psychology is to make explicit the implicit theories of everyday life and to extend those theories using *theory-guided* empirical research.
- According to Kelly's PCT, people can be thought of as intuitive scientists (*man-the-scientist*), who use their *personal constructs* to make predictions about, and explain, behaviour. To understand other people's behaviour, we must know what constructs they are putting to the test.
- In the experimental situation, subjects formulate hypotheses about the experimental hypothesis being tested; this relates to Orne's *demand characteristics*.
- In traditional psychology, the experimenter is of higher status and 'in charge', whereas within a PCT framework, research is a co-operative venture between 'equals'; the *process* of research is much more important than the results obtained.
- According to Humphrey, human beings have evolved as natural psychologists (*Homo psychologicus*). What makes humans distinctive as a species is our ability to read the minds of other human beings.
- Based on introspection, we use our knowledge of our own thoughts/feelings as a guide for understanding how others are likely to be thinking/feeling.
- Consciousness is a biological adaptation which has evolved to enable us to perform this introspective psychology. The development in children of a 'theory of mind' is consistent with this evolutionary view.

Suggestions for further reading

Bannister, D. and Fransella, F. (1980) *Inquiring Man*, 2nd edn. Harmondsworth: Penguin.

Humphrey, N. (1986) *The Inner Eye* (especially Chapter 2), London: Vintage.

Kelly, G.A. (1955) *A Theory of Personality: The psychology of personal constructs*, New York: Norton.

Attribution

Attribution and everyday psychology

We saw in the previous chapter that Fritz Heider (1958) regarded the 'ordinary' person, the 'person-in-the-street' (i.e. the non-psychologist), as a *naive scientist*, someone who actively tries to make sense of the world – in particular, the social world, the world of behaviour. He believed that a fundamental feature of *commonsense psychology* is the belief that underlying people's overt behaviour are causes, and it is these causes, and not the observable behaviour itself, which represent the meaning of what people do.

Causes can be of two main kinds, *dispositional* or *personal* (internal), and *situational* or *environmental* (external), and a major 'task' that we face as 'everyday psychologists' is to decide which type of cause (abilities, emotions, personality, motivation, attitudes, or other internal causes, *or* the behaviour of other people, demands of the situation, physical aspects of the environment, or other external causes) best accounts for the behaviour we are trying to explain. This decision process is called the *attribution process* and Heider's insights into the process form the basis for *attribution theory*: the latter is the scientific psychologist's attempt to explain the former.

Causes and perceived causes

Before getting any deeper into the details of attribution theory and the way it has been used in psychology, it is important to make a distinction that is crucial for appreciating the nature of the attribution process and the attempts by psychologists to explain it.

When we talk about 'the causes' of behaviour, the implication is that we *know* what is responsible for the observed behaviour, that our explanation is accurate, adequate and sufficient. By contrast, when we talk about 'perceived causes', we are referring to what we *believe* is responsible for the observed behaviour and acknowledging that our explanation might be mistaken. While we might be willing to accept this distinction at the theoretical level, in practice we often confuse our beliefs with 'the truth'. For example, we may be 'convinced' that someone acted for a particular reason, or that 'so-and-so is the murderer', subsequently only to be proved wrong. There are really two issues involved here.

1 However sure we are about the truth of something, this does not in itself mean that it *is* true; subjective certainty does not guarantee objective truth.

2 It is often very difficult to say exactly what is the cause (or causes) of behaviour in an objective way. Indeed, the whole of psychology can be seen as an attempt to find out 'what makes us tick', with different theories offering very different (and sometimes conflicting) accounts.

When attribution theorists try to explain the lay person's explanations of behaviour, they are not concerned with the accuracy or validity of these everyday explanations, but simply with how they are reached – the process rather than the product. In fact, some of the most important research and theory dealing with the attribution process has focused on the biases involved in people's attempts to make sense of behaviour (their own as well as others'), the term implying that the resulting explanations are very likely to depart from 'the truth' (however that may be established).

Hence, 'Attribution theory is concerned with the cognitive processes individuals use to understand and predict their own behaviour, as well as that of others. Specifically, the focus is on the perceived "cause" of a person's behaviour' (Moghaddam et al. 1993).

Figure 2.1 This advertisement show how easy it is to confuse the truth: it looks as though the policeman is chasing the Black man at first glance, but in fact both are chasing a criminal

Attribution theory and theories of Attribution

Fiske and Taylor (1991) distinguish between attribution theory and theories of attribution. *Attribution theory* deals with the general principles that govern how the social perceiver selects and uses information to arrive at causal explanations or judgements for events (i.e. behaviour) in a wide variety of domains. *Theories of attribution*, on the other hand, draw on the principles of attribution theory and make predictions about how people respond in particular life domains.

However, attribution theory does not refer to a single body of ideas and research, but to a collection of diverse theoretical and empirical contributions which share several common concerns. Fiske and Taylor identify six different theoretical traditions, which form the backbone of attribution theory:

1 Heider's (1958) *commonsense psychology* (see Chapter 1);
2 Jones and Davis's (1965) *correspondent inference theory*;
3 Kelley's (1967, 1972, 1973) *covariation model*;
4 Schachter's (1964) theory of *emotional lability* (or *cognitive labelling theory*);
5 Bem's (1967, 1972) *self-perception theory*, and
6 Weiner's (1979, 1985) *motivational theory of attribution*.

Identifying these major theoretical strands also helps to identify some of the major *life-domains* (to use Fiske and Taylor's term) to which attribution principles have been applied.

Commonsense psychology

The title of Heider's 1958 book was *The Psychology of Interpersonal Relations*. In it, he was attempting to apply the Gestalt theory of physical object perception to the perception of people (social perception or, more specifically, *interpersonal perception*, the perception of *others*). The attribution process is usually discussed in the context of impression formation: most of our impressions of others are based on what they actually do and the situations in which they do it. Unless we are able to make a judgement as to the internal or external causes of someone's behaviour, we cannot really use behaviour as a basis for forming impressions – only when we make an *internal attribution* are we using behaviour as an indication of what the actor is like.

According to Fiske and Taylor (1991), Heider's major contribution was to 'define many of the basic issues that would later be explored more systematically in further theoretical ventures', in particular, those of Jones and Davis, and Kelley, which will be summarized below.

Theory of emotional lability

Schachter's theory of emotional lability (cognitive labelling theory) represents perhaps one of the first attempts to apply attributional principles to a domain other than interpersonal perception, namely, the subjective experience of emotion; specifically, how do we come to label our physiological arousal in one way rather than another? Although the behaviour of other people may influence this labelling process, Schachter is concerned with the individual's emotional experience, not our perception of emotion in others. We shall discuss Schachter's research below.

Self-perception theory

While the name of Bem's self-perception theory suggests that it is directly relevant to social perception (albeit not to the perception of others), it is in fact a theory of *attitude change* which draws on Heider's basic distinction between internal and external causes. This too will be discussed later in the chapter.

Internal and external causes

Whether the cause is judged to be internal (generated by the actor) or external (produced by the situation) is referred to as the *locus* of a cause. As important as this is, it is not sufficient. For example, if you fail an exam, even if you accept that it was 'your fault' (e.g. you cannot blame it on a really difficult paper or being badly taught), the specific internal cause that you (and others) believe was responsible is important. If you attribute your failure to the really bad headache you had that morning, at least you can console yourself that, had it not been for the headache, you may well have passed, and others are likely to take a similar view. However, if you believe that you failed simply because you lack the necessary ability, the implications for the future are very different from the first explanation.

Although both headaches and lack of ability are *internal* causes, the former is a transient, temporary state, while the latter is a stable, permanent feature of a person's make-up. Both Jones and Davis, and Kelley, argue that causal analysis is most informative when stable causes are identified, such as personal dispositions (of which academic ability is one). So we have now identified a second important dimension of causality, namely *stability*. But the attribution process is not solely about understanding why something has happened; it is also about (i) trying to predict what will happen in the future (understanding/explanation and prediction are two major aims of science), and (ii) trying to understand what controls future events (Heider, 1958; Kelley, 1967) (control being the third main aim of science; see Chapter 3 on the idiographic–nomothetic debate). If you attribute your exam failure to not working hard enough and allowing yourself to be distracted by social life instead of revising, this is at least something over which you have control, whereas your (perceived) lack of ability is not. So *controllability* is a third important dimension of causality.

Such *self-attributions* are important for behaviour because they are associated with differences in feelings of self-confidence and expectations of future success and failure. If you believe that not working hard enough was the reason for your failure, you are likely to try harder next time, because removing the cause of failure should improve the chances of success. However, there's not much you can do to 'remove' your basic lack of ability! Much the same can be shown for a number of challenges that people face in the field of health. For example, cigarette smokers who see themselves as more 'addicted' have lower expectations of their ability to give up and may be less likely to try. 'Thus, the way we describe

Figure 2.2 Cigarette smokers who see themselves as more addicted have lower expectations of their ability to give up and may be less likely to try – despite increasingly strong health warnings

ourselves will reflect what we think others expect, or are entitled to expect, of us as well as what we expect of ourselves' (Eiser, 1994).

Drawing on these observations and assumptions, Weiner has explored domains such as impression management (our attempts to influence the impressions formed of us), achievement motivation, and helping behaviour. We shall discuss all three domains later in the chapter. (We should also note here that Bem's self-perception theory could be renamed *self-attribution* theory – see below.)

Other domains to which attribution principles have been applied include prejudice, depression, and marital relationships. (See Figure 2.3.)

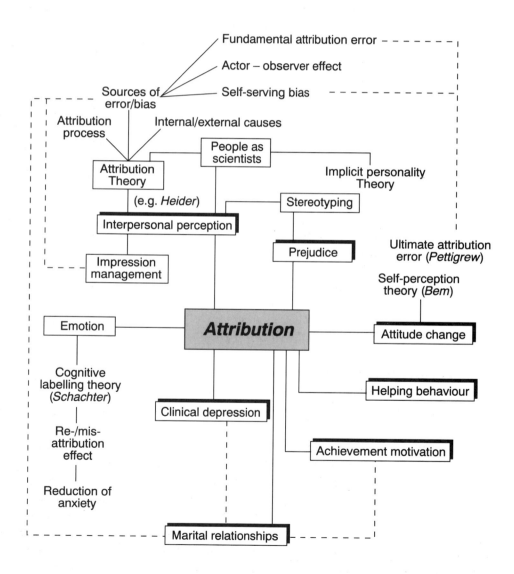

Figure 2.3   Some of the domains to which attribution theory principles have been applied

Correspondent inference theory

This is concerned primarily with whether a person's behaviour will be attributed to some disposition (i.e. a stable cause) of the actor rather than to accidental or extenuating (situational) factors. An attribution or inference is 'correspondent' when the disposition attributed to an actor 'corresponds' to the behaviour from which this disposition is inferred.

For example, if someone gives up his or her seat on the bus to allow a pregnant woman to sit down, and we infer that the actor is 'kind and unselfish', we are making a correspondent inference, because both the behaviour and the disposition can be labelled in the same way: 'kind and unselfish'. But if we attribute the behaviour to compliance with someone else's behaviour (the person giving up his seat is a man whose wife has *told* him to give up his seat), then we might infer some other disposition about him (e.g. 'he is weak and likes to be dominated by others'); however, this disposition does *not* correspond to the behaviour from which it is inferred (i.e. it is not a correspondent inference) (Gross, 1994).

According to Jones and Davis (1965), a precondition for a correspondent inference is the attribution of *intentionality* (i.e. the behaviour was deliberate) and they specify, in turn, two criteria or conditions for this: the actor must be perceived as having:

1 *knowledge* that the act would have the observed effects, and
2 the *ability* to produce the observed effects.

According to the theory, the aim of the attribution process is to infer that both the observed behaviour, and the intention to behave in that way, correspond to the actor's dispositions. How is this done? Briefly, it is done through the *analysis of uncommon* (or non-common) effects, and the use of other cues – in particular, *choice*, *social desirability*, *social role*, and *prior expectations*.

Covariation model

Kelley's (1967, 1972, 1973) covariation model is concerned primarily with whether the cause of some behaviour is internal or external; as far as the latter is concerned, a distinction is made between the external target of the behaviour (usually, but not invariably, another person) and the external circumstances surrounding the behaviour (Zebrowitz, 1990). However, this describes the end result of a process. The model really begins with the question: what information do people use to arrive at one or other kind of attribution?

When the perceiver has information from multiple sources, the principle of covariation is used: an effect (the behaviour to be explained) is attributed to a condition (cause) that is present when the effect is present, and absent when the effect is absent. (This is based on a statistical technique – analysis of variance or ANOVA – which examines the changes in a dependent variable, the *effect*, in an investigation involving two or more independent variables, the *conditions*.)

There are three main conditions, and three kinds of causal information which correspond to them – *consensus*, *distinctiveness*, and *consistency*; it is the permutation of high or low consensus, distinctiveness and consistency which leads the perceiver, logically, to make an internal or external attribution. But what happens when not all three kinds of information are available?

Kelley (1972) himself acknowledged that the ANOVA model was 'idealized', and that there are many occasions when the perceiver lacks the information, time or motivation to examine multiple observations. In these cases, the perceiver uses *causal schemata*, which are ready-made beliefs, preconceptions and even theories, built up from experience, about how certain kinds of causes interact to produce a specific kind of effect (Hewstone & Antaki, 1988).

Limitations of attribution theory

As we have seen, Kelley recognized a major limitation of his original model, and introduced the concept of causal schemata in an attempt to 'plug the hole'. Despite this, Gahagan (1991) believes that scant attention has been paid to a very important issue for attribution theorists – namely, under what circumstances does the lay psychologist act like a scientific psychologist, carefully and systematically drawing inferences about the causes of behaviour, and when does he or she simply use some ready-made explanation?

A study relevant to this question is one by Lalljee et al. (1982), which showed that explanations of *unexpected* behaviour tend to be more complex than for expected behaviour: if the situation is familiar and the behaviour is unexpected, we are likely to make an *internal* attribution, while if the situation is unfamiliar and the behaviour is also unfamiliar, we are likely to make an *external* attribution.

Lalljee (1981, cited by Gahagan, 1991) argues that even something as apparently straightforward as consistency information (i.e. is the behaviour we are trying to explain a 'one-off', or does the person regularly behave like this?) is problematical. Even assuming that we have knowledge of the actor's previous behaviour, 'consistency' can mean very different things, depending on the nature of the behaviour. For example, getting divorced four times in five years would strike us as much more frequent than, say, jogging four times in three years! We might draw very different inferences about the actor in these two cases if that were all we knew about them.

All three major theories (Heider, Jones & Davis, and Kelley) adopt the perspective of the perceiver as a naive scientist, and, as such, all three tend to see the lay person as a logical and rational thinker, who arrives at attributions in much the same way as his or her professional counterparts.

Indeed, Kelley's ANOVA model was presented as a *normative* model: it showed how perceivers *should* make accurate causal attributions. However, the research has shown that perceivers do not usually act like scientists, following such detailed, formal, logical rules. Instead, they make attributions quickly, using much less information and showing clear preferences for certain sorts of explanation.

There is the need, therefore, for more *descriptive* models – that is, more accurate accounts of how people actually go about making attributions – and this has been at least partly achieved by exploring the biases involved in the attribution process. These include the *fundamental attribution error* (Ross, 1977), the *actor–observer effect* (Jones & Nisbett, 1971), and the *self-serving bias* (Miller & Ross, 1975), and together they seem to provide a better descriptive analysis of causal attribution than do complex, normative models (Hewstone & Antaki, 1988).

When attribution principles are applied to particular domains of behaviour, such as emotional experience and attitude change, the fundamental distinction between internal and external causes is used, in more or less the way that Heider originally made it.

In other cases, such as impression management, achievement motivation and helping behaviour, depression and marital relationships, the more complex analysis proposed by Weiner (i.e. where the locus, stability and controllability of causes are all taken into account) is used.

In the examples of depression and marital relationships, the self-serving bias is also used to explain the nature of the behaviour involved, while the fundamental attribution error has been used to help explain certain aspects of prejudice.

The rest of this chapter is devoted to discussing how all these different aspects of attribution theory and research have been applied to a wide range of behaviour and experience.

Attribution and emotion

Two of the earliest theories of emotion were the James-Lange (1884, 1890) and the Cannon-Bard (1927). According to the former, our emotional experience is the *result* of perceived bodily changes (not their *cause*, as would be claimed by the 'commonsense' view). So, for example, we feel *frightened* of the bear *because we run away from it*, whereas common sense would say that we run away because we are frightened: 'the bodily changes follow directly the perception of the exciting fact, and . . . our feeling of the same changes as they occur *is* the emotion' (James, 1890).

According to Cannon, there are four major faults with the James-Lange theory, two of which are of particular relevance here.

1 It implies that for each subjectively distinct emotion there is a corresponding set of physiological (bodily) changes which enable us to

Figure 2.4 According to the James-Lange theory, we feel frightened because we are running away from something and are not running away because we are frightened

attach a label to the emotional experience. Against this, Cannon (1927) argued that 'the same visceral changes occur in very different emotional states and in non-emotional states'.

2 Even if there were identifiable patterns of physiological response associated with different subjective emotions, such physiological changes themselves do not necessarily produce emotional states – there is more to emotion than just bodily arousal.

The Cannon-Bard theory proposes that the emotional experience is quite independent of the physiological changes involved: the emotion-producing stimulus is processed by the thalamus (a part of the brain through which all sensory information is processed), which sends impulses to the cortex, where the emotion is consciously experienced, *and* to the hypothalamus (a different part of the brain which plays a major role in controlling the activity of the autonomic nervous system and the endocrine-hormonal system), which sets in motion certain autonomic physiological changes.

According to Schachter (1964), Cannon was wrong in thinking that bodily changes and emotional experience are independent, while the James-Lange theory is mistaken in claiming that physiological changes cause the feeling of emotion. But the James-Lange theory correctly sees physiological changes as *preceding* the emotional experience, because the latter depends both on physiological changes and on the interpretation made of those changes: we have to decide which particular emotion we are feeling, and the label we give to our arousal depends on what we attribute that arousal to. See Box 2.1.

Box 2.1 Schachter and Singer 'adrenaline' experiment

In what is now considered one of the classic experiments of psychology, Schachter and Singer (1962) gave participants what they were told was a vitamin injection in order to see its effects on vision; in fact, it was adrenaline.

Group A participants were told the real side-effects of the injection (palpitations, tightness in the throat, tremor, sweating, etc.), those in Group B were given false information (itching and headache), those in Group C were given no information (true or false), and Group D participants were given a saline injection (and were otherwise treated like Group C).

While waiting for a 'vision test', each participant sat in a waiting room with a confederate (supposedly another participant). For half the participants in each condition, the confederate acted either in a happy, frivolous way (euphoria) or very angrily (anger). The dependent variable – the participants' emotional experience – was measured by (i) how much they joined in with the confederate's behaviour, and (ii) self-report scales.

The results were very much in line with predictions.

1 If an individual experiences a state of physiological arousal for which there is no immediate explanation (it *cannot be attributed* to the injection), he or she will 'label' this state and describe it in terms of the cognitions available. This means that exactly the same state of arousal could receive very different labels (euphoria or anger – Groups B and C).

2 If an individual experiences a state of physiological arousal for which there is a completely appropriate explanation (it *can be attributed* to the injection), he or she will label this state accordingly, and will largely ignore other available cognitions (Group A).

3 Given the same circumstances, an individual will react emotionally, or describe his or her feelings as emotions, only to the extent that he or she experiences a state of physiological arousal (Groups A, B and C).

While the last point is saying that physiological arousal is necessary, point 1 is saying that *both* the arousal and the cognitive labelling are necessary; the nature of the arousal is unimportant – it is how we interpret that arousal that is crucial (hence, the theory is sometimes called the 'Two-factor theory of emotion'). Our interpretation depends on the attribution we make: what caused that state of arousal? If we can attribute it to an injection (which has elements of both internal and external causation), then we need go no further in looking for an explanation. Group A participants experienced arousal which did not need to be given an *emotion interpretation* because it could be given a perfectly adequate *physiological* one.

But the arousal for Groups B and C was not adequately explained. Neither group could attribute it to the injection, because either they experienced symptoms which were different from what they were told to expect, or they didn't know what to expect. For them, their arousal was ambiguous; there was no ready-made explanation available (i.e. the injection). This explains their 'susceptibility' to the cognitive cues provided by the (rather extreme) behaviour of the confederate.

Despite failures to replicate the 1962 study and criticisms of the methodology and the conclusions drawn from it, Schachter's cognitive labelling theory has had a considerable influence on the study of emotion (Parkinson, 1987). One of the implications of the theory is that emotional reactions induced by, say, a threatening experience can be reattributed to a neutral or less-threatening source. Schachter has demonstrated that our attributions for our emotional arousal are malleable: it is possible for us to mis-label our feelings and to draw mistaken conclusions about the causes of those feelings. This is called the *mis-attribution effect* (Ross & Nisbett, 1991). The Group B and C participants in the adrenaline experiment all attributed their arousal to something other than the drug that was the actual cause.

A classic demonstration of the mis-attribution effect is a study by Nisbett and Schachter (1966). Participants were given a sugar-pill placebo, which they were told was a drug that would affect them in one of two ways, either (i) tremors, shaky hands, pounding heart, and other symptoms associated with fear arousal, or (ii) itching, headache and other symptoms unrelated to fear. The 'drug' was given just before the participants experienced a series of intense electric shocks – they had to indicate at what point the shocks became painful and when they became intolerable. As predicted, those in the first group reported first experiencing pain at a higher shock level and showed a higher tolerance level than those in the second group. Why? Because they mis-attributed their fear symptoms to the drug (which were, in fact, induced by the shock), actually *reducing* the fear.

This suggests that, by inducing people to reattribute their arousal from a threatening source to a neutral or less threatening one, they can be helped to function more effectively in settings which currently induce anxiety (Fiske & Taylor, 1991). So what began as a laboratory-based, experimental approach to emotional arousal (the mis-attribution paradigm; Valins, 1966) has profound clinical implications, since it provides the potential for a general model for the treatment of emotional disorders (Valins & Nisbett, 1972).

One of the criticisms of the mis-attribution effect (Fiske & Taylor, 1991) is that laboratory studies seem to be more successful than actual clinical investigations; a suggested reason for this difference is itself to do with attribution, namely that people with real problems already have a stable explanation for their arousal and do not search for alternatives, making them less susceptible to mis-attribution.

Reference to the treatment of clinical problems through re-attribution techniques is also relevant to an analysis of depression, which we will discuss below.

Attribution and attitude change

Bem's self-perception theory (1967, 1972) is best understood as a major alternative to one of the most widely debated and tested theories of attitude change, namely Festinger's (1957) *cognitive dissonance theory*. Briefly, what Festinger proposed was that whenever we simultaneously hold two (or more) cognitions which are psychologically inconsistent, we experience dissonance, a negative drive state, a state of 'psychological discomfort or tension' which motivates us to reduce it and so achieve consonance. For example, if we have acted in a way that is inconsistent with our beliefs or attitudes, we are likely to experience dissonance; one cognition will correspond to the behaviour, and the other(s) will correspond to the relevant belief or attitude. According to the theory, dissonance may be reduced by changing our cognitions, often through adding one or more (such as regarding our behaviour in a different light); this is what is meant by attitude change.

Perhaps the most famous dissonance experiment is the 'one dollar – twenty dollar' experiment (Festinger & Carlsmith, 1959), in which college students spent thirty minutes working on two extremely dull and repetitive tasks. Later, they were offered either one or twenty dollars to try to convince the next 'participant' (in fact, a confederate) that the tasks were interesting and enjoyable. Finally, they were asked to assess the tasks, and this was taken to indicate the extent of their attitude change (based on the assumption that their initial attitude was that the tasks were extremely dull and boring). As predicted by *dissonance theory* (but contrary to the commonsense prediction of *incentive theory*; Janis et al., 1965), the one-dollar group showed the greater attitude change. The explanation is that the large, twenty-dollar incentive gave those participants ample justification for their counter-attitudinal behaviour, so that they experienced very little dissonance (and, therefore, little motivation to change their attitude). The one-dollar group, on the other hand, experienced considerable dissonance (and, therefore, considerable motivation to reduce it through attitude change), because they could hardly justify their counter-attitudinal behaviour in terms of the negligible reward.

Despite several successful replications of these findings, the theory has been criticized on many grounds, and one of its most outspoken critics has been Bem. He claims that dissonance as such is neither a necessary nor sufficient explanation, and (as a behaviourist) he rejects any reference to hypothetical, intervening variables (which, by definition, cannot be directly observed and measured). According to his self-perception theory,

> *'self-attributions' follow much the same logic as the attributions we make about other people. In other words, statements about our own mental or personal characteristics do not reflect any 'privileged access'... but are simply* explanations *of our own observable behaviour, no different in principle from those that could be made by a fully-informed outside observer. We see ourselves ... as we would see someone else who behaved as we did in the same situation.*
>
> (Eiser, 1994)

Any self-report of an attitude is an inference from observation of one's own behaviour and the situation in which it occurs. If the situation contains cues (say, the offer of a large, twenty-dollar reward) which imply that we might have behaved that way regardless of how we personally felt (we tell someone else how interesting the task is even though it is terribly boring), then we make no inference that our behaviour reflected our true attitude. But in the absence of obvious situational pressures (we are only offered one dollar), we assume that our attitudes are what our behaviour suggests they are.

In attributional terms, the twenty-dollar group can easily make a *situational attribution* ('I did it for the money'), whereas the one-dollar group have to make a *dispositional attribution* ('I did it because I must have really enjoyed it').

Bem's way of testing his theory is a form of experiment which he calls *interpersonal simulation*, in which he presents 'observer' participants with a summary description of the procedure used in some well-known dissonance experiment (such as that of Festinger and Carlsmith) and then asks them to estimate the original participants' attitudinal response. Usually, this is done quite accurately, with the 'observers' being less likely to assume a match between the behaviour and attitude of the twenty-dollar participants than in the case of the one-dollar group.

The reasoning is, if a non-involved observer (simulator) can reproduce the results obtained with actual experimental participants, then it is not necessary to believe that any internal, motivational state (i.e. dissonance) is involved in the one-dollar group's change in attitude: they simply observe their own behaviour, find no obvious situational explanation and ask themselves, in effect, 'What must my attitude have been in order for me to describe the task as enjoyable?' Answer? 'I must have enjoyed it after all!' – a dispositional attribution.

The responses given by real and observer participants should, according to Bem, be identical, because, in an important sense, they are all only observers (Shaver, 1987). However, the actual participants are observers of *their own behaviour*, while the 'observers' are assessing *someone else's behaviour*, and, according to the *actor – observer effect*, the former are more likely to make a situational attribution, and the latter a dispositional attribution. (Recall that this is one of the major sources of bias in the attribution process, more of which below.)

The self-serving bias and depression

The *actor – observer effect* (AOE; Jones & Nisbett, 1971) refers to the actor's tendency to explain his or her own behaviour in terms of situational factors and the observer's tendency to explain the actor's behaviour in terms of dispositional factors. The observer's bias corresponds to another major source of bias, namely the *fundamental attribution error* (Ross, 1977) or *lay dispositionism* (Ross & Nisbett, 1991), defined as the tendency to underestimate the impact of situational factors and to overestimate the role of dispositional factors in controlling behaviour.

While there is support for the AOE (e.g. Nisbett et al., 1973; Storms,

1973), it sometimes simply fails to fit the facts. If something goes wrong or we receive negative feedback about something we have done, we typically blame it on the situation (or somebody else), as predicted by the AOE. But what about *positive* feedback and achievements – do we normally attribute these to the situation as well, rather than to our own efforts and abilities? No – we usually want to take the credit for our successes (*self-enhancing bias*) while not wishing to accept the blame for our failures (*self-protecting bias*). Together, these are referred to as the *self-serving bias* (Miller & Ross, 1975): 'in an attempt to maintain or improve self-esteem, self-attributions may deny responsibility (i.e. externalize) for failure and take credit for (i.e. internalize) success. It has been shown that there is a predictable pattern between the dimensions of self-esteem and self-attribution in adults . . . and in children . . .' (Burgner & Hewstone, 1993).

An interesting exception to this general rule is the clinically depressed person. Having conducted research with dogs, Seligman (1974) explained depression in people in terms of *learned helplessness*. When the dogs were faced with repeated, uncontrollable, aversive stimulation (usually in the form of electric shocks), all attempts to escape eventually stopped, even after escape had become practically possible. Seligman observed many similarities between the helplessness syndrome in laboratory animals and depressed patients, including passivity in the face of stress, and a number of experiments with humans seemed to replicate the original animal findings.

However, the helplessness model of depression was seen as inadequate, for a variety of reasons. For example, the experience of being unable to control the outcome of one particular situation (helplessness) does not inevitably lead to clinical depression in most people, and some studies involving people indicated that helplessness sometimes actually improves performance (Davison & Neale, 1994).

So what other factors are involved? The original model was revised, the major change being the introduction of *attribution principles* (Abramson et al., 1978; Abramson & Martin, 1981). When we experience failure, we try to explain it (just as we try to explain our successes), and this is perfectly 'normal'. What is associated with depression is a particular pattern of attributions, or *attributional style* ('a tendency to make particular kinds of causal inferences, rather than others, across different situations and across time'; Metalsky & Abramson, 1981, quoted in Fiske & Taylor, 1991), based on three key dimensions, namely *locus* (internal or external), *stability* (stable or unstable), and *global* or *specific*. (This overlaps with Weiner's theory, outlined above, but his includes 'controllability' instead of global/specific.)

The depressed person believes that his or her failure is (i) caused by internal factors; (ii) reflects stable, long-term, relatively permanent factors; and (iii) reflects a global, pervasive, deficiency, i.e. failure applies to all or most aspects of his or her life (see Figure 2.5). People who are diagnosed as being clinically depressed are more likely to display this pattern when given, for example, the Attributional Style Questionnaire (Seligman et al., 1979), but just as important is the belief that the person who is prone to become depressed may display this attributional style; it is thought to play a mediating role between negative life events and adverse physical and mental health outcomes. When such depression-prone people experience stressors, they are more likely to develop the symptoms of depression and their self-esteem is shattered (Peterson & Seligman, 1984, cited in Davison & Neale, 1994).

Davison and Neale also refer to studies that show characteristic differences in how men and women cope with stress. Men typically engage in activities that distract them from their depression, while women are less active, tending to ponder over their situation, and blaming themselves for being depressed. This reinforces the state of depression and negative mood, perhaps by interfering with attempts to solve problems.

	Successes	Failures
Depressed	External Unstable Specific	Internal Stable Global
Non-depressed	Internal Stable Global	External Unstable Specific

Figure 2.5 Attributional styles for success and failure in depressed and non-depressed people (Based on Abramson et al., 1978; Abramson & Martin, 1981)

Attributional style, achievement motivation, and gender

The gender difference in depression noted above, in particular the tendency of women to blame themselves for their problems, is very relevant for an understanding of achievement motivation (or 'need for Achievement', nAch) (Murray, 1938; McClelland et al., 1953), i.e. the need to be successful, especially where this entails doing as well or better than someone else (Paludi, 1992).

According to Weiner's (1972) *cognitive attribution theory of achievement motivation*, the key difference between high- and low-achievement individuals is the different attributions they make regarding the causes of their success and failure. High nAch scorers make internal attributions for their success. They take charge of their own achievements – they believe themselves to be the cause of their successes (because of ability and hard work) – while low scorers attribute their successes to external causes (such as an easy exam or a mistake in the marking) and their failures to internal ones (such as lack of ability).

These patterns of attribution are, of course, consistent with those for non-depressed and depressed people respectively, and what is particularly interesting is the finding that there are gender differences in both domains. Women are about twice as likely as men to suffer from depression (with learned helplessness and lack of personal and political power being popular explanations for this difference; Davison & Neale, 1994), and women are also more likely to make external attributions (such as luck) for success, and internal attributions (such as low ability) for failure. Women also tend to reverse this pattern when explaining men's successes and failures (Paludi, 1992).

This pattern of self-attribution (typical of depression-prone people and women – who are often the same people) which attributes success to external factors and failure to internal factors, is *self-derogatory/self-derogating*: if self-attributions reflect, and affect, self-esteem, then we might expect that individuals belonging to social groups perceived as inferior (such as women), would have low self-esteem and a self-derogatory pattern of attributions compared with those who belong to the dominant social group (men) (Burgner & Hewstone, 1993). As we have seen, women are more likely to display a self-derogating pattern, and men are more likely to display a self-enhancing pattern (consistent with the self-serving bias).

Burgner and Hewstone refer to studies (such as that published by Lochel in 1983) which show these gender differences among children as young as four. In their own research, they tried to extend Lochel's findings to ethnic minorities (Asians in Britain), predicting that members of such groups would show the same self-derogating pattern as do girls, and that there would be an interaction between gender and ethnic background. They gave Asian and white children (mean age, five years, three months) a number of (non-sex-stereotyped) tasks to perform and then asked them to explain their successes and failures.

Lochel's original findings were confirmed, but there was no evidence of an ethnic difference. Both boys and girls used 'can' and 'know' attributions, but boys used these to explain their success only, while girls used them for both success and failure. This is likely to increase boys' experience of positive affect and self-esteem following success ('I succeeded because I know how to do it'), while protecting them from negative affect following failure. However, girls used these attributions less than boys to explain success and slightly more to explain failure ('I failed because I don't know how to do it'), which may account for increased negative affect and lower self-esteem following failure. Boys were also significantly more likely than girls to use 'difficulty' explanations following failure (i.e. a self-protecting attribution to external, uncontrollable factors): 'The rather depressing picture of self-enhancing attributions for boys and self-derogating attributions for girls parallels the results from the adult literature and needs to be considered within the broader context of sex-role socialization and the social divisions between the sexes' (Burgner & Hewstone, 1993). (See Chapter 6, on feminism.)

Attributional style and marital relationships

If depressed people, and women and girls, display similar attributional styles when explaining their successes and failures, another domain in which such a style has been found is in married couples' relationships. Research has shown that when members of married couples try to account for their partner's behaviour, both positive and negative, they tend to use a pattern of attribution which is associated with the overall state of the marital relationship (Bradbury & Fincham, 1990; Brehm & Kassin, 1990 cited in Brehm, 1992). Figure 2.6 shows the typical attributions made for happy and unhappy couples; it should be apparent that these patterns match exactly those for depressed and non-depressed people when explaining their successes and failures (see Figure 2.5). Figure 2.7 shows these patterns in a different way and also indicates that those of happy couples are *relationship-enhancing*, while those of unhappy couples are *distress-maintaining*.

	Partner's behaviour	
	Positive	**Negative**
Unhappy couples	*External* *Unstable* *Specific*	*Internal* *Stable* *Global*
Happy couples	*Internal* *Stable* *Global*	*External* *Unstable* *Specific*

Figure 2.6   Attributional styles for partner's behaviour in happily and unhappily married couples (Based on Bradbury & Fincham, 1990)

Like depressed people, those involved in unhappy marriages tend to make attributions that are contrary to what the self-serving bias implies is 'normal', while those who are happily married (like non-depressed people) show attributional styles that are consistent with it. (Strictly, the self-serving bias refers to self-attributions, but, by extension, it can also be applied to others who are emotionally significant for us.)

Shaver (1985) makes the important distinction between *causal* attributions and *responsibility* attributions, the former referring to factors seen as *producing* an event (morally neutral), the latter referring to a person's perceived *accountability* for an event (not morally neutral). So, for

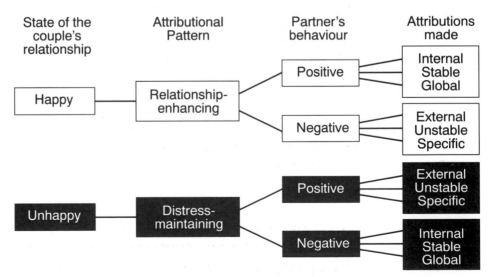

Figure 2.7   Attributions made by happy and unhappy couples (From Brehm, 1992)

Figure 2.8 Unhappy couples tend to attribute selfish motives and negative behaviour to their partner, which intensifies the unhappiness in the relationship over time

example, you might have been the one to cause the fire (causal attribution) but it might not have been your fault, because it was an accident, or somebody else's negligence or carelessness was to blame (responsibility attribution).

In general, unhappy couples are more likely to regard their partner as selfishly motivated and behaving with negative intent; they blame their partner for negative events, making both a causal and a responsibility attribution (Bradbury & Fincham, 1990). These findings suggest that 'these attributions act as screen – magnifying behaviours consistent with the state of the relationship while filtering out discrepant relationships. Over time, such a screen should intensify the initial emotional quality of the relationship. The happy should get happier, and the miserable more miserable' (Brehm, 1992). However, this assumes that the kind of attributions made to the partner can produce differences in satisfaction. Is it possible that attributions are simply produced by the state of the relationship without having any direct influence themselves?

Brehm believes that the available research raises the possibility that causal attributions for the partner's behaviour *may* have an influence on subsequent satisfaction with the relationship. There is also considerable evidence that dissatisfaction with one's marriage leads to depression, so could distress-maintaining attributions made by unhappy couples stem from their depressed mood? Although this is unlikely, such attributions may become associated with depression over time, and are likely to increase hostile, non-cooperative behaviour at times of conflict, which is likely to increase stress. This may, in turn, lead to depression (Brehm, 1992).

It would certainly be very unusual if one partner's attributions about the other partner's behaviour did not influence the former's cognitive, affective and behavioural reactions to the latter. As we noted earlier, attributions can also be seen as expectancies about future behaviour, and there is considerable evidence that an observer's expectancies may influence perceptions of, and behaviour towards, the actor, which, in turn, may alter the actor's behaviour, mood and attitudes, including self-concept (Sacco et al., 1993).

Sacco and Dunn (1990, cited in Sacco et al., 1993) found that the failures and personal problems of hypothetical depressed people were attributed (by college students) to more dispositional causes, while their successes were attributed to more situational causes. Sacco et al. wanted to study similar attributions within naturally occurring relationships involving a clinically depressed partner. In line with their prediction, they found that husbands of depressed wives (relative to those with non-depressed wives) made more dispositional attributions about negative events occurring to their wives, but, contrary to predictions, they did not make more situational attributions for positive events. They also reported more negative affect in reaction to negative events, and indicated less marital satisfaction.

One of the interesting features of this study is that, while previous research has focused on attributions about marital behaviours directed at the partner making the attributions (e.g. 'your spouse criticizes something you do'), here the relationship between attributions and marital distress was also found for negative events that did not directly affect the partner (e.g. 'a friend acts in a hostile way towards your wife') (Sacco et al., 1993).

The self-serving bias as a cultural phenomenon

We have been discussing the attributional patterns of certain groups of people – depressives, women and unhappily married couples – as deviating from the self-serving bias, implying that this form of bias constitutes a *norm*, an expected, 'proper' way of explaining one's successes and failures (and those of one's husband or wife).

However, could it be that this bias is only normal in particular cultures, rather than being a universal norm (see Chapter 8, on cross-cultural psychology)? According to Moghaddam et al. (1993), there are two assumptions about culture involved in the apparently straightforward self-serving principle:

1 people have a strong need to judge themselves favourably;
2 a positive self-image is derived from biased attributions related to the *self*.

Are there entire cultures where a self-derogating (or self-effacing) attributional style (that is, where it is self-derogating/effacing only relative to the norm of the self-serving bias) is normal?

When discussing cross-cultural psychology, a basic distinction is made between *individualist* and *collectivist* cultures (corresponding to Western and Eastern cultures respectively), and a major distinguishing feature is how much focus is put on the self relative to the in-group. If people derive much of their esteem not from individual achievement but from collective or group identity, then esteem can well be maintained by attributions serving the group rather than the individual. Kashima and Triandis (1986), for example, found that Japanese students are less likely to be self-serving than American students (at least for certain dimensions of achievement-oriented experiences), reflecting the much greater emphasis on mutual support and effort towards group aims, rather than individual achievement.

In a comparison of American and Asian students (from Hong Kong, Japan, Korea, the Philippines, Vietnam, Indonesia and

1 Internal:

Perceived cause = **Self**

2 In-group/self-inclusion:

Perceived cause = **In-group, including oneself**

3 In-group/self-exclusion:

Perceived cause = **In-group, but *not* oneself**

4 External:

Perceived cause = **An agent, external to oneself *and* in-group**

Figure 2.9   A four-way classification of the self-serving bias (Based on Moghaddam, 1993)

Malaysia), all attending a large US university, Yan and Gaier (1994) found that Americans attributed academic achievement significantly more often to ability, and they also seemed to believe that effort is more important for success than lack of effort for failure. By contrast, the East Asian and South-East Asian students attributed effort much more equally to success and failure; if anything, it was seen a more important in relation to failure. These findings are consistent with the individualist nature of the USA culture and the collectivist nature of Eastern cultures. In the latter, the individual is not 'inner directed' but is controlled by the need not to lose face: 'Face is lost when the individual, either through his action or that of people closely related to him, fails to meet essential requirements placed upon him by virtue of the social position he occupies' (Hofstede, 1980, quoted in Yan & Gaier, 1994).

'The minute an examination of the self-serving bias in other cultural contexts suggests a more collective orientation, it forces consideration of the whole internal/external distinction, which lies at the heart of attribution theory' (Moghaddam et al., 1993). If we now add a person's group as a potential unit of attribution, a new classification scheme for attribution becomes necessary, comprising four categories, as shown in Figure 2.9. This more group-oriented classification would seem to better accommodate cultures that are more collectivist, and where the group – family, role or cultural – takes precedence over the self as a unit of analysis. It allows for the traditional self-serving bias (e.g. internal attribution for positive events), a group-serving bias (e.g. in-group/self-exclusion attribution for positive events), or a self-serving bias in a more collective cultural context (e.g. in-group/self-inclusion for positive events) (Moghaddam et al., 1993).

According to Markus and Kitayama (1991), perceiving a boundary between the individual and the rest of the social environment (as involved in the internal/external cause distinction) is distinctly Western in its cultural orientation. They describe this Western view as one where the individual is 'an independent, self-contained, autonomous entity who (a) comprises a unique configuration of internal attributes (e.g. traits, abilities, motives and values) and (b) behaves primarily as a consequence of these internal attributes' (quoted in Moghaddam et al., 1993). (This is relevant to the trait–situation debate – see Chapter 4.)

Markus and Kitayama use the term *connectedness* to describe the perspective of non-Western cultures (instead of the more common 'collectivist'). What these observations suggest is that the internal/external distinction, the very cornerstone of attribution theory, needs to be re-examined. This is not to discredit attribution, but to try to understand it as a culturally relative phenomenon (Moghaddam et al., 1993).

Attributional bias, discrimination and prejudice

Discussion of this more group-oriented classification of attribution is relevant to the work of Crocker and Major (1989, cited in Moghaddam et al., 1993), who are particularly interested in the attributions of those who belong to groups that are potential victims of discrimination. They argue that members of stigmatized groups are constantly confronted with attributional ambiguity: such individuals are never sure if their bad (or, indeed, their good) treatment from others is due to their own behaviour or the fact that they belong to that particular group. Such constant ambiguity can result in feelings of insecurity and frustration, but surprisingly, it is precisely this ambiguity that allows members of stigmatized groups to maintain a positive self-image. How? Instead of *internalizing* failure and other negative experiences, they can attribute them to discrimination (an *external* attribution, consistent with the self-serving bias).

An extension of the self-serving bias can help us understand prejudice and discrimination from the point of view of the prejudiced person (the bigot). There appears to be a *positivity bias for intimate others*, such that we grant them the benefit of the doubt by attributing positive actions to dispositional causes and negative actions to situational causes (Taylor & Koivumaki, 1976, cited in Pettigrew, 1979).

However, granting members of a disliked out-group the benefit of the doubt may not be so common. Taylor and Koivumaki suggest that 'a person who is disliked or hated may well be viewed as responsible for bad behaviours and not responsible for good ones. In other words, we may find a corresponding "negativity" effect for disliked others.' It is this possibility of a *negativity effect* extended to the intergroup level that forms the basis of what Pettigrew (1979) calls the *ultimate attribution error* (based, of course, on the fundamental attribution error – FAE – see above).

Part of the bigot's prejudice is a stereotyped view of the out-group and this needs to be protected from a positive evaluation of any of its members. If a member of the out-group is seen as behaving in a socially undesirable way, consistent with the stereotype, the FAE is enhanced (and the stereotype reinforced). Often, when race and ethnicity are involved, these attributions will take the form of believing that the negative behaviours of the individual are the result of immutable, genetic characteristics of the group in general – 'the bedrock assumption of racist doctrine', the *ultimate attribution error* (Pettigrew, 1979).

Attribution and impression management

We saw early in the chapter that making dispositional attributions is an integral part of the process of forming impressions of others. But it would be mistaken to think that we just let others form impressions of us without our trying to influence that process: because we usually wish to make a *favourable* impression, we try to present ourselves to others 'in such a way as to obtain favourable reactions or more generally to look good in terms of cultural ideals or their private values' (Turner, 1991).

This process of trying to influence how others see us is called *impression management* (or self-presentation), and two ways of trying to create favourable impressions of us in others, both of which are explicable in terms of attributional principles, are *excuse giving* and *confessing* (Weiner, 1992).

It is often in our own interests to manipulate others' perceptions of our responsibility for our behaviour, in order to control or alter their affective reactions towards us – that is to say, to make them make a particular kind of attribution about our behaviour. If we have 'broken a social contract', by, for example, arriving late for an appointment, a lesson, or even a date, we usually blame our lateness on something (or somebody) else. What we call 'making an excuse' involves 'substituting a false cause for a true cause', the word *excuse* meaning 'from' (*ex*) 'cause' (*cuse*) (Weiner, 1992).

Through trying to get the other person to make an *external attribution* about our socially unacceptable behaviour, we are trying to prevent or reduce an angry, disapproving, response:

> *To ward off these negative consequences, people may withhold the truth (lie), substituting explanations they anticipate will lessen anger. These good or functional excuses relieve the transgressor of personal responsibility. That is, excuses for a broken social contract are given to foster the perception that the wrongdoer is a 'moral person'. This certainly increases the likelihood that the relationship will be maintained.*
>
> (Weiner, 1992)

When we confess (as when we apologize), we are actually accepting responsibility and personal blame, 'Yet this admission of responsibility has the paradoxical effect of reducing responsibility and eliciting forgiveness' (Weiner, 1992).

Why should this be?

In terms of Jones and Davis's correspondent inference theory, 'the linkage between the negative act and the correspondent inference of unfavourable personality characteristics of the actor is lessened by the carrying out of a confession. That is, the behaviour and the intention that produced it are less likely to be perceived as corresponding to some underlying dispositional property of the person' (Weiner, 1992).

Attribution and helping behaviour

In one of the most famous field experiments to investigate *bystander intervention*, Piliavin et al. (1969) had actors stage a collapse in a New

Figure 2.10 Getting drunk is perceived as a controllable cause of need, and alcoholics are often seen as the most responsible for their own predicament

---

You know drink driving is dumb, so why do you do it? It's something you'd be embarrassed to admit to. Isn't it? But when you get done that's exactly what you have to do. Admit you're a loser. First you admit it to the police and the judge. They see people like you every day. Then you've got to admit to your boss you've got a one year ban, a five grand fine and insurance that costs more than your car does. And your friends? They think you're a mug, although they won't say it to your face. They'll just say it when you're not around. Don't drink and drive, or you may live to regret it. Issued by The Portman Group.

You really believe you won't get caught drink driving? How can you be so arrogant? What makes you so special? You probably even know someone who's been done, and you're no different. An idiot. When you do get caught, you face a ban of up to one year, a fine of up to five grand and insurance premiums that could treble. And you could be locked up. But then there's no getting through to some people. Don't drink and drive, or you may live to regret it. Do not drink and drive. Or you may live to regret it. Issued by The Portman Group.

Figure 2.11 Drink-drivers are held legally and morally responsible for the consequences of their actions

---

York subway train compartment. They manipulated several variables in order to see their effect on helping behaviour, the most relevant to our discussion of attribution being whether the 'victim' who collapses was either apparently ill or apparently drunk.

It was found that an individual who appears to be ill was significantly more likely to receive help than one who appears to be drunk, even when the immediate help needed is of the same kind. Piliavin et al. explained this finding by arguing that the costs of helping the drunk are higher (greater disgust) and the costs of not helping are lower (less self-blame and censure, since he is partly responsible for his own plight).

It is this last point that is crucial here; one of the major determinants of the decision to go to the aid of another person is the *perceived* cause of the need for help (Weiner, 1992). Piliavin et al. were only proposing this explanation of the greater help received by the ill victim as an 'after-the-fact interpretation', but is there any evidence that perceived causes are an element in the 'cost–reward matrix' involved in the decision to help or not to help?

A common experimental procedure is for a student to receive a request for academic help from a supposed classmate, with the reasons for the request being manipulated. One early study (Berkowitz, 1969) involved two reasons, experimenter error (external locus) or the classmate taking it easy (internal locus); more help was offered in the former case.

Barnes et al. (1979) varied two dimensions of causality independently: (i) controllability (the classmate asked to borrow notes either because of low ability – uncontrollable – or lack of effort – controllable) and (ii) stability. The uncontrollable cause was much more likely to elicit help, especially if this was seen as a stable characteristic. Since *both* controllability and stability involve an internal locus, the results suggest that it is controllability which is the crucial variable (rather than internal locus).

As applied to the Piliavin et al. study, getting drunk is perceived as a controllable cause of a need – people typically are held responsible for their alcohol consumption. When alcoholics are rated along with other stigmatized groups (such as the mentally ill, homosexuals, and obese people), they are often seen as the most responsible for their own predicament (Weiner, 1992). This is highlighted in campaigns against drink-driving, where, although the driver is clearly not intentionally harming his or her victim, because the harm is a consequence of a freely chosen, controllable act, he or she is held responsible – both legally and morally – for those consequences (Gross, 1994).

According to Weiner (1992), if witnesses regard the behaviour of the victim as uncontrollable (if, say, the victim is ill), they are more likely to respond sympathetically, which, in turn, makes it more likely that they will help; but if they consider it to be controllable (the victim is drunk), they are more likely to respond angrily, and help will be less forthcoming.

Clearly, not all forms of illness will be seen as equally uncontrollable, and some may be seen as highly controllable (preventable), as in the case of lung cancer or heart disease, which are linked to smoking. There is currently a debate taking place in Britain about the rights and wrongs of accepting patients for heart surgery (and other forms of treatment for major illnesses) when they continue to smoke or otherwise reduce the chances of the treatment being successful.

While these are clearly ethical issues, an understanding of the cognitive and affective processes involved when people debate them may throw light on the opinions expressed and the conclusions reached. Prominent among those cognitive processes are the attributions made concerning causation, controllability, and responsibility. (See Chapter 12, on free will and determinism.)

Summary

- According to Heider, a fundamental feature of *commonsense psychology* is the belief that *causes* underlie people's overt behaviour.
- The *attribution process* refers to the *naive psychologist's* attempt to explain behaviour in terms of *dispositional/personal* (internal) or *situational/environmental* (external) causes.
- *Attribution theory* refers to the attempt by psychologists to understand the attribution process; it is the process itself (and the 'perceived' cause), rather than its accuracy ('the' cause), that they are interested in.
- A distinction has been made between attribution theory and *theories of attribution*.
- Attribution theory refers to a collection of diverse theoretical traditions, notably Heider's commonsense psychology, Jones and Davis's *correspondent inference theory*, Kelley's *covariation model*, Schachter's *emotional lability/cognitive labelling theory*, Bem's *self-perception theory*, and Weiner's *motivational theory of attribution*.
- Attribution principles have been applied to: interpersonal perception, the subjective experience of emotion, attitude change, self-attributions, impression management, achievement motivation, helping behaviour, prejudice, depression and marital relationships.
- *Correspondent inference theory* is concerned primarily with whether

a person's behaviour will be attributed to some disposition of the actor, rather than to situational factors.

- An attribution or inference is correspondent when the disposition attributed to an actor 'corresponds' to the behaviour from which it is inferred.
- A precondition for a correspondent inference is the attribution of *intentionality* which, in turn, depends on *knowledge* that the act would have the observed effects and the *ability* to produce them.
- Correspondent inferences are drawn through *the analysis of uncommon effects*, *choice*, *social desirability*, *social role*, and *prior expectations*.
- The covariation model begins by asking: *What information do people use to arrive at an internal or external attribution*? The three main kinds of causal information are *consensus*, *distinctiveness* and *consistency*.
- *Causal schemata* are also used to arrive at an attribution, to supplement these.
- Attribution theory is criticized for portraying naive scientists as being much more rational and logical than they really are; study of *attributional biases* seem to provide a better descriptive analysis of causal attribution. These include: the *fundamental attribution error*, the *actor – observer effect*, and the *self-serving bias*.
- According to Schachter's cognitive labelling theory, emotional experience depends both on physiological changes and on how these are interpreted. The famous 'adrenaline' experiment shows that we have to 'decide' which particular emotion we are feeling, the label we give to our arousal depending on to what we attribute that arousal.
- An important implication of Schachter's theory is the *mis-attribution effect*, which, in turn, has therapeutic/clinical implications, especially the treatment of anxiety disorders.
- Bem's self-perception theory is a major alternative to Festinger's theory of attitude change, *cognitive dissonance theory*.
- It claims that *self-attributions* are explanations of our own observable behaviour, essentially the same as attributions we make about others.
- Bem tested his theory using *interpersonal simulation*.
- The actor–observer effect and the fundamental attribution error are two major sources of bias in the attribution process. The former may apply to negative behaviour, but the self-serving bias can explain attributions for both negative *and* positive behaviour.
- An exception to the self-serving bias is the person who is *clinically depressed*. The earlier *helplessness model* of depression was replaced by a model based on attributional principles, namely an *attributional style*, in which failures are explained in terms of *internal*, *stable* and *global factors*.
- A corresponding attributional style is found among people who score

low on *need for Achievement* (nAch); by contrast, high scorers make internal attributions for their successes.

- This *self-derogatory/self-derogating* pattern of self-attribution is also more common among women in general, and women are also more likely to be depressed and to score low on nAch.
- Gender differences in attributional style appear as early as three or four years of age. This is linked to gender differences in overall levels of self-esteem.
- Happily married couples show *relationship-enhancing*, and unhappily married couples show *distress-maintaining*, patterns of attribution when explaining their partners' positive and negative behaviour.
- Unhappy couples are also more likely to blame their partners (*responsibility attribution*) and not just make a *causal attribution*.
- The self-serving bias may be a characteristic of *individualist* cultures, and not a universal norm. Indeed, the whole internal/external cause distinction is distinctly Western in its cultural orientation.
- Members of minority groups can maintain a positive self-image by attributing their failures etc. to discrimination and other external factors.
- A negativity effect applied to whole groups forms the basis of the *ultimate attribution error*, the fundamental assumption of racist doctrine.
- Two forms of *impression management/self-presentation* are *excuse giving* and *confessing*. Both involve the attempt to make the other person make an external attribution about our socially unacceptable behaviour, thus reducing our personal responsibility.
- One of the major influences on people's decision to offer help to another person is the *perceived cause* of the need for help, with controllability being a crucial variable.

Suggestions for further reading

Ross, L. & Nisbett, R.E. (1991) *The Person and the situation: Perspectives of social psychology* (especially Chapter 3), New York: McGraw Hill.

Weiner, B. (1992) *Human Motivation: Metaphors, theories and research* (especially Chapters 6 and 7), Newbury Park, Calif.: Sage.

The idiographic and nomothetic approaches to the study of behaviour

Psychology: the study of individuals or the study of people?

Of all the methods traditionally used by psychologists to study human beings, it is the case study which has most often been criticized for being unscientific (or the least scientific), on the grounds that, since only one 'case' is being studied, it is not, therefore possible to generalize the results – that is, we cannot base our theories of what *people* are like on the study of *individuals*.

According to the same argument, the *experiment* is the most powerful method of research, partly because it does allow us to generalize (notwithstanding the criticisms of artificiality etc.). This is possible only because the characteristics of particular subjects/participants, being controlled through the use of experimental design, are irrelevant: it is group averages that are statistically analysed and what the investigator is interested in, not individual performance.

Consequently, if psychologists want to find out about people, the last thing they should do is to study . . . *people!* This might seem like an absurd conclusion to reach, but is it also an inevitable one?

A number of points need to be made here.

1 Imagine a chemist refusing to generalize the results of an investigation on the grounds that the particular sample of the chemical used was not typical or representative: however absurd that may sound, it is the equivalent of the situation with regard to the psychological case study.

2 It follows from point 1 that human beings are different from chemicals (and other aspects of the physical world) in at least one major respect, namely, they are not all identical or interchangeable but display great variability and variety.

3 Different psychologists have interpreted (and studied) the nature and extent of this variability and variety in different ways. A convenient way of identifying these different approaches is to quote Kluckhohn and Murray (1953): 'Every man is in certain respects like all other men, like some other men, and like no other men.'

How we are *all like each other* is a way of referring to *general psychology*, the study of basic psychological processes, with the emphasis very much on the process, such as memory, perception and learning. It is almost as if the *process* occurs in some disembodied way, with the memorizer, perceiver or learner being almost irrelevant, or at least unnecessary, for an understanding of the process being investigated. This is part of what goes on in the name of psychology, so it must be to do with the study of people – but is it?

The nomothetic approach

Ways in which we are like *some* other human beings is the subject matter of *individual differences*. While this approach acknowledges that humans are definitely not like chemicals, it also claims that there is only a limited, relatively small number of ways in which people differ from each other, sometimes referred to as *group norms*. Examples include personality, intelligence, age, gender, ethnic and cultural background.

This is a way of studying people using a *nomothetic approach* (from the Greek *nomos*, meaning 'law'). If psychologists can establish the ways in which we are like some others, then they can also tell us how we are *different from* others – these are two sides of the same coin. In either case, a comparison is being made between people and this is usually done using *psychometric tests*. The results of these tests are then analysed using a statistical technique called *factor analysis*, which is used to identify the basic factors or dimensions which constitute for example, personality or intelligence. Once these have been identified, the basis for comparing people with each other has been established. Factor-analytic theories of intelligence include Spearman's (1904, 1967) *Two-factor theory*, Burt's (1949, 1955) and Vernon's (1950) *hierarchical model*, Thurstone's (1938) *primary mental abilities* and Guilford's (1959) *structure of intellect*. Eysenck (1953, 1965) and Cattell (1965) are probably the best known factor-analytic personality theorists.

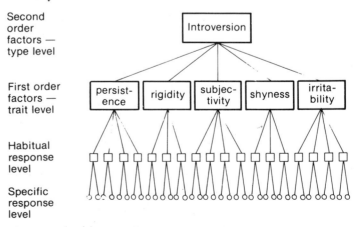

Figure 3.1 Eysenck's hierarchical model of personality in relation to the introversion dimension (After Eysenck, 1953)

The idiographic approach

Ways in which we are *unlike anyone else* is the subject matter of those psychologists who adopt an *idiographic approach* (from the Greek *idios* meaning 'own' or 'private'). This is the study of *individual norms*, the study of people as unique individuals. Gordon Allport (1937, 1961) is perhaps the main advocate of an idiographic approach, with the humanistic personality theories of Maslow (1954, 1968) and Rogers (1951, 1961), and Kelly's (1955) *personal construct theory* representing this approach and embodying many of its basic principles and assumptions.

Some points for consideration

1 Are the nomothetic and idiographic approaches mutually exclusive – do we have to choose between them? Are there any theories of personality which embody *both* approaches?

2 Does it make sense to talk about a totally unique person, someone whose personality has *nothing* in common with that of any other?

3 Must we agree with Allport (1937) that, since all science is nomothetic, and since psychology should be concerned with the study of individuals, therefore, psychology cannot be a science?

4 Have we found a solution to the riddle concerning the study of people: that psychologists, in order to learn about people, should not study people? If we distinguish between people as individuals and people as groups, then perhaps we have; we have to be clear whether our aim is to find out about this particular person (idiographic) or how this person compares with others (nomothetic). Putting this in a slightly different way, the idiographic approach takes the individual as its basic unit of analysis, while for the nomothetic approach it is groups of individuals (see Figure 3.5). In the former, the obtained data are a sample of the individual's total set or population of emotions, cognitions, personality traits (as expressed through behaviour) and so on, while in the latter, the obtained data are specified traits or behaviour as measured in a sample of individuals drawn from some larger population of individuals. It is the difference between a population of many (nomothetic) and a population of one (idiographic).

If the answers to question 1 above are 'no' and 'yes' respectively, and if the answer to question 2 is 'no', then we should regard the process of studying individuals as individuals as being inseparable from the process of comparing individuals with each other.

By the same argument, if the answer to question 3 is 'no', then we should be willing to accept that generalizing from the individual case, as well as generalizing about the same individual, are legitimate scientific activities; i.e. the nomothetic and idiographic approaches are compatible with each other.

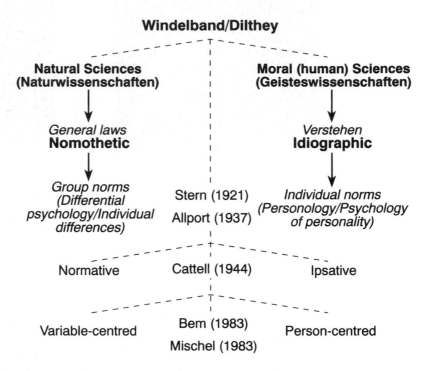

Figure 3.2 The nomothetic-idiographic distinction and its relationship to other, corresponding distinctions

Historical background

The distinction between idiographic and nomothetic approaches is related to a distinction made, independently, by two nineteenth-century German philosophers, Dilthey and Windelband, between two kinds of science. The *Naturwissenschaften* (natural sciences), such as physics and chemistry, aim to establish general laws, allowing predictions based on statements about cause-and-effect relationships, while the *Geisteswissenschaften* ('moral sciences'), such as philosophy, the humanities, history, biography and literary criticism, and 'social science', involve *Verstehen*, an intuitive, empathic understanding. (See Figure 3.2.)

The natural sciences are concerned with the natural world, and so quite appropriately *explain* it in terms of 'natural laws' ('laws of nature'), and analyse it into elements. But the moral or human sciences require an understanding of human mental activity (i.e. consciousness), stressing the inner unity of individual life and the person as an articulated whole (Valentine, 1992). Rather than treating the individual case as incidental to the discovery of general laws, the social sciences focus primarily on the

Figure 3.3 The nomothetic and idiographic distinction is related to the distinction made in the nineteenth century between *Naturwissenschaften* (natural sciences) and *Geisteswissenschaften* (moral sciences), which can be recognised as the distinction between the scientist in the laboratory and the philosopher in his/her armchair

particular (whether this be a person, historical event, or literary work). Windelband, together with another German, Rickert, went on to argue that all the disciplines concerned with 'man and his works' should not – and by their very nature cannot – generalize, but must devote themselves to the understanding of each particular case (Holt, 1967).

Corresponding to the distinction between the natural and human sciences is that between a *variable-centred* and *person-centred* approach (Bem, 1983; Mischel, 1983), and that between a *normative* ('compared with others') and *ipsative* ('compared with the self') approach (Cattell, 1944) (see Figure 3.2). According to Holt (1967), this sweeping statement reflects a number of false beliefs, still widely held, about the nomothetic – idiographic distinction, some of which we shall now consider. We should note that (i) these are false beliefs as held by those of an idiographic persuasion, and (ii) a distinction is commonly made between *personology* (the psychology of personality) and *differential psychology* (the psychology of individual differences; Holt, 1967). These correspond to the idiographic and nomothetic approaches respectively.

The goal of personology is understanding, while that of nomothetic science is prediction and control.

According to Holt (1967), all the highly developed sciences aim at prediction and control *through* understanding, and these three goals cannot be separated: 'Most scientists, as contrasted with technologists, are themselves more motivated by the need to figure things out, to develop good theories and workable models that make nature intelligible, and less concerned with the ultimate payoff, the applied benefits of prediction and control that understanding makes possible' (Holt, 1967).

He argues that many psychologists, subscribing to this misconception of natural science as totally rigorous, objective, and machine-like, try to emulate this nomothetic approach. It is because of, rather than despite, the 'intrinsically difficult and ambiguity-ridden' nature of psychology, that this view of natural science is so appealing, especially to behaviourist psychologists.

However, the kind of understanding involved in *Verstehen*, namely an attempt to know something from the inside, by non-intellectual means, as directly as possible, through trying to gain an empathic feeling of it, is non-explanatory, and is 'a subjective effect properly aimed at by artists, not scientists' (Holt, 1967).

But even accepting Holt's argument regarding the importance of understanding in natural science, and the important difference between 'scientific' and 'non-scientific' understanding, isn't this only half the story – does it necessarily follow that prediction and control are appropriate aims for psychology (as they clearly are for physics and chemistry, along with explanation and understanding)?

George Miller (1969) for one, believes that control is inappropriate, at least in the sense of one person (the experimenter/investigator/therapist) assuming a powerful, directing role in relation to another (subject/patient). Radical critics of mainstream, particularly behaviouristic, psychology (especially Skinner's 'radical behaviourism') see the attempt to apply to human behaviour, principles and methods derived from the laboratory study of rats and pigeons, as the ultimate kind of mechanistic, dehumanizing approach (e.g. Heather, 1976; Shotter, 1975). (See Chapter 11.)

Not only is *understanding* the appropriate aim for psychology (as opposed to control), but it is *self*-understanding which, according to Miller, psychology should be striving to provide people with – this is what he means when he advocates 'giving psychology away'.

Attempts to realize these aims are perhaps best seen in psychotherapy, much of which is an attempt to change individuals' perception of themselves and increase their self-understanding/insight. It also aims at increasing autonomy and independence (Lindley, 1987, cited in Fairbairn, 1987), i.e. *taking control of one's own life* (a very different form of control compared with its meaning in the natural sciences) (but see Chapter 10).

The proper methods of personology are intuition and empathy, which have no place in natural science.

Holt (1967) rejects this claim by pointing out that all scientists make use of intuition and empathy as part of the most exciting and creative phase of their work, namely when deciding what to study, what variables to control, what empirical strategies to use, and when making discoveries within the structure of empirical data. To the extent that such processes are inevitably involved in science, which is, first and foremost, a human activity, no science can be thought of as wholly objective (see Chapters 1 and 11). The failure to recognize the role of these processes, and the belief in the 'objective truth' produced by the use of the 'scientific method', can result in theories and explanations which can work to the detriment of certain individuals and social groups (as in the 'race and IQ debate'; see Chapter 10, on ethics).

While 'hard science' may appear softer when the role of intuition is acknowledged, it is also nomothetic psychology which has been most guilty of the 'crimes' of racism, ethnocentrism and sexism (see Chapters 6 and 8).

The concepts of personology must be individualized, not generalized, as are the concepts of natural science.

General laws aren't possible in personology, because its subject matter is unique individuals which have no place in natural science.

These two beliefs are dealt with together, because they lie at the very heart of the nomothetic – idiographic debate. They relate to two fundamental questions.

1 Does it make sense to talk about a wholly unique individual?
2 What is the relationship between individual cases and general laws/principles in scientific practice?

THE WHOLLY UNIQUE INDIVIDUAL

Allport (1961) distinguished between three types of personal traits or dispositions, *cardinal, central* and *secondary*. Briefly, *cardinal traits* refer to a particular, all-pervading disposition (such as greed, ambition or lust) which dictates and directs almost all of an individual's behaviour. In practice, these are very rare. *Central traits* are the basic building blocks which make up the core of the personality and which constitute the individual's characteristic ways of dealing with the world (by being honest, loving, happy-go-lucky for example). A surprisingly small number of these is usually sufficient to capture the essence of a person. *Secondary traits* are less consistent and influential than central traits and refer to tastes, preferences and so on which may change quite quickly and do not define 'the person' as central traits do.

These *individual traits* are peculiar (idiosyncratic) to each person, in at least three senses.

1 A trait that is central for one person may only be a secondary trait for another and irrelevant for a third. What makes a trait central or secondary is not what it is, but how often and how strongly it influences the person's behaviour (Carver & Scheier, 1992).
2 Some traits are possessed by only one person; indeed, there may be as many separate traits as people to have them.

3 Even if two different people are given (for convenience) the same descriptive label (for example, 'aggressive'), it may not mean the same for the individuals concerned, and to that extent, it is not the same trait.

For Allport, since personality dispositions reflect the subtle shadings that distinguish a particular individual from all others, they must often be described at length ('little Susan has a peculiar anxious helpfulness all her own'), instead of by a single label ('helpful').

What all this means, for Allport, is that it is very difficult to compare people:

> *Suppose you wish to select a roommate or a wife or a husband, or simply to pick out a suitable birthday gift for your mother. Your knowledge of mankind in general will not help you very much . . . [Any given individual] is a unique creation of the forces of nature. There was never a person just like him and there will never be again . . . To develop a science of personality we must accept this fact.*
> (Allport, 1961, quoted in Carver & Scheier, 1992)

While the idiographic approach contends that people are not comparable (everyone is, in effect, on a 'different scale'), comparing people in terms of a specified number of traits or dimensions (in order to determine individual differences) is precisely what the nomothetic approach involves. According to this view, traits have the same psychological meaning for everyone, so that people only differ in the extent to which the trait is present. For example, everyone is more or less introverted, which means that everyone will score somewhere on the introversion–extroversion scale: the difference between individuals is one of degree only (a quantitative difference). By contrast, the idiographic approach sees differences between people as qualitative, as being differences in kind.

Allport himself recognized that people *can* be compared with each other, but in terms of *common traits* (as distinct from individual traits). Although every person is unique, there are basic modes of adjustment which are applicable to all members of a particular cultural, ethnic or linguistic group. These basic modes of adjustment (common traits) are 'those aspects of personality in respect to which most people within a given culture can be profitably compared . . . [and are] indispensable whenever we undertake to study personality by scales, tests, ratings, or any other comparative method' (Allport, 1961, quoted in Ewen, 1988). At best, they can only provide a rough approximation to any particular personality. For example, many individuals are predominantly outgoing or shy, yet 'there are endless varieties of dominators, leaders, aggressors, followers, yielders, and timid souls . . . When we designate Tom and Ted both as *aggressive*, we do not mean that their aggression is identical in kind. Common speech is a poor guide to psychological subtleties' (Allport, 1961, quoted in Ewen, 1988). The nomothetic approach, for Allport, can only portray human personality in an oversimplified way: even the traits that people seem to share with one another always have a personal flavour which differs from individual to individual.

So how valid is the notion of a wholly unique person? According to Holt (1967), to describe an individual trait, we either have to create a new word (neologism) for each unique trait, or we use a unique configuration of already-existing words. While the former would make ordinary communication impossible, let alone science, the latter is a concealed form of nomothesis, a 'fallacious attempt to capture something ineffably individual by a complex net of general concepts' (Allport, 1937, quoted in Holt, 1967).

Disagreement between Allport and those of a nomothetic persuasion is not so much to do with whether or not they believe in the idea of uniqueness, but rather the way it is defined. Eysenck, for example, sees uniqueness as reflecting a unique *combination* of levels on trait dimensions, with the dimensions themselves being the same for all: 'To the scientist, the unique individual is simply the point of intersection of a number of quantitative variables' (Eysenck, 1953, quoted in Carver & Scheier, 1992).

As we have seen, this is a definition of uniqueness in terms of common traits; for Allport, this is a contradiction in terms, since only individual traits capture the individuality of individuals.

Agreeing with Holt, Brody (1988, quoted in Eysenck, 1994) argues that: 'If the trait applies only to one person, then it cannot be described in terms that apply to more than one person. This would require one to invent a new language to describe each person or, perhaps, to develop the skills of a poet to describe an individual.'

According to Krahé (1992), the idiographic claim that there are unique traits that apply to only one individual is undoubtedly false, if taken literally, anyway: traits are defined as differential constructs referring to a person's position on a trait dimension relative to that of other people. But at the other extreme, Krahé believes that the traditional (nomothetic) view of traits as explanatory constructs which apply to everyone, is equally misguided.

For Holt (1967), the nomothetic – idiographic distinction is based on a false dichotomy: all descriptions involve some degree of generalization, so that when we describe an individual case, there is always (at least implicitly) a comparison being made with other instances of the category or class to which the individual belongs. To describe this person, we must already have (and be applying) our concept of a person; if our concept of a person includes their uniqueness, this at least is something that everyone has in common and is perfectly consistent with Eysenck's (nomothetic) concept of uniqueness. Indeed, could we even recognize a person who was totally unlike any other, in any respect, as a *person*?

THE RELATIONSHIP BETWEEN INDIVIDUAL CASES AND GENERAL PRINCIPLES

When Windelband distinguished between *Naturwissenschaften* and *Geisteswissenscaften* in 1894, the mechanistic science of the time operated on the principle that science does not deal with individual cases. The individual case is not lawful, since laws were seen as empirical regularities; based on Plato's *idealism* and Popper's *essentialism*, an *average* is the only fact and all deviations from it are merely errors (Holt, 1967).

Putting this another way, since it is not possible to generalize from a single case, and since the aim of science is to formulate general laws and principles, the study of single cases is not a valid part of scientific practice. But is this a valid view of science as it is practised today? Are there different senses in which generalization can take place? Given the false dichotomy between the nomothetic and idiographic approaches, how should we understand the relationship between individual cases and general laws or principles?

Holt (1967) himself pointed out that, while we cannot carry out the complete scientific process by the study of one individual, 'in certain of the disciplines concerned with man, from anatomy to sensory psychology, it has usually been assumed that the phenomena being studied are so universal that they can be located for study in any single person'.

However, no matter how intensively prolonged, objective and well controlled the study of a single case may be, we can never be sure to what extent the findings will apply to other people: unless and until the investigation is repeated with an adequate sample, we cannot know how 'typical' the single case actually is. This is the logic behind the study by psychologists of *groups* of people, so that personality and other individual differences do not 'get in the way' of the key individual variable under investigation.

But while the reasons behind this practice may be clear, are they necessarily valid? The objections from an idiographic theorist like Allport should now be obvious, but a nomothetic theorist such as Eysenck will also object, although for very different reasons. Precisely because he emphasizes the basic dimensions of personality, in terms of which every person can be compared, he believes that any investigation which attempts to exclude them or render them irrelevant (through rigorous use of experimental design) is inadequate. For example, (i) main experimental effects apply only to *means*, preventing predictions about individual cases; (ii) any theories or explanations based on such studies may only have very limited validity; they may not generalize to samples with particular scores on important personality dimensions; (iii) failure to take individual differences into account may result in main experimental effects being swamped or obscured.

Eysenck (1966, cited in Valentine, 1992) sees the dimensional approach (or typologies) as a compromise between the false extremes of the experimentalist, who seeks to establish general functional relationships (the nomothetic approach) where personality differences are largely excluded, and the idiographic personality theorist, who 'embraces the concept of the individual so whole-heartedly that it leaves no room for scientific generalization, laws, or even predictability of conduct' (Eysenck, 1966, quoted in Valentine, 1992).

For a number of writers, the dichotomy between single case and group studies is a false one. For example, according to Newcombe and Marshall (1988, cited in Valentine, 1992), the importance of an effect is not simply related to sample size but is a function of theoretical context. Again, an individual case can be, and often is, the subject of scientific investigation. Where data from individual subjects are seen as reliable and representative, single-subject designs are considered acceptable (Valentine, 1992).

While, from the idiographic perspective, the very notion of an individual being 'representative' is itself contentious (because it implies the opposite of unique), the fact that the study of individual cases goes on at all within 'mainstream', nomothetic psychology indicates that the study of individuals may not, in and of itself, be incompatible with the aim of psychological science to *generalize* about behaviour.

Indeed, for Thorngate (1986, quoted in Hilliard, 1993), the study of averages is often ill-suited to providing information about what people 'in general' do, since it typically cancels out systematic patterns in individual persons. (This is similar to Eysenck's criticism of experimental psychology, discussed above, regarding the irrelevance of individual differences.) Rather than searching for nomothetic laws based on averaged data, their discovery requires a strategy in which the uniqueness of individuals is preserved: 'To find out what people do in general, we must first discover what each person does in particular, then determine what, if anything, these particulars have in common . . . Nomothetic laws lie at the intersection of idiographic laws; the former can be discovered only after we find the latter' (Thorngate, 1986, quoted in Hilliard, 1993).

In other words, the generality of the findings would not be determined through group aggregates (finding the average for a large number of individuals), but by replication on a case-by-case basis. Thorngate is arguing that the two approaches are complementary and interdependent. 'Although single-case methodology has been identified with an exclusive idiographic focus in the minds of many, this identification is simply not warranted. Most single-case research clearly involves determining the generality across subjects of the relationships uncovered at the individual, or idiographic, level' (Hilliard, 1993).

Figure 3.4 The individual dove acts as its own control in the Skinner Box and represents single-case research

Hilliard gives as a prime example of such methodology Skinner's use of single-case research to study the principles of operant conditioning. One feature of such research is the fact that the individual rat or pigeon acts as its own control, since its behaviour is measured before, during and after the reinforcement contingencies are applied. Of course, the individuality of the animals used in such research is of no concern to the researchers: the aim is to formulate generalizations applicable to *all* members of those species (and, indeed, to other species as well), and/or to test general laws/principles which have already been proposed.

Sometimes, single cases may be all that is available to the investigator, as in neuropsychology, where patients who suffer brain injury and disease are patients first, and subjects/participants second. While they may be intensely interesting in themselves, they are usually studied for what they can tell us about the normal functioning of the brain and nervous system. Unless an adequate baseline for comparison is provided, such as the patient's

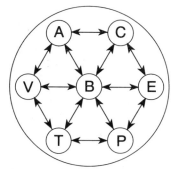

a) Basic unit of study = the individual

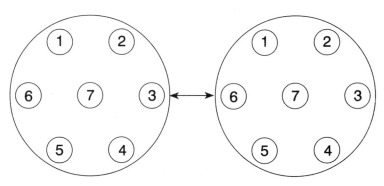

b) Basic unit of study = the group

Figure 3.5 Differences in the kind of generalization involved in the (a) idiographic and (b) nomothetic approaches. In the idiographic approach, data collected represent samples from an individual's total population of characteristics (A, attitudes; B, behaviour; C, cognition; E, emotion; P, physiological make-up; T, traits; V, values), and the norms that operate are **individual norms**, generalizing within the individual. In the nomothetic approach, data collected represent either (i) samples from the total population of the characteristic in question (e.g. 'How do high E (extroversion) scorers compare with low E scorers on some task?'), or (ii) samples from the total population of performance on some task with individual differences held constant (e.g. the independent variable is exposure to high or low stress). In both cases, this gives **group norms**, generalizing across or between individuals.

performance before the illness or injury, or scores from the normal population on standarized tests, the results are scientifically uninterpretable. Without replication, it is difficult to know whether the results are generalizable: such data are insufficient to establish general laws. However, even if the study of individual cases doesn't allow the testing of hypotheses, it may at least help to formulate them (Valentine, 1992).

The results from studies of individuals may also offer the potential for generalizing to other attributes or behavioural characteristics of the individual being studied. Idiographic research is aimed at generalizing *within* the individual, while nomothetic research seeks to generalize *across* individuals (see Figure 3.5). According to Krahé (1992), there is no inherent conflict between these aims; they are complementary, rather than mutually exclusive research strategies.

> *Nomothetic procedures are important for investigating individual differences and differences in performance among groups of subjects, but provide no information on processes within individuals. Idiographic approaches, on the other hand, provide information about processes within individuals, but provide no information on individual differences or on the generality of findings across individuals. Thus, each procedure has its advantages and limitations, and neither is a substitute for the other.*
>
> (Epstein, 1983, quoted in Krahé, 1992)

Not only is this a view of the two approaches being equally valid and necessary; it is also a way of thinking about generalization in relation to individuals.

As we saw earlier, the nineteenth-century scientific belief, that the average is the only fact and that the individual case is not lawful, led Windelband to make the distinction between the natural and 'human' sciences, and it is from this distinction that the whole nomothetic–idiographic debate emanates. Logically, there is no reason to equate 'generalization' with the study of 'groups', although that is precisely the equation made by the nomothetic approach. Allport was interested in the study of individual norms (as distinct from group norms); both involve 'going beyond' the data which have actually been collected and making predictions about future 'performance': this can either be the future performance of other individuals not included in the sample studied (group norms/nomothetic approach), or the future performance of the same individual (individual norms/idiographic approach).

According to Hilliard (1993), there has been a recent widespread resurgence of interest in single-case designs within psychotherapy research. There is a plethora of terms used for such designs, including: *single case*, N *of 1*, *case study*, *small* N, *idiographic*, *intensive*, *discovery-oriented*, *intrasubject* and *time-series*. He believes that such a variety of terms can lead to confusion and argues that single-case research is best viewed as a subclass of intrasubject research in which the focus is on the unfolding, over time, of variables within individual subjects.

Consistent with this revival is the view that it is perfectly possible to apply systematic, reliable, quantitative, or experimental methods to the study of individual cases; for example, factor analysis can be applied to individual as well as to group data (Krahé, 1992). Not only is this a scientifically valid approach, but there has been a proliferation of quantitative and experimental studies of the single case (Runyan, 1983, cited in Krahé, 1992).

Reconciling the nomothetic and idiographic approaches

From the preceding discussion, it seems that psychologists are increasingly coming to believe that the two approaches, far from being opposed and mutually exclusive, are in fact complementary and interdependent. As Krahé (1992) puts it, 'there seems to be a growing consensus that it is possible, in principle, for idiographic and nomothetic approaches to join forces so as to contribute to a more comprehensive analysis of the issues of personality psychology'.

Even Allport, the leading advocate of the uniqueness of the individual, did not reject the nomothetic approach out of hand. For example, when discussing the nature of psychology as a science, he says that:

> *Science aims to achieve powers of understanding, prediction and control above the level of unaided common sense. From this point of view it becomes apparent that only by taking adequate account of the individual's total pattern of life can we achieve the aims of science. Knowledge of general laws . . . quantitative assessments and correlational procedures are all helpful: but with this conceptual (nomothetic) knowledge must be blended a shrewd diagnosis of trends within an individual . . . Unless such idiographic (particular) knowledge is fused with nomothetic (universal) knowledge, we shall not achieve the aims of science, however closely we imitate the methods of the natural and mathematical sciences.*

(Allport, 1960)

Also in relation to the aims of science, Jaccard and Dittus (1990, cited in Krahé, 1992) argue that it is untrue that a strictly idiographic approach is directly opposed to the identification and development of universal laws of human behaviour. The idiographic researcher, like the nomothetic, is interested in explaining behaviour, and to do this, both seek a general theoretical framework that specifies the constructs that should be focused upon and the types of relationships expected among these concepts. The essential difference between them is that one applies the framework to a single person, while the other applies it to people in general. They share the same scientific aim.

Both Allport and Windelband made it very clear that one and the same issue can, in principle, be considered either from an idiographic or nomothetic perspective, depending on the nature of the question under investigation (Krahé, 1992), while, according to Epstein (1983, cited in Krahé, 1992), the two approaches 'do not present different solutions to the same problem but solutions to different problems'.

Perhaps the most radical departure from the traditional individual differences (nomothetic) approach to the study of personality, has been Lamiell's (1981, 1982, 1987) *idiothetic* approach. This represents an attempt to integrate the aims of both approaches.

Idiographic methods, old and new

We began the chapter by pointing out the limitations (as judged from a nomothetic point of view) of the case study. While one of the standard criticisms of Freud's psychoanalytic theory is to do with his reliance on the case study, we have also seen that this method is central to neuro-psychology. Perhaps it is not the case-study method itself which is of limited scientific value, but rather the use that researchers make of it, the data that are obtained, and the resulting theories and hypotheses.

A more specific idiographic method is the *Q-sort*, originally devised and developed by Butler and Haigh (1954) and Stephenson (1953), but best known as it was used by Carl Rogers (Rogers & Dymond, 1954), for assessing an individual's self-concept, especially in the context of psychotherapy. Although there are many variations, the basic procedure involves giving people a large set of cards, that contain self-evaluative statements (such as 'I am intelligent', 'I often feel guilty', 'I am ambitious'), phrases or single words. The person is asked to sort the cards into piles, one pile containing statements etc. that 'are most like you', another containing statements that 'are least like you', and other piles representing gradations in between these two extremes. While the two 'extreme' piles may only comprise a single card, those in between are allowed to have more, with those in the middle having the most.

The technique forces the sorter to decide what he or she is like by comparing qualities with each other, whereas in (nomothetic) rating scales, each response is separate and unrelated to the others – all the descriptions apply equally well. This is impossible in the Q-sort (Carver & Scheier, 1992).

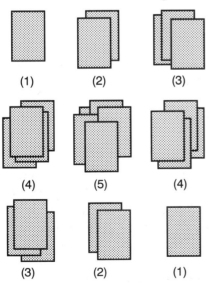

Figure 3.6 The Q-sort is used to assess an individual's self-concept

This same basic technique can be used to assess: 'The

kind of person I am (now)', 'The kind of person I used to be', allowing an assessment of changes in the self-image over time, and 'The kind of person I would like to be', a measure if the person's ideal self. Comparing self-image and ideal self can be used as a measure of the progress of therapy, since the greater the similarity between the two, the greater the degree of *congruence*, one of the goals of Rogers's *client-centred therapy*. The Q-sort is repeated several times during the course of therapy (see Chapter 12).

The *repertory grid technique* (or 'rep grid') was used by Kelly to investigate a person's system of constructs – that is, the individual's unique set of concepts and perceptions through which he or she interprets and predicts the world, both social and physical.

There are different forms of the test, but the basic method involves:
1 writing a list of the most important people in your life (*elements*),
2 choosing three of these elements,
3 deciding how two of these are alike and different from the third, the resulting description being a construct, expressed in a bipolar way (for example, affectionate–not affectionate),
4 applying the construct to all the other elements
5 repeating steps 2 – 4 until either the person has produced all the constructs he or she can, or until a sufficient number has been produced as judged by the investigator.

All this information can be collated in the form of a grid, hence the name. The grid can be factor-analysed, in order to reveal any overlap between the person's constructs, and, although it is primarily an idiographic technique, it can be used nomothetically, as Bannister and Fransella (1966, 1967) have done with thought-disordered schizophrenics. Their Grid Test of Thought Disorder contains standardized elements and constructs (supplied by the investigator), and the test has been standardized on large numbers of similar patients, allowing individual scores to be compared with group norms.

Like the Q-sort, the rep grid has been used to study how patients participating in group psychotherapy change their perception of each other (and themselves) during the period of therapy. The group members and themselves are the elements, and constructs are supplied (Fransella, 1970). It has been used extensively by Fransella (1972) with people being treated for severe stuttering.

According to Krahé (1992), the traditional range of methodologies (both idiographic and nomothetic) for studying personality has been substantially enriched by the growing acceptance of idiographic research methods. Building on the work of Allport (1937) and Murray (1938), 'the study of individual lives has recently been rediscovered as a central task for personality theorists committed to the personological tradition' (Krahé, 1992). Krahé discusses several new concepts and units of analysis designed to capture an individual's characteristic way of dealing with the multiple tasks, themes and events of life; these concepts include Little's *personal projects*, Emmons's *personal strivings*, and the *life tasks* of Cantor and Langston.

Conclusions: a different way of looking at the research process

Regardless of the details of particular new methodologies, according to Krahé (1992) the major implication of the resurgence of interest in the idiographic approach is a new conception of the relationship between the investigator and the person 'under investigation'.

The traditional (nomothetic) perception of the process of psychological inquiry involves a clear-cut division of roles, whereby the investigator formulates hypotheses, produces operational definitions, and selects appropriate measuring instruments, while the subject delivers valid data by dutifully completing the measuring instruments. Interaction between the two is limited to (i) instructions, and (ii) debriefing.

From the idiographic perspective, this role division is neither appropriate nor fruitful: it makes little use of the competence of the individual as an expert on his or her own personality.

Some investigators have explicitly advocated that the person whose personality is being studied should play a more active and cooperative role in the research process. For example, Hermans and Bonarius (1991, cited in Krahé, 1992) use the term *co-investigator* (cf. Kelly's personal construct therapy, in which the client is likened to a PhD student, with the therapist as his or her supervisor), and *collaborative research* and *new paradigm research* are becoming increasingly influential (see Coolican, 1994, and Chapter 11). The very use of the term *participant*, instead of 'subject' (see, for example, British Psychological Society, 1990, 1993), reflects a change in the thinking of psychologists about the research process, especially its ethical features. Not only is the term 'subject' degrading and dehumanizing (see Heather, 1976), but it could be argued that if a person is not studied as a unique individual (individual norms), but only in order to establish group norms, then he or she is not being treated fully as a person (see Chapter 10).

This, of course, is an ethical criticism of the nomothetic approach to research from an idiographic perspective. But just as there has been considerable reconciliation in recent years between the methodologies of the two approaches, so there is the promise that this reconciliation will make the study of human personality a more meaningful, and a more ethically acceptable, undertaking.

Summary

- One respect in which human beings differ from elements of the physical world is that they are not all identical or interchangeable, but display great variability and variety.
- The ways in which *we are all alike* is the subject matter of *general*

psychology.

- The ways in which *we are like some other people* is the concern of *individual differences*, which is concerned with *group norms*, such as personality, intelligence, age, gender, ethnic and cultural background.
- The study of individual differences involves a *nomothetic approach*, according to which people are compared in terms of a limited number of factors or dimensions, established by *factor analysis*. Examples include: Spearman's *two-factor theory* of intelligence, the *hierarchical model* of intelligence (Burt and Vernon), and the personality theories of Eysenck and Cattell.
- The ways in which *we are unlike anyone else* is the concern of the *idiographic approach*, which studies *individual norms*. Examples include: Allport's *trait theory*, Maslow's and Rogers' *humanistic personality theories*, and Kelly's *personal construct theory*.
- The idiographic–nomothetic distinction is related to that between the *Geisteswissenschaften* ('moral sciences') and the *Naturwissenschaften* (natural sciences) respectively. The latter are concerned with establishing general laws which enable predictions to be made about the natural world, while the former involve *Verstehen*, which focuses on individual cases and does not permit generalization.
- Holt argues that the three goals of prediction and control (*differential psychology/individual differences*) and understanding (*personology/psychology of personality*) cannot be separated.
- There is much debate as to whether prediction and control are appropriate aims for psychology, and *self-understanding* may be more appropriate than *understanding* (best seen in psychotherapy).
- Intuition and empathy are not unique to personology but play a part in all scientific work, making science less than wholly objective.
- Allport distinguished between three kinds of *individual traits*, namely *cardinal*, *central*, and *secondary*. Because these are peculiar (idiosyncratic) to each person, it is impossible to use them to compare people; however, they can be compared in terms of *common traits*.
- The idiographic approach sees differences between people as qualitative, while the nomothetic approach sees them as merely quantitative.
- The claim that an individual can be totally unique is very controversial.
- Uniqueness can be defined in different ways. Eysenck sees uniqueness as reflecting a unique *combination of levels on trait dimensions* (which are the same for everybody).
- The idiographic–nomothetic distinction is based on a false dichotomy: all descriptions involve some degree of generalization.

- Eysenck criticizes the (extreme nomothetic) attempt to eliminate individual differences from experimental studies, in order to establish general functional relationships, as well as the (extreme idiographic) emphasis on the individual which prevents generalization, laws, or even the prediction of behaviour.
- The dichotomy of *single case* versus *group studies* is a false one, with individual cases often being used in psychological research, indicating that the study of individuals may not be incompatible with making generalizations about behaviour.
- Most single-case research involves determining the *generality across subjects* of the relationships uncovered at the individual level, such as in Skinner's study of operant conditioning, in which the individual rat or pigeon acts as its own control.
- Sometimes, single cases may be all that is available to the investigator, as in neuropsychology. But an adequate baseline must be provided if the data from such single cases are to be scientifically useful.
- Even if the study of individual cases does not allow the testing of hypotheses, it may at least help to formulate them.
- Idiographic research aims at generalizing *within* the same individual (*intrasubject*), while nomothetic research aims at generalizing *across* different individuals (*intersubject*). The two approaches are complementary, rather than mutually exclusive.
- There has recently been a widespread revival of interest in single-case designs within psychotherapy research, as well as a proliferation of quantitative (including factor analysis) and experimental studies of the single case.
- Even Allport advocated the use of both idiographic and nomothetic methods in the pursuit of science's aim to achieve powers of understanding, prediction and control above the level of unaided common sense.
- Lamiell's *idiothetic* approach represents an attempt to integrate the aims of both the idiographic and nomothetic approaches.
- The case study is often cited as the least scientific of all the methods used by psychologists; this may reflect the use that researchers make of it, and the resulting data and theories, rather than the method in itself.
- The *Q-sort* is an idiographic method, best known as used by Rogers for assessing an individual's self-concept in the context of psychotherapy.
- Kelly's *repertory grid technique* (or 'rep grid') is used to identify a person's unique set of constructs. It can be used nomothetically, as with thought-disordered schizophrenics, patients in psychotherapy, and people being treated for severe stuttering.
- Several new concepts and units of analysis have been designed to

capture an individual's characteristic way of dealing with life's tasks, themes and events, including *personal projects*, *personal strivings*, and *life tasks*.
- The major implication of the resurgence of interest in the idiographic approach is a new view of the relationship between the investigator (who used to be 'in control') and the person being studied ('the subject'). The latter is now seen as an expert on his or her own personality, and is much more of a *co-investigator* or *collaborator/colleague* in the research process.
- The use of the term 'subject' has ethical implications, with *'participant'* being increasingly preferred, reflecting the changes in attitude towards the people taking part in research and the nature of the research itself.

Suggestions for further reading

Allport G.W. (1962) The general and the unique in psychological science, *Journal of Personality*, 30, 405–22.

Holt, R.R. (1962) Individuality and generalization in the psychology of personality, *Journal of Personality*, 30, 377–404. (This is an alternative to the 1967 reference, which is a revised version of the 1962 article which appeared in a book on personality, edited by Lazarus and Opton – see References at back.)

Krahé, B. (1992) *Personality and Social Psychology: Towards a synthesis* (especially Chapters 6, 7 and 9), London: Sage.

Traits and situations as causes of behaviour

Commonsense views of personality

It would seem to be part of 'commonsense' psychology, i.e. the lay person's everyday understanding of behaviour, that people behave in a largely reliable (consistent), and hence predictable way. As a general rule, if you ask someone to predict another person's behaviour, the response will depend on how well (or otherwise) he or she knows (or feels they know) the other person: complete strangers are impossible to predict, while with close relatives and friends it is much easier. Why?

Part of what we mean by saying that we know somebody well, is that we are able to identify the traits and characteristics that comprise that person's *personality*. In turn, we take these traits to be relatively permanent features of the person, which, collectively, at least, make someone the person he or she is. Logically, it follows that people will behave consistently, and predictably, on different occasions and in different situations. Since personality is constant, so behaviour will be consistent:

Personality traits → Consistency of behaviour →Predictability of behaviour

'Our experience with other people – as well as with ourselves – tells us that there is a certain regularity, consistency and uniqueness in the behaviours, thoughts and feelings of a person which define his or her personality' (Krahé, 1992). But is this all there is to it? Even in terms of our commonsense psychology, isn't the issue more complex than the picture presented so far?

Surely it is, since another feature of our commonsense psychology is the view of people as being less than one hundred per cent predictable. Indeed, we might regard someone who was so predictable as somehow being not quite human, robot-like, more of an automaton than a person. We *expect* people to be different at different times, to show changes in mood, thought and behaviour, within certain limits. And what sets those limits? To some degree they are set by our general concept of a person ('people are not robots'), but also by our familiarity with particular individuals. This latter point relates to what we said above about what it means to say we know

Figure 4.1 We might regard someone who was one hundred per cent predictable as somehow not quite human, more of an automaton than a person

someone well – our knowledge (or, perhaps more accurately, our beliefs) of another's personality is based on interactions with that person and observations of his or her behaviour over a large number of occasions, in a variety of situations. So we will have witnessed the variations in their behaviour, as well as the regularities, with the latter being used to draw our inferences about 'the kind of person' he or she is.

Consistency of behaviour and psychological abnormality

If part of our concept of a person is the element of unpredictability or inconsistency of behaviour, then anyone who shows excessive consistency may, to that extent, be judged as displaying abnormal behaviour. Indeed, the behaviour of individuals whom clinicians tend to work with may be highly predictable on the basis of some underlying trait or disposition; clinical problems may, in fact, be associated with a rigidity or inflexibility to changing conditions (Wachtel, 1977). But at the other extreme, people who 'shift with the wind' may also be subject to emotional disorder, such as overdependence on the environment as a guide to behaviour: 'To be totally at the mercy of one's surroundings, like a rudderless ship, would seem to pose as many problems as being insensitive to varying environmental demands (Phares, 1979)' (Davison & Neale, 1994). So, we could suggest that a criterion of psychological normality is a balance between consistent behaviour (usually taken to reflect the influence of personality traits) and inconsistent behaviour (usually taken to reflect the influence of situational factors). (See Chapter 7.)

Personality and social psychology

Traditionally, it has been personality psychologists who have been committed to the view that individuals can be characterized by enduring qualities which distinguish them from others and which make their behaviour highly consistent and predictable across a range of situations (high *intra-individual consistency*). By contrast, social psychologists have emphasized the impact on individuals of social situations, which can account for high *inter-individual consistency*. These two kinds of consistency relate to weak and strong situations respectively (Mischel, 1977): *weak situations* allow people to express their personal qualities easily – they 'leave room' for individual differences (they are fairly 'open-ended') – while *strong situations* force behaviour into specific channels making individual differences (largely) irrelevant (they are highly structured), demonstrating that most people behave in the same way in a particular situation. Some of the most famous (and controversial) studies in social psychology, if not in psychology as a whole, involve strong situations, such as Asch's studies of conformity, Milgram's studies of obedience, and

Figure 4.2 Zimbardo's prison simulation experiment showed that it is the prison environment which makes inmates and guards behave as they do and not their predisposed character traits, whilst at a party everyone is free to behave as they please; the environment is open or weak

Zimbardo's study of a simulated or 'mock' prison. While there is evidence of individual differences in all three studies, what they have in common is their focus on the power of social situations to make individuals behave in similar ways (that is, to create inter-individual consistency).

To take the 'prison-simulation experiment' as an example, the study investigated why prisons induce in staff and inmates alike such destructive, dehumanizing and pathological behaviour. The conventional, widely held view (the *dispositional hypothesis*) is that prison guards are 'sadistic, uneducated and insensitive', while prisoners, by definition, are antisocial; it is these personal qualities of the people who populate prisons which makes them the kind of institutions they are. What the prison-simulation experiment aimed to do (see, for example, Haney et al., 1973) was to reject the dispositional hypothesis in favour of a *situational* explanation, which states that it is the physical, social and psychological conditions of prisons which are to blame, not the people in them.

Haney et al. believed that they had found very convincing evidence in support of the situational explanation, based largely on the abnormal reactions of both prisoners and guards who were volunteers, selected for their non-criminal, non-sadistic, psychologically well-adjusted personalities, and randomly selected to their respective roles. In this way, the characteristics of the people were being controlled, leaving only the prison environment to account for the pathological reactions which developed. Like Milgram's obedience studies before it, the prison-simulation experiment provoked considerable upset, both on the part of other psychologists and on the part of the general public, but Zimbardo (1973) believes that this was caused only in part by ethical concerns: 'another part of . . . [the] power [of experiments like those of Milgram and Zimbardo] lies precisely in their demonstration of how strong situational determinants are in shaping behaviour' (Zimbardo, 1973). (For a fuller discussion of the prison-simulation experiment, see Gross, 1994.)

Such dramatic studies demonstrate that predicting the behaviour of individuals on the basis of personal dispositions has its limits, set by the demands of strong situations. Equally strong, although far less dramatic, are all kinds of everyday situations in which the norms or rules of behaviour are very clearly defined and widely accepted (at least by those who are familiar with the culture), thus making *conformity* the 'easy' option, and making the expression of personal qualities almost irrelevant. Personality psychologists do not deny the role of situational factors, and social psychologists acknowledge the part played by individual differences; there has been a certain convergence between them in recent years. However, there is still a great divergence between them, social psychology still being very strongly biased towards *situationist* models of explanation, and personality psychology still favouring *dispositionism* (Krahé, 1992).

Some key issues in the study of personality

Consistency

As we have already seen, central to the concept of personality is the consistency and predictability of behaviour. What is commonly referred to as the *consistency controversy* was sparked in 1968 when Walter Mischel declared that his review of a wide range of personality domains gave evidence of very little support for the concept of intra-individual consistency. He argued that the average correlation between different behavioural measures designed to tap the same personality trait was typically between 0.1 and 0.2, often lower. He also argued that correlations between scores on personality scales designed to measure a given trait, and behaviour in any particular situations meant to tap that trait, rarely exceed 0.2 to 0.3; hardly any studies produced coefficients (either between individual pairs of behavioural measures or between personality scale scores and individual behavioural measures) exceeding the 0.3 'barrier'.

Effectively, this undermined the whole concept of a personality trait, since it is precisely the possession of traits which, according to personality theorists, accounts for consistency and predictability. And if you remove the usefulness of the trait concept, according to Mischel, you are left only with situational influences to account for the inconsistency of individual behaviour: the same person behaves differently in different situations because different situations require different behaviour, and are associated with different kinds of reinforcement. So, from this (rather extreme) situationist perspective, intra-individual *inconsistency* is exactly what you would expect!

Interactionism

While Mischel's attack on the concept of consistency produced a severe crisis of confidence in the field of personality (Krahé, 1992), Mischel came in for criticism of his own, largely in terms of the methodological flaws in many of the studies he reviewed in reaching his conclusions. These criticisms helped him to modify his views, so that he moved away from situationism towards an interactionist perspective. Essentially, this sees behaviour as a joint function of both the person and the situation:

$$\text{Behaviour} = \text{Person} \times \text{Situation}$$

As Ross and Nisbett (1991) point out, Mischel never did argue that the absence of behavioural consistency across situations proves that there are no measurable or predictable individual differences. On the contrary, he stressed that individuals might show responses that are very consistent within the same situation. Thus, specific responses to specific situations might be very stable over time. Hartshorne and May's (1928) study of an apparently unwatched child's tendency to copy from an answer book during a general knowledge test is an example of this. Indeed, stability coefficients (correlations between two measures of the same behaviour on different occasions) often exceed 0.4. However, Mischel did believe that strong individual differences between people are limited to these very specific responses and situations, while the 'consistency debate' seemed to be about broad, cross-situational traits (such as 'honesty').

The 'formula' above for interactionism is interesting in as much as it relates to another major debate within social psychology, which mirrors the current debate within the field of personality, namely *attribution theory* – specifically, the actor–observer effect (AOE) and the fundamental attribution error (FAE); (see Chapter 2).

The AOE (Jones & Nisbett, 1971) refers to the lay person's bias towards explaining other people's behaviour in terms of dispositional or internal causes (this, in fact, is the FAE; Ross, 1977), and his or her own behaviour in terms of situational or external causes. By describing these as biases (the 'error' in the FAE is itself rather inaccurate; Fiske & Taylor, 1991), we are implying that an unbiased, logical, objective analysis of social behaviour will always show that both the personal dispositions of the actor and features of the situation contribute to what the actor does, albeit in different ways and to varying degrees and proportions. This can be seen in terms of weak and strong situations; dispositional factors play a much greater role in the former than in the latter, but, as we have already said, even in strong situations like Milgram's obedience experiment and the prison-simulation experiment, not everyone behaves in an identical way.

Applications of the term 'interactionism'

So interactionism seems to be the only logical, as well as empirically reasonable, view to take (as opposed to extreme dispositionism or extreme situationism). But are there different kinds of interactionism, or at least different ways of thinking about what an interaction between the person and the situation might mean? According to Carver and Scheier (1992), there are four main ways in which the term has been used.

One of these relates to the distinction between weak and strong situations, which we have already discussed.

A second relates to the 'formula', which we considered above; this is probably the most common understanding of the term and is associated with the research of psychologists such as Endler and Magnusson (1976), Pervin (1985) and Snyder and Ickes (1985). It is tied to the analysis-of-variance (ANOVA) understanding of how two (or more) variables (or classes of variables) influence an outcome (as used in Kelley's covariation model of attribution, for example; see Chapter 2). When a situation and a trait are examined in the same study, three systematic sources of influence on behaviour result:

1 Sometimes variations in the situation have an overall (and fairly predictable) effect (corresponding to strong situations and high interindividual consistency).

2 Sometimes variations on a trait dimension have an overall effect (corresponding to weak situations and low inter-individual consistency).

3 Sometimes variations in the situation affect different people in different ways. This may be instead of the first two points and/or in addition to them. Either way, it is the interaction between person and situation that produces weak overall effects (low correlations) for both trait and situation. While the traditional dispositional view of behaviour (as held by personality theorists) sees the trait (such as the tendency to dominate others) as being the crucial factor, interactionists argue that the expression of this tendency will inevitably be influenced by situational factors (for example, authoritarian personalities bully less powerful or important people, but are submissive to more powerful or important people; Argyle, 1983).

A typical study, aimed at testing the trait and interactionist models, involves observing, or asking for reports of, the behaviour of a number of individuals in a number of situations, and calculating how much of the variation can be explained by person factors, how much by situational factors, and how much by interaction between them. The general pattern of results that emerges from this kind of study, involving a variety of different populations, traits and situations, is very clear: situations are at least as important as persons, and P × S interactions are more important than either (Argyle, 1983; Bowers, 1973). While it is now recognized that this kind of research cannot determine whether personality or situation is more important, the results nevertheless clearly favour the interactionist position (Argyle, 1983).

The third of Carver and Scheier's (1992) definitions describes how one of the limitations of the ANOVA approach to studying interaction effects is that it is largely laboratory-based, where people are placed into identical situations. While this might be very convenient for the investigators, it may not be ecologically valid. It may not reflect what goes on outside the laboratory situation, where people exercise considerable choice over which situations or environments they expose themselves to. Because the choices people make depend partly on personality differences, the choosing of situations represents a kind of interaction which is very different from what is involved in the second application of interactionism, described above.

In their fourth definition, Carver and Scheier (1992) cite evidence that people differ in the kinds of responses that they evoke in others, that introverts and extroverts tend to steer conversations in different directions, and that people manipulate one another, using tactics such as charm, coercion and 'the silent treatment'. All these effects of people serve to change the situation, so that the situation is different for different individuals involved. This reciprocal influence between persons and situations is another way of looking at person–situation interaction (Carver & Scheier, 1992).

The psychological situation

Of course, other actors are an important part of situations but it is individual differences between actors which, as we have seen, also contribute to how a particular situation is experienced by the various participants. In other words, not only are personality differences essential for any understanding of people's behaviour in particular situations, but there is a very real sense in which the situation is defined in terms of the individuals involved.

Rather than trying to define the situation in an objective way, independently of the actors involved, it is the psychological situation which constitutes a critical determinant of behaviour: the psychological meaning of a situation for the individual (how it is perceived) is a crucial factor in predicting behaviour and accounting for regularities in behaviour across situations (Krahé, 1992).

The trait dimension

Reference to the psychological situation suggests at least a partial explanation of the lack of behavioural consistency claimed by Mischel in 1968: if people fail to show consistent behaviour across situations, couldn't this be because those situations might not all have the same meaning for the individuals concerned (which they 'should' have – and need to have – according to the researchers who define those situations in an objective way)? In other words, only if the perceptions of actors and those of researchers coincide, can there be any possibility of finding consistency.

A solution to this problem was proposed by Bem and Allen (1974). While essentially conceding Mischel's basic claim about low consistency when a random sample of people responds to some fixed set of trait-relevant situations, they argued that a rather more restricted trait theory might still be valid, namely the view that at least some traits can be appropriately applied to at least some people. That is, instead of claiming that everyone is more or less equally consistent and predictable according to whichever traits one chooses to measure, Bem and Allen argued that most people are probably consistent on some behavioural dimensions but not others, and people will differ regarding which traits are consistent for them and which are not.

The traditional trait approach (the target of Mischel's attack) adopts a nomothetic approach, assuming that every person can be meaningfully assigned a score on every personality dimension, while Bem and Allen were advocating an idiographic approach, focusing on the unique aspects of a given individual's personality configuration (Ross & Nisbett, 1991; see Chapter 3). To do this, one must first identify the particular traits that 'apply' for the individual in question (or, alternatively, identify particular individuals for whom the trait of interest is truly applicable): 'one must conduct one's search for behavioural consistency recognizing that only a subset of trait dimensions usefully characterizes any given individual, and that only a subset of individuals can be characterized in terms of any given trait dimension' (Ross & Nisbett, 1991).

What made Bem and Allen's theoretical approach different was the assumption that consistency will be shown only by people striving to meet personal standards, trying to convey a consistent impression to others, or actively monitoring their behaviour in an attempt to achieve consistency, and that it will only be manifested in the particular situations perceived as relevant by those individuals.

However, what Bem and Allen advocated and what they actually did were not the same thing. What they did was to stipulate two specific traits, friendliness and conscientiousness, then classified all the available actors as high or low in consistency on these traits (based on self-ratings and ratings by peers and parents). This is essentially a nomothetic approach. The idiographic alternative, which is what they originally advocated, would have involved deriving trait dimensions, and situations relevant to those dimensions, from the participants themselves.

As far as both traits are concerned, the high-consistency individuals' peer ratings, parent ratings and self-ratings correlated highly with each other (the average correlation coefficient being 0.61 for friendliness, and 0.48 for conscientiousness) and (although less highly) with the relevant behavioural measures (the average for friendliness being 0.47, and for conscientiousness, 0.36). In all cases, coefficients for the low-consistency individuals were lower.

Regarding correlations between the relevant behavioural measures, for friendliness, the high-consistency individuals scored 0.73, and the low-consistency individuals scored 0.30. (clearly in line with predictions). However, for conscientiousness, the results were −0.04 and −0.19 respectively (clearly not what they expected or hoped to find).

Carver and Scheier (1992) point out that attempts to replicate Bem and Allen's results have met with very mixed fortunes. However, what their view of consistency represents is an important *moderator variable*, something which links personal dispositions and actual behaviour and can account for the very low levels of consistency found in earlier studies and on which Mischel based his attack of the trait approach. Another such moderator variable is *self-monitoring* (Snyder, 1987), according to which (i) high self-monitors are expected to show low cross-situational consistency, since these individuals adapt their behaviour to suit the demands of the situation, and (ii) low self-monitors are expected to show high cross-situational consistency, since they tend to 'be themselves' regardless of the demands of the situation. If people can validly be classified as high or low self-monitors, this means that some people are less or more consistent in general than others.

Aggregated observations

If Bem and Allen were trying to defend the trait concept against Mischel's attack, another response has been to argue that, instead of measuring single instances of behaviour and calculating the correlations between these (individual) instances, we should take the average of several different individual measures ('items') and calculate the correlations between these aggregated observations. The main advocate of this view is Epstein (for example, Epstein, 1979), who argues that only by taking an *average* can we obtain a reliable or accurate measurement of a disposition, because only in this way will random or extraneous factors partially cancel each other out. Individual behaviours, like single items on a test of any kind, are highly unreliable and are likely to reflect the influence of several systematic and random factors other than the underlying personality disposition under investigation. This is a purely statistical argument, one which Mischel himself had made in 1968 (Ross & Nisbett, 1991).

According to the Spearman-Brown 'prophecy formula' championed by Epstein, if we took 25 measures of, say, extroversion, for each individual, found the mean, then correlated this mean with that for a different set of 25 measures, we would obtain a correlation of 0.83. If we did the same for a mere nine measures, we would still obtain a correlation of 0.63.

Not surprisingly, Epstein's argument was greeted enthusiastically by personality test researchers, for it seemed to explain why standardized pencil-and-paper self-reports, and peer ratings, generally produce high levels of stability over time and at least moderate levels of inter-rater agreement: these kinds of assessment are likely to be the product of many observations, made on different occasions, in a variety of situations (Ross & Nisbett, 1991).

Long-term consistency

While Epstein has been criticized, a very important implication of his argument is that to measure consistency in the short term (based on one or two observations made close together in time) is to miss the point. The widely held definition of a personality trait is that it is a latent tendency or disposition which plays a causal role in determining both specific patterns of individual behaviour and individual differences in people's reactions to a given situation. Gordon Allport (1937), one of the pioneers of personality research and a major trait theorist, argued that a person with a particular disposition will only behave in a particular way if he or she meets with situations that actualize that disposition, allowing it to be expressed. Not only does this represent a form of interactionism, but it implies that if we observe a person on just one or two occasions, we will not have given particular traits 'enough of a chance' to manifest themselves; it is only in the long term that intra-individual consistency can be meaningfully measured. Short-term inconsistency, but long-term consistency, is exactly what is predicted by trait theories of personality.

The constructionist approach

Another strand in the complex fabric of the 'trait debate' is to shift the focus away from the actor and onto the observer: instead of denoting dispositional qualities of the individual, traits are conceptualized as cognitive categories used by the perceiver to interpret an individual's behaviour across different situations. Therefore, consistency is construed by the perceiver, as much as manifested by the actor: judgements of an individual's personality depend as much on the interpretative activity of the perceiver as on the observed behaviour itself (Krahé, 1992).

While not rejecting the trait concept, the constructionist view maintains that personality does not have an objective reality independent of the observer, or of the cultural and historical context in which both the actor and observer are located. According to Hampson (1988), the process of personality construction is seen as a form of communication through which the actor, observer and the self-observer ideally arrive at a shared impression about the actor: 'In this sense, personality should not be located *within* persons, but *between* and *among* persons. (Hampson, 1988, quoted in Krahé, 1992.)

In relation to our role of self-observer, *self-monitoring* is a key process (see 'The trait dimension', above). Also, the constructionist approach has led to a revival of research on *social desirability scales*, which may be measuring two distinct qualities, self-deception and impression management (Deary & Matthews, 1993).

Personality factors

Finally, let us return to 'the beginning of the story', so to speak. According to Krahé (1992), despite its troubled history, 'the trait concept presents itself in remarkably good shape at the beginning of the '90s.' Since the 1980s, there has been a vast amount of research involving a search for a small but comprehensive number of basic trait dimensions which can account for the structure of personality and individual differences. The results suggest that personality can be adequately described by five broad constructs, commonly referred to as the 'Big Five', namely: *Neuroticism Extroversion, Openness, Agreeableness* and *Conscientiousness* (McCrae &

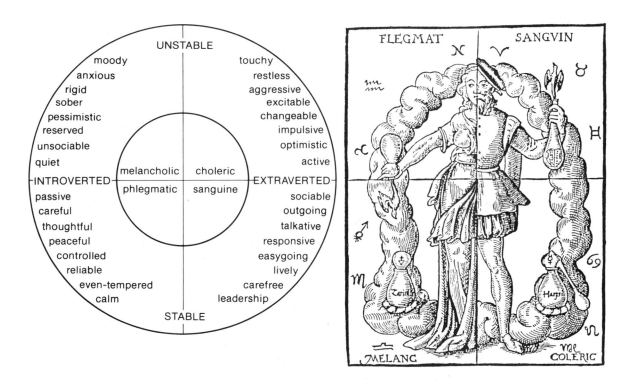

Figure 4.3 Personality has been dissected into component parts for thousands of years; what is interesting is how these ideas relate to the modern concept of personality traits, as shown by Eysenck's dimensions of personality (From Eysenck, 1965)

Costa, 1989); the first two are almost identical to these dimensions as used in Eysenck's personality theory.

While different versions of the Big Five have been proposed, the five-factor model has provided a unified framework for trait research (Costa & McCrae, 1993). However, this approach faces some of the same basic problems as more traditional theories, notably those of Eysenck and Cattell, and this stems from the fact that they all rest upon the use of the statistical technique of factor analysis (FA)

One of the sources of debate and disagreement between, say, Eysenck and Cattell has been to do with the 'best' method of FA to use, which in turn determines the *number* of factors (or basic trait dimensions) to be extracted from the mass of data derived from self-reports, observer ratings and so on. Even if there is much more general agreement now among personality psychologists than there used to be about the number of factors which should be sought, there remains the fundamental problem of the meaning of the factors which are extracted (Kline, 1993; Krahé, 1992).

> *The labelling of factor solutions is a largely intuitive process whereby the investigator typically inspects the items with high loadings on a given factor and then chooses a label that in his or her view contains the gist of the total range of items making up the factor. Thus, it is not surprising that different studies have arrived at different qualitative interpretations of their obtained five factor solutions.*
>
> (Krahé, 1992)

Ultimately, personality factors, however many or few, must be identified from their correlations with external criteria (Kline, 1993).

Finally, Bentall (1993), a clinical psychologist, asks if personality theory has anything to offer in the context of helping or understanding people with psychological problems. He argues that the Big Five seems to suffer from many of the disadvantages of traditional diagnostic approaches in psychopathology, the following in particular:

1 While these personality dimensions are described as 'natural' categories, the labels used to designate them seem to reflect the value systems of the researchers. For example, the anxious (neurotic), introverted, reserved etc. person 'stands condemned as a lesser human being. Should any liberal society tolerate this way of classifying individuals?' (see Chapters 6 and 11). The use of assessment techniques derived from the Big Five model in job selection, for example, raises serious ethical and political questions.

2 While the 'consistency debate' has focused almost exclusively on 'normal' behaviour, as far as problem behaviour is concerned, it is often the inconsistencies which are most striking, such as the breakdown in normal functioning following some major life event.

Conclusions

Surely, for a theory of personality to even begin to be adequate, it must apply to both the consistencies and inconsistencies, the short and the long term, the predictable and the unpredictable features of behaviour. It must also be able to explain both normal and abnormal behaviour, as well as the emotional, cognitive, social and interpersonal components of behaviour, all within the cultural and historical context in which a person's personality is perceived and judged.

> *Today's view isn't a picture in which traits exert a* constant *influence on behaviour . . . Rather, trait differences sometimes matter a lot and sometimes don't matter at all. People also display traits by choosing situations, not just by reacting to situations forced on them. This dynamic approach to understanding the role of traits in the constantly varying social environment recognizes complexities in behaviour that formerly were ignored. As a result, this picture is widely seen as a distinct improvement over simpler conceptions of the effects of traits.*

(Carver & Scheier, 1992)

Summary

- Part of our commonsense understanding of behaviour is the belief that people behave in fairly consistent, and hence predictable, ways, across a range of situations (high *intra-individual consistency*). This is attributed to their *personality*, which refers to the relatively permanent features of a person's make-up.
- Another commonsense belief is that people are *not completely predictable*; they are changeable, within certain limits, those limits being set by (i) our general concept of a person, and (ii) our familiarity with particular individuals.
- Both excessive predictability/consistency and excessive unpredictability/inconsistency may be indicators of psychological abnormality.
- Personality psychologists have tended to stress high *intra-individual consistency*, while social psychologists have stressed the impact of social situations, accounting for high *inter-individual* consistency.
- These two kinds of consistency relate to *weak* and *strong situations* respectively.
- Many famous (and controversial) studies in social psychology involve strong situations, such as Asch's conformity experiments, Milgram's obedience experiments, and the prison-simulation experiment of Zimbardo et al.

- Such experiments show that the validity of predicting the behaviour of individuals on the basis of personal dispositions is limited by the demands of strong situations.
- Despite recent convergence between personality psychology and social psychology, the former still strongly favours *dispositionism* and the latter *situationism*.
- Mischel sparked the *consistency controversy* by claiming that there was very little evidence of intra-individual consistency: correlations between (i) different behavioural measures meant to tap the same personality trait and (ii) scores on personality scales and on behaviour in situations designed to measure a given trait, rarely exceed the 0.3 'barrier'.
- This undermined the whole concept of a personality trait and introduced a *situationist* perspective into personality psychology, which predicts intra-individual inconsistency.
- Criticisms of Mischel led him to modify his views, towards an *intractionist* perspective, which sees behaviour as a joint function of both the person and the situation.
- This corresponds to two major sources of bias in relation to attribution, namely the *actor–observer effect* and the *fundamental attribution error*.
- While interactionism might be the only logical and empirically reasonable view to take, there are different ways of thinking about what a person–situation interaction might mean.
- The general pattern of results found in studies aimed at testing the trait and interactionist models, is that situations are at least as important as persons, and person × situation interactions are more important than either.
- In real life, people choose the situations to which they expose themselves. This represents a kind of interaction and reduces the *ecological validity* of laboratory experiments, in which situations are imposed by the experimenter.
- People change the situation by virtue of their personality, the responses they evoke in others and so on; this represents another form of interaction.
- Rather than trying to define situations independently of the actors involved, it is the *psychological situation* which is the crucial influence on behaviour.
- Bem and Allen proposed a restricted trait theory, according to which at least some traits can be applied to at least some people, so that most people are probably consistent on some behavioural dimensions but not others. People will differ regarding which traits are consistent for them and which are not.
- Consistency will be shown by people only with respect to traits that are personally relevant and in situations perceived as relevant to

those traits.
- Empirical support for Bem and Allen is mixed, but their view of consistency represents an important *moderator variable*, another example being *self-monitoring*.
- Instead of measuring single instances of behaviour and calculating the correlations between them, we should take the average of several individual observations and calculate correlations for these *aggregated* measures.
- To measure consistency in the short term misses the point as far as how a 'trait' is commonly understood; intra-individual consistency is a long-term phenomenon.
- Consistency is also viewed as construed by the perceiver, as much as manifested by the actor. This *constructionist approach* maintains that personality does not exist objectively, but is a form of communication.
- The 'Big Five' personality trait factors comprise: *Neuroticism, Extroversion, Openness, Agreeableness* and *Conscientiousness*.
- There remains the fundamental problem of the meaning of the factors extracted by the use of factor analysis.
- The value of personality theory in relation to people with psychological problems has been questioned, in particular the Big Five, which seem to reflect the value systems of the researchers and overemphasize consistency relative to inconsistency.

Suggestions for further reading

Krahé, B. (1992) *Personality and Social Psychology: Towards a synthesis* (especially Chapters 1, 2, 3, 4, 5, and 8), London: Sage.
Mischel, W. (1968) *Personality and Assessment*, New York: Wiley.
Mischel, W. (1977) The interaction of person and situation. In Magnusson, D. & Endler, N.S. (Eds), *Personality at the Crossroads: current issues in interactional psychology*, Hillsdale, N.J: Lawrence Erlbaum.

Heredity and environment

Framing the questions

The debate about the roles of heredity and environment (or *nature* and *nurture*) is one of the longest lasting, as well as one of the most heated and controversial, both inside and outside psychology. Whether it is within a religious, philosophical, political, or scientific context, the debate is concerned with some of the most fundamental questions that human beings (at least those from Western cultures) ask about themsleves: How do we come to be the way we are, what makes us develop in the way we do?

I have deliberately expressed these questions in very general, abstract terms, in order to highlight an ambiguity involved: are they concerned with the human species as a whole, relative to other species, or are they concerned with individual differences between human beings – that is, individuals relative to each other?

In a broad, general sense, the nature–nurture debate involves both types, or level, of question. For example, is language an innate (inborn) ability which is unique to the human species – is it a 'natural' (biologically given) ability which will appear, under 'normal' environmental conditions, in people with normal brains? Similar questions have been asked about perception and aggression.

In the cases of language and perception, the focus is on what people have in common, as members of the human species, in contrast with other species. Clearly, if language is a species-specific ability, then the focus of research and theorizing will be on the nature of that ability, exactly what it is that is innate or biologically 'given', how the brain is specialized for language and so on. Chomsky's (1965, 1968) *language acquisition device (LAD)* is perhaps the prime example within modern psychology of such an approach.

In the case of aggression, both types of question have been posed: 'Are human beings the naturally most aggressive species on the planet?' represents the same level as the first question regarding language, while 'Why are some people more aggressive than others?' represents the other level, the one that which focuses on individual differences. According to

Plomin (1994), it is in the latter sense that the nature–nurture debate takes place.

However, having established the 'individual differences' level at which the debate takes place, there is another, equally important distinction which needs to be made between the kinds of questions that are asked. In order to appreciate this distinction, we need to take a brief look at the philosophical roots of the nature–nurture debate.

Nativism, empiricism and interactionism

As the word implies, *nativism* refers to the philosophical theory which sees nature (heredity) as determining certain abilities and capacities, rather than learning and experience. A nativist who has had an enormous impact on psychology is the French philosopher, René Descartes (1596–1650). At the opposite philosophical extreme is *empiricism*, associated mainly with seventeenth-century British philosophers, in particular John Locke (1632–1704). Locke believed that, at birth, the human mind is a *tabula rasa* (or 'blank slate'); the blank slate is gradually 'filled in' by learning and experience.

At the risk of some oversimplification, these two doctrines represent polar opposites; they take the view that it is either nature (nativism) or nurture (empiricism) which accounts for human abilities: they are either innate or learnt.

Most present-day psychologists (and biologists) would reject such an extreme, either/or approach to such a complex issue, mainly on the grounds that the two theories are attempts to answer the wrong question: to ask, 'Is it nature or nurture?' is to ask an oversimplified question which will inevitably produce an oversimplified answer. Also, Descartes and Locke were asking the question at the level of 'the whole species', and not at the level of individual differences.

However, despite these two observations, the influence of nativism and empiricism within psychology is very clear to see, particularly, but by no means exclusively, in the early days of the discipline. The Gestalt psychologists were Germans and Austrians (notably Wertheimer, Köhler and Koffka) studying perceptual processes, mainly during the 1920s and 1930s, who believed that the basic principles of perceptual organization are innate, with perceptual experience having very little, if any, influence.

One of the American pioneers of child psychology, Arnold Gesell (1925) introduced into psychology the concept of *maturation*, genetically programmed sequential patterns of change (Bee, 1989), according to which all babies and children will pass through the same series of changes, in the same order and at more or less the same rate. A third, and more recent, example of a nativist theory is Chomsky's LAD which was referred to earlier.

Empiricism has had its impact within psychology in many different forms, but an early and extremely influential theory is *behaviourism*, whose American founder, John Watson (1878–1958), leaves the reader in no doubt as to the behaviourist position regarding the nature–nurture debate when he declares:

> *Give me a dozen healthy infants, well-formed, and my own specified world to bring them up in and I'll guarantee to take any one at random and train him to become any type of specialist I might select – a doctor, lawyer, artist, merchant-chief and, yes, even into beggarman and thief, regardless of his talents, penchants, abilities, vocations and race of his ancestors.*
>
> (Watson, 1925/1926, quoted in Soyland, 1994)

He also claimed that 'there is no such thing as an inheritance of capacity, talent, temperament, mental constitution and character', and again,

> *The behaviourists believe that there is nothing from within to develop. If you start with the right number of fingers and toes, eyes, and a few elementary movements that are present at birth, you do not need anything else in the way of raw material to make a man, be that man genius, a cultured gentleman, a rowdy or a thug.*
>
> (Watson, 1928, quoted in Plomin, 1994)

This extreme form of empiricism (or *environmentalism*) was perpetuated in the operant conditioning research of B.F. Skinner (1904–90).

So, if extreme nativism and empiricism, whether in the form of philosophical or psychological theories, choose between nature and nurture, a more complex way of posing the question is to ask, 'How much?' This, of course, presupposes that both nature and nurture are involved, a view which, as we noted above, most psychologists would subscribe to. Indeed, for most behavioural scientists, it is probably inconceivable that there is no interaction between them (Plomin, 1994).

In turn, the 'How much?' question is linked, almost inevitably, to the 'individual differences' form of the debate. For Galton, the issue was clearly about the *relative importance* of heredity and environment, and he left us in no doubt as to which he considered to be the more important: 'There is no escape from the conclusion that nature prevails enormously over nurture when the differences in nurture do not exceed what is commonly to be found among persons of the same rank in the same country' (Galton, 1883, quoted in Plomin, 1994).

Finally, if 'How much?' represents an improvement on the rather crude, oversimplified 'Which one?', it is still concerned with trying to measure or quantify the contributions of genetic and environmental factors. This has been the main focus of *behavioural* (or quantitative) *genetics*, which attempts to establish the extent to which differences between, for example, people's intelligence are due to differences in their genetic make-up (i.e. it aims to establish a *heritability estimate* for intelligence). The methods used in behavioural genetics include *twin studies*, *adoption studies*, and other studies of *family resemblance*.

One reason for the emphasis on 'How much?' is the availability of these methods – they make it relatively straightforward to establish heritability estimates. Much more difficult is a third question about the nature–nurture relationship, which follows logically from the second, namely, 'How do they interact?' (Anastasi, 1958; Plomin, 1994). This is concerned with *qualitative* issues, the ways in which heredity and environment influence each other. Much of the rest of this chapter will be concerned with some of the different attempts to understand this interaction.

The nature of 'nature'

Within *genetics* (the science of heredity), 'nature' refers to what is typically thought of as inheritance, which denotes differences in genetic material (chromosomes and genes) which are transmitted from generation to generation (from parents to offspring). Just as in 1865 the 'father' of genetics, Gregor Mendel, explained the difference between smooth and wrinkled seeds in garden peas in terms of different genes, so in modern human genetics the focus is on genetic differences among individuals. 'Nature' in this context does not refer to the nature of the human species, what we all have in common genetically with other human beings (and indeed with other primates), but rather to *genetically produced differences* among individuals within the (human) species. This was certainly the way in which the term 'nature' was used by Francis Galton (a cousin of Charles Darwin), who in 1883 coined the phrase *nature–nurture* as it is used in the scientific arena (Plomin, 1994).

Figure 5.1   Gregor Mendel (1822–1884) the 'father' of genetics

Genetics and evolution

The raw material of evolution is genetic variability: individuals with genes that help them to survive changing environmental conditions will be more likely to produce offspring (who also possess those genes), whereas those individuals lacking such genes will not. In this way, new species develop, and species-specific characteristics (including behaviours) are those which have enabled the species to evolve and survive.

However, as Plomin (1994) points out, the links between such species-typical evolution and genetic sources of individual differences are much looser than is often assumed. He cites the examples of *Sociobiology* (e.g. Wilson, 1975), *evolutionary psychology* (e.g. Buss, 1991), and *developmental psychology* (e.g. Harper, 1992), all of which are mainly concerned with differences between species, although attempts have been made to incorporate individual differences (for example, by Dawkins, 1983). It is easy to make the mistake of assuming that evolution implies genetic variation within a species, and vice versa. Taking the example of language again, if acquisition of language is a human species-specific behaviour, hardwired by evolution to occur if the minimal environment encountered by our species during development (most importantly, another language user) is present, then we can say that our species is a natural language user. However, this does not imply that differences among individual language users in their language ability are also genetic in origin: such differences could be entirely due to environmental factors (Plomin, 1994).

> *The causes of average differences between species are not necessarily related to the causes of individual differences within groups. Moreover, characteristics that have been subject to strong directional selection will not show genetic variability because strong selection exhausts genetic variability. In other words, when genetic variability is found among individuals within our species for a particular trait, it is likely that the trait was not important evolutionarily, at least in terms of directional selection.*

> (Plomin, 1994)

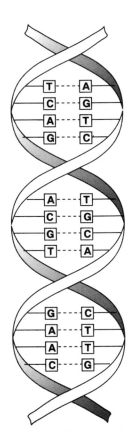

thymine is bound to adenine
cytosine is bound to guanine

Figure 5.2 The structure of a DNA molecule represented schematically. This shows its double-stranded coiled structure and the complementary binding of nucleotide bases, guanine to cytosine and adenine to thymine (From Pinel, 1993)

Heredity: chromosomes, genes and DNA

Now that we have established what nature is not, let us take a closer look at what it is; clearly this is important if we are to try to understand the relationship between nature and nurture.

The basic units of hereditary transmission are *genes*. Genes are large molecules of deoxyribonucleic acid (DNA), extremely complex chemical chains, comprising a ladder-like, double helix structure (discovered by Watson and Crick in 1953; see Figure 5.2). The genes, which occur in pairs, are situated on the *chromosomes*, which are found within the nuclei of living cells. The normal human being inherits twenty-three pairs of chromosomes, one member of each pair from each parent. The twenty-third pair are the sex chromosomes, which comprise two Xs in the case of females, and an X and a Y in males. (See Figure 5.3.)

The steps of the gene's double helix (or spiral staircase, Plomin, 1994) consist of four nucleotide bases (adenine,

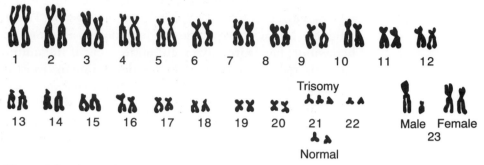

Figure 5.3   A sample karyotype. The 21st chromosome has one too many chromosomes, a common problem. This is called a 'trisomy'. The 23rd chromosome pair is shown with both male and female versions. In a normal karyotype, only one such pair would be found
(From Ruch, 1984)

thymine, cytosine and guanine) which can occur in any order on one side of the double helix, while the other side is fixed, such that adenine always pairs with thymine, and cytosine always pairs with guanine. Taking just one member of each of the twenty-three pairs of chromosomes, the human *genome* (the total complement of genes) comprises more than three billion nucleotide base pairs (Plomin, 1994).

Two major functions of genes are self-duplication, and protein synthesis.

Self-duplication

DNA copies itself by unzipping in the middle of the spiral staircase, with each half forming its complement. In other words, when a cell divides, all the genetic information (chromosomes and genes) contained within the cell nucleus is reproduced, so that the 'offspring' cells are identical to the 'parent' cells. This process is called *mitosis* and applies only to non-gonadal cells (the body's non-reproductive cells such as skin, blood and muscle cells).

The reproductive or germ cells (ova in females and sperm in males) duplicate through the process of *meiosis*, whereby each cell only contains half the individual's chromosomes and genes. Which member of a chromosome pair goes to any particular cell seems to be determined randomly. The resulting germ cells (called *gametes* in their mature state), therefore, contain twenty-three chromosomes, one of which will be either an X (female) or a Y (male). When a sperm fertilizes an ovum, the two sets of chromosomes combine to form a new individual with a full set of forty-six chromosomes. If both parents contribute an X chromosome, it will be female, whereas if the father contributes a Y (remember that the mother only has Xs), it will be male. It is the father, therefore, who determines the sex of the baby. (See Figure 5.4.)

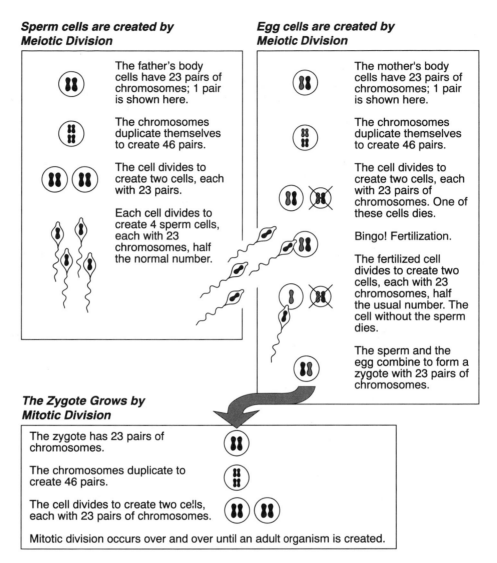

Figure 5.4   Mitotic and meiotic cell division (From Pinel, 1993)

Protein synthesis

The 'genetic code' was cracked in the 1960s. Essentially, DNA controls the production of ribonucleic acid (RNA) within the cell nucleus. This 'messenger' RNA moves outside the nucleus and into the surrounding cytoplasm, where it is converted by ribosomes into sequences of amino acids, the building blocks of proteins and enzymes. Genes that code for proteins and enzymes are called *structural genes*, and they represent the foundation of classical genetics (Plomin, 1994). The first single-gene disorders discovered in the human species involved metabolic disorders caused by mutations (spontaneous changes) in structural genes. A much-cited example is phenylketonuria, which will be discussed below in relation to gene–environment interaction.

However, most genes are *regulator genes*: they code for products that bind with DNA itself, and serve to regulate other genes. Unlike the structural genes which are 'deaf' to the environment, the regulator genes communicate closely with the environment and change in response to it (Plomin, 1994).

The nature of nurture: what is the environment?

When the term 'environment' is used in a psychological context, we normally think of all those influences, or potential sources of influence, that lie outside the individual's body, in the form of other people, opportunities for intellectual stimulation and social interaction, as well as the physical circumstances of the individual's life ('environs' = 'surroundings').

For most babies and young children, the immediate family is the environmental context in which their development takes place, although the nature of this immediate environment is itself coloured and shaped by the wider social and cultural setting in which the family exists.

In other words, we normally view the environment as:

1 external to the individual;
2 post-natal (i.e. something which becomes important after birth);
3 a way of referring to a whole set of (potential) influences which impinge on a passive individual, who is shaped by his or her environment, without in any way shaping or contributing to that environment.

On all three counts, this seems to be a mistaken view.

As far as points 1 and 2 are concerned, while the nature–nurture debate is normally conducted at the level of the immediate family and the society and culture within which it is embedded, 'opportunities for gene–environment interaction arise long before the birth process . . . [and] individual differences in environmental conditions have a modifying influence upon the expression of genetic inheritance' (McGurk, 1975).

For example, at any particular moment in time, any one cell has a specific location within a cluster of other cells, but, with repeated mitosis, that location is forever changing as the cell's environment (the total number of cells in the cluster) continues to grow. At an even more micro-level, the cell nucleus (which contains the genetic material) has as its environment the cytoplasm of the cell. Strictly speaking, 'heredity' refers only to the particular set of chromosomes and genes which combine at the moment of fertilization; anything that occurs from that moment on is environmental (Kirby & Radford, 1976).

This, of course, includes all the influences acting on the developing *embryo* (as the 'baby' is called during the first eight weeks of pregnancy; thereafter it is the *foetus*), such as hormones, drugs taken by the mother, accidents, mother's diet and so on. From a psychological perspective, the

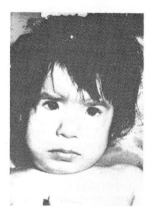

Figure 5.5 Alcohol consumption during pregnancy can result in Foetal Alcohol Syndrome; the baby may be intellectually impaired, hyperactive and suffer from a very short span of attention. Physical abnormalities can also be present such as a relatively small head, a short nose and low nasal bridge as can be seen here

importance of this pre-natal, biological environment relates to the damaging effects which it can have on the brain development of the unborn child. For example, of commonly taken drugs, alcohol is the most clearly damaging. It is toxic to brain cells during the first ten weeks of pregnancy, and *Foetal alcohol syndrome* refers to intellectual impairment, hyperactivity, and attention difficulties associated with very high levels of alcohol consumption (Rutter & Rutter, 1992).

As far as point 3 is concerned, the focus is on the social (and cultural) environment (as opposed to the biological), as well as the physical. This, as we have seen, is the level at which the nature–nurture debate normally takes place. If it is inaccurate to see the individual as at the mercy of the environment (as Watson, for one, would have us believe), then we need to ask, *In what ways does the individual influence or contribute to his or her environment?*

Watson's extreme brand of environmentalism sees 'the environment' as existing largely independently of the individual, a passive receptacle for environmental influences, and, as we saw earlier, it relates to the 'Which one?' question in the nature–nurture debate.

An alternative view of what the environment is, relevant to the 'How?' question (which, remember, assumes that both heredity and environment contribute to the development of individual differences), is to see people as *making their own environments* (Scarr, 1992). This runs counter to what most parents believe about the impact they have on their children, as well as what the mainstream of developmental psychology teaches: 'each child constructs a reality from the opportunities afforded by the rearing environment, and . . . the constructed reality does have considerable influence on variations among children and differences in their adult outcomes' (Scarr, 1992).

Eliciting a response

One way in which people influence or contribute to their environments is through evoking or eliciting a certain response from other people. This may be due either to their behaviour or to particular biological characteristics.

An example of the latter is gender; if people have stereotyped views and expectations regarding the differences between boys and girls, then these are likely to be expressed through different ways of relating to boys and girls, simply because they are male or female. A good example of such differential treatment are the 'baby X' experiments (Smith & Lloyd, 1978, cited in Rutter & Rutter, 1992). Toddlers were dressed in unisex snowsuits and then given names to indicate gender, half the time in line with their actual gender, half the time not. When adults played with them, they treated them differently, according to what they believed the toddler's gender to be.

What this demonstrates is that a person's biological make-up (or, at least, others' perception of it) becomes part of the person's environment, because other people's reactions to our biological make-up is part of our (social) environment. Indeed, anything about us which may form the basis for others' stereotyped perceptions and reactions towards us, be it physical attractiveness, ethnic, racial or national background, or any physical disability, is as much a part of our environment as it is part of our biological make-up.

However, these examples all relate to static aspects of our make-up. What about more dynamic aspects, such as temperament and behaviour? For example, children with a very sunny, easy-going and cheerful disposition are more likely to elicit friendly interactions with others than miserable or 'difficult' children. It is widely accepted that some children are easier to love (Rutter & Rutter, 1992). Research has shown that aggressive boys not only behave more aggressively, but also *elicit* more hostile behaviour in other boys (Patterson, 1982, cited in Rutter & Rutter, 1992). Their actions help to create a vicious cycle of negative interactions: when aggressive behaviour meets with a hostile response, this makes it more likely that further aggression will occur, and so on (Rutter & Rutter, 1992).

To the extent that all these characteristics are, to some degree, influenced by genetic factors, all the above examples illustrate *gene–environment correlations* (Rutter & Rutter, 1992; Scarr, 1992): aggressive children tend to experience aggressive environments because they tend to evoke aggressive responses in others. Looking at the environment in this way helps to explain why it is that different individuals have different experiences.

Shared psychosocial experiences

Another way of looking at how people influence or contribute to their environment is to distinguish between shared and non-shared psychosocial experiences (Rutter & Rutter, 1992).

When the environment is being discussed as a set of (potential) influences that impinge on the individual, it is often 'broken down' into factors such as overcrowding, poverty, social class or socio-economic status (SES) (which is correlated with the first two, as well as with other indicators), family break-up, marital discord, and so on. In studies of, say, intelligence or aggression, children are often compared with each other in terms of these environmental factors, which are then correlated with the behaviour or ability. So, for example, it may be concluded that children from low SES backgrounds are more likely to behave in antisocial ways and to be labelled as juvenile delinquents.

When families are compared in this way, it is assumed that children from

Figure 5.6 The Thatchers are prime examples of the variances in personality, ability and psychological make-up to be found within families; both children have shown themselves to be not only very different from each other, but also from their parents, and all four members of the family follow completely different careers

the same family will all be similarly and equally affected by those environmental factors. However, for most characteristics, most children within the same family are not very similar; in fact, they are often extremely varied in personality, abilities, and psychological disorders. According to Rutter and Rutter (1992), this observation is most striking when two adopted children are brought up in the same family: 'they are usually very little more alike when they grow up than any two people picked at random from the general population' (Rutter & Rutter, 1992).

This substantial within-family variation is exactly what we would expect to find if it is non-shared influences which are the crucial ones: differences between children in the same family will be associated systematically with differences between their experiences. One of the few major studies of this relationship is Dunn and Plomin's (1990) *Separate Lives*. In that book they argue that family-wide influences (such as SES, and marital discord) cannot influence behavioural development unless their impact is experienced differently by each child.

A more specific way of trying to account for these findings is by distinguishing between relative and absolute differences between children in how they are treated. Dunn and Plomin (1990) found that the ways in which parents respond differently to their different children (*relative differences*) are likely to be much more influential than the overall characteristics of the family (*absolute differences*). For example, it may matter very little whether children are brought up in a home that is less loving or more punitive than average, whereas it may matter considerably that one child receives less affection or receives more punishment than his or her sibling.

These findings imply 'that the unit of environmental transmission is not the family, but rather micro-environments within families' (Plomin & Thompson, 1987, quoted by Scarr, 1992). Consistent with these findings is the view that, so long as children are brought up in good-enough, supportive, non-deprived, non-abusive or non-neglectful environments, the particular family in which they are raised makes very little difference to their personality and intellectual development. Most families provide sufficiently supportive environments that children's individual genetic differences will develop (Scarr, 1992); this could account for (i) temperamental differences between children; (ii) why parents treat different offspring differently (the relative differences); and (iii) the differences in the experiences of different children.

Even though Dunn and Plomin's findings are only preliminary, and there are many qualifications which need to be made about them (see Rutter & Rutter, 1992, for a discussion), they represent a very important explanation of how the experiences of different individuals might differ: to the extent that people's experiences differ, their environments are different.

The constructionist view

Dunn and Plomin (1990) imply that to try and define the environment independently of the person who is experiencing it is futile, since every person's experience is different. An extreme behaviourist approach would see the structure of experience as given in the environment, which provides stimuli that impinge and shape the individual regardless of who they are. But according to constructionist views, people shape their own experiences: we don't merely respond differently to our environments (which implies a fairly passive role), but we actively create our own experiences. As we shall see in Chapter 8, cross-cultural psychology is based on the assumption that no sociocultural environment exists apart from the meaning that human participants give it (Shweder, 1990). Nothing real 'just is'; realities are the product of how things get represented, embedded, implemented, and reacted to (Scarr, 1992). Similarly, with individual differences within cultures: 'Different people, at different developmental stages, interpret and act upon their environments in different ways that create different experiences for each person. In this view, human experience is a construction of reality, not a property of a physical world that imparts the same experience to everyone who encounters it' (Scarr, 1992).

A concept that is closely related to the constructionist view of experience is that of *internal models*. (See Chapter 9, on attachment through the life cycle.) The effect of some environmental event depends on the individual's interpretation of it; the meaning given to it, as opposed to the objective nature of the event. The interpretation of the event reflects the individual's internal models, which refer to assumptions and expectations about the world, relationships with others, the self and so on, through which all subsequent experience is filtered. The concept of internal models helps to explain the continuity of behaviour over time, as well as why the 'same' experience seems to have such varying effects on different individuals (Bee, 1994).

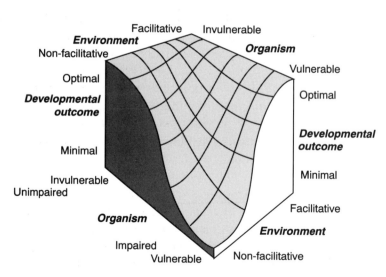

Figure 5.7 Horowitz's model of the interaction of a child's environment with protective factors and vulnerabilities. The surface of the curve illustrates the level of a developmental stage, such as IQ or social skills. According to this model, if a low-birthweight child is reared in a poor environment then it is likely that that child will do less well than other children reared with a different combination of vulnerabilities and environment

Facilitativeness

A further way of trying to answer the 'How?' question is to consider the idea of vulnerability or susceptibility to environmental influence; this represents an important kind of gene–environment interaction (Rutter & Rutter, 1992). In describing the environment, Horowitz (1987, 1990, cited in Bee, 1994) uses the term *facilitativeness*: a highly facilitative environment is one in which the child has loving and responsive parents, and is provided with a rich array of stimulation. When different levels of facilitativeness are combined with a child's initial vulnerabilities or susceptibilities, there is an interaction effect. For example, a resilient child (one with many protective factors and few vulnerabilities) may do quite well in a poor environment; equally, a vulnerable child may do quite well in a highly facilitative environment. Only the vulnerable child in a poor environment will do really poorly. (See Figure 5.7.)

This interactionist view is very well supported in a thirty-year longitudinal study which took place on the Hawaiian island of Kauai. (See Box 5.1.)

Box 5.1 Werner's 'Children of the Garden Island'

Starting in 1955, Werner and her colleagues studied all the children born on the island (nearly 700 of them) in a given period, following them up when they were one, two, ten, eighteen and thirty-one to thirty-two years old.

Werner became interested in a number of 'high risk' or 'vulnerable' children, who – despite exposure before the age of two to four or more of the following: reproductive stress (either difficulties during pregnancy and/or during labour and delivery), discordant and impoverished home lives, including divorce, uneducated, alcoholic or mentally disturbed parents – went on to develop healthy personalities, stable careers and strong interpersonal relationships. There were two main kinds of protective factors which contributed to their resilience.

CONSTITUTIONAL FACTORS

These included, temperamental characteristics which elicit positive responses from family and strangers, such as a fairly high activity level, a low degree of excitability and distress, and a high degree of sociability. The resilient individuals were typically described, as infants, as 'active', 'affectionate', 'cuddly', 'easy-going', and 'even-tempered', with no eating or sleeping habits which caused distress to their carers.

ENVIRONMENTAL FACTORS

There were four or fewer children in families of resilient individuals, with two or more years between themselves and the next child. In spite of poverty, family discord, or parental mental illness, resilient individuals were able to establish a close attachment to at least one carer, who might be a grandparent, older sibling, aunt or uncle, or a regular baby-sitter. They also found a great deal of emotional support from outside the family, were popular with their classmates, and had at least one close friend. School became a home away from home, a refuge from a disordered household.

Of the seventy-two children who were classified as resilient, sixty-two were studied after reaching their thirties. As a group, they seemed to be coping well with the demands of adult life, three-quarters had received some college education, nearly all had full-time jobs and were satisfied with their work.

> *As long as the balance between stressful life events and protective factors is favourable, successful adaptation is possible. When stressful events outweigh the protective factors, however, even the most resilient child can have problems.*
>
> (Werner, 1989)

These findings challenge the traditional assumption that there is a simple and direct link between early experiences and later development (Werner, 1989).

SOME PROVISIONAL CONCLUSIONS REGARDING THE GENE–ENVIRONMENT RELATIONSHIP

Although we are not free to choose the womb we are born in, or the school we go to, this is clearly not because it is our genes which determine these things (Dobzhansky & Penrose, 1955, cited in Plomin, 1994). However, as we have seen, the environment comprises more than such macro-environments: we are free to choose and create the *micro*-environments that form the bulk of our immediate, ongoing, experience:

> *Socially as well as cognitively, children select, modify, and even create their experiences. Children select environments that are rewarding or at least comfortable,* niche-picking. *Children modify their environments by setting the background tone for interactions, by initiating behaviour, and by altering the impact of environments . . . Children can make their own environments. That is, they can create environments compatible with their own propensities,* niche-building.
>
> (Plomin, 1994)

Gene–environment interaction

Physical characteristics

According to Jones (1993), most modern geneticists regard the 'Which one?' question as largely meaningless and the 'How much?' question as dull. The reason for this is that:

> *Nearly all inherited characteristics more complicated than a single change in DNA involve gene and environment acting together. It is*

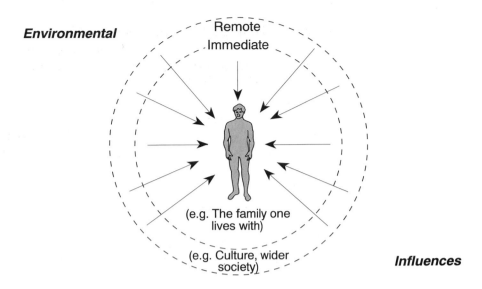

Figure 5.8a   Traditional, extreme behaviourist/environmentalist view of the environment as a set of external, post-natal influences acting upon a purely passive individual

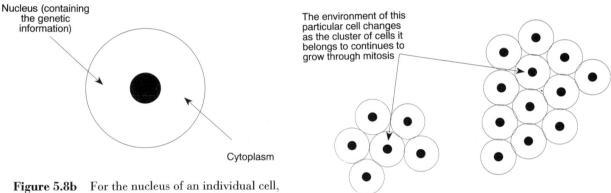

Figure 5.8b   For the nucleus of an individual cell, the environment is the surrounding cytoplasm

Figure 5.8c

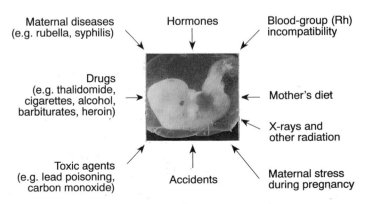

Figure 5.8d   The pre-natal, biological environment

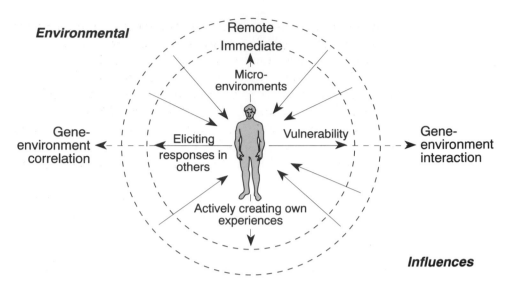

Figure 5.8e   The post-natal, socio-cultural environment with the individual portrayed as actively influencing the environment as much as he/she is influenced by it

> *impossible to sort them into convenient compartments. An attribute such as intelligence is often seen as a cake which can be sliced into so much 'gene' and so much 'environment'. In fact, the two are so closely blended that trying to separate them is more like trying to unbake the cake.*

(Jones, 1993)

Genetically speaking phenylketonuria (PKU) is a simple characteristic, since it refers to a bodily disorder caused by the inheritance of a single recessive gene from each parent. In its non-PKU state, the body produces the amino acid phenylalanine hydroxylase which converts phenylalanine (a substance found in many foods, particularly dairy products) into tyrosine. In the presence of the two recessive PKU genes, this process fails to work properly, and phenylalanine builds up in the blood, depressing the levels of other amino acids. As a result, the developing nervous system is deprived of essential nutrients, leading to severe mental retardation and, eventually, death. The relationship between what the child inherits (the two PKU genes – the *genotype*) and the actual signs and symptoms of the disease (high levels of phenylalanine in the blood, mental retardation – the *phenotype*) appears to be straightforward, direct and inevitable: given the genotype, the phenotype will occur.

However, a routine blood test soon after birth can detect the presence of the PKU genes, and an affected baby will be put on a low-phenylalanine diet, thus preventing the disease from developing. In other words, an environmental intervention will prevent the phenotype from occurring; the link between genotype and phenotype is not so direct and straightforward after all.

The special diet does not change the structure of the PKU genes themselves (which are *structural* genes; see above), or their functioning in response to the environment, yet they are prevented from producing the bodily effects which they would otherwise, inevitably, produce. '[The] nature [of children born with PKU genes] has been determined by careful nurturing and there is no answer to the question of whether their genes or their environment is more important to their well-being' (Jones, 1993).

Jones points out that there are hundreds of human variants which show the same interaction between heredity and environment, many of which are medically important. He refers to a whole new science of *pharmacogenetics* which studies individual differences in response to drugs (including alcohol and tobacco).

'Cancer' covers a multitude of conditions, all due to a failure to control cell division, and cancer genetics is a discipline in its own right. Very often, the chances of contracting cancer depend both on one's genes and on the environmental circumstances one is exposed to, such as nicotine, aspects of diet, radiation, and carcinogenic (cancer-producing) chemicals.

Behavioural characteristics

If there is no one-to-one relationship between genotype and phenotype in the case of the genetically simple PKU, how much more likely is it that complex characteristics and behaviours, such as intelligence, schizophrenia and homosexuality, will involve a highly complex interaction between heredity and environment?

Much of the most controversial and heated debate within psychology, past and present, has focused on precisely these characteristics, with the level of debate being predominantly 'How much?' However, in recent years, biologists, particularly in the USA and Britain, have made a number of claims to have identified the genes for, amongst other things, criminality, manic–depression, schizophrenia, alcoholism, high intelligence, and homosexuality (Horgan, 1993). In terms of the 'three questions', this research is not directly, or explicitly, aimed at answering any of them. However, while in principle the search for the genetic cause of complex human behaviours is consistent with all three, in practice, it seems to be most closely relevant to 'Which one?'

Horgan (1993) quotes Watson, the co-discoverer of the double-helix structure of DNA and the former head of the Human Genome Project (the massive international attempt to identify every single human gene), who recently claimed, 'We used to think that our fate was in our stars. Now we know, in large part, that our fate is in our genes'. Horgan (1993) also cites Koshland, an eminent biologist and editor of the influential journal *Science* (the journal of the American Association for the Advancement of Science), who in a recent editorial declared that the nature–nurture debate is 'basically

Figure 5.9 These German girls from 1934 demonstrate the stereotype of the Nazi ideal of fitness and health

over', since scientists have shown that genes influence many aspects of human behaviour. He also claims that genetic research may help to eliminate society's most intractable problems, including drug abuse, homelessness, and violent crime. Horgan believes that this illustrates that 'Eugenics is back in fashion'.

The term *eugenics* (from the Greek for 'good birth') was coined by Galton in 1883, and it embodied the idea that human society could be improved through 'better breeding'. Beginning in the 1920s, the American Eugenics Society sponsored 'Fitter Families Contests' at state fairs; just as cows and sheep were judged, so were people. Eugenicists helped to persuade more than twenty states to authorize the sterilization of men and women in prisons and psychiatric hospitals, and they also urged the Federal Government to restrict immigration of 'undesirable' races (Horgan, 1993). Intelligence tests, which had been developed for the selection of soldiers during the First World War, were then used to justify the exclusion of certain nationalities, including those from Eastern Europe, from entry into America during the 1920s and 1930s. It was, of course, precisely those groups which suffered at the hands of the Nazis, who took eugenics to its horrifying extreme by exterminating six million Jews and other 'undesirables' in the gas chambers. (See Gould, 1981; Gross, 1994.)

Is homosexuality genetically determined?

LeVay and Hamer (1994) discuss research which claims to have identified a segment of the X chromosome which is likely to be the site of the genes responsible for 'swaying', if not 'determining', sexual orientation. The research which they discuss is a *linkage study*, based on the finding that genes that are close together on a chromosome are almost always inherited together. Therefore, if there is a gene that influences sexual orientation, it should be 'linked' to a nearby DNA marker that tends to travel along with it in families. (A *marker* is a segment of DNA that indicates locations on a chromosome.) Out of forty pairs of gay brothers, thirty-three pairs showed the same marker, located at the tip of the long arm of the X chromosome, in a region known as Xq28, a concordance (similarity) rate that is statistically significant. (See Figure 5.10.)

'The most straightforward interpretation of the finding is that chromosome region Xq28 contains a gene that influences male sexual orientation. The study provides the strongest evidence to date that human sexuality is influenced by heredity because it directly examines the genetic

X Chromosome   **Xq28 (Shared region)**

Figure 5.10   The Xq28 region of the X chromosome (From LeVay and Hamer, 1994)

information the DNA' (LeVay & Hamer, 1994). However, LeVay and Hamer recognize that these are only initial findings, and that, as well as the need for replication, the gene itself has not yet been isolated. Xq28 is about four million base pairs in length; although this represents less than 0.2 per cent of the total human genome, it is still long enough to contain several hundred genes: searching for the 'gay genes' is like looking for the proverbial 'needle in a haystack' (LeVay & Hamer, 1994).

Despite these qualifying observations, Byrne (1994), for one, warns against drawing inappropriate conclusions from this research. As he points out, genes in themselves specify proteins, not behavioural or psychological phenomena. Although we know virtually nothing about how complex psychological phenomena are embodied in the brain, it is conceivable that particular DNA sequences might somehow cause the brain to be wired specifically for homosexual orientation. However,

While attempts to replicate these preliminary findings continue, researchers and the public must resist the temptation to consider them in any but the most tentative fashion. Perhaps more importantly, we should also be asking ourselves why we as a society are so emotionally invested in this research ... Perhaps the answer to the most salient questions in this debate lie not within the biology of human brains but rather in the cultures those brains have created.

(Byrne, 1994)

Figure 5.11 A rare photograph of Simon LeVay (a homosexual who claims to have found a biological factor in sexual orientation)

Finally, it is interesting to consider some of the social and political implications of research into the genetics of behaviour.

The genetic theory of intelligence, especially the claim that racial differences are due to genetic differences (see, for example, Jensen, 1969) has always been condemned by those of a left-wing persuasion, since it is seen as reinforcing, and even fuelling, the racism and racial inequalities that are responsible for the intellectual differences in the first place.

However, in the case of homosexuality, the picture is much less clear-cut. If scientific evidence shows that homosexuality is genetically determined, this means that gays (and, presumably, lesbians too) do not choose their sexual orientation; they 'cannot help it'. But this could be used, by those who oppose homosexuality, against gays and lesbians: if they cannot choose to be different (that is, heterosexual), then they are more of a threat, rather than less. The genetic view is usually a chance to blame the victim, a way of excusing injustice (Byrne, 1994).

Many gays and lesbians fight for the right to choose their sexual preference, so it may be very surprising to find LeVay, a homosexual and eminent biologist, advocating the search for 'gay genes'. He believes that, if the search is successful, the scientific evidence will make society as a whole more, not less tolerant, precisely because it will show that homosexuals don't choose to 'be that way'. However, he also recognizes that 'increasing knowledge of biology may eventually bring with it the power to infringe on the natural rights of individuals and to impoverish the world of its human diversity. It is important that our society expand discussions of how new scientific information should be used to benefit the human race in its entirety' (LeVay & Hamer, 1994).

Summary

- The debate about heredity and environment (or the *nature–nurture debate*) is concerned with some of the most fundamental questions that human beings ask about themselves.
- In its broadest sense, the debate is both about the human species as a whole (compared with other species) and about individual differences between people.
- Plomin believes that it is at the level of individual differences that the nature–nurture debate takes place.
- *Nativists* (such as Descartes) believe that heredity determines certain abilities and capacities, whereas *empiricists* (such as Locke) believe that the mind, at birth, is a *tabula rasa*, which is gradually 'filled in' by learning and experience.
- Examples of nativism in psychology include the Gestalt psychologists, Gesell's concept of *maturation*, and Chomsky's LAD.
- *Behaviourism* represents a very influential and extreme form of empiricist theory within psychology.
- To ask, 'Is it nature or nurture?' is to ask an oversimplified question about a very complex issue. 'How much?' is a more complex question, concerned with the relative importance of heredity and environment; it presupposes that both are involved, consistent with an *interactionist* position.
- The 'How much?' question is linked to the 'individual differences' form of the debate, and it is still concerned with trying to quantify their relative contributions. This is the main focus of *behavioural genetics*, which uses methods such as *twin studies, adoption studies*, and other studies of *family resemblance*.
- 'How do they interact?' is a third question, which is concerned with qualitative issues, i.e. the ways in which heredity and environment influence each other.
- Within *genetics*, 'nature' refers to 'inheritance': differences in chromosomes and genes transmitted from parents to offspring.
- While genetic variability is the raw material of evolution, evolution does not imply genetic variation within a species, and vice versa.
- The basic units of hereditary transmission are *genes*, large molecules of *DNA*. They occur in pairs and are situated on the *chromosomes*.

- Genes have two major functions: *self-duplication* and *protein synthesis*. The body's non-reproductive cells duplicate through *mitosis*, while the reproductive/germ cells duplicate through *meiosis*.
- Genes come in two forms, *structural* and *regulator*. Structural genes code for proteins and enzymes and form the basis of classical genetics. Regulator genes (the majority) communicate closely with the environment and change in response to it.
- In a psychological context, 'environment' usually implies external, post-natal influences impinging on a passive individual. This is a very inaccurate view.
- The environment of individual cells is the cluster of cells to which it belongs, and the cytoplasm of the cell is the environment for the cell nucleus. Everything that happens after fertilization is environmental.
- Instead of seeing the environment as separate from the individual, people may be seen as making their own environments. This can happen by (i) eliciting a certain response from other people, due to behaviour or biological characteristics (*gene–environment correlations*); (ii) non-shared psychosocial experiences; (iii) attaching their own meaning to events or experiences; (iv) an interaction between the *facilitativeness* of the environment and the individual's *vulnerabilities* (*gene–environment interaction*).
- The thirty-year longitudinal study by Werner et al. of nearly seven hundred children in Hawaii supports the hypothesis of interaction between individual vulnerability and environmental facilitativeness very well.
- A distinction is made between macro-and micro-environments; children cannot choose the former but can choose or create the latter, through *niche-picking* and *niche-building*.
- Even genetically very simple characteristics, such as the disease PKU, involve an interaction with the environment, such that the effects of the gene (the *phenotype*) can be prevented by environmental intervention: the link between the *genotype* and phenotype is not direct and straightforward.
- *Pharmacogenetics* studies interactions between individuals and drugs, and *cancer genetics* studies the interactions between genes and environment as they affect the risks of developing cancers.
- Biologists have recently made claims to have identified the genes for criminality, manic-depression, schizophrenia, alcoholism, high intelligence, and homosexuality. These are interpreted as ending the nature–nurture debate – in favour of nature.
- These claims appeal to supporters of *eugenics*.
- LeVay and Hamer cite a *linkage study*, showing the same *marker* in thirty-three out of forty pairs of gay brothers. They conclude that a

region of the X chromosome probably contains a gene that influences male sexual orientation, although the gene itself has not been identified.
- But genes specify proteins, not behavioural/psychological phenomena.
- This kind of research raises fundamental questions: why is the research seen as so important, what are its social and political implications, will society become more or less tolerant of homosexuality if it is found that 'gays can't help it'?

Suggestions for further reading

Horgan, J. (1993) Eugenics revisited, *Scientific American*, June, 92–100.
Plomin, R. (1994) *Genetics and Experience: The Interplay between nature and nurture*, Thousand Oaks, Calif.: Sage.
Rutter, M. and Rutter, M. (1992) *Developing Minds: Challenge and continuity across the life span* (especially Chapters 2, 3 and 6), Harmondsworth: Penguin.

Psychology, women and feminism

6

At first sight, it may not seem obvious what a chapter with the title 'Psychology, Women and Feminism' will be about, or why such a chapter should be necessary.

In a very real sense, what it is about is precisely what makes it necessary, namely the very strong and pervasive masculinist bias within psychology, which, in turn, reflects – and to some degree may contribute to – the superior power and status of males in Western society.

Feminism is a social and political movement that arose outside of psychology (often used synonymously with the Women's Movement of the 1970s in particular); however, many who would describe themselves as feminists were, and are, academics who criticized their particular discipline, including psychology, for being 'gender blind' (Kelly, 1988). If what feminists have in common is a condemnation of the oppression of women (in any and all its forms), then we would expect that those engaged in occupations and professions (including psychology) will be critical of such treatment of women as it goes on within their occupation or profession.

However, feminist thinkers and writers are not just against oppression of and discrimination against women, they are also *for* the recognition of the achievements, contributions and the experience of women as being valid and important in its own right, and not just something to be understood and evaluated in comparison with men. *Feminist psychologists*, therefore, are female psychologists who criticize psychology as a discipline, in its methods, its theories, and its applications, from a feminist perspective.

What is feminist psychology?

According to Wilkinson (1989), definitions of feminist psychology vary widely, in both substance and inclusiveness. For example, in the USA, 'feminist psychology' and the 'psychology of women' are often used synonymously: psychological research on women, and its practitioners, are automatically described as 'feminist'; however, in the UK, these are generally more clearly distinguished.

This chapter as a whole explores some of the major criticisms of psychology made from a feminist perspective. Briefly, these include the following.

1 A great deal of psychological research is conducted on all-male samples, but then it either fails to make this clear or reports the findings as if they applied to women and men equally.

2 Some of the most influential theories within psychology as a whole are based on studies of males only, but are meant to apply equally to women and men.

3 If women's behaviour differs from that of men, the former is often judged to be pathological or abnormal or deficient in some way, since the behaviour of men is, implicitly or explicitly, taken as the 'standard', the norm against which women's behaviour is compared.

4 Psychological explanations of behaviour tend to emphasize biological (and other internal) causes, as opposed to social (and other external) causes, thereby giving (and reinforcing) the impression that psychological sex differences are inevitable and unchangeable, and at the same time reinforcing widely held stereotypes about men and women. As well as being objectionable in themselves, such stereotypes contribute to the oppression of women.

5 Heterosexuality, both in women and men, is taken – either implicitly or explicitly – to be the norm, so that homosexuality is seen as abnormal.

In short, feminist psychologists see psychology as being *sexist* – regarding women as inferior to men and discriminating against them because they are women – and *heterosexist* – regarding gay men and lesbian women as abnormal and discriminating against them because they are gays or lesbians. They also consider that although, as a science, psychology claims to be 'neutral', 'objective', and 'value-free', it is in fact *value-laden*, taking men as the 'universal' standard, the centre around which everything else revolves. So, apart from being sexist and heterosexist, psychology is also *androcentric* (male-centred), as far as feminist psychologists are concerned.

Sexism within the psychology profession

In 1974, Bernstein and Russo published an article in *American Psychologist* called 'The history of psychology revisited: Or, up with our foremothers'. It consisted largely of a quiz, which their psychology colleagues failed miserably! The questions were as follows.

(i)   Who were the first persons to use the term 'projective technique' in print?

(**Answer:** Lois Murphy and Ruth Horowitz.)

(**ii**) Who was the first person to develop child analysis through play?

(**Answer:** Hermine von Hug-Hellmuth.)

(**iii**) Who developed the Cattell Infant Intelligence Test Scale?

(**Answer:** Psyche Cattell.)

(**iv**) What do the following have in common?
The Bender–Gestalt Test, the Taylor Manifest Anxiety Scale, the Kent–Rosanoff Word Association Test, the Thematic Apperception Test (TAT), and the Sentence Completion Method.

(**Answer:** A woman was either the senior author or the sole author of each test/method.)

(**v**) The following are the last names of individuals who have contributed to the scientific study of human behaviour. What else do these names have in common?
Ausubel, Bellak, Brunswick, Buhler, Dennis, Gardner, Gibson, Glueck, Harlow, Hartley, Hoffman, Horowitz, Jones, Kendler, Koch, Lacey, Luchins, Lynd, Murphy, Premack, Rossi, Sears, Sherif, Spence, Staats, Stendler, Whiting, Yarrow.

(**Answer:** They are the surnames of female social scientists.)

While you may have recognized some of the names in question v, this may only be because they have more famous and familiar husbands with whom they have jointly published research (for example, Gardner & Gardner, Harlow & Harlow, Kendler & Kendler, Luchins & Luchins, and Sherif & Sherif), so that you automatically infer that the 'Harlow' in the list is Harry Harlow (of rhesus monkey fame) and that the 'Sherif' is Muztafer Sherif (of the autokinetic effect in conformity fame).

Similarly, there is a strong tendency to assume that a psychologist whose name is unfamiliar to you is male: even though statistically it is very likely that you will be correct, this is not the basis for making such assumptions. Instead, it reflects a *masculinist* bias, the belief that the contributions made by men to psychology are more important than those made by women. As Scarborough and Furumoto (1987, cited in Paludi, 1992) state, the history of psychology is the history of male psychology.

If the names in the answers to questions i–iv are not what you would call 'household names', this is precisely because the psychological literature's treatment of women psychologists has kept them invisible (Paludi, 1992).

> *The histories written by psychology's academicians are neither accurate nor complete, neglecting as they do the most important contributions made by women . . . they do not include Mary Calkin's theory of self nor her invention of the method of paired associates, they do not mention Christine Ladd-Franklin's developmental theory*

of colour vision . . . Additionally, they fail to mention the monumentally important books of Margaret Washburn on animal behaviour . . . and they totally ignore Magda Arnold's comprehensive theory of emotions and Margaret Harlow's contribution to an understanding of the importance of tactile stimulation in mothering.

(Stevens & Gardner, 1982, quoted in Paludi, 1992)

Figure 6.1 Mary Calkins and Margaret Washburn; if these women are not household names, it is because psychological literature's treatment of women psychologists has kept them invisible

Mary Calkins was also the first person to explicitly recognize, and vividly describe, primacy-recency effects in memory (although she never actually used these terms) (Jackson, 1992).

Jackson (1992) points out that during the earliest days of the discipline of psychology (the mid-1800s), discrimination against women was overt: they were simply banned from participating. Calkins was excluded, in 1890, from a graduate psychology programme, on the grounds that she was a woman. Similarly, both Calkins and Ladd-Franklin were refused their PhDs, even though they had completed their theses.

Washburn was the first white American woman to receive a PhD in psychology, in 1908 (1904, according to Paludi, 1992); Inez Prosser was the first black American woman, receiving her PhD in 1933 (Jackson, 1992)! Washburn was also the second woman President of the American Psychological Association (APA), in 1921, but despite this, she was denied an academic post at a research university (Paludi, 1992).

The rediscovery of women psychologists

Their colleagues' poor performance on their quiz led Bernstein and Russo (1974) to conclude that women psychologists need to be rediscovered. According to Paludi (1992), in response to the neglect of women's contributions to psychology and to the recognition that women's history has the potential to transform women's self-understanding, a subfield of *women's history in psychology* has evolved in recent years. This draws on Lerner's (1979) model, namely (i) finding lost or overlooked women and putting them back into the history (*compensatory history*); (ii) noting women's contributions (*contribution history*); (iii) noting how history is constructed through a male (*androcentric*) perspective and reconstructing it from the perspective of women (*reconstruction history*).

In the USA, the Association for Women in Psychology was formed in 1969, and in 1973, the APA formed the Division of the Psychology of

Women (Division 35), which publishes its own journal, *The Psychology of Women Quarterly* (PWQ).

Parlee (1991) asks how far the PWQ has helped to develop a psychology for women or a psychology of gender that is different from mainstream (or 'malestream') psychology. Compared with mainstream journals, articles in the PWQ have (i) more often involved women of different ages, sexual orientations and from different ethnic backgrounds, (ii) less often involved just experimental research designs, and (iii) have paid somewhat more attention to the context of behaviour (as opposed to biological or personality variables). (Points ii and iii are discussed in more detail below.) However, Parlee feels that these differences represent only a superficial change.

This view is endorsed by Wilkinson (1989), who asks why there has been a lack of change within mainstream psychology in response to the 'feminist critique'. The answer, she says, is essentially to do with legitimacy; feminist research is not seen by the mainstream to be 'legitimate science', and so it is largely dismissed. Not only is it not seen as legitimate, but, because of the commitment of feminist research to social and political change for the benefit of women, it provides a convenient 'handle' for the labelling of feminist research as 'purely political'. This false polarization of 'science' and 'politics' removes the need to take femininst arguments seriously and protects mainstream researchers from having to acknowledge the political dimension of his or her practice (Wilkinson, 1989). (See Chapters 5 and 11.) The Division of the Psychology of Women also has a section on the Psychology of Black Women, as well as committees on the Psychology of Latinas and Asian-American Women.

In her Presidential Address to the APA in 1987, Bonnie Stricklund pointed out that women now constitute about one third of all employed psychologists and more than half of those gaining PhDs in psychology each year. Compared with the overt discrimination of the early years of psychology, this represents a radical change. She predicted that psychology will become the first science to be 'feminized', i.e. it will have more women than men. This, she claimed, will allow the investigation of a set of research problems that weren't consistent with, or couldn't be solved by, the androcentric paradigm, such as women's friendships with other women, rape, sexual harrassment, battered women, eating disorders, and sexism within psychopathology (Paludi, 1992). In the UK the British Psychological Society (BPS) has a Psychology of Women Section (POWS), set up in 1987, and there also exists the more informal Women in Psychology organization.

One manifestation of sexism within psychology is the devaluation (by men) of the areas of the discipline in which women are traditionally more numerous and which they seem to prefer, compared with the traditionally 'male' areas. The former include person-oriented/service-oriented fields, such as educational, developmental, and clinical psychology, and counselling, while the latter are the academic–experimental areas, including learning and cognitive psychology, which are regarded (by men) as more scientifically rigorous and intellectually demanding (Paludi, 1992). This is consistent with the more general observation that professions dominated by women are seen as low status (at least by male practitioners) (Wilkinson, 1989).

Could it be that women are 'channelled' into certain fields of psychology, which are then defined as 'inferior', simply because they are populated mainly by women? People who play a key role in this process are 'gatekeepers,' individuals, such as heads of university psychology departments, who have the power and authority to decide who is employed, to teach and do research, and in what areas of the discipline. In psychology, the gatekeepers are usually men.

Heterosexism in the psychology profession

Many radical feminists, both within and outside psychology, are lesbians. Not surprisingly, lesbian feminist psychologists tend to focus their criticisms on the neglect of the topic of homosexuality, and discrimination against lesbians and gays, both staff and students.

According to Celia Kitzinger (1990), homosexuality hardly features in undergraduate psychology courses. She quotes Louise Clarke (1989), a lesbian student at one of the 'new' universities in London, who says that: 'There are . . . lesbians/gay men in every college of higher education, whose needs are barely acknowledged, let alone met. Our existence should be acknowledged and reflected not just in the lecture room, but also in the curriculum.'

Kitzinger goes on to say that for gay and lesbian students and staff alike, academic psychology departments can be deeply oppressive places. Although teaching unions have anti-discrimination policies and oppose Section 28 of the Local Government Act (outlawing 'promotion' of homosexuality and the teaching of the 'acceptability of homosexuality as a pretended family relationship'), universities still embody anti-gay attitudes. Psychologists who 'come out' run the risk of verbal abuse and threats of violence. Kitzinger advocates that policies be implemented that are comparable to those dealing with gender, race, and disability discrimination, to protect lesbians and gays wherever psychologists work.

While the APA has a Gay and Lesbian Studies Division (set up in 1984), there is no equivalent in the BPS. However, the POWS may provide the opportunity for developing lesbian and gay psychology, although this is likely to have a very limited impact on mainstream psychology: 'Ultimately, it is only when psychologists as a profession are willing to take heterosexism seriously that we will be able to tackle discrimination and oppression, both within our own discipline, and in the world at large' (Kitzinger, 1990).

The feminist critique of science

If certain areas of psychology (such as cognitive) are regarded (by men) as being scientifically more rigorous and intellectually demanding, we need to ask just what it is that's meant by 'scientifically rigorous'. What is the view of science that is assumed by those who would make such a claim? What is the 'malestream' or androcentric account of the nature of science?

Basically, it sees the scientist as pursuing 'the truth' through the use of highly controlled, experimental methods. The scientist is able to discover what the world is really like, in some objective sense – that is, in the sense that we can find out how things are when they are not being observed and measured by scientists. Because the scientist is only interested in objective truth ('facts'), science, according to this perspective, is said to be *value-free*: the scientist's values and biases do not influence the scientific process. This positivistic approach applies as much to the study of people as it does to the physical world.

But can scientific enquiry be neutral, totally free of bias, wholly independent of the value-system of the human scientists who are doing the science?

> *Decisions about what is, and what is not, to be measured, how this is done, and most importantly, what constitutes legitimate research are made by individual scientists within a socio-political context, and thus science is ideological. Science is perhaps better viewed as 'a discourse that narrates the world in a special way' . . . Scientific psychology has reified concepts such as personality and intelligence – and the scientific psychology which 'objectively' and 'rationally' produced means of measuring these reifications has been responsible for physical assaults on women such as forced abortions and sterilizations.*

(Prince & Hartnett, 1993)

Prince and Hartnett point out that, between 1924 and 1972, over 7,500 women in the state of Virginia alone were forcibly sterilized – in particular, 'unwed mothers, prostitutes, the feeble-minded, children with discipline problems'; the criterion in all cases was the woman's mental age as measured by the Stanford–Binet intelligence test (Gould, 1981). The crucial point that they are making, of course, is that when some human ability or quality, such as intelligence, is treated as if it had a separate, independent, objective, existence (that is, when it is *reified*), such that it can be measured in an objective way; scientific 'findings' relating to that ability or quality can then be used to promote and justify discrimination against groups in society. But intelligence, personality and so many more of the 'things' psychologists study are *hypothetical constructs*, abstract concepts used to help explain and predict behaviour, but not directly, or literally, observable.

The very decision to study intelligence, and to develop tests designed to measure it, indicates that (some) psychologists believe that not only is this possible, but (much more relevant to the view of science as value-free) that it is important to do so! Such decisions are not made in a politico-cultural vacuum, and so cannot be seen as objective, neutral and value-free. As Weisstein (1993b) says, 'our ideas are filtered through our cultural and social categories, the ongoing social context and our own social rank'. Far from advocating that psychology should be value-free, objective and 'scientific', many feminist psychologists argue that we should stop denying the role of values and acknowledge that psychological investigation must always take wider social reality into account. They call for a new *value-laden approach to research*: unless and until psychology 'comes clean' about its values and biases, it will never be able to adequately reflect the reality of its subject matter, namely, human beings.

In the 1993 Preface to her classic *In a Different Voice*, Carol Gilligan (1982) says that at the core of her work on moral development in women and girls was the realization that within psychology, and in society at large, 'values were being taken as facts'. She continues:

> . . . in the aftermath of the Holocaust . . . it is not tenable for psychologists or social scientists to adopt a position of ethical neutrality or cultural relativism – to say that one cannot say anything about values or that all values are culturally relative. Such a hands-off stance in the face of atrocity amounts to a kind of complicity.

(Gilligan, 1993)

While the example she gives is clearly extreme, it helps to illustrate the argument that, not only do psychologists (and other scientists) have a responsibility to make their values explicit about important social and political issues, but failure to do so may (unwittingly) contribute to prejudice, discrimination and oppression.

The masculinist bias

The major 'sin' of mainstream psychology has been to deny the part played by values, resulting in the *masculinist bias* which permeates so much of the discipline. This takes a number of forms.

'Women want first and foremost to be mothers'

As we have seen, most psychologists are male, and the predominant research methodology used is the experiment, which is supposed to be objective and value-free. But we have also seen that deciding what is worth investigating is itself a value judgement, and this is particularly clear when male psychologists investigate aspects of female behaviour, such as motherhood.

For example, according to Bettelheim (1965, quoted in Weisstein, 1974), 'we must start with the realization that, as much as women want to be good scientists or engineers, they want first and foremost to be womanly companions of men, and to be mothers'. Similarly, Bowlby (1953) linked motherhood inextricably to being at home, white twenty to thirty years old, middle class and married. But what about the parent and infant studies of non-married, single, gay, lesbian, and black parents (Jackson, 1992)?

Figure 6.2 The fact that Eve was made from Adam's rib illustrates the point that men are the standard by which women are all too often judged

The male standard

Men are taken as some sort of standard or norm, against which women are compared and judged. According to Tavris (1993),

> *In any domain of life in which men set the standard of normalcy, women will be considered abnormal, and society will debate woman's 'place' and her 'nature'. Many women experience tremendous conflict in trying to decide whether to be 'like' men or 'opposite' from them, and this conflict is itself evidence of the implicit male standard against which they are measuring themselves. This is why it is normal for women to feel abnormal.*

She gives three examples.

1 Women and men have the same moods and mood swings but only women get theirs packaged into a syndrome. Women's hormones have never been reliably related to behaviour, competence, or anything to do with work, while men's *are* related to a variety of antisocial behaviours. Despite this, women may suffer from pre-menstrual syndrome, but there is no male equivalent (such as 'hyper-testosterone syndrome').

2 In 1985, the American Psychiatric Association proposed two new categories of mental disorder for inclusion in the revised (third) edition of *Diagnostic and Statistical Manual of Mental Disorders* (DSM-III-R), the official classification system used by American psychiatrists. One of these was *masochism*. In DSM-II this was described as one of the psychosexual disorders in which sexual gratification requires being hurt or humiliated. The proposal was to extend the term so that it became a more pervasive personality disorder, in which a person seeks failure at work, at home, and in relationships; rejects opportunities for pleasure; puts others first, thereby sacrificing one's own needs, playing the martyr, and so on. While not intended to apply to women exclusively, these

Figure 6.3 John Wayne is seen by many as the ultimate 'macho man'

characteristics are associated predominantly with the female role. Indeed, Caplan, in 1985, appeared before an American Psychiatric Association hearing on the proposed disorder and argued that it represented a way of calling psychopathological the behaviour of women who conform to social norms for a 'feminine woman', the 'good wife syndrome' (Caplan, 1991). In short, such a diagnostic label was biased against women and perpetuated the myth of women's masochism. After a year-long debate, the label was changed to *self-defeating personality disorder* and was put in the appendix of DSM-III-R, under the heading 'Proposed Diagnostic Categories Needing Further Study'. As Zimbardo (1992) argues, this example shows the political and ideological implications of diagnosing certain behaviour patterns as mental disorders. (See Chapter 7.) At the same time, there was no proposal for a parallel diagnosis for men who conform to social norms for a 'real' man (the John Wayne type, or 'macho personality disorder'). However, in 1991, Pantony and Caplan formally proposed that 'delusional dominating personality disorder' be included in DSM-IV, which was at the time being prepared (and was subsequently published in 1994). The Committee soundly rejected the proposal, on the grounds that 'there is no clinical tradition' for such a disorder (Caplan, 1991; Tavris, 1993).

3 When men have problems, including drug abuse, and behave in socially unacceptable ways, as in rape and other forms of violence, the causes are looked for in their upbringing, while women's problems are the result of their psyche or their hormones. This corresponds roughly to an internal attribution in the case of women, and an external attribution in the case of men, with the further implication that for men, it could have been different (they are the victims of their childhoods etc.), while for women it couldn't (because 'that's what women are like'). (See Chapter 2, on attribution.)

According to Tavris (1993), the view that man is the norm and woman is the opposite, lesser or deficient (the problem) constitutes one of three currently competing views regarding what she calls the 'Mismeasure of Woman' (meant to parallel Gould's. 'The Mismeasure of Man', 1981, a brilliant critique of intelligence testing; see Gross, 1994). It is the view which underlies so much psychological research designed to discover why women aren't 'as something' (moral, intelligent, rational) as men. It also underlies the enormous self-help industry, whereby women consume millions of books advising them how to be more beautiful, independent, or whatever. Men, being normal, feel no need to 'fix' themselves in corresponding ways (Tavris, 1993).

Consistent with this view is a study by Broverman et al. (1979, cited in Jackson, 1992), who asked several psychiatrists to define a healthy adult, a healthy adult male, and a healthy adult female. Responses regarding the first two were very similar, the character being defined by traits such as assertiveness, aggression, ambition, and task-oriented. But healthy women were viewed as being caring, expressive, nurturing and affiliative. Women, therefore, are in a double bind. As healthy women, they fall outside the norm for healthy adults; if they assume male characteristics, they step outside the definition of a healthy woman (Jackson, 1992).

Accentuating the sex differences

In psychology in general, but perhaps in the study of gender in particular, there is a strong bias towards publishing studies which have produced 'positive' results, i.e. where the null hypothesis has been rejected. So, in the case of gender, studies which find sex differences will be published, while those that do not, will not. The far more convincing evidence for 'sex similarity' is, therefore, ignored, creating the very powerful impression that differences between men and women are real, widespread, and 'the rule'. Indeed, the very term 'sex similarities' sounds rather odd (Jackson, 1992; Tavris, 1993; Unger, 1979).

The male norm as the standard

'The bias of seeing women's behaviour as something to be explained in relation to the male norm makes sense in a world which takes the male norm for granted' (Tavris, 1993). Moreover, the male norm frames the very questions that investigators ask; the answers to these questions then create the impression that women have 'problems' or 'deficiencies' if they differ from the norm.

Tavris (1993) gives some examples of typical findings from the literature on psychological sex differences:

- Women have lower self-esteem than men do.
- Women do not value their efforts as much as men do.
- Women are less self-confident than men.
- Women are more likely to say they're hurt than to admit they're angry.
- Women have more difficulty developing a 'separate sense of self'.

Most people would agree that it is desirable for women to have high self-esteem, to value their efforts more, and so on. So such studies usually conclude with discussion of 'the problem' of why women are so insecure and what can be done about it.

But had these studies used women as the basis of comparison, the same findings might have produced different conclusions about what the 'problems' are.

- Men are more conceited than women.
- Men overvalue the work they do.
- Men are not as realistic as women in assessing their abilities.
- Men are more likely to accuse or attack others when unhappy, instead of stating that they feel hurt or looking for sympathy.

- Men have more difficulty in forming and maintaining relationships.
If these 'translations' of the first set of statements sound biased and
derogatory, this is precisely the point that Tavris is trying to make:
describing women's deficiencies is not usually seen as biased and
derogatory, because the male norm is the standard against which women
are being judged. As soon as a female norm is used to set the standard, the
bias becomes apparent: only then do we become aware of the bias that was
there all the time!

'Why has it been so difficult to notice the same negative tone in the way
we talk about women? The answer is that we are used to seeing women as
the problem, and to regarding women's differences from men as deficiencies
and weaknesses' (Tavris, 1993). Tavris argues that, after centuries of
trying to 'measure up', many women feel exhilarated by having female
qualities and experiences valued and celebrated. *Cultural feminists*, while
regarding man as the norm, see woman as *opposite but better* ('the
solution'); this represents the second current version of the 'mismeasure of
woman'.

Sexism in research

Pointing out the sexist bias in psychological research is as much an ethical
criticism as it is a scientific and practical one: we have already seen how
damaging to women sexist research can be.

The APA Board of Social and Ethical Responsibility for Psychology set
up a Committee on Nonsexist Research, which reported its findings as
Guidelines for Avoiding Sexism in Psychological Research (Denmark et al.,
1988).

According to Denmark et al., gender bias is found at all stages of the
research process: (i) question formulation; (ii) research methods and
design; (iii) data analysis and interpretation; (iv) conclusion formulation.
The principles set out in the *Guidelines* are meant to apply to other forms
of bias too – race, ethnicity, disability, sexual orientation and socio-
economic status.

QUESTION FORMULATION

Gender stereotypes that are associated with the topic being studied can bias
the questions that are asked (and the research outcomes). For example,
leadership is often defined in terms of dominance, aggression, and other
styles that stress stereotypically male characteristics. To correct this
problem, researchers should recognize the existence of a range of leadership
styles, including those that stress egalitarian relationships, negotiation,
conflict resolution, and consideration of others.

Again, questions derived from, or constrained by, existing theory and
research based on male samples, thus not taking into account women's
experiences, are likely to result in explanations of female behaviour that are
not very meaningful. For example, the hypothesis that aggressive stimuli

increase sexual arousal is based on results using male participants only; it is essential to either use female participants as well as male, or to point out the difficulties of generalizing these results to women.

Finally, it is assumed that topics that are relevant to white males are more important and 'basic', whereas those relevant to white females, or ethnic minority females or males, are more marginal, specialized or applied. For example, the effects of TV violence on aggression in boys is considered basic research, whereas research on the psychological correlates of pregnancy or the menopause is not. (This relates to what we noted earlier regarding the value-laden nature of psychology and the need to recognize the biases involved in research, instead of trying to deny them.)

RESEARCH METHODS AND DESIGN

The selection of research participants is often based on stereotypic assumptions, and doesn't allow for generalizations to other populations. For example, in studies of contraception, female-only samples are used, on the assumption that males are not (or need not be) responsible for contraception. But both sexes should be studied before drawing any conclusions about the factors that influence the use of contraception.

Sometimes male samples are used because of practical convenience. For example, male animals are often preferred as subjects in experiments because the oestrous cycle in females disrupts responses in certain types of behavioural or biological tests. Generalization to females must then be done only with great caution.

In a surprisingly large number of studies, the sex and race of the participants, researchers, and any confederates who may be involved, are not specified. As a consequence, potential interactions between these variables are not accounted for. For example, men tend to display more helping behaviour than women in studies involving a young female confederate who needs help. These findings could be a function of either the sex of the confederate or an interaction between the confederate and the participant rather than sex differences between the participants (which is the usual conclusion that is drawn).

DATA ANALYSIS AND INTERPRETATION

As we noted in 'Accentuating the sex differences', above, when sex differences are *not* found, the findings tend to remain unreported. Not only should they be, but, conversely, when any non-hypothesized sex differences are found, they should be reported. In both cases, the findings should be reported so that replications can be carried out.

Sex differences are sometimes claimed to be present when a significant correlation is found between two variables for, say, men, but not for women. Instead of testing to see if there is a significant difference between the two correlations, it is simply *assumed*, because the findings fit the stereotypes.

Finally, significant sex differences may be reported in a very misleading way, because the wrong sort of comparisons are being made. For example, 'The spatial ability scores of women in our sample is significantly lower than those of men, at the 0.01 level'. We might conclude from this that women cannot or should not become architects or engineers. However, 'Successful architects score above 32 on our spatial ability test . . . engineers score above 31 . . . 12 per cent of women and 16 per cent of men in our sample score above 31; 11 per cent of women and 15 per cent of men score above 32'. What conclusions would you draw now?

CONCLUSION FORMULATION

Results based on one sex only are then applied to both. This can be seen in some of the major theories within psychology, notably Erikson's theory of life-span development, and Kohlberg's theory of moral development. Grosz (1987, quoted in Wilkinson, 1989) would describe these as 'phallocentric' theories, which involve 'the use of general or universal models to represent the two sexes according to the interests and terms of one, the male'.

Discussing Erikson's theory, which was based on the study of males only, Gilligan (1982) states that 'psychological theorists . . . implicitly adopting the male life as the norm . . . have tried to fashion women out of a masculine cloth . . . In the life cycle . . . the woman has been the deviant'.

On the one hand, Erikson (1950, 1968) describes a series of eight developmental stages that are meant to be universal; that is, they apply to both women and men, in different cultures, and so on. For example, the conflict between *identity* and *role confusion* (which occurs during adolescence) precedes that between *intimacy* and *isolation* (young adulthood). On the other hand, he (1968) acknowledges that the sequence is different for the female: she holds her identity in abeyance as she prepares to attract the man by whose name she will be known, by whose status she will be defined, the man who will rescue her from emptiness and loneliness by filling 'the inner space'. For men, achieving a sense of identity precedes intimacy with a sexual partner. For women these tasks seem to be fused; intimacy goes along with identity: 'the female comes to know herself as she is known, through her relationships with others' (Gilligan, 1982).

Yet despite his observation of sex differences, Erikson's *epigenetic chart* of the life-cycle stages remains unchanged: 'identity continues to precede intimacy as male experience continues to define his [Erikson's] life-cycle concept' (Gilligan, 1982).

Similarly, Kohlberg's (1969) six-stage theory of moral development was based on a twenty-year longitudinal study of eighty-four boys (starting in 1955), but he claims universality for his stage sequence. Girls and women rarely attain a level of moral reasoning above the third stage ('Good boy–nice girl' orientation) which is supposed to be achieved by most adolescents and adults. This leaves females looking decidedly morally deficient. But Gilligan's studies of females lead her to argue that men and women have qualitatively different conceptions of morality. When presented with hypothetical moral dilemmas, such as the famous case of Heinz (whose wife is dying from cancer and can only be saved by a drug which Heinz can only obtain by stealing it), while both boys and girls typically want his wife to live, the 'female' solution is to 'find some other way' besides stealing the drug, and the emphasis is put on the notions of care, responsibility and relationships. By contrast, males are more likely to condemn the druggist for asking so much money for the drug (which is his invention), stressing rights and rules.

Also, sex differences in performance on a specific task or behaviour are interpreted as reflecting sex differences in a global ability or characteristic. For example, it is concluded that males are more *field-independent* than females (that is, males have the ability to ignore the context by picking out a part of a picture from the picture as a whole). But this is found only for embedded figure tests and rod-and-frame tests, and not on tactile and auditory tests.

Finally, group (mean) scores indicating sex differences often obscure important individual differences within each sex. Group averages must not be used to justify any inequality of opportunities.

What's different about feminist research?

From a feminist standpoint, researchers must become actively involved in the research process, taking the perspective of the participants; they are not detached investigators but became an integral part of the whole process. According to the Task Force of APA Division 35, feminist research in psychology tends to be 'co-operative, participative . . . interdisciplinary [and] non-hierarchical . . . [beginning] with personal experience' and recognizing that 'truth is not separate from the person who speaks it' (quoted in Wilkinson, 1989).

The very terms used by psychologists, such as *subject*, *manipulate* and *control*, imply the masculinist-biased nature of the field: the dominance, status and power of the experimenter and the subordinate role of the participant (Paludi, 1992). (See Chapter 10, on ethics.) Most psychologists have been, and still are, trained within a paradigm which is positivistic and behaviouristic, being taught that:

> . . . effects derived from orderly determinist causes, that the subjective aspects of behaviour were irrelevant, and that the best studies required maximal distance between experimenter and subject . . . If I thought of sex professionally at all, I saw it as a variable which could neither be manipulated or controlled and therefore of very little scientific interest. Even the rats were male.
>
> (Unger, 1984, quoted in Unger, 1993)

According to Tavris (1993), two new directions taken by feminist researchers in recent years are (i) looking outward at gender in context, and (ii) looking inward at gender as narrative.

Gender in context

This relates to the debate within the psychology of personality as to the relative influence of individual traits and situational factors on behaviour (see Chapter 4). It can be seen as the application of that debate to the particular issue of gender differences.

It is widely believed among feminist psychologists that a major figure in the debate is Weisstein (1993a). While she was not the first person to discuss the role of ideology and social context in the construction of the female psyche (that person probably being Simone de Beauvoir in 1953), her article entitled 'Psychology Constructs the Female' was the first to provide a challenge to psychology's *essentialist views* regarding maleness and femaleness (Unger, 1993).

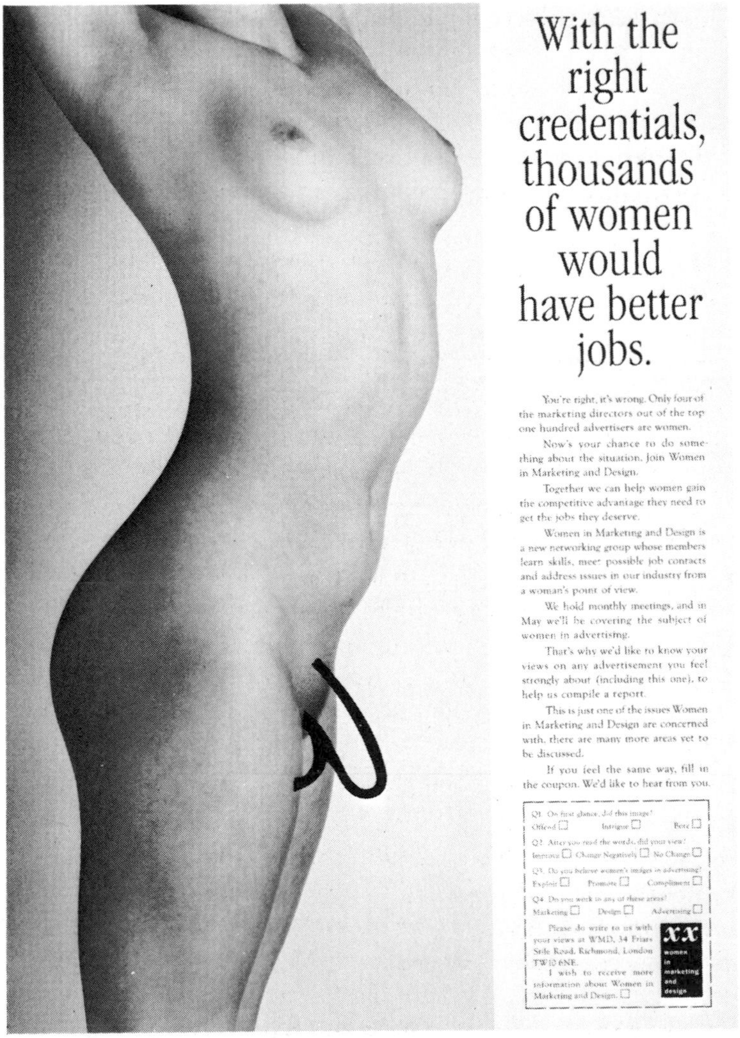
With the right credentials, thousands of women would have better jobs.
You're right, it's wrong. Only four of the marketing directors out of the top one hundred advertisers are women.
Now's your chance to do something about the situation. Join Women in Marketing and Design.
Together we can help women gain the competitive advantage they need to get the jobs they deserve.
Women in Marketing and Design is a new networking group whose members learn skills, meet possible job contacts and address issues in our industry from a woman's point of view.
We hold monthly meetings, and in May we'll be covering the subject of women in advertising.
That's why we'd like to know your views on any advertisement you feel strongly about (including this one), to help us compile a report.
This is just one of the issues Women in Marketing and Design are concerned with, there are many more areas yet to be discussed.
If you feel the same way, fill in the coupon. We'd like to hear from you.
Q1. On first glance, did this image?
Offend Intrigue Bore
Q2. After you read the words, did your view?
Change Negatively No Change
Q3. Do you believe women's images in advertising?
Exploit Promote Compliment
Q4. Do you work in any of these areas?
Marketing Design Advertising
Please do write to us with your views at WMD, 34 Friars Stile Road, Richmond, London TW10 6NE.
I wish to receive more information about Women in Marketing and Design.
xx
women in marketing and design

Figure 6.4 This Cowan Kemsley Taylor advertisement was censored by every national newspaper. It appeared once, in *Girl about Town* magazine

The central argument in Weisstein's critique was that psychology can have 'nothing of substance to offer' to either 'a study of human behaviour' (male or female) or a vision of 'human possibility', because it insists on looking for 'inner traits' when it ought to be looking 'for social context'.

In doing so, psychology has functioned as 'a pseudo-scientific buttress for our cultural sex-role notions', which include not only our ideas about the 'nature of women', but also about the 'nature of homosexuality'; thus, psychology has helped to justify and reinforce many of the prejudices which are inherent in a 'patriarchal social organization', such as the USA (and Western culture in general).

By placing the emphasis on internal, individual causes of

behaviour, psychologists, unwittingly, help to promote a view of society which is composed of so many individuals removed from the political, economic and historical context in which human behaviour takes place. It reinforces the popular view that 'people are as they are', including, of course, the 'nature' of women and men, making behavioural change virtually impossible.

> *Psychology may be so predisposed as a discipline to individualize and decontextualize the phenomena it studies (including gender, sexuality, race and class) that it necessarily depoliticizes those phenomena and thereby functions both as a collaborator in the social reproduction of the status quo and as an obstacle to social change.*
>
> (Bem, 1993)

Bem gives the example of 'battered woman's syndrome'. Although it has helped battered women in the USA to conduct a legal defence when accused of murdering their batterers and has captured some of the helplessness that they undoubtedly feel, it has achieved this by pathologizing the women themselves, rather than trying to expose the institutional context in which they live and in which their ultimate act of self-defence occurs.

A less individualized and depoliticized approach would be to argue not that the woman herself is sick (which necessarily deflects attention away from the 'sickness' of her institutional context), but to argue that there is something fundamentally male-centred about the USA legal definition of self-defence: a defendant may be found innocent of homicide (murder) only if he or she perceived imminent danger of great bodily harm or death and responded to that danger with only as much force as was necessary to defend against it. Feminist legal scholars point out that this definition fits the scenario in which two men are involved in an isolated episode of sudden violence much better than the battered woman scenario. She is put at an immediate and fundamental disadvantage by virtue of the fact that her victimization has been taking place over an extended period of time, such that the perceived danger may be no greater at the time the killing takes place than it has been on many previous occasions; the act is the culmination of (usually) years of terror.

Bem is probably best known for her work on *androgyny*, the blending within the same individual man or woman of masculine and feminine characterisics, during the 1970s, and the later *gender schema theory* (1984), which sees androgyny as a disposition to process information in accordance with relevant non-sex principles (in contrast with traditional 'masculine' men and 'feminine' women, who spontaneously think of things in sex-typed terms).

By the mid-1980s, Bem began to feel 'theoretically hemmed in', partly because of her own 'overly narrow focus on how gender stereotypes in the head constrain both sexes' (Bem, 1993). This left out the social institutions that push women and men into different and unequal roles and the (rather obvious) fact that, because most societies are male-dominated, women are a lot more constrained by these social institutions than men are.

In 1993, Bem wrote a book called *The Lenses of Gender*, which she describes as 'a contextualized and constructivist analysis of how biology, culture, and individual psyche all interact in historical context to systematically reproduce not only the oppression of women, but of sexual minorities too'. In it, she argues that there are hidden assumptions embedded in cultural discourses, social institutions, and individual psyches that shape not only perceptions of reality, but the material aspects of reality itself (for example, unequal pay, inadequate day-care facilities for children). These assumptions take the form of three kinds of lenses, (i) *androcentrism*, or male-centredness, which we have already discussed at length; (ii) *gender polarization*, which superimposes a male–female dichotomy on almost every aspect of human experience (such as modes of dress, social roles, ways of expressing emotion, experiencing sexual desire); (iii) *biological essentialism*, which rationalizes and legitimizes the other two lenses by treating them as the inevitable consequences of the intrinsic biolgical nature of women and men.

Bem's *enculturated lens theory* tries to explain how we either acquire the culture's lenses and construct a conventional gender identity, or we construct a gender-subversive identity: 'We must reframe the debate on sexual inequality so that it focuses not on the differences between women and men but on how male-centred discourses and institutions transform male–female difference into female disadvantage' (Bem, 1993).

SO HOW *IS* GENDER CONSTRUCTED?

Weisstein's (1993a) article foreshadowed the paradigm shift within psychology from the view that reality constructs the person to the view that the person constructs reality (Buss, 1978, cited in Unger, 1993). She, together with a few other pioneers, explicitly used the term 'social constructionism' to question the bases of psychological knowledge.

One form that this construction of gender can take is through social expectations of behaviour, both other people's expectations of our behaviour and our expectations of our own behaviour. More specifically, expectations can influence behaviour through the self-fulfilling prophecy; Weisstein cites classic studies by Rosenthal and his co-workers (Rosenthal, 1966; Rosenthal & Jacobson, 1968) which demonstrate how expectations can change experimental outcomes: 'even in carefully controlled experiments, and with no outward or conscious difference in behaviour, the hypotheses we start with will influence enormously the behaviour of another organism' (Weisstein, 1993a). (Rosenthal's experiments and their implications for the objectivity of scientific psychology are discussed further in Chapter 11.)

Weisstein also discusses Milgram's obedience experiments as demonstrating the very powerful influence of the social situation on the behaviour of individuals (see Chapter 4, on the trait–situation debate).

In line with this continuing shift towards studying the importance of context, more recent studies of gender have consistently shown that the behaviour that we associate with 'gender' depends more on what an individual is doing than on biological sex (e.g. Eagly, 1987).

Risman (1987, cited in Tavris, 1993) compared the 'parenting' skills and personality traits of single fathers, single mothers, and married parents. Having responsibility for children was as strongly related to 'feminine' traits (such as nurturance and sympathy) as being female was. The single fathers were more like mothers than like married fathers, but this was not because they were atypical as a group of nurturant men – they had custody of their children because of widowhood, the wife's desertion, or the wife not wanting custody. In other words, many of them had single parenthood 'thrust upon them', and did not have personality traits that predisposed them to being good parents.

Similarly, Maccoby (1990, cited in Tavris, 1993) re-analysed studies which used to show that little girls are 'passive' and little boys are 'active'. She concluded that boys and girls do not differ, as groups, in some consistent, trait-like, way: *their behaviour depends on the gender of the child they are playing with*. There is gender segregation, such that girls (as young as three) are only passive when a boy is present, but they are just as independent as boys when in an all-girl group.

Results such as these suggest that 'gender, like culture, organizes for its members different influence strategies, ways of communicating and ways of perceiving the world. The behaviour of men and women often depends more on the gender they are interacting with than on anything about the gender they are – a process that West and Zimmerman (1987) call "doing gender"' (Tavris, 1993).

However, a major aspect of the context of people's lives is the power they have (or lack) in influencing others and in determining their own lives. Clearly, the 'two cultures' of women and men are not equal in power, status and resources. Tavris (1993) believes that many behaviours and personality traits thought to be typical of women (such as 'women's intuition' – the ability to 'read' non-verbal cues – and the tendency to blame themselves for their shortcomings and to have lower self-esteem than men) turn out to be typical of women – and men – who lack power; they seem to be the *result* of powerlessness, not the cause.

Gender as narrative

The other major recent direction that feminist research has taken is to focus on the life story, which Sarbin (1986) describes as the key metaphor in understanding human behaviour. Our plans, memories, love affairs and hatreds are guided by narrative plots, with women and men differing greatly in the narrative plots they tell about their lives. (These can be seen as an important move towards idiographic methods of studying gender, and away from the nomothetic methods used by psychologists wanting to establish gender differences from the androcentric perspective, see Chapter 3, on the idiographic–nomothetic debate.)

Where do the narratives come from? What functions do they serve for the storyteller? Why do so many women today feel safe telling stories that place their fate in the stars or premenstrual syndrome, rather than in their own hands – or society's? However, life stories can change; how and why they do is at the heart of psychology and politics (Tavris, 1993).

So are women and men different – and if so, how?

According to the third of the current versions of the mismeasure of woman, this is seen as being no problem, because man is the norm and woman is just like him. Tavris (1993) cites Tiefer (1992) who argues that this assumption pervades the diagnosis of sexual disorders in DSM: 'Men and women are the same, and they're all men'.

Tavris believes that the study of gender has entered a 'transformationist' era (Crawford & Mararcek, 1989), whereby we should 'stand back from the fray' and accept that we shall never know the essence of male and female: these are endlessly changing and depend both on the eye of the observer and the conditions of our lives. Instead of asking, 'Do men and women differ?' (which is literal and limited), this approach asks, 'Why is everyone so interested in differences? Which differences? What function does *belief* in differences serve? What are the consequences of believing that women are emotionally and professionally affected by their hormones, but men aren't, or that women are the love experts and that men are incapable of love and intimacy? Where do these beliefs come from and who benefits (and loses) from them?'

While cultural feminism is an important step forward in the study of gender, it runs the risk of replacing one set of stereotypes with another. The 'woman is better' school, like the 'woman is deficient' school, assumes a fundamental opposition between the sexes. Thinking in opposites leads to what philosophers call 'the law of the excluded middle': most actual women and men fall somewhere in between the stereotypical opposites regarding psychological qualities, abilities, traits and so on.

The debate about gender and gender differences is not whether or not women and men differ: of course they do. As in the debate about racial differences in IQ, what is controversial is how such differences, when they are found, should be interpreted. Do they reflect permanent, biological, intra-individual traits and characteristics, or should they be understood in relation to life experiences, social contexts, resources and power, which can and do change culturally and historically? 'By setting aside predetermined categories, we have learned that there is no one right way to be lesbian, straight or gay, no one right way to *be*' (Tavris, 1993).

Concluding comments: what's better about feminist psychology?

Wilkinson (1989) maintains that there are three major improvements that feminist psychology can make to mainstream psychology:

1 it identifies hitherto unrecognized sources of bias (such as Gilligan's critique of Kohlberg);
2 it increases critical thinking;
3 it broadens the scope of research by (a) looking at under-researched areas (such as violence against women), and (b) by generating new ways of looking at old problems.

This, in turn, offers the possibility of an 'extra dimension' to psychological knowledge: by looking at human experience from women's perspective, we can enrich and extend our understanding of the whole of human functioning and its possibilities (Wilkinson, 1989).

Summary

- *Feminism*, as a social and political movement, condemns the oppression of women and strives for the recognition of women's achievements, contributions and experience as valid and important in its own right.
- *Feminist psychologists* criticize psychology from a feminist perspective.
- 'Feminist psychology' and the 'psychology of women' are often used synonymously in the USA, but are usually more clearly distinguished in the UK.
- Femininst psychologists see psychology as *sexist* and *heterosexist*, *value-laden* and *androcentric*.
- The *masculinist bias* holds the contributions made by men to psychology to be more important than those made by women; the history of psychology is the history of *male* psychology.
- In the early days of psychology, women were discriminated against quite overtly.
- *Women's history in psychology* is the field of study comprising: *compensatory history*, *contribution history*, and *reconstruction history*.
- A number of organizations have been set up by, especially for, women, including: the Association for Women in Psychology, the APA Division of the Psychology of Women (which has a Section on the Psychology of Black Women), the BPS Psychology of Women Section, and Women in Psychology.
- The 'feminist critique' has had little impact on mainstream psychology, because it is not seen as legitimate science and is

dismissed as 'purely political'.

- Despite the growing numbers of female psychologists, they are still found working in predominantly *person-oriented* and *service-oriented* areas, compared with the traditionally male *academic* and *experimental* areas.
- This could reflect sexism among male psychologists who regard 'female' areas of psychology as scientifically and intellectually inferior; 'gatekeepers' are also predominantly male.
- Many radical feminist psychologists are lesbians, who criticize mainstream psychology for its heterosexism.
- The feminist critique of science challenges the fundamental assumptions of the *positivist* approach, which sees scientific enquiry as objective, value-free, unbiased, independent of the value system of the human scientist.
- When psychological constructs, such as intelligence and personality, are *reified*, 'scientific findings' relating to them can be used to promote and justify discrimination against social groups.
- Psychologists' decisions about what they should study reflect values, and are related to a particular politico-cultural context.
- Feminist psychologists advocate a *value-laden approach* to research, so that values will no longer be mistaken for facts. If psychologists fail to make their values explicit about important social and political issues, they may (unwittingly) contribute to prejudice and discrimination.
- The *masculinist bias* can take the form of: (i) deciding what is worth investigating about women; (ii) taking men as a standard against which to compare and judge women, such that women's differences from men come to be seen as deficiencies and weaknesses; (iii) only publishing the results of studies which have found evidence of sex differences.
- Gender bias can be found at all stages of the research process – *question formulation*, *research methods/design*, *data analysis/interpretation*, and *conclusion formulation*.
- Gender stereotypes associated with the topic being studied (e.g. leadership) can bias the questions that are asked.
- Questions derived from theory based on *male-only samples* are likely to produce explanations of female behaviour that are not very meaningful. Some of the major theories within psychology, such as Erikson's theory of life-span development and Kohlberg's theory of moral development, are based on male-only samples but are meant to apply to males and females equally.
- Topics that are relevant to white males are seen as more important and 'basic' than for females or other social or ethnic groups.
- Results regarding sex differences are often interpreted in line with stereotyped expectations, or they may be reported in a very

misleading way, because the the wrong sort of comparisons are being made.

- Sex differences in performance on a specific task or behaviour are often interpreted as reflecting a difference in some global characteristic.
- Group (mean) scores indicating sex differences often obscure important individual differences within each group.
- Feminist researchers become actively involved in the research process, taking the perspective of the participants; they reject the detached experimenter role, and do not see themselves as of higher status, or more powerful, than the 'subject'.
- Feminist critics of mainstream psychology believe that it has overemphasized internal, individual causes of behaviour and neglected social context; this helps to reinforce the status quo and the belief that people cannot change.
- Bem describes three kinds of 'lenses' (assumptions which shape perceptions of reality and material aspects of reality itself), *androcentrism*, *gender polarization*, and *biological essentialism*.
- Her *enculturated lens theory* sees gender identity as being constructed in a way that disadvantages women.
- One way in which gender is constructed is through *social expectations* of behaviour, specifically *self-fulfilling prophecies*.
- Research evidence suggests that the behaviour we associate with gender depends more on what an individual is doing than on biological sex. Also, the behaviour of men and women often depends more on the gender they are interacting with than on anything about their own gender.
- Many personality traits thought to be typical of women are, in fact, typical of *people who lack power*, and so are the result, not the cause, of powerlessness.
- Feminist research tends towards idiographic methods, such as the recent focus on the *life story*.
- According to *cultural feminism*, women are *opposite but better* than men, who are the norm. This threatens to replace one set of stereotypes with another, and assumes a fundamental opposition between the sexes (leading to the *law of the excluded middle*).
- The crucial question is not whether sex differences exist but how they should be interpreted.

Suggestions for further reading

Paludi, M.A. (1992) *The Psychology of Women*, Debuque Iowa: WCB Brown & Benchmark.

Tavris, C. (1993) The mismeasure of women, *Feminism & Psychology*, 3(2), 149–68. (There are a number of other important articles in the same issue of *Feminism & Psychology*.)

Normality and abnormality

Most of this chapter will be devoted to trying to define the terms 'normal' and 'abnormal' and to establish the relationship between them. While it is always important to be clear what is meant by the terms we use in discussion of any psychological topic, here it is essential, because the whole field of *abnormal psychology* rests upon the assumption that a distinction can be made between normality and abnormality.

As with many terms and concepts, examples can help to get a discussion started and may help to raise some of the important issues. So, if you were asked to give some examples of the kinds of behaviour and experiences which fall under the heading of abnormal psychology, you would probably include: *schizophrenia, anxiety, panic attacks, homosexuality, sexual fetishes, depression, hallucinations.* While the list of possible examples is very much longer, these make it reasonably clear what the field of abnormal psychology is about, what the 'scope' of the field is. However, giving examples is the easy bit! What we really want to know is: What do they all have in common which makes us want to call them abnormalities in the first place? Does there have to be anything that links them, or can they all illustrate abnormality for different reasons? Do psychologists and psychiatrists consider the meaning of normality and abnormality, or do they just assume that, say, schizophrenia is abnormal and concentrate on investigating its causes, diagnosing and treating it? Is it possible to define and diagnose abnormality in an objective way, without allowing our values to bias the judgements that we make? What are some of the practical and ethical implications of labelling a person's behaviour as abnormal?

Trying to give answers to these very complex questions will form the basis of this chapter.

Abnormality, deviance and difference

According to Littlewood and Lipsedge (1989), every society has its own characteristic pattern of normative behaviour and beliefs, i.e. expectations about how people should behave as well as what they should think. These norms define what is acceptable and permissible, as well as what is desirable. It might be useful to think of a scale or continuum, as shown in Figure 7.1.

Unacceptable.......Tolerable.......Acceptable/permissible.......Desirable.......Required/obligatory

Figure 7.1   The continuum of normative behaviour

At the left-hand end of the scale, we are dealing with behaviour that is either illegal (such as burglary, fraud) or that breaches fundamental moral or religious principles (adultery, abortion) or both (child sexual abuse, rape, bigamy). While there is usually little room for disagreement as to whether or not something is illegal, there will usually be more debate about the immorality of (illegal) acts: the vast majority of people will condemn child abuse and rape (including, very often, the perpetrator of the act), but people have very different views regarding the smoking of marijuana. (The current climate of opinion in the UK, including that of the police, is towards the legalization of soft drugs; however, whether this reflects a change in moral opinion is another issue.)

Behaviour that is deemed *tolerable* is at the fringes of illegality and/or immorality; examples might include gambling, drinking (large amounts of) alcohol, going to strip-tease clubs, joining a squat, and living with one's sexual partner (as opposed to getting married).

Getting married is, of course, also *acceptable/permissible*, and *desirable*, as far as most people are concerned. To the extent that most people will get married (at least once in their lives), that we usually assume that adults are married (unless we have good reason to believe otherwise), and that there is an implicit judgement made about people who don't get married ('there must be something wrong with them'), getting married can also be seen as *required/obligatory*.

This example brings us back full circle to what is unacceptable: this was defined earlier in terms of illegality and immorality, but perhaps there is another criterion by which we make this judgement. Clearly, it is not illegal to remain single (there is no actual, literal, law against it), nor is there any religious or moral law that is being broken (assuming that instead of being married one isn't cohabiting or 'living in sin'). But still it is somehow socially unacceptable, it is 'not quite right', it may make us feel a little uneasy, less sure about how to relate to this person than we are when interacting with individuals who are married.

Our first reaction to learning that someone is unmarried might be to wonder if he or she is gay or lesbian, which represents both a perfectly logical explanation but at the same time raises even more fundamental questions about acceptability and normality (see below). Similarly, if the person is painfully shy, or badly disfigured or disabled, or a nun or a priest, we can easily understand his or her unmarried state.

But what if none of these explanations is available to us? This is when the unacceptability of the 'behaviour' becomes an issue: being married is, for most people, part of their definition of 'reality', the 'natural order' of things. Perhaps the unacceptability of schizophrenia, homosexuality, and the other examples given above, also lies in the way in which they threaten and challenge our basic view of the world, what Scheff (1966) called *residual rules*, the 'unnameable' expectations we have regarding such things as 'decency' and 'reality'. Because these rules are themselves implicit, taken for granted, and not articulated, behaviour that violates them is found strange and sometimes frightening – but it is usually very difficult to say why. Similarly, Becker (1963) believes that the values on which psychiatric intervention is based are, generally speaking, middle-class values regarding decent, reasonable, proper behaviour and experience. These influence the process of diagnosis of patients, who, in state-funded (National Health Service) hospitals, at least, are mainly working class. (We shall return below to the question of the objectivity of psychiatric diagnosis.)

In addition to the breaking of residual rules, the mere fact of being different may at least contribute to the unacceptability of schizophrenics and others deemed 'abnormal'. If every society has its own characteristic pattern of normative behaviour and beliefs, then 'outsiders' (those who deviate from these norms), even if they are not seen as physically dangerous, are threatening simply because they are different. As a way of confirming our own identity (which is so much bound up with these norms), we push the outsiders even further away, and 'By reducing their humanity, we emphasize our own' (Littlewood & Lipsedge, 1989).

'Outsiders in our midst' include criminals (those who break the 'law of the land'), those whose behaviour and beliefs conflict with our moral code, and those, like the mentally ill, who break residual rules. All three groups can be regarded as *deviants*, since their behaviour is considered to deviate from certain standards as held by the person making the judgement. While criminal behaviour is sometimes seen as being caused by psychological disturbance, it is important to distinguish between *social deviance* (non-conformity) and mental disorder or abnormality: 'Neither deviant behaviour, e.g., political, religious, or sexual, nor conflicts that are primarily between the individual and society, are mental disorders unless the deviance or condition is a symptom of a dysfunction (i.e. impairment of function) in the person' (Eysenck, 1994). This is a quote from the revision of the third edition of the *Diagnostic and Statistical Manual of Mental Disorders* (abbreviated to DSM-III-R), published by the American Psychiatric Association in 1987. It is the official system for classifying and diagnosing mental disorders used by American psychiatrists, and we shall have many occasions to discuss this (and the latest edition, DSM-IV, published in 1994) throughout the rest of the chapter. (Also see Chapter 6, on feminism.)

Although some *clinical psychologists* and *psychiatrists* are interested in the causes and treatment of criminality as a form of social deviancy, the main focus of abnormal psychology is the kind of unacceptable behaviour and experience which are variously called *mental illness, emotional disturbance, behaviour disorder, mental disorder*, or *psychopathology* (literally, 'disease of the mind', or psychological abnormality).

Criteria for defining psychological abnormality

So far, the discussion has suggested a number of possible criteria for defining psychological abnormality, as well as considering their usefulness and validity. In this section, we shall take another look at these criteria (although from a slightly different angle), as well as discuss some additional ones. Many of these have been proposed by a number of different writers (e.g. Davison & Neale, 1994; Miller & Morley, 1986; Rosenhan & Seligman, 1989), and so particular points will not always be attributed to specific writers.

The statistical rarity criterion (or deviation from the average)

According to this criterion, what is average determines what is normal: behaviour is abnormal to the extent that it falls outside the middle ranges (what the majority of people do) – that is to say, it is *extreme*.

Take the example of 'mental retardation'. As measured by IQ test scores, those with a score below 70 or 75, who represent the lowest two per cent (approximately) of the whole population (Fig. 7.2), are considered to be retarded; their scores are, clearly, extremely low and so, according to this criterion, their intelligence is *abnormally* low.

But what about those individuals whose scores are extremely high? According to this criterion, they should be thought of as equally abnormal because their scores (the two per cent (approximately) scoring 130 and above) are as extreme as those scoring 75 and below. Those who score extremely high are usually described as 'gifted', a somewhat more positive label

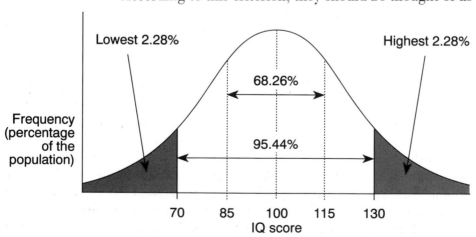

Figure 7.2   Normal distribution curve for IQ, given a mean of 100 and a standard deviation of 15 IQ points

than 'mentally retarded', yet the two groups are statistically equally abnormal. Clearly, there is more to abnormality than mere statistics!

Also, just how far from the population mean does an individual need to be to be considered abnormal? As Miller and Morley (1986) point out, any chosen cut-off point is necessarily arbitrary; what's the significance of 75/70 as the boundary between mental normality and retardation?

A further problem with this criterion is that most kinds of abnormality that psychologists are interested in (see the list above) simply cannot be measured in the way that intelligence can (or, at least, is). In other words, the statistical criterion assumes that psychological characteristics in general can be viewed as *dimensional* (measured on at least an ordinal scale), such that individual scores can all be placed somewhere on the same scale. This in itself is a complex and controversial issue in relation to the normality – abnormality debate, which we shall return to below.

Abnormality as personal distress

From the perspective of the individual, abnormality is the subjective experience of intense anxiety, unhappiness, depression or a whole host of other forms that personal distress or suffering can take. While this may often be the only indication that anything is wrong (and may not necessarily be obvious to others), it may be a sufficient reason for someone to seek professional help. As Miller and Morley (1986) say, 'people do not come to clinics because they feel that they have met some abstract definition of abnormality. For the most part they come because their feelings or behaviour cause them distress.'

However, the converse may also sometimes be true. Someone whose behaviour is 'mad', as far as others are concerned, may be unaware of how others see him or her and may experience little or no subjective distress. This 'lack of insight' (self-awareness or understanding) is often taken to be a characteristic of *psychotic mental disorder* (as opposed to neurotic disorder), and is a kind of 'the fish is the last to discover water' syndrome.

Abnormality as others' distress

It might at first seem very strange, if not illogical, to define one person's abnormality in terms of another person's distress. But, as we have seen above, the person seen by others as behaving abnormally may be the last to recognize that there is a problem, so that others' concern acts as a counterbalance to the lack of concern in the former. This criterion also suggests that, as with all behaviour, abnormality is *interpersonal*, and not simply *intrapersonal/intrapsychic*. Behaviour is something that takes place between people, in social situations, and is not merely a reflection of personal qualities or characteristics of the individual actor. (This, of course, is a reference to the trait–situation debate that was discussed in Chapter 4).

From a practical and an ethical point of view, this criterion can be seen as double-edged: others' distress may be both a 'blessing' (literally a lifesaver on occasions, for someone lacking insight into his or her own self-destructive behaviour, for example) and a curse (for example, a parent's distress regarding a son or daughter's homosexuality, with which the son or daughter may feel perfectly comfortable). While the former may be termed *empathic concern*, where the 'helper' has an altruistic desire to reduce the other's distress, in the latter, personal distress produces an *egoistic desire* to reduce one's own distress. The question is, whose distress is really the focus of the attempt to intervene?

One of the most outspoken critics of conventional, medical psychiatry during the heyday of the *anti-psychiatry* movement in the 1960s was the Scottish psychiatrist R.D. Laing. According to his *family interaction model* (1961), schizophrenia can only be understood as something that occurs between people, rather than as something taking place inside a person as maintained by the medical model (see below). Schizophrenia refers to an *interpersonal ploy* used by some people (parents, doctors, psychiatrists) in their interactions with others ('the schizophrenic').

To understand individuals, we must study not individuals but interactions between individuals and this is the subject matter of *social phenomenology*. The family interaction model was consistent with research by Bateson et al. (1956), which showed that schizophrenia arises within families which use 'pathological' forms of communication – in particular, contradictory messages (*double binds*), as in the case where a mother induces her son to give her a hug, but when he does so, tells him 'not to be such a baby'.

More directly relevant to the 'distress criterion' is a later explanation of schizophrenia, namely Laing's (1967) *conspiratorial model*, according to which schizophrenia is a label, a form of violence perpetrated by some people against others. The family, general practitioners, and psychiatrists conspire against schizophrenics in order to keep them in check:

Figure 7.3 Peter Sutcliffe, The Yorkshire Ripper. Was he mad – or just bad?

by treating them as patients who are sick, 'imprisoning' them in a psychiatric hospital, where they are degraded and invalidated as human beings, these people are able to maintain their definition of reality (the *status quo*). (*Residual rules* again?) The threat posed by the behaviour and experience of the 'patient' is contained within a medical framework: 'if they act and think like that *they must be sick*, which means that we are all right and everything is still all right with the world as we know it.'

According to his *psychedelic model* (1967), Laing argued that the schizophrenic is, in fact, an exceptionally eloquent critic of society and schizophrenia is 'itself a natural way of healing our own appalling state of alienation called normality'.

Abnormality as unexpected behaviour

What Davison and Neale (1994) mean by this, is that it is abnormal to react to a situation or an event in ways that could not be predicted, or reasonably expected (given what we know about human behaviour). For example, anxiety disorders are diagnosed when the anxiety is 'out of proportion to the situation'.

Although this might seem to be a very reasonable and useful criterion, it could be claimed that it raises as many questions as it answers. In particular, who is to say what is 'in proportion'? Is this just another form of deviation from the average, whereby what is a reasonable, acceptable, response is simply how *most people* would be expected to respond? By this criterion, *under*-reacting is just as abnormal as *over*-reacting, and yet the way Davison and Neale describe it suggests very strongly that it is only an over-reaction that is seen as a problem. So we need to ask, by what other criteria do we judge a reaction to be normal or abnormal?

Abnormality as highly consistent or highly inconsistent behaviour

If we have generalized expectations about how people are typically going to react to particular (kinds of) situation, as when we define abnormality as unexpected behaviour, then a person's behaviour is predictable to the extent that we know about the situation. However, not all situations are equally powerful influences on behaviour, and so cannot be used equally to predict a person's behaviour; in some situations, individual differences play a much larger role in influencing behaviour, and this makes behaviour *less* predictable. Consequently, it is 'normal' for any individual's behaviour to be partially predictable (*high intra-individual consistency*) and, at the same time, partially unpredictable (*low intra-individual consistency*).

If we accept this argument, then it is reasonable to further argue that it is abnormal for a person to display either extremely predictable behaviour or extremely unpredictable behaviour. If someone acts so consistently that they seem to be unaffected by the situation, including the other people involved, this would strike most people as very odd; it's almost as if we are dealing with more of a machine than a person! Someone who is paranoid, for example, might see the world almost entirely in terms of others' malevolent intentions, which may, in turn, elicit certain kinds of responses in others. These responses from others may reinforce the attribution of negative intent, thus producing a vicious cycle.

Equally, someone who, for whatever reason, is very unpredictable certainly makes interaction very difficult, since our dealings with others requires us to make assumptions and expectations about their responses. Schizophrenics are often perceived, by the lay person, as embodying this kind of unpredictability, which is unnerving and unsettling. Again, this perception, together with the related expectation of unpredictability, may to some degree contribute to that unpredictability.

What is important to note, in both cases, is that the assessment being made is as much a reflection of the perceiver who is making the judgement, as it is a reflection of the person whose behaviour is being judged. Perhaps the term *consistency* refers more to the actor's behaviour, while *predictability* refers more to the perceiver's judgement. Whichever term is used, the basic argument is the same – namely, that to understand behaviour, we must always take the actor *and* the situation (including other people) into account. (This way of looking at normality and abnormality was discussed in Chapter 4 in relation to the trait–situation debate.) We shall return to this point later on when we look at the process of psychiatric diagnosis.

Abnormality as maladaptiveness or disability

When people's behaviour prevents them from pursuing and achieving their goals, or does not contribute to their personal sense of well-being, or prevents them from functioning as they would wish in their personal, sexual, social, intellectual and occupational life, it may well be seen as abnormal for that reason. For example, drug abuse (or substance-use disorders) is defined mainly by how the substance abuse produces social and occupational disability, such as poor work performance and serious marital arguments. Phobias can be maladaptive or disabling in this way; for example, fear of flying might prevent someone from taking a job promotion (Davison & Neale, 1994).

So, according to this criterion, it is the *consequences* of the behaviour which lead us to judge the behaviour to be abnormal, rather than the behaviour itself. At the same time, such behaviours may be very distressing for the person concerned; by their nature, phobias are negative experiences because they involve extreme fear, regardless of any practical effects brought about by the fear.

Figure 7.4 Schizophrenia often brings with it confused and nonsensical thought patterns. Artist Brian Charnley's growing thought disorder during a period of schizophrenia is reflected in this series of self-portraits. As he becomes increasingly disturbed, his self-image reduces to the point where he perceives himself as no more than a tiny door

An interim summing-up: what have we learnt so far?

We have now considered six criteria for defining behaviour as abnormal:
1 involves a *comparison* with other people's behaviour
3 involves looking at the *consequences* for others of the behaviour in question,
4 involves another kind of *comparison* with others' behaviour,
5 also involves making *comparisons* between both the actor and others, and between the actor and him/herself on different occasions, and
6 is concerned with the *consequences* for the actor of his or her behaviour.
What about the second criterion? While the other criteria could be seen as having an external focus (they look outwards from the behaviour in question towards something else), the personal distress criterion has an internal focus: it begins and remains with the person whose behaviour is in question.

While it is generally agreed that it is impossible to give a simple definition of abnormality that captures it in its entirety (see, for example, Davison & Neale, 1994), and that no single criterion is necessary (see Zimbardo, 1992), this distinction between external and internal focus is important: discussions of abnormality often seem to assume that certain behaviours and experiences are abnormal in and of themselves, without any reference to any external criterion. Examples might include all those included in our original list, although some of these such as homosexuality, will be considerably more controversial than others when seen from this perspective. None of the criteria we have discussed so far addresses this issue.

The case of homosexuality: normal or abnormal?

Let us apply the criteria we have discussed so far to the case of homosexuality, in order to expose their limitations and to introduce some important additional ones.

As far as criterion 1 is concerned, it is very likely that most people, especially those who consider that homosexuality is abnormal, believe that homosexuals and lesbians represent a very small minority of the adult population. But even if it were discovered that a majority of adults were homosexual (or had had at least one homosexual relationship), most people would continue to believe it to be abnormal: the very use of the term '*queer*' conveys the negative attitude towards homosexuals, since its other main meaning is 'ill'. In other words, there's more to judging homosexuality to be abnormal than simply regarding it as a deviation from the average.

In relation to criterion 2, while there are undoubtedly some homosexuals who experience conflict and distress about their sexuality, there are probably as many for whom being gay or lesbian feels as 'right' as being heterosexual does for most 'straights'. This, together with the fact that many of those who are in conflict are so because of society's *homophobic* attitudes (the irrational fear and extreme intolerance of homosexuality) and *heterosexism* (inequality and discrimination based on people's sexual preference or orientation), suggests that 'being homosexual' is not distressing in itself. Experiencing distress is not an inherent feature of preferring members of one's own sex as sexual partners, as it is for the person with a phobia, for example; indeed, it is as likely to be as pleasurable as is a heterosexual's sexual attraction to someone of the opposite sex.

Assuming that homosexuals themselves do not typically, or inevitably, experience distress, why should other people do so 'on their behalf', which is what happens, according to criterion 3? It is clearly false to assume that homosexuals 'don't realize what they're doing' (as in, say, the case of drug addicts or others engaging in self-destructive behaviour), so that they need to be 'saved from themselves'. We need to look elsewhere for the source of others' distress.

Such an explanation is most unlikely to be found in criterion 4. It doesn't make very much sense to see homosexuality as an over-reaction to some event. What could such an event be? If it were discovered, for example, that homosexuals have typically experienced some kind of trauma in early childhood which caused their homosexuality, we would not want to then call this outcome an over-reaction; it would instead be seen as a 'normal' reaction to that kind of trauma. (Although 'normal' here might seem to beg the question, the idea of homosexuals as a group all reacting in the same way at least suggests that the reaction is not a deviation.)

Research may not have found any evidence for traumatic events as a causal influence on the development of homosexuality, but Bieber et al. (1962) claim to have found a difference between male homosexuals and heterosexuals, namely that the former are brought up by a 'close-binding intimate mother' and a father who displays 'detachment-hostility'. This difference is referred to as a *pathogenic* ('disease-producing') factor, which is responsible for the pathological condition of homosexuality. But we only judge this pattern of childrearing to be pathological if we have already judged its outcome to be pathological – that is, only if we already regard homosexuality to be abnormal will we regard any difference between homosexuals and heterosexuals (and which we think causes homosexuality) as itself abnormal (Davison & Neale, 1994). This is clearly a circular argument and begs the whole question of the normality or abnormality of homosexuality.

As far as criterion 5 is concerned, there is no reason to believe that homosexuals, as a group, compared with heterosexuals, are any more or less consistent or predictable in their overall behaviour, so this criterion does not move us on any further in our search for the reasons behind the belief that homosexuality is abnormal.

This leaves just criterion 6. Unlike the case of someone with a phobia, the negative consequences (maladaptiveness or disability) suffered by homosexuals are not to do with being homosexual, but stem from society's response to the homosexual. Whereas someone with a phobia of flying might be unable to visit far-away lands as a direct result of the phobia (almost as an extension of the phobia), quite independently of any external factors or influences, the homosexual is confronted by homophobia and heterosexism, which are not part of being homosexual. It is social attitudes towards homosexuals which constitute the maladaptiveness/disability of homosexuality, not the 'handicapping' nature of being gay.

So we are left still needing to know by what criteria homosexuality is judged to be abnormal. This brings us on to the 'deviation from the norm' criterion.

Abnormality as deviation from the norm

This implies that, regardless of how other people behave (i.e. the statistical criterion), abnormality involves not behaving, feeling or thinking as one should. 'Norms' have an 'oughtness' about them: they convey expectations about behaviour such that what is normal is 'right', 'proper', 'natural', 'desirable' and so on. (See Figure 7.1.)

Clearly, these terms all convey value judgements; they are not neutral, value-free, objective descriptions or assessments of behaviour but reflect beliefs concerning what are essentially moral or ethical issues.

Sometimes, it is very obvious how a particular behaviour deviates from a norm, and it is equally obvious what the norm is. For example, murder is a crime, and the law which makes it a crime embodies the moral law – 'Thou shalt not murder'. As with most crime, the behaviour is labelled as 'bad', making clear that legal or moral norms have been breached.

However, there is no law against being schizophrenic, or having panic attacks, or being depressed; nor is it obvious what moral law or ethical principle is being broken in these cases. It seems that we might be dealing, once more, with residual rules (see above).

Up until the 1960s, in the UK, homosexuality among consenting adults was illegal. That law, presumably, embodied the pre-Christian Jewish and early Christian condemnation of sex outside marriage and for any purpose except reproduction, even as an expression of love between husband and wife (Doyle, 1983). Now it is legal (at least between consenting adults over the age of 18), but homophobia and heterosexism continue to reflect these religious roots.

So behaviour may be judged abnormal quite independently of its legal status (including its legal history) because it seems to breach certain fundamental religious or moral principles, even though it may not be easy to identify these principles or even to articulate them. However, in Western culture, unlike in many non-Western cultures, a sharp distinction is made between legal, religious and medical aspects or definitions of normality: illness, disease and pathology, in all its forms (bodily and psychological), are dealt with by the medical profession. They are the province of doctors and psychiatrists (as opposed to priests); thus, psychopathology or mental disorder has become medicalized. Religion and illness are in separate 'cultural compartments'; illness is an entirely secular matter.

However, many human situations and forms of human distress that are conceptualized in the West as 'illness' are seen in religious and/or philosophical terms in Indian culture, for example, which also stresses that harmony between the person and his or her group indicates health. In African culture, the concept of health is more social then biological:

> *In the mind of the African, there is a more unitary concept of psychosomatic interrelationship, that is, an apparent reciprocity between mind and matter. Health is not an isolated phenomenon but part of the entire magico-religious fabric; it is more than the absence of disease. Since disease is viewed as one of the most important social sanctions, peaceful living with neighbours, abstention from adultery, keeping the laws of gods and men, are essentials in order to protect oneself and one's family from disease.*
>
> (Lambo, 1964, quoted in Fernando, 1991)

And again, 'for Africans, the whole of existence is a religious phenomenon; man is a deeply religious being living in a religious universe' (Mbiti, 1969, quoted in Fernando, 1991). The spiritual and physical worlds are not separate entities, as they are in Western culture; mind and body do not exist separately, and no distinction is made between 'bodily illness' and 'mental illness'.

However, although ideas about health and illness vary across cultures on a number of parameters, every culture possesses a concept of illness as some kind of departure (or deviation) from health. Having said that, 'The overall world view within a culture, appertaining to health, religion, psychology and spiritual concerns determine the meaning within that culture of "madness", mental illness and mental health' (Fernando, 1991). So thinking about, and treating, psychological abnormality from a medical, biological, perspective is itself a cultural phenomenon.

This brings us to an eighth major criterion of abnormality, namely *abnormality as mental illness or mental disorder*. Because of the close connection between this and the 'deviation from the norm' criterion, I shall discuss them together in much of the remainder of this chapter.

The objective nature of mental disorders: do they exist?

At the heart of the 'abnormality as mental illness' criterion is the *medical model*. The use of the term *psychopathology* to refer to the particular kind of deviancy which psychiatrists and clinical psychologists are concerned with ('mad', not 'bad') reflects the medical model. Also central to the model is the classification and diagnosis of mental disorders, the treatment of psychiatric patients in psychiatric hospitals and other medical terminology (Maher, 1966).

All systems of classification stem from the work of Emil Kraepelin (1913), who published the first recognized textbook of psychiatry in 1883. He proposed that certain groups of symptoms occur together sufficiently often to merit the designation 'disease' or 'syndrome', and he went on to describe the diagnostic indicators associated with each syndrome. His classification helped to establish the organic (bodily) nature of mental disorders, and this is an integral feature of the medical model.

Although Kraepelin's system laid the foundation for all subsequent classification systems (in particular, DSM in America, and the World Heath Organization's *International Classification of Diseases*), psychiatrists have, until very recently, distinguished between (i) *organic mental disorders*, in which biological factors are clearly involved (usually taken to be causal factors), such as Alzheimer's disease and senile dementia, and (ii) *functional mental disorders*, in which the role of biological factors is much less obvious. What 'functional' conveys is that there is no demonstrable physical basis for the abnormal behaviour and that something has gone wrong with the way the person functions in the network of relationships that make up his or her world (Bailey, 1979).

This distinction is related to another which has traditionally been made (and which has also been recently dropped), namely that between *neurosis* and *psychosis*. In terms of the first distinction, the great majority of neuroses and psychoses have traditionally been thought of as functional disorders; the examples given above of organic disorders have usually been referred to as *organic psychoses*. Although neuroses and psychoses have not been defined in terms of the role of biological factors (otherwise all psychoses would be organic, and all neuroses functional), the difference in the way they have typically been treated strongly suggests the underlying view regarding their likely causes: while neuroses (such as phobias, panic attacks, obsessive-compulsive behaviour) are mainly treated using psychological techniques (psychotherapy, behaviour therapy), psychoses (schizophrenia, manic depression) are mainly treated using physical methods (major tranquillizing and other powerful drugs, and electroconvulsive therapy).

The important point here is that most biologically orientated psychiatrists (who are the large majority of psychiatrists as a whole) have always believed that schizophrenia (and the other functional psychoses) is, in fact, organic, and that it is only a matter of time until medical science discovers the biological causes and mechanisms involved.

This argument is supported by classic cases such as general paresis of the insane (GPI). This was recognized as a clinical syndrome (in summary, dementia) long before the physical cause was discovered (namely, untreated syphilis). This discovery represents an important landmark in the history of psychiatry because it stimulated a search for organic causes of other syndromes (Gelder et al., 1989). Also, many illnesses which were once thought to have a supernatural or psychological origin have now become generally accepted as physical; for example, epilepsy was for centuries thought to be of divine origin (Littlewood & Lipsedge, 1989).

But against this view, socially orientated psychiatrists argue that mental disorders, such as GPI, always had an 'organic feel' about them – they are only found associated with easily recognized bodily abnormalities. And, conversely, Charcot and Freud helped hysteria (for so long thought to be caused by abnormalities of the womb) to be generally accepted as psychological in origin (Littlewood & Lipsedge, 1989).

If mental disorders 'exist' in some objective sense – that is, independently of cultural norms and values and world-views – then the most likely candidates will come from those believed to be organic in origin. Just as modern medicine is based on the assumption that physical illness is the same throughout the world, and that definition, classification, causation and diagnosis are largely unaffected by cultural factors, so biologically orientated psychiatrists contend that psychoses, in particular schizophrenia and depression, are also 'culture-free'.

The cross-cultural study of mental disorder

During the 1970s and '80s, psychiatrists and clinical psychologists became increasingly interested in 'cultural psychiatry', 'transcultural psychiatry', or 'comparative psychiatry'. The central issue in the cross-cultural study of psychopathology is whether phenomena such as schizophrenia are (i) *absolute* (found in all cultures in precisely the same form); (ii) *universal* (present in some form in all cultures, but subject to cultural influence regarding what factors bring them on, how they are expressed, and so on); (iii) *culturally relative* (unique to particular cultures and understandable only in terms of those cultures) (Berry et al., 1992).

Absolute phenomena

Of the three possibilities, this is the only one that corresponds to a 'culture-free' view of abnormality. But even in the case of a disorder which may appear to be totally 'biological', such as the physiological response to alcohol, cultural factors seem to play a part. For example, cultural norms regarding what, where and how much to drink result in quite different expressions of alcohol use across cultural groups: 'We may conclude that it makes little sense to even consider a culture-free abnormal behaviour, since cultural factors appear to affect at least some aspects of mental disorders, even those that are so closely linked to human biology' (Berry et al., 1992).

Universality

This is a more likely candidate for capturing the nature of psychopathology, and this is supported, in particular, by studies of schizophrenia and depression. We shall look only at the former here. Schizophrenia is the most commonly diagnosed mental disorder in the world, and of the major disorders, the largest number of culture-general symptoms has been reported for schizophrenia (see, for example, World Health Organization, 1973, 1979; Draguns, 1980, 1990). These two findings constitute one of the major arguments for the biological basis of this disorder.

The core symptoms include: (i) poor insight into the reasons for one's problems and one's current thinking; (ii) thinking aloud; (iii) incoherent speech, one phrase or sentence apparently bearing no relationship to others; (iv) giving unrealistic information that would be contradicted by objective facts if the person were able to consider them; (v) widespread, bizarre and/or nihilistic delusions (feeling that existence is useless and nothing is worth is living for); (vi) flattened mood and limited ability to form emotional ties with others (Brislin, 1993).

According to Brislin (1993), even with this large core of culture-general symptoms, there are at least three possible ways in which culture-specific factors can influence schizophrenia: (i) the form that symptoms will take; (ii) the specific reasons for the onset of the illness; (iii) the prognosis.

THE FORM THAT SYMPTOMS WILL TAKE

When schizophrenics complain that their minds are being invaded by unseen forces, in North America and Europe these forces keep up to date with technological developments. So, in the 1920s, these were often voices from the radio, in the 1950s they often came from the television, in the '60s it was satellites in space, and in the '70s and '80s spirits were transmitted through microwave ovens. In cultures where witchcraft is considered common, the voices or spirits would be directed by unseen forces under the control of demons.

Citing Katz et al. (1988), Brislin points out that the exact form taken by the symptoms of schizophrenia can be understood by looking at predominant cultural values. In Ibadan, Nigeria, the symptoms shown by schizophrenics emphasized a highly suspicious orientation towards others, with many bizarre fears and thoughts. This reflects how many Nigerians view illnesses: it is normal to view illness as caused by unseen evil forces and sometimes those forces are directed at a person by enemies and witches. This paranoid aspect of the schizophrenic's symptoms are an exaggeration of this normal view, a distortion of the 'normal' state.

This is an extremely interesting finding in the context of the whole nature of psychological abnormality. One way in which neurosis and psychosis have been distinguished is to say that, while neurotic behaviour is continuous with 'normal' behaviour (there is only a quantitative difference between them, a difference in degree), psychotic behaviour is discontinuous with 'normal' behaviour (there is a qualitative difference). This corresponds to the *dimensional* and the *categorical* views of abnormality respectively. This would mean that the schizophrenic's delusions and hallucinations are different kinds of experience from that of non-schizophrenics. The findings of Katz et al. suggest that this traditional distinction may need to be revised. We should also note that psychiatric classification is based on a categorical view of abnormality, a view that many, such as Zimbardo (1992) and Eysenck (1970), would not accept. According to Miller and Morley (1986), this dimensional view has considerable appeal, especially for psychologists, but it is difficult for the clinician to cope with more than one or two dimensions, and dimensional systems often end up being converted into categories before the information they provide can be usefully related to individuals. No dimensional system has ever gained widespread acceptance (Miller & Morley, 1986).

REASONS FOR THE ONSET OF ILLNESS

One view of schizophrenia is that we inherit a predisposition towards the disorder (we are 'at risk') while the actual symptoms are triggered by stress (see Draguns, 1990). Day et al. (1987, cited in Brislin, 1993) studied schizophrenia in nine different locations in the USA, Asia, Europe and South America. Acute schizophrenic attacks were associated with stressful events, which could be described as external to the patients (and not initiated by them), and they tended to cluster within a two- to three-week period before the onset of obvious symptoms (such as the unexpected death of spouse, losing one's job, and parental divorce). Some stressful events were interpretable only if the researchers had considerable information regarding the cultural background of the sample.

THE PROGNOSIS

Lin and Kleinman (1988, cited in Brislin, 1993) found that the prognosis for successful treatment of schizophrenia was better in non-industrialized than industrialized societies. Why should this be? Wouldn't we expect the opposite to be true, given the superior resources available in the latter? To be a functioning member of a 'highly industrialized' nation, certain skills are needed which are very difficult for the schizophrenic to demonstrate, and many of the core symptoms involve relating to others. Individualism is valued in highly industrialized societies (see Chapter 8, on cross-cultural psychology), and it is up to the individual to develop rapport and emotional ties with others. Yet there is no automatic support group available to help with this. In the past, there might have been the nuclear family, but its members are often so affected by divorce and intrafamilial conflict that it can be a source of stress rather than support.

> *Along with this heavy emphasis on independence, self-reliance, and personal freedom, individualistic value orientations also tend to foster*

fierce competition, frequent life changes, and alienation, and they do not usually provide the kind of structured, stable, and predictable environments that allow schizophrenic patients to recuperate at their own pace and to be reintegrated into the society.

(Lin & Kleinman, 1988, quoted in Brislin, 1993)

In contrast, the slower lifestyle and more integrated collectives commonly found in less industrialized nations may provide a more supportive environment for schizophrenics, including the greater likelihood of finding productive work (for example, in the family farm or business). This is clearly important for developing a sense of self-worth. Also, 'colleagues' will be more tolerant of mistakes than would an employer or colleagues in large, impersonal organizations. Brislin (1993) concludes: 'As part of their socialization, people learn to express psychological disturbances in ways that are acceptable within their culture, in ways that will be understood, and in ways that will evoke sympathy from others.'

What Brislin seems to be implying is that (i) there is a crucial element of learning involved in abnormality, although this does not, of course, rule out the role of biological factors; (ii) abnormal behaviour and experience are not random, arbitrary or meaningless but make perfectly good sense in terms of the culture in which they are manifested; and (iii) there is a continuity between normal and abnormal behaviour (including schizophrenia), since both are, at least in part, acquired through the same process of socialization.

Although these observations are consistent with how universal abnormality has been defined by transcultural psychiatrists, Berry et al. (1992) point out two major limitations of the studies which provide the bulk of the evidence.

1 Studies such as the International Pilot Study of Schizophrenia (World Health Organization, 1973), which compared the prevalence of schizophrenia in Columbia, Czechoslovakia, Denmark, India, Nigeria, Taiwan, the UK, the USA, and (the former) USSR, involved the use of diagnostic instruments, concepts and researchers etc. which all belonged to Western psychiatry.

2 The patient populations involved were not representative of world cultural variation (and were themselves, to some extent, acculturated to a Western way of life); 'Hence, one cannot exclude entirely the possibility that the definition of schizophrenia will have to be further informed by cultural variations that are insufficiently studied so far' (Berry et al., 1992).

Cultural Relativity

A large number of studies have found that, in a wide range of non-Western cultures, there are apparently unique ways of 'being mad' (Berry et al., 1992) – there are forms of abnormality that are not documented and recognized within the classification systems of Western psychiatry. These 'exotic' disorders are usually described and interpreted in terms which relate to the particular culture in which they are reported, with the local, indigenous, name being used, which gradually enters the (Western) psychiatric literature.

These *culture-bound syndromes* (CBS) are studied, perhaps not surprisingly, mainly by anthropologists, who focus on 'culture-specific' disorders, stressing the differences between cultures; in contrast, psychiatrists tend to focus on 'universal' disorders, stressing the similarities. So, when a 'new' condition is observed in some non-Western society (that is, among people perceived as being alien to Western culture), the syndrome itself is perceived as alien to the existing classification system, sufficiently 'outside' the mainstream that it may be unclassifiable. The fact that they may be quite common within a particular culture makes no difference – if they are limited (or apparently limited) to other cultures, they are excluded from the mainstream classification of mental disorder. Since the disorder occurs in groups that are seen as alien in primarily racial terms, the concept of a CBS is, therefore, one that has been generated by the ideology of Western psychiatry: 'psychopathology in the West is seen as culturally neutral and psychopathology that is distinctively different from that seen in the West as "culture-bound" ' (Fernando, 1991).

Again, researchers distinguish between modern, scientific psychiatry and traditional *ethnopsychiatry* (the study of culture-relative or culture-specific disorders), seeing the former as telling us about authentic illness, while the latter tells us about illness that is contaminated/distorted by culture.

Fernando (1991) believes that anthropology and psychiatry have colluded in regarding psychiatric disorders which are seen in Western (white) societies as being on a different plane from those seen in non-Western (black, 'primitive') societies: 'When culture "distorts" a syndrome beyond a certain point, a CBS is identified. Practitioners go along with this approach seeing symptom constellations in the West as the standard and those in other cultures as anomalies' (Fernando, 1991). This represents a form of *ethnocentrism* within Western psychiatry, and in keeping with this view, Fernando (1991) believes that the concept of the CBS has a distinctly racist connotation.

Similarly, Littlewood and Lipsedge (1989) argue that it is wrong to look at beliefs about madness in other cultures as if they are only more or less accurate approximations to a 'scientific' (accurate, objective) description. A cultural understanding of mental disorder is as important in Western as in any other culture, and, indeed, some general features of those 'ritual patterns' usually classed as CBSs are applicable to Western neurosis (Littlewood & Lipsedge, 1989). It has been suggested that anorexia nervosa and premenstrual syndrome (see Chapter 6, on feminism) may be Western CBSs (Fernando, 1991).

Figure 7.5 A modern-day interpretation of the 'berserker'; Michael Douglas in *Falling Down*, where a 'normal' man goes on the rampage in retaliation against the frustrations of everyday life

Ironically, in at least two cases, CBS names have become part of the common vocabulary in English-speaking Western societies. *Amok* involves wild, aggressive behaviour, usually short-lived, and usually confined to males, involving attempts to kill or injure. It was identified in Malaysia, Indonesia and Thailand, the Malay word *amok* meaning 'to engage furiously in battle'. It has obvious similarities to the Viking behaviour called *berserker*, practised just before going into battle (Berry et al., 1992). You don't have to come from South-East Asia, or be a Viking, in order to 'run amok' or 'go berserk'!

The culture-bound nature of psychiatry

If Western psychiatry is, inevitably, influenced by Western cultural beliefs and values (since it is part of that culture), then it cannot claim to be objective, scientifically 'detached', and value-free in the way that it does. If we accept this argument, it should follow that (i) psychiatric definitions and classification of mental disorders will change over time, reflecting changes in cultural beliefs and values; and (ii) the process of psychiatric diagnosis will be influenced by wider cultural beliefs and values.

CHANGING VIEWS OF HOMOSEXUALITY

Psychological abnormality has not always been explained and dealt with in Western culture by medicine. During the Middle Ages (roughly AD 500–1500), when religion was the dominant force in almost all aspects of European life, what we now call mental disorder was seen as possession by the Devil. It was the time of witch-hunts and burning witches at the stake, the Spanish Inquisition and brutal exorcisms to drive the Devil out (Holmes, 1994). The 1500s marked the beginning of widespread recognition that disturbed people needed care, not exorcism and condemnation, but it wasn't until the middle of the 1800s that 'modern' psychiatry began to emerge, seeing psychological abnormality as comparable to bodily, physical illness, having organic origins (*somatogenesis*).

We noted earlier that psychiatrists (at least those in America) have recently dropped the traditional distinction between organic and functional disorders. So, in the latest edition of the American 'bible' of psychiatry, DSM-IV, the category 'Organic Mental Disorders', which had appeared in DSM-III-R (published in 1987) has been omitted and replaced by 'Delirium, Dementia, Amnestic and Other

Figure 7.6 During the Middle Ages, what we would now call mental disorder was seen as possession by the Devil or as witchcraft

Cognitive Disorders'. According to Davison and Neale (1994), the thinking behind this change is that the term 'organic' implies that the other major categories do not have a biological basis. Since research has shown the influence of biological factors through a whole range of disorders, it is no longer considered appropriate to use the term 'organic'; it is now thought to be misleading. (To this extent, mental disorder is even more medicalized than it has ever been.)

This shows that mental disorders and the way they are classified are not 'set in stone'. Assuming that the behaviour and experience of people with disorders do not change radically, at least within the same cultural group, over relatively short periods of time, it is not the 'reality' of mental disorder that changes but how psychiatrists define and interpret that reality. As we have seen, those definitions and interpretations reflect wider cultural beliefs and values, and there is perhaps no better demonstration of this process than the example of homosexuality.

DSM-II (1968) included homosexuality as a sexual deviation. In 1973, the Nomenclature Committee of the APA, under pressure from many professionals and gay activist groups, recommended to the general membership that the category should be removed and replaced with *sexual orientation disturbance*. This was to be applied to gay men and women who are 'disturbed by, in conflict with, or wish to change their sexual orientation'. The change was approved, but not without vehement protests from several eminent psychiatrists who maintained the traditional view that homosexuality is inherently abnormal.

When DSM-III was published in 1980, another new term, *ego-dystonic homosexuality* (EDH), was used, referring to a person who is homosexually aroused, finds this arousal to be a persistent source of distress, and wishes to become heterosexual. Since homosexuality itself was no longer a mental disorder, there was no discussion in DSM-III of predisposing factors (as there was for all disorders). But predisposing factors for EDH were included, and were, primarily, those negative societal attitudes (homophobia and heterosexism) which have been internalized by the homosexual individual. So, according to DSM-III, a homosexual is abnormal if he or she had been persuaded by society's prejudices that his or her sexual orientation is inherently abnormal, but at the same time it denied that homosexuality in itself is abnormal (Davison & Neale, 1994)!

For whatever reasons, very little use was made of the EDH category. Less surprisingly, no such category as 'ego-dystonic *heterosexuality*' has ever been used (Kitzinger, 1990)!

When DSM-III was revised (DSM-III-R, 1987), the APA decided that even the watered-down EDH should no longer be included. Instead, 'Sexual Disorder Not Otherwise Specified' includes 'persistent and marked distress about one's sexual orientation'. This has been retained in DSM-IV.

Rather than searching for why some people prefer members of their own gender as sexual mates and rather than investigating and applying methods for changing homosexuals' orientation in the direction of heterosexuality, clinicians and researchers might better focus on how people in general deal with their sexuality . . . Fewer and fewer state laws legislate against homosexuality; as these legal proscriptions are eliminated, social biases may also slowly mollify. As a consequence of all these changes, the very societal conditions that underlie distress about one's sexual orientation may disappear and with them . . . the last vestige of homosexuality from the list of recognized mental disorders.

(Davison & Neale, 1994)

PSYCHIATRIC DIAGNOSIS AS A SOCIAL PROCESS

Fernando (1991, based on Kendell, 1975) maintains that the diagnostic interview consists, primarily, of (i) taking the patient's history, and (ii) assessing the patient's current 'mental state'.

The history is often thought of as comprising objective facts, but, in reality, it is a highly selected account of whatever information has been acquired from the patient and others – it is the psychiatrist who does the crucial sorting out. The psychiatrist also influences the content of the history, in two interrelated ways. Firstly, the type and extent of information given by the patient and others are fashioned by the perceptions of the psychiatrist about the people providing the information, and vice versa. For example, if a black Asian patient says little about an arranged marriage (because he or she thinks it will be disapproved of by the white psychiatrist), this will usually be interpreted as a negative quality (secretiveness or deviousness) of the patient, rather than a quality of the doctor. Secondly, the picking and choosing that occurs during the history-taking depends on the beliefs, value judgements, understanding, and knowledge of the psychiatrist. White, middle-class psychiatrists are unlikely to have personal experience of predominantly black areas (such as Harlem in New York, Tower Hamlets in London, and St Paul's in Bristol), and so will be unaware of the pressures impinging on black people who live there. This is likely to result in a misinterpretation of their lifestyles and behaviour, which often reinforce their racist attitudes.

The assessment of the patient's 'mental state' is probably the major determinant of the final diagnosis. What the patient reports of his or her experiences is taken to depict an inner state of mind. The validity of such an inference is dubious at the best of times (even when there is excellent rapport and full understanding between patient and psychiatrist). In a multicultural setting, it is highly unlikely that such rapport exists: 'The meanings attached to experiences and perceptions, the concept of illness, and the overall significance of the interview situation . . . are but some of the parameters along which variation must occur when cultural differences are present between the participants of an interaction' (Fernando, 1991).

Deductions made from an 'examination' of the mental state cannot be viewed as equivalent to a medical description of the state of a bodily organ: these organs are described in terms which have (at least some degree of) objective validity: 'What a doctor "finds" in a "mental state" is as much a reflection of the observers as the so-called patient. It is the result of an interaction rather than a one-sided observation' (Fernando, 1991).

Summary

- The whole field of *abnormal psychology* rests upon the assumption that a distinction can be made between *normality* and *abnormality*.
- It is relatively easy to give examples of psychological abnormality, but it is much more difficult to provide precise definitions.
- Every society has its own pattern of normative behaviour and beliefs; all behaviour can be placed somewhere on a continuum, running from *unacceptable*, through *tolerable*, *acceptable/permissible*, to *desirable* and *required/obligatory*.
- Although 'unacceptable' usually implies 'illegal' or 'immoral', it may also convey 'contrary to our basic view of the world'/'not decent and proper' (*residual rules*). Because these rules are implicit, we cannot easily say why schizophrenia, homosexuality etc. are strange, frightening and so on.
- *Deviants* (members of our own society who deviate from society's norms) include criminals, those who break moral 'laws', and the mentally ill (who break residual rules).
- We must distinguish between *social deviance* and *mental disorder/abnormality*; according to DSM-III-R, only the latter involves an *impairment of function* in the person.
- The *statistical rarity criterion* (or *deviation from the average*) states that behaviour is abnormal to the extent that it differs from what most people do – the average. It assumes that psychological characteristics in general are *dimensional*.
- *Abnormality as personal distress* refers to the experience of intense anxiety, unhappiness, depression or any other form of personal, subjective suffering. But those judged to be suffering from *psychotic mental disorder* may not experience any distress at all.
- Defining abnormality as *other people's distress* suggests that, as with all behaviour, abnormality is *interpersonal*. But it may be motivated by a selfish desire to reduce one's own distress rather than by an altruistic desire to reduce the 'sufferer's' distress.
- According to Laing's *conspiratorial model*, schizophrenia is a label applied by people (the family, GPs, psychiatrists) to protect them against the threat posed by the patient's behaviour/experience.
- *Abnormality as unexpected behaviour* raises as many questions as it answers; e.g why should over-reacting seem any more abnormal than under-reacting?

- Behaviour that is either *extremely predictable* or *extremely unpredictable* may be judged as abnormal; in the latter case, this is partly due to the difficulty in interacting with such people.
- *Abnormality as maladaptiveness/disability* focuses largely on the *consequences* of behaviour – that is, on what it prevents the individual from achieving, personally, sexually, socially, intellectually or occupationally.
- The distinction between criteria of abnormality which have an external focus and those with an internal focus is important, since discussion of abnormality often assumes that certain behaviours/experiences are abnormal in and of themselves.
- According to the 'deviation from the norm' criterion, abnormality involves not behaving, feeling and/or thinking as one should. This involves value-judgements and relates to residual rules.
- Although now no longer illegal, homosexuality still breaches certain fundamental religious or moral principles; homophobia and heterosexism continue to reflect these religious roots.
- In Western culture, unlike many non-Western cultures, a sharp distinction is made between legal, religious and medical definitions of normality; illness, disease and pathology are dealt with by the medical profession, so that mental disorder has become medicalized.
- In African culture, the concept of health is more social than biological, and mind and body are not seen as separate: no distinction is made between bodily and mental illness.
- While every culture possesses a concept of illness as a deviation from health, it is the overall world view within a culture which determines the meaning of 'madness', mental illness and mental health.
- Defining and treating psychological abnormality from a medical/biological perspective is itself a cultural phenomenon.
- At the heart of the 'abnormality as mental illness' criterion is the *medical model*. This involves the classification, diagnosis and treatment of *psychopathology*.
- All systems of classification stem from Kraepelin, who helped to establish the *organic* nature of mental disorders, which have traditionally been contrasted with *functional* disorders, in which the role of biological factors is much less obvious.
- Another traditional distinction is that between *neurosis* and *psychosis*. Although these categories are not defined in terms of the role of biological factors, psychoses are mainly treated using physical methods, which implies that they are, in fact, biologically caused.
- If mental disorders 'exist' independently of cultural norms and values, the most likely candidates are the (organic) psychoses, in particular, schizophrenia and manic-depression.
- The central issue in cultural/transcultural/comparative psychiatry is

whether phenomena such as schizophrenia are *absolute*, *universal* or *culturally relative*.

- 'Absolute' here means 'culture-free', and this view of abnormality is generally thought to be untenable.

- Of all the major mental disorders, the largest number of *culture-general symptoms* has been reported for schizophrenia. It is also the most commonly diagnosed mental disorder in the world.

- But there are at least three ways in which culture-specific factors could influence schizophrenia: (i) *the form the symptoms will take*; (ii) *the specific reasons for the onset of the illness*; and (iii) *the prognosis*.

- In Western psychiatry, *psychosis* in general has been seen as *discontinuous* with normal behaviour, i.e. there is a qualitative difference, implying a *categorical* view of abnormality. By contrast, *neurosis* is seen as *continuous* with normal behaviour, implying a *dimensional* view.

- But in Nigeria, for example, the paranoid aspect of the schizophrenic's symptoms are an exaggeration of the 'normal' view of illness.

- Psychiatric classification in general is based on a categorical view of abnormality.

- Some stressful events, as triggers of schizophrenic symptoms, can only be understood within the context of the patient's cultural background.

- The prognosis for successful treatment is better in non-industrialized than industrialized societies. This is attributable to the greater support available in *collectivist*, non-industrialized cultures.

- The evidence which supports the view of abnormality as universal is of limited value, because of the use of culturally biased diagnostic instruments and samples.

- Many studies have found, in a wide range of non-Western cultures, unique ways of 'being mad'. These *culture-bound syndromes* are excluded from mainstream, Western psychiatric classification, according to which psychopathology is seen as *culturally neutral*.

- This exclusion of culture-bound syndromes represents a form of *ethnocentrism*, since 'Western symptoms' are seen as the 'standard'.

- A cultural understanding of mental disorder is as important in Western as in any other culture.

- Western psychiatry is influenced by Western cultural beliefs and values, and so is not objective and value-free as it claims to be. This is reflected in changing views amongst psychiatrists regarding the 'status' of homosexuality as a mental disorder.

- The cultural nature of psychiatry can also be seen if psychiatric diagnosis is understood as a social process. Assessment of the patient's 'mental state' is not equivalent to a medical description of a bodily organ, but is the product of an interaction between individuals who will often possess widely divergent beliefs, values and cultural experience.

Suggestions for further reading

Davison, G.C. & Neale, J.M. (1994) *Abnormal Psychology*, 6th edn., New York: John Wiley & Sons.

Miller, L & Morley, S. (1986) *Investigating Abnormal Behaviour*, London: Lawrence Erlbaum Associates.

Cross-cultural psychology

Culture as part of the nature–nurture debate

When discussing the *heredity–environment* (nature–nurture) issue in
Chapter 5, we made a distinction between two levels at which the debate
has taken place.

1 The level of the species: Are particular abilities, such as using language,
   unique to human beings, and if so, are they part of our biological make-
   up, or are they an acquired ability, or do they involve an interaction
   between biological factors and environmental ones?
2 The level of the individual, or, more accurately, the individual
   differences level. How do we account for the fact that people vary in, say,
   intelligence? Are these differences largely due to differences in genetic
   make-up between people, or to differences in their environmental
   experience, or to an interaction between the two?

The concept of *culture and cultural differences* provides a third level at
which the nature–nurture issue may be debated, intermediate between the
other two. All human beings are born into a particular cultural
environment, and culture (to be defined below) may be regarded as
something which makes human beings different from other species. This
corresponds to level 1. To the extent that different cultures provide their
members with different experiences, they represent an important source of
individual differences; this, of course, corresponds to level 2. So culture is
part of the experience of every human being (and is a distinctive feature of
human behaviour), but at the same time cultures differ, so that people have
different experiences (and display different behaviour) depending on the
particular culture in which they grow up. To ask in what ways differences
in culture are related to differences in behaviour, is to ask about
nature–nurture at level 3.

A useful way of thinking about culture and environment is
Bronfenbrenner's (1979, 1989) *ecological model*, intended mainly to help
explain child development, according to which there are four levels, with
interactions possible both within and between:

1 *the microsystem*: the immediate setting in which the individual is directly involved; for instance, face-to-face interactions between a mother and child;
2 *the mesosystem*: the total system of microsystems which impinge on a particular child; for example, experiences at school and at home are bound to influence each other;
3 *the exosystem*: interactions between settings in which at least one setting does not directly involve the individual; for example, the child's home and the parents' place of work;
4 *the macrosystem*: the overall system of micro-, meso- and exosystems that characterize a particular culture or subculture.

'The ecological environment is conceived as a set of nested structures, each inside the next, like a set of Russian dolls' (Bronfenbrenner, 1979). So, interactions between two individuals, such as mother and child, are influenced by the social context within which they occur (usually, the family). In turn, the family exists and functions within a broader social setting (such as socio-economic status or racial background), which is itself part of an even broader, cultural context.

What is cross-cultural psychology?

The study of microsystems has mainly been carried out by psychologists, while the 'larger' units (meso-and exosystems) have traditionally been the focus of sociologists and anthropologists. To the extent that *cross-cultural psychologists* are interested in studying variability in behaviour among the various societies and cultural groups around the world (Smith & Bond, 1993), they have more in common with sociologists and social anthropologists than with other (more traditional) psychologists. In terms of Bronfenbrenner's model, it is precisely the interrelationships between the different levels which makes the cross-cultural approach different from that of other psychological approaches to the study of behaviour.

According to Jahoda (1978), the immediate (and modest) goals of cross-cultural psychology are (i) to describe varieties of social behaviour encountered in different cultural settings and to try to analyse their origins; and (ii) to sort out what is similar across different cultures and, thus, likely to be our common human heritage (the universals of human behaviour). This theme of *cultural difference* and *cultural similarity* is one to which we shall return later in the chapter.

A slightly different emphasis is given in Triandis's (1980) definition: 'Cross-cultural psychology is concerned with the systematic study of behaviour and experience as it occurs in different cultures, is influenced by culture, or results in changes in existing cultures.'

As well as being important and interesting in itself, cross-cultural psychology is important for another reason: it helps to correct the fundamental bias within psychology as a whole (including social psychology, which 'ought to know better') of *ethnocentrism*, the strong human tendency to use our own ethnic or cultural group's norms and values to define what is 'natural' and 'correct' for everyone (Triandis, 1990), to define 'reality'.

What this means, in essence, is that psychology as a discipline has been dominated by psychologists from America, Britain, and other Western cultures, and the large majority of participants in psychological research have been members of those same cultures. What's more, the vast majority of participants in psychological research are university undergraduates studying psychology!

'Historically, both researchers and subjects in social psychological studies have shared a lifestyle and value system that differs not only from that of most other people in North America, such as ethnic minorities and women, but also the vast majority of people in the rest of the world' (Moghaddam et al., 1993). Yet the findings from this research, and the theories based upon it, have been applied to *people in general*, as if culture makes no difference. An implicit, assumed, equation is made between 'human being' and 'human being from Western culture', and this is commonly referred to as the *Anglocentric* or *Eurocentric bias*.

When members of other cultural groups have been studied, it has usually been so that they can be compared with Western samples, using the behaviour and experience of the latter as the standard. (This is an exact parallel to the masculinist or androcentric bias in mainstream psychology, whereby men's behaviour and experience have been taken, by male psychologists, as the standard against which women have been judged. See Chapter 6, on feminism.)

In both cases (the *Anglocentric* and *masculinist biases*), it is the failure to recognize and acknowledge the bias, the 'direction the psychologist is coming from', which creates the misleading and false impression that what is being said about behaviour can be generalized without qualification. Cross-cultural psychologists do not equate 'human being' with 'member of Western culture', because for them, cultural background is the crucial *independent variable*.

> *Social psychology has through most of its history been a predominantly North American enterprise. Within the USA and Canada there exists a great diversity of cultural groups, so it is entirely possible that research undertaken there will prove to reflect the cultural variability to be found in other parts of the world. However, we can only be sure that this is so if we make thorough tests in which the different cultural groups involved in particular studies are clearly and separately identified.*

> (Smith & Bond, 1993)

Smith and Bond analysed two major social psychology textbooks, one American (Baron & Byrne, 1991), and one British (Hewstone et al., 1988), to see in which countries the studies referred to were carried out. In the former, a full ninety-four per cent were American, and even in the latter (whose authors are all European), sixty-eight per cent are American. This seems to illustrate very well the cultural bias of social psychology.

Even in textbooks published in other languages, including India, Japan, and Spain, the influence of North American sources is still very strong. Smith and Bond estimate (very crudely) that of all the social psychologists in the world, seventy-five per cent are North American, and according to someone else's estimate, sixty-four per cent of all the world's researchers in the whole of psychology are Americans. While this may not be a problem in, say, physics, it very definitely is in the study of behaviour (particularly social behaviour): instead of an objective, universal account of behaviour, what is being presented is a predominantly North American, and to a lesser degree, European, picture. Cross-cultural psychology is designed to make us aware that there is a distinction!

This is not to say that the search for universal principles of human behaviour is, in itself, invalid. It is certainly consistent with the 'classical' view of natural science, according to which the scientist's ultimate goal is to discover laws of nature, to which there are no exceptions (see Chapters 3 and 11). Furthermore, if universal principles of behaviour are to be found, they can be found by anyone, regardless of race, gender or social class. But this could only be achieved if the researchers adopted a non-ethnocentric approach:

> . . . *if researchers can generate and address research questions without being limited by the characteristics, such as values and perceptions, of their own culture. Unfortunately, ethnocentrism, involving a belief in the superiority of one's own cultural group, has influenced research in social psychology so that even some of the most established findings in social psychology do not stand up to the test when assessed in cultures outside North America.*

> (Moghaddam et al., 1993)

We shall consider some examples of these apparent social psychological 'facts' later in the chapter, but we must now examine the central concept of culture.

What is this thing called culture?

For once, there is widespread agreement (and this a rare commodity in psychology) about the definition of this term (although things will become more complicated later on). Based on Herskovits's (1948) conclusions, culture is usually defined as the 'man-made part of the environment' (Segall et al., 1990), or (more politically correctly), the 'human-made part of the environment' (Moghaddam et al., 1993). According to Triandis (1990), it has two major aspects: *objective* (roads, bridges, cooking pots and military weapons, musical symphonies and poetry; these examples are given by Moghaddam et al.) and *subjective* (beliefs, attitudes, norms, roles and values). The examples above of objective aspects suggest that this category should be subdivided into *physical/material* and *social/non-material*.

Thus, culture is the part of the environment that is made by humans; in turn, culture helps to 'make' humans: 'In essence, humans have an interactive relationship with culture: we create and shape culture, and are in turn influenced by our own cultural products' (Moghaddam et al., 1993).

While our culture is already 'there' when we arrive in the world (we are born into our culture), this does not mean that it is a static thing. Jahoda (1978) cites the famous geneticist, Waddington, who referred to culture as an 'information-transmitting system', which provides humans with an evolutionary system distinct from the biological one governing the animal world: 'There is no evidence that our Stone Age ancestors were biologically very different from modern man, and most of the vast transformations that have taken place appear to have been the outcome of cultural evolution which is social rather than genetically transmitted' (Jahoda, 1978).

Of course, the rate of cultural evolution is far greater in some societies than others. A fairly common distinction is made between Western culture, which is characterized by very rapid change (of both material and social/non-material aspects of culture) and traditional (non-Western) culture, where the rate of change is very much slower. In turn, 'traditional' has come to mean something like 'resistant to the influence of Western culture', but this seems to be a matter of degree only; nowhere is immune from Western influence.

Broadly speaking, 'culture' can refer to groups of nations (for example, the USA, Canada, and all the member states of the European Union are 'Western'), or a single one, or it can refer to sub-units (or subcultures) within a nation, such as tribes, social classes, and castes.

Although the family is the key mechanism for transmitting the culture, it is never the sole one. In tribal groups, for example, preparation for initiation ceremonies into adulthood is usually undertaken by the 'elders', who do not belong to the families (nuclear or extended) of those undergoing the initiation. Similarly, in Western cultures, teachers and other adults involved in the educational system, together with the mass media, are key agents of socialization, especially as the child gets older.

Rohner (1984, cited in Smith & Bond, 1993) makes the important distinction between *culture* and *social system*. The former refers to an organized system of meanings which members attribute to the persons, objects and events comprising that culture, while the latter refers to the behaviours found within a culture. *Society* is defined as 'the largest unit of

Figure 8.1   The national culture of Northern Ireland is dominated by the subculture of religion

a territorially bounded, multi-generational population, recruited largely through sexual reproduction, and organized around a common culture and a common social system' (Rohner, quoted in Smith & Bond, 1993). This definition acknowledges the degree to which culture and social system are interwoven.

Much cross-cultural research is in fact based on 'national cultures', which, of course, often comprise a number of separate subcultures; these may be demarcated by religion (as in Northern Ireland), by language (in Belgium) or by race (in Malaysia and Singapore). But studies in this area often provide little more detail about the participants than the name of the country (national culture) in which the study was done.

When this is done, there are two 'penalties' that we pay (according to Smith and Bond, 1993). Firstly, when we compare national cultures, we can lose track of the enormous diversity found within many of the major nations of the world, and differences found between any two countries might well also be found between carefully selected subcultures within those countries. Secondly, there is the danger of implying that national cultures are unitary systems, free of conflict, confusion and dissent. This, of course, is rarely the case.

So, if we should distinguish between *culture* and *country/national culture*, how can we define 'culture'? Or, as Brislin (1993) puts it, what are the fundamental features of culture? Brislin proposes a checklist of twelve features (some of which overlap with the definitions we have already considered; see Box 8.1).

Box 8.1   A checklist of fundamental features of culture (based on Brislin 1993)

1 Culture consists of ideas, values and assumptions about life that guide specific behaviour.
2 Culture consists of those aspects of the environment that people make (but people's responses to aspects of the environment that are natural, such as the climate, also constitute part of the environment).
3 Culture is transmitted from generation to generation, with the responsibility being given to parents, teachers, religious leaders, and other respected elders in a community.
4 There will be childhood experiences that many people in a community remember happening to them.
5 Aspects of one's culture are not commonly discussed by adults; since culture is widely shared and accepted, there is little reason to.

6 Culture can become clearest in well-meaning clashes – that is, in interactions among people from very different backgrounds. Each may behave quite 'normally' as far as their own culture is concerned, but not as judged by the other culture.

7 Culture allows people to 'fill in the blanks' when presented with a basic sketch of familiar behaviours or situations.

8 Cultural values remain despite compromises and slip-ups. Even though we can list exceptions, the cultural value is seen as a constant that continues to guide specific behaviours.

9 People react emotionally when cultural values are violated, or when a culture's expected behaviours are ignored.

10 There can be both acceptance and rejection of a culture's values at different times in a person's life. For example, rebellious adolescents and young adults come to accept a culture's expectations after having children of their own.

11 When changes in cultural values are contemplated, people are likely to react by saying, 'this will be difficult and time-consuming'. (In other words, people tend to resist cultural change.)

12 When comparing proper and expected behaviour across cultures, it is possible to observe certain sharply contrasting beliefs or orientations; for example, the treatment of time, and the clarity of rules or norms for certain complex behaviours.

Since Brislin's checklist is to do with the fundamental features of culture, the emphasis is on *what different cultures have in common*. It is only point 12 which relates to *differences between cultures*: one way of trying to distinguish between cultures is to see how the concept of time is used and understood in different cultures. However, as important as it is, time represents a fairly specific feature of cultural life. Are there any more general features or dimensions which can help to understand the differences between cultures?

Dimensions of cultural difference

Two very useful attempts to identify the key dimensions in terms of which cultures differ, and so may be compared, are those of Hofstede (1980) and Triandis (1990).

For Hofstede (1980), culture is 'the collective programming of the mind which distinguishes the members of one group from another'. He conducted a large-scale study of several thousand IBM employees in forty different countries and identified four dimensions:

1 *power distance*: the amount of respect and deference that is shown by those in both superior and subordinate positions;

2 *uncertainty avoidance*: the focus on planning and stability as ways of dealing with life's uncertainties;

3 *individualism–collectivism*: whether one's identity is defined by personal choices and achievements (individualism) or by characteristics of the collective groups to which one is more or less permanently attached (collectivism);

4 *masculinity–femininity*: the relative emphasis on achievement (masculinity) or interpersonal harmony (femininity).

We should be careful to note here what we mean when a culture is described as, say, individualist. (i) We do not mean that any two members of the culture must be equally individualist, or that either one of them must necessarily be more individualist than someone from a collectivist culture. We are looking at the mean score of a large number of individual scores. (ii) We mean that it displays individualism to a greater degree than collectivism, and more than a collectivist culture does. These are dimensions, rather than categories or types, so that it is the manifestation of these characteristics and behaviours relative to each other and relative to other cultures that matters. (See Figure 8.2.)

In 1983 Hofstede expanded his sample to include fifty national cultures. Although he omitted the former Soviet Bloc countries, as well as most of Africa, in terms of global coverage, his study is unrivalled, and the individualism–collectivism dimension has attracted many cross-cultural researchers in recent years (Smith & Bond, 1993).

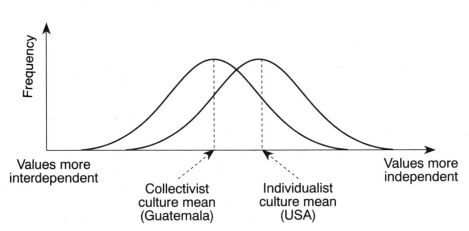

Figure 8.2   Hypothetical distributions of interdependent/independent value scores in a collectivist and an individualist national culture

Cultural syndromes

One of these cross-cultural researchers is Triandis, who replicated some of Hofstede's results with fifteen samples from different parts of the world (Triandis et al., 1986, cited in Triandis, 1990).

Triandis sees 'culture' as comprising *cultural syndromes*, which he defines as 'a pattern of values, attitudes, beliefs, norms and behaviours that can be used to contrast a group of cultures to another groups of cultures'. Three major cultural syndromes are *cultural complexity*, *individualism–collectivism*, and *tight vs loose cultures*.

CULTURAL COMPLEXITY

The more complex the culture, the more people must pay attention to *time*, which, interestingly enough, is one of the examples given by Brislin (1993; see above). This is related to the number and diversity of the roles that members of the culture typically play, so that the more numerous and diverse the roles, the more important it is that time be allocated in an appropriate way. There is evidence that cultures that are more industrialized and technological, such as Japan, Sweden and the USA, are more focused on time. To this extent, therefore, more industrialized and technological cultures are more complex cultures. The *concept* of time also differs between cultures: typically, in the West, time is seen as *linear* (it 'travels' in a straight line, from past, through present, to future), while in many non-Western cultures, it is seen as *circular* (i.e. it occurs in recurring cycles).

Another feature of complexity is *specificity vs diffusion*: the more complex the culture, the more specific roles become. For example, because of the role of religion in certain cultures (such as the Arab world in general, and Iran), a person's religion is a major determinant of his or her social behaviour. In Western cultures, however, there is a fairly clear demarcation between the religious and the non-religious (the secular).

INDIVIDUALISM VS COLLECTIVISM

Triandis believes that, of the score of dimensions of cultural variation which have been proposed, this is the most promising, in the sense of being the most likely to account for a great deal of social behaviour. As we saw when first describing this dimension, people in every culture have both types of tendency, but the relative emphasis in the West is towards individualism and in the East towards collectivism.

The basic distinction has been popular in most of the social siences for about 100 years: *Gemeinschaft–Gesellschaft* in sociology, and an individual vs relational value orientation in anthropology

When Triandis et al. (1986) replicated some of Hofstede's findings, they found four additional factors related to the main construct: *family integrity* ('Children should live at home with their parents until they get married'), and *interdependence* ('I like to live close to my good friends') are both related to *collectivism*, while *self-reliance with hedonism* ('If the group is slowing me down, it's better to leave it and work alone; the most important thing in my life is to make myself happy') and *separation from in-groups* (indicated by agreement with items showing that what happens to extended family members is of little concern) are both related to *individualism*. Other 'defining attributes', according to Triandis (1990), are as follows.

1 Collectivists pay much more attention to an identifiable in-group and behave differently towards members of that group compared with out-group members. The in-group can best be defined by the *common fate* of its members; often, it is the unit of survival, or the food community, so

that if there is no food, all in-group members starve together. In most cultures, the family is the main in-group, but in some, the tribe or country can be just as important, and in still others, the work group (for example, in Japan, reflecting the incredible economic success enjoyed by that culture).

2 For collectivists, in-group goals have primacy over individual goals, and it is the other way round for individualist cultures; the former often perceive the latter as 'selfish'.

3 Collectivists' behaviour is regulated largely by in-group norms, while that of individualists is regulated largely by personal likes and dislikes and cost–benefit analyses. Thus for 'traditional' behaviours, such as having children, *norms* (which have an outward-looking, group reference) should be more important in collectivist cultures, whereas *attitudes* (which have an inward-looking, personal reference) should be more important in individualist cultures. Lower-class groups, in most societies, are more collectivist than upper-class groups. This difference will not necessarily apply to 'non-traditional' behaviours – for example, whether or not to attend school, since formal schooling is a relatively recent development in many cultures.

4 Collectivists emphasize social hierarchy much more than individualists; usually the father is 'head of the household' and women are generally subordinate.

5 Collectivists emphasize harmony and 'saving face'. They favour homogeneous in-groups, in which there are no internal disagreements, so that a 'united front' is shown to out-groups. But in individualist cultures, disagreements within the in-group are acceptable and often help to 'clear the air'.

6 Collectivist cultures stress in-group fate and achievement, and interdependence within it. Self-reliance in a collectivist culture implies, 'I'm not a burden on the in-group', whereas in an individualist culture it conveys, 'I can do my own thing'. There is generally much more emotional detachment from the larger in-group in individualist cultures.

7 For collectivists, the *self* is an appendage, or extension, of the in-group, whereas for individualists it is a separate and distinct entity. When asked to complete statements that begin 'I am . . .', collectivists typically give more in-group related answers ('I am a son', 'I am a Roman Catholic'), individualists typically give more personal-attribute answers ('I am kind', 'I am hard-working'). In collectivist cultures, people usually belong to a small number of in-groups and are influenced very much by them; in individualist cultures, behaviour is rarely greatly influenced by any one in-group in particular because there are usually so many, and they often make conflicting demands on the individual.

8 In collectivist cultures, *vertical relationships* (such as parent–child) take priority over *horizontal relationships* (such as spouse–spouse) when there is a conflict between them. The reverse is true in individualist cultures. Collectivists stress family integrity, security, obedience and conformity,

whereas individualists stress achievement, pleasure and competition. Consistent with these differences, individualist cultures use childrearing methods which encourage autonomy and self-reliance, while collectivist cultures encourage children to be obedient and dutiful, and to make sacrifices for the in-group.

Roughly speaking, *capitalist* politico-economic systems are associated with *individualism*, and socialist societies are associated with *collectivism*. There is also evidence which shows that urban environments, compared with rural ones, *within* the same societies, seem to encourage competitiveness, one of the major features of individualism (Smith & Bond; 1993; see Figure 8.2).

TIGHT VS LOOSE CULTURES

In *tight* cultures, people are expected to behave according to clearly defined norms and there is little tolerance of deviation from those norms; in *loose* cultures, there is a good deal of freedom to deviate. (This is relevant to the whole question of *normality/abnormality*, including mental disorder. See Chapter 7.)

The concept of tightness has much in common with Hofstede's (high) *uncertainty avoidance* (see above). Japan is the prototype of a tight culture (although tightness is not a feature of every aspect of social life), and Thailand is the prototype of a loose culture.

Tightness is also associated with cultural homogeneity, i.e. where there is very little mixing of ethnic groups from a variety of cultural backgrounds, and where the culture is relatively 'pure'. By contrast, looseness is associated with cultural heterogeneity and marginality, and Hofstede found evidence of looseness (low uncertainty avoidance) in Hong Kong and Singapore, two cultures in which East (China) meets West (Britain).

In addition to these three major dimensions of cultural diversity, Triandis (1990) discusses three more specific dimensions.

1 *Masculinity vs femininity* is also one of Hofstede's four main dimensions, which he described in terms of work-related goals, with Japan being masculine and Sweden feminine.

  An interesting similarity is that between masculinity and individualism, on the one hand, and femininity and collectivism on the other: masculine cultures stress getting the job done, achievement, progress, advancement, being strong and effective, while feminine cultures stress quality of life, good interpersonal relationships, nurturing, concern for others, being kind and caring. (See Chapter 6, on feminism.)

2 Regarding *emotional control vs emotional expressiveness*, in cultures such as in Japan, where people are expected to express mostly pleasant emotions (even in unpleasant situations), people do very well in controlling their emotions. By contrast, in cultures such as those Southern Europe, where people are not expected to control their emotions, they often feel good about expressing themselves openly.

  There is some evidence that people in Africa, and places near Africa,

Figure 8.3 In cultures where people are not expected to control their emotions, they often feel good about expressing themselves openly

express their emotions freely, and that the further people live from where human beings first developed, the more emotional control they have. If human beings originated in Africa (a widely held belief among anthropologists), then as they migrated to remote corners of the world, they had to learn to control the unfriendly environments they encountered – and themselves. Self-control became a value, and emotional control was a manifestation of that value.

3 *Contact vs no-contact cultures* refers to cultural differences in terms of what Hall (1959, 1966) called *proxemic rules*, which prescribe the amount of physical distance that is appropriate between people in everyday interactions, according to the situation and the relationship between the people involved. How close we are 'allowed' to sit or stand next to others (particularly those we are meeting for the first time) constitutes an important feature of non-verbal communication; misunderstandings between members of different cultural groups (and unfavourable first impressions) can arise from a failure to appreciate the appropriate proxemic rules which apply on a particular occasion (see Table 8.1).

Table 8.1 Major dimensions of cultural difference

Power distance	Hofstede (1980)
Uncertainty avoidance	Hofstede (1980)
Tight vs loose cultures	Triandis (1990) Triandis et al. (1986)
Individualism–Collectivism	Hofstede (1980) Triandis (1990) Triandis et al. (1986)
Masculinity–Femininity	Hofstede (1980) Triandis (1990) Triandis et al. (1986)
Cultural complexity	Triandis (1990) Triandis et al. (1986)
Emotional control vs emotional expressiveness	Triandis (1990) Triandis et al. (1986)
Contact vs no-contact cultures	Triandis (1990) Triandis et al. (1986)

Doing cross-cultural research: conceptual and methodological issues

The emic–etic distinction

As we have seen, cross-cultural psychology (like psychology as a whole) involves the study by (mostly) members of one cultural group (Western psychologists) of members of non-Western cultural populations. This perhaps makes it inevitable (even if it doesn't make it justifiable) that when a Western psychologist studies members of some other culture, he or she will use theories and measuring instruments that have been developed in the 'home' culture. These can be used for studying both cross-cultural differences *and* universal aspects of human behaviour (the 'psychic unity of mankind', a phrase popular in the early twentieth century). For example, aggression is a cultural universal – but how it is expressed may be culturally specific (Gross, 1994).

Similarly, in discussing the nature of psychological abnormality, there are good reasons for believing that schizophrenia is a universal mental disorder, such that there are core symptoms which are found in a wide range of cultural groups, but that, at the same time, culture-specific factors seem to influence the form the symptoms will take, the specific reasons for the onset of the illness, and the likely outcome of the illness (the prognosis) (Brislin, 1993). (See Chapter 7.)

The distinction between culture-specific and universal behaviour is one version of what has come to be known in cross-cultural psychology as the *emic–etic distinction*, which also refers to problems inherent in the cross-cultural use of instruments developed in a single culture (Segall et al., 1990). The terms 'emic' and 'etic' are based on the distinction made in linguistics between *phonemics*, the study of universal sounds as they contribute to the meaning of a language, and *phonetics*, the study of universal sounds used in human language, independently of their relationship to meaning.

So, as applied to the study of cultures (as distinct from the study of languages), 'etics' refers to culturally general concepts, which are easier to understand (because, by definition, they are common to all cultures), while 'emics' refer to culturally specific concepts, which include all the ways that specific cultures deal with etics. It is the emics of another culture that are often so difficult to understand (Brislin, 1993).

According to Pike (cited in Berry et al. 1992), who first made the emic–etic distinction in 1954, the terms should be thought of as referring to two different viewpoints regarding the study of behaviour. The etic approach studies behaviour from outside a particular cultural system, and the emic approach studies behaviour from the inside (Segall et al., 1990).

While both viewpoints represent part of cross-cultural psychology, does the distinction help us to understand how research is actually carried out?

According to Berry (1969), research has to begin somewhere and, inevitably, this usually involves an instrument or observational technique rooted in the researcher's own culture (that is, an emic for that culture). When such an emic is brought in from an outside culture, is assumed to be valid in the alien culture, and so is seen as a valid way of comparing the two cultures, an *imposed etic* is being used (Berry, 1969).

Many attempts to replicate American studies in other parts of the world involve an imposed etic; they all assume that the situation being studied has the same meaning for members of the alien culture as it does for members of the researcher's own culture (Smith & Bond, 1993). The number of failures to replicate the findings obtained using American samples illustrates very clearly that this assumption is often false! (We shall look at some examples of such failures at the end of the chapter.)

An (imposed) etic approach is the more likely one to be used, since the researcher brings with him or her ready-made theories and measuring instruments in an attempt to identify universal behavioural patterns. But this is also the approach which involves the danger of the researcher imposing his or her own cultural biases and theoretical framework on the behaviour of people from a different cultural group – what is dangerous is that those biases and framework may simply not 'fit' the phenomena being studied, resulting in their distortion. Related to this is perhaps an even more serious danger, namely ethnocentrism (see above).

Brislin (1993) gives the example of 'raising responsible children' as an etic, and 'encouraging independent thinking' as an emic designed to achieve it. While the etic may be reasonable, in that it is relevant to all cultures, it is simply wrong to believe that the emic will also be – different cultures may use very different means to achieve the same goal. We cannot simply assume that 'one's own emics are *part of* the culturally-common etic'. This is, of course, an imposed etic.

Another example given by Brislin is the concept of intelligence. The etic, he suggests, is 'solving problems, the exact form of which hasn't been seen before', a definition which is likely to be generally acceptable across cultures (partly because it is at least consistent with the fact that what constitutes a 'problem' differs from culture to culture). However, is the emic of 'mental quickness' (for example, as measured by timed IQ tests) universally valid? Among the Baganda people of Uganda, for example, intelligence is associated with slow, careful, deliberate thought (Wober, 1974, cited in Brislin, 1993). Nor is quick thinking necessarily a valid emic for all schoolchildren within a culturally diverse country like the USA (Brislin, 1993).

Some possible solutions to the 'imposed etic' problem

Instead of using imposed etic measures, Berry (1969) outlines a strategy for reaching a more valid set of *derived etic* generalizations; this strategy basically consists of a number of parallel emic studies within a series of national cultures. This focuses on culture-specific phenomena, such as the behaviours, values, customs and traditions of the particular national cultures included. This is the approach typically used in ethnographic anthropological research (*ethnography* being 'fieldwork'), which provides a rich source of information about the culture, which can then be used as a basis for cross-cultural psychology (Berry et al., 1992). Typically, participant observation is used, together with local people serving as informed observers, as well as local test construction, in an attempt to tap the culture's own indigenous system of classification or 'subjective culture' (Triandis, 1972).

If the subjective culture of different national cultures show similarities (that is, if there is a convergence between the results obtained within each culture), we can be more confident that we have identified processes which are equivalent, and we are in a position to make a derived etic generalization, at least with regard to the particular cultures which have been sampled (Smith & Bond, 1993).

The problem of equivalence

The emic–etic distinction implies that social psychology cannot discover cultural universals unless it adopts a cross-cultural approach. The methods used by psychologists need to be adapted so that researchers can study the same processes in different cultures (Moghaddam et al., 1993).

But how do we know that we are studying the same processes? What does 'same' mean in this context? For Brislin (1993), the question is: 'Do the concepts being investigated, and especially the way the concepts are being measured, have the same meaning in the different cultures?' He describes three approaches which have been used to deal with this fundamental issue of *equivalence*.

TRANSLATION EQUIVALENCE

Discovering if concepts can be easily expressed in the languages of the different cultures being studied represents a first step in dealing with the issue of equivalence. If material does not translate well, this might be because emic aspects are involved with which the translators are unfamiliar. Alternatively, there may not be readily available terms in the language to capture certain aspects of the concept being translated.

A common method used in trying to overcome this problem is *back-translation*. The material say, a questionnaire on childrearing practices in the original language (usually English) is carefully prepared, then a bilingual person translates it into the target language. A second bilingual person (unfamiliar with the efforts of the first) then translates it from the target language (back) into English. The two English versions are then examined in order to see what 'comes through' clearly. If the two English versions are equivalent, it is assumed that the target-language version is adequate. By studying the back-translated original-language (English) version, researchers can gain insights into what can and cannot be easily expressed in the target language. (See Figure 8.4.)

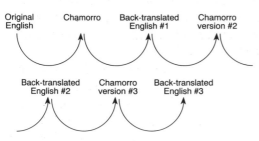

Figure 8.4 An example of back-translation between English and Chamorro (the native language of Guam, an island in the northern Pacific) (From Brislin, 1993)

CONCEPTUAL EQUIVALENCE

The material that proceeds smoothly through the multiple steps of back-translation is said to be *translation equivalent*. Conceptual equivalence begins with the assumption that there will most likely be different aspects of a concept that serve the same purpose in different cultures. This often begins by identifying the etic aspects, followed by a further identification of the emic aspects related to the etic in the various cultures being studied.

To take an earlier example, the etic for 'intelligence' might be 'solving problems the exact form of which haven't been seen before', while the emic might include 'mental quickness' (USA and Western Europe), 'slow, careful, deliberate thought' (the Baganda people, of Uganda; Wober, 1974), and 'responsibility to the community (getting along well with others)' (the Chi-Chewa people of Zambia; Serpell, 1982). All these emics are conceptually equivalent; they all form part of the definition of intelligence as used by respected adults in the various cultures, and might be elicited by asking such adults, 'Which young people in your community are considered intelligent?'

METRIC EQUIVALENCE

While conceptual equivalence centres on the analysis of different behaviours which can all demonstrate the same general concept, *metric equivalence* centres on the analysis of the same concepts across cultures, based on the assumption that the same scale (after proper translation procedures have been carried out) can be used to measure the concept.

For example, after careful translation, an IQ test produces a score of, say, 120 for an American woman and for a woman in Chile. The assumption is that the intelligence scale (metric) is measuring exactly the same concept (intelligence) in the two countries, and that a score in one country can be directly compared with that in another.

But is this necessarily a valid assumption to make? Even if translation has been carried out satisfactorily, this is no guarantee of conceptual equivalence, and, surely, this is the most important criterion by which to assess the cross-cultural equivalence of an IQ test (as well as being a requirement for metric equivalence). In discussing translation equivalence, we are looking at a method which has actually been used in cross-cultural research, and which is not particularly controversial, whereas conceptual and metric equivalence are largely theoretical and are much more controversial: they raise more questions than they answer.

Even if conceptual equivalence can be established (and we have seen that there is research that provides evidence of conceptually equivalent emics for 'intelligence'), there remains the question of who constructs the test – a Western psychologist (in which case the test must be translated, but still begging the question of metric equivalence) or a local test constructor (which removes the need for translation). In either case, we seem to be left with the question of whether the test is *culture-fair*.

According to Frijda and Jahoda (1966, cited in Segall et al., 1990), a culture-fair test (i) could be a set of items which are equally unfamiliar to all possible persons in all possible cultures, so that everyone would have an equal chance of passing (or failing) the items; or (ii) could comprise multiple sets of items, modified for use in each culture to ensure that each version of the test would contain the same degree of familiarity. This would give members of each culture about the same chance of being successful with their respective version. The first option is a virtual impossibility; the second option is possible in theory, but in practice very difficult to construct: 'The effort to devise culturally-fair testing procedures will probably never be completely successful. The degree to which we are measuring the same thing in more than one culture, whether we are using the same or different test items, must always worry us' (Segall et al., 1990).

The view that 'tests of ability are inevitably cultural devices' (Cole, 1985) suggests a further problem faced by those attempting to achieve cross-cultural equivalence. What none of the three types of equivalence takes into account is *the meaning of the experience of taking an intelligence test* (what we could perhaps call 'experiential equivalence'). Taking tests of various kinds is a familiar experience for members of Western culture, both within and outside the educational context, but what about cultures in which there is no generally available schooling? How can we measure intelligence independently of people's responses to taking the test itself?

The very nature or form of the *tasks* involved in an intelligence test (as distinct from the content) is something that has a cultural meaning, as illustrated by Glick's report of research with the Kpelle people (1975, cited in Rogoff & Morelli, 1989). Participants were asked to sort twenty objects into groups. They did this by using *functional* groups (e.g. knife with orange, potato with hoe), instead of *category* groups, which the experimenter thought more appropriate. When their way of classifying the objects was challenged, they often explained that this was how a wise man would do it. 'When an exasperated experimenter asked finally, "How would a fool do it?", he was given back sorts of the type that were initially expected – four neat piles with food in one, tools in another, and so on' (Glick, 1975, quoted in Rogoff & Morelli, 1989).

This is a kind of 'putting two fingers up' at the researcher for being ethnocentric, imposing an etic, and making culturally inappropriate assumptions. Being asked to perform a task outside of its usual context (from practical to abstract) could so easily produce the conclusion that the people being studied lack the basic ability to classify, when it is the inappropriateness of the task that is at fault.

Advantages of cross-cultural research

It has become almost a truism amongst cross-cultural researchers that the development of concepts and theories of human behaviour demands that behaviour be studied all over the world. This might seem like common sense, but as we have already seen in this chapter (and in others in this book), psychologists often seem to believe that it is perfectly legitimate to investigate behaviour in one culture (or using one gender), and then to generalize to other cultures (or to the other gender).

HIGHLIGHTING IMPLICIT ASSUMPTIONS

An important function of cross-cultural research has been to allow investigators to look closely at the impact of their own belief systems ('folk psychology') on scientific theories and research paradigms. When participants and researchers are from the same population, interpretations of development (or whatever aspect of behaviour is being studied) may be constrained by implicit cultural assumptions.

Working with people from a quite different background can make us aware of aspects of human activity that normally we would not notice, either because they are missing in the 'new' culture or because they are arranged in a different way. In this way, we become aware of our assumptions, helping us to recognize that human functioning cannot be separated from its contexts, both cultural and more immediate (Rogoff & Morelli, 1989). The case of the Kpelle being asked to sort objects is a very insightful (and amusing) example of this.

SEPARATING BEHAVIOUR FROM CONTEXT

One of the consequences of researchers being unable to stand back from their own cultural experience is that, when studying behaviour within their own culture, there is the tendency to focus on the behaviour, rather than on the situation or context, and to see the behaviour as reflecting personal dispositions of the actor (the fundamental attribution error; Ross, 1977; see Chapter 2). They are so familiar with those situations and contexts that it is difficult for them to appreciate the impact that they have on behaviour. This may be seen when minority group children within the USA are compared with mainstream children: not taking cultural context into account, and assuming that mainstream (white, middle-class) skills and upbringing are normal and superior, results in a 'deficit model' view of minority groups, who are seen as needing intervention to compensate for their deficiencies (Rogoff & Morelli, 1989).

However, when studying other cultures, it may be far easier to make this separation of behaviour from situational context, since many situations will be new, unfamiliar and fresh in their eyes (Brislin, 1993). This increased sensitivity to context may help to counteract the ethnocentrism that is found when studying minority groups within the researcher's own national culture.

EXTENDING THE RANGE OF VARIABLES

Figure 8.5 A researcher would have to go a long way to find a corner of the Earth which did not have access to television

Studying members of only one, or a small number and range of cultures, limits the range of variables and concepts that can be explored. For example, trying to find out what effect having a TV set in the home has on school achievement is very difficult to do by just studying American or British samples, since the vast majority of families have (at least) one!

Again, research suggests that members of individualist cultures (which includes the vast majority of psychologists) are much more likely to explain behaviour in terms of personality traits (and so see behaviour as consistent across situations), while those from collectivist cultures use a more complex analysis, whereby the same person may act differently in different situations (see for example, Schweder, 1991, cited in Brislin, 1993). The point here is that if only individualist cultures were studied, we would regard the explanation of behaviour as reflecting personality traits as a universal tendency (Brislin, 1993; see Chapter 4, on traits vs situations).

SEPARATING VARIABLES

Cross-cultural research can also help to separate out the effects of variables that may usually be confounded within a particular culture: 'Cross-cultural research . . . allows psychologists to use cultural variation as a natural laboratory to attempt to disentangle variables that are difficult to tease apart in the US and to study conditions that are rare in the US' (Rogoff & Morelli, 1989). For example, how do gender differences manifest themselves under different cultural conditions? To what extent is cognitive development a function of schooling, as distinct from age (two variables that cannot be separated where schooling is freely available and compulsory)?

A very famous example is Freud's theory of the Oedipus complex, as it applies to little boys, according to which the son experiences extreme jealousy of his father (over the father's 'possession' of the mother) and at the same time extreme fear of the father (who is more powerful and, in the child's view, will punish him by castration if he continues to compete with the father for the mother's affections).

Malinowski (1929) found that amongst the Trobriand Islanders of the South Pacific it is the mother's brother, not the child's father, who is the major figure of authority, although the father continues to have a normal sexual relationship with the mother. Under these circumstances, sons tend to have a very good relationship with their father, free of the love–hate ambivalence which Freud saw as an inevitable feature of the Oedipus complex. But the relationship with the uncle is not usually so good.

This suggests that not only is the Oedipus complex not universal, as Freud claimed it was, but sexual jealousy and rivalry, as a major component in the whole 'family drama', may play a much less important role than he believed.

TESTING THEORIES

Finally, a major function of cross-cultural research is to test out theories which have been developed in the West, in order to see whether they apply to other cultural groups. Most of the major theories within psychology, such as those of Freud and Piaget, are meant to be universal, but we have already considered one example of a cross-cultural study which casts doubt on the universal nature of the Oedipus complex, one of the fundamental elements of Freud's psychosexual theory of personality.

The USA is still the world centre of psychology, and of social psychology in particular, but some of the models of social behaviour which have come out of the USA may have little relevance or appeal in a different cultural context. For example, Thibaut and Kelley's (1959) analysis of social relationships in terms of the exchange of rewards is a 'kind of rational, market-based mode . . . [which] is shaped by the values of middle-class, US culture, and often it is only when people from other backgrounds become familiar with middle-class, US culture that such models make sense to them' (Moghaddam et al., 1993).

Especially from the late 1960s, European social psychology has developed its own character, with Tajfel (regarded generally as the 'father' of European social psychology) and Harré in England, Moscovici in France, and Doise in Switzerland, among the leading figures. It has become more *social* than its American counterpart, in the sense that there is a greater focus on larger societal issues, such as intergroup relations, unemployment, and ideology (Moghaddam et al., 1993).

Festinger's (1957) *Cognitive Dissonance Theory* has generated an enormous amount of research and theorizing in America, but there is evidence that it does not explain behaviour very well in some non-Western cultures, including Japan. For example, how well a person handles a supposed 'inconsistency' is considered a sign of maturity and broad-mindedness. Japanese children are brought up to accept inconsistency, whereas the focus of the theory is on the ways in which people attempt to reduce the dissonance which results from perceived inconsistencies.

According to one estimate, only about thirteen per cent of all the research reported in the leading American journals of social psychology are field studies. Because these are conducted in contexts that are culturally richer than laboratory studies, we need to be even more attentive to the role of cultural factors when interpreting the results (Moghaddam et al., 1993).

A good example of this is the famous 'Robber's Cave' experiment of

Figure 8.6 The famous 'Robber's Cave' experiment of intergroup conflict involved boys at summer camp in America, a culturally significant factor

intergroup conflict involving boys at a summer camp in America (Sherif et al., 1961). The very fact that it was conducted in this setting is significant, since boys' summer camps play a certain role in North American culture which is not found elsewhere. The study also illustrates the importance of taking into account what the participants see as the appropriateness of different types of behaviour in certain settings. The boys interpreted the situation as one where both competition *and* cooperation for scarce resources were appropriate; which strategy was used depended on which best served their material interests (they competed for the knives which were awarded to the winners of the tournament, but cooperated by, literally, pulling together to get their bus out of the mud). Such interpretations have a cultural bias (Moghaddam et al., 1993).

Diab (1970, cited in Smith & Bond, 1993) replicated the study in Lebanon. This tried to follow the procedure used by Sherif et al. as closely as possible (using a summer camp setting, with eleven-year-old boys, and the same planned stages of group formation, intergroup competition, and, finally, group cooperation). Two randomly created groups of nine (Muslims and Christians in each group) developed very different 'cultures': 'The Friends' were warm and cooperative, while 'Red Genie' were highly aggressive and competitive, and stole things, from one another as well as from The Friends. It proved impossible to get the two groups to cooperate in stage three (as Sherif et al. had managed to do); when Red Genie lost the tournament, they stole the knives, threatened The Friends with them, and tried forcibly to leave the camp. The study had to be abandoned.

As Tyerman and Spencer (1983), having failed to find any spirit of competition in their replication involving English Boy Scouts, point out, the culture of each specific group will depend not just on externally imposed incentives of competition and co-operation, but also on established traditions and local cultures which form a background to specific events within each group. As we have said, the summer camp is a North American phenomenon, although we could find 'stimulus equivalents' in other cultures. However, the formation of friendships rigidly within one's own age group is more characteristic of industrialized societies, compared with traditional cultures, where friendships tend to be extensions of family networks. Such cultural differences help to explain why it has proved so difficult to replicate Sherif et al.'s study outside of North America (Moghaddam et al., 1993).

Some concluding comments

As we noted when discussing culture-fair intelligence tests, the participant's familiarity with taking tests of any description, together with his or her concept of a test and understanding of the test situation, are all crucial factors to be taken into account when evaluating his or her performance on the test. Similarly, the tradition of political polls and consumer surveys cannot be taken for granted when conducting research outside Western countries; social science may not be practised at all, or it may be highly politicized. These factors make it essential that novel methodologies (instead of questionnaires and laboratory experiments) be developed, relationships with cultural informants be carefully nurtured, and careful training of participants take place before data collection actually begins: 'In all cases, the cultural context of "doing social science" must be thoughtfully assessed by the social scientist to ensure that the outcome of the resulting research has a claim to validity' (Smith & Bond, 1993).

Summary

- The concept of *culture/cultural differences* represents a third level at which the nature–nurture debate takes place, intermediate between (i) the *species* level, and (ii) the *individual differences* level.
- According to Bronfenbrenner's *ecological model*, there are four interacting levels: *microsystem, mesosystem, exosystem* and *macrosystem*.
- *Cross-cultural psychologists* study variability in behaviour among the various societies and cultural groups around the world. They have more in common with sociologists and anthropologists than with other, more traditional, psychologists.
- Cross-cultural psychologists are also interested in the *universals* of human behaviour.
- Cross-cultural psychology helps to correct *ethnocentrism* within psychology as a whole, including social psychology, whereby an implicit equation is made between 'human being' and 'human being from Western culture' (the *Anglocentric/Eurocentric bias*).
- For cross-cultural psychologists, cultural background is the crucial *independent variable*. Their aim is to show that the account of behaviour being presented by psychology is a predominantly North American (and, to a lesser degree, European) one, rather than an objective, universal one.
- *Culture* is usually defined as the man/person-made part of the environment, both the *material* and *non-material/social aspects*. Human beings both create culture and are influenced by it.
- Culture is not static, but provides humans with an evolutionary

system distinct from the biological system of animals. Cultural evolution is social rather than genetically transmitted.

- 'Traditional' cultures experience a much slower rate of change than is normal in Western culture.
- While the family is the key agent of socialization, both in Western and non-Western cultures, it is never the only one.
- A distinction is made between *culture* and *social system*. Much cross-cultural research is based on *national cultures* (denoted by the name of a country); this obscures the enormous diversity *within* a national culture and implies that national cultures are unitary, harmonious systems.
- Hofstede identified four central dimensions of culture: *power distance, uncertainty avoidance, individualism–collectivism, masculinity–femininity*.
- Overlapping with these are Triandis's *cultural syndromes*, namely *cultural complexity, individualism–collectivism, tight vs loose cultures*. He also discusses three more specific cultural dimensions: *masculinity vs femininity, emotional control vs emotional expressiveness, contact vs no-contact cultures*.
- When Western psychologists study members of other cultures, they use theories/measuring instruments which have been developed in the 'home' culture. These can be used to study both cultural *differences* and *universals*.
- The distinction between culture-specific and universal behaviour is one version of the *emic–etic distinction*. 'Etics' refers to culturally general concepts; 'emics' refers to culturally specific concepts.
- The etic approach studies behaviour from outside a particular cultural system, whereas the emic approach studies behaviour from the inside.
- When Western psychologists use an instrument or observational technique from their own culture (an emic for that culture) to study another culture, an *imposed etic* is being used.
- An imposed etic approach is involved when attempts to replicate American studies are made in other countries; it assumes that the situation being studied has the same meaning in all the cultures being tested. This assumption is likely to distort the phenomena being studied, and is related to ethnocentrism.
- One solution to the imposed etic problem is to reach a more valid set of *derived etic* generalizations, by conducting a number of parallel emic studies in a variety of national cultures, focusing on culture-specific phenomena.
- Psychologists need to adapt their methods so that they study the same processes in different cultures. This raises the fundamental issue of the equivalence of meaning.
- Three approaches used to deal with this issue are *translation*

equivalence (often using *back-translation*), *conceptual equivalence*, and *metric equivalence*.

- Translation equivalence is a prerequisite for conceptual equivalence (but does not guarantee it), just as conceptual equivalence is a prerequisite for metric equivalence. While the first is actually used and not particularly controversial, the other two are largely theoretical proposals and are much more controversial.
- Metric equivalence is related to the issue of the *culture-fairness* of psychological tests.
- A fourth kind of equivalence which must be taken into account is *the meaning of the experience* of taking, say, an intelligence test ('experiential equivalence').
- Cross-cultural research allows investigators to examine the influence of their own beliefs and assumptions, revealing how human behaviour cannot be separated from its cultural context.
- Being able to stand back from their own cultural experience allows researchers to appreciate the impact of situational factors on behaviour; they are thus less likely to make the fundamental attribution error and to use a 'deficit model' to explain the performance of minority group members.
- Cross-cultural research expands the range of variables and concepts that can be explored, and allows the separation of the effects of variables that may be confounded within a particular culture.
- Only by conducting cross-cultural research can Western psychologists be sure whether their theories and research findings are relevant outside of their own cultural context. Thibaut and Kelley's exchange theory of relationships, Festinger's cognitive dissonance theory of attitude change, and Sherif et al.'s 'Robber's Cave' experiment have all failed the replication test outside of North American settings.

Suggestions for further reading

Brislin, R. (1993) *Understanding Cultures Influence on Behaviour*, Orlando, Fla.: Harcourt Brace Jovanovich.

Moghaddam, F.M., Taylor, D.M. & Wright, S.C. (1993) *Social Psychology in Cross-Cultural Perspective*, New York: W.H. Freeman & Co.

Smith, P.B. & Bond, M.H. (1993) *Social Psychology across Cultures: Analysis and perspectives*, Hemel Hempstead, Herts.: Harvester Wheatsheaf.

Attachment and separation through the life cycle

Considering how often we use the word 'attached' in everyday language, when referring both to people and objects, it is perhaps very surprising that psychologists have, at least up until recently, confined the term to the earliest emotional ties that human (and non-human) beings form to those who care for them. While the *primary* use of the term in everyday life is related to other people, it is certainly not restricted to describing our feelings for our parents, but can refer to a whole range of emotional bonds, with romantic partners, friends (of both sexes), our own children and so on. In a *secondary* use of the term, we often confess to being attached to our pets, as well as a whole variety of physical objects (including books, souvenirs and mementos, houses and motor cars).

So what is the common element? Perhaps it is the significance that these things have for our self-concept, our sense of who we are as a person; they help define who we are. Clearly, some will be much more important in this way than others, and it is when we are separated from them, either temporarily or permanently, that we realize just how important they are. Indeed, if attachments are vital to our self-concept, it follows that loss of these attachment objects will threaten that self-concept, requiring an adjustment on our part, a redefinition of our sense of ourselves. Permanent loss of our most significant attachments will require a major, perhaps fundamental, adjustment, while some losses may upset us only briefly, especially if we are able to replace what we have lost.

The most significant attachments in our lives are the people who are irreplaceable, and it is this feature of our relationships which makes the process of readjustment so essential. So attachment and separation are two sides of the same emotional coin and, as I will try to show in this chapter, they are interrelated processes which are not confined to infancy and early childhood but which recur throughout our lives.

Figure 9.1   People can become very emotionally attached to their pets, resulting in emotional trauma if the pet should die or be lost

What is attachment?

Ainsworth (1989) defines an attachment as affectional bond that is 'a relatively long-enduring tie in which the partner is important as a unique individual and is interchangeable with none other.' In common with other affectional bonds, there is a desire to maintain closeness to the partner, but a unique feature of attachments is that the attachment figure provides a sense of security and comfort which, in turn, provide the confidence needed to engage in other activities, to explore and investigate the environment. The attachment figure thus represents a safe or secure base for approaching what is unfamiliar, unknown and even threatening.

This feature of attachments can be seen very clearly in the case of *securely attached* one-year-olds in the 'strange situation' (Ainsworth et al., 1978); they typically play quite happily in an unfamiliar room, with unfamiliar toys and in the presence of a stranger, so long as the mother is present. However, when the mother leaves the room, the child is distressed, stops playing, cannot be comforted by the (female) stranger, greets the mother very warmly on her return, and only after being cuddled by her, can he or she resume playing and exploring. The presence of mother will largely be ignored by the securely attached child, although he or she will need reassurance every so often that she is still there. This lack of attention to the mother is evidence of the security and safety that she provides.

By contrast, the *insecure–anxious avoidant* child largely ignores the mother, but this is because of indifference towards her, as demonstrated by the fact that the child's play and general behaviour are little affected whether she is present or absent. Just as the securely attached child largely takes the attachment for granted, so do adults (Weiss, 1991). However, even relatively brief separations result in *separation distress*, and the death of a partner usually results in deep, persisting grief, in which separation protest is a major component. In turn, one feature of separation protest is a sense of hopelessness and fear: 'In adults as well as children, attachments appear to be relationships critical to continuing security and so to the maintenance of emotional security' (Weiss, 1991). Indeed, Weiss (1991) defines attachments as relationships whose loss produces grief, and defines loss as 'an event that produces persisting inaccessibility of an emotionally important figure'.

Clearly, then, in terms of both attachments and reactions to their loss, both young children and adults seem to have much in common. Indeed, while both Bowlby and Ainsworth are best known (and even only known) for their study of attachment and separation in young children (they both used the term *safe base* in that context), attachment theory, which they developed both independently and together, leads to two very significant hypotheses: (i) attachment behaviour characterizes human beings throughout life; and (ii) patterns established in childhood parent–child relationships tend to structure the quality of later bonds in their adult relationships, and may account for why some people even seem to avoid this presumably 'natural' inclination (Bartholomew, 1993). Is there an adult counterpart, therefore, to the anxious–avoidant child referred to above? We shall return to this question later in the chapter.

Attachments, affectional bonds and other relationships

While attachments are affectional bonds, not all affectional bonds are necessarily attachments. For example, having defined attachments in terms of the security and safety which they provide, parents do not normally derive these from their children; if they did, the relationship might well (and justifiably) be regarded as unhealthy, since it is one of the functions of their relationship with their (marriage) partner (*sexual pair bond*) to provide these. For this reason, Ainsworth prefers the view that, while children are *attached* to their mothers, mothers have *bonds* with their children.

However, it is quite appropriate to describe the affectional bonds between sexual partners as attachments, since they do share so many basic features with children's attachments to their parents. And it might be considered appropriate to describe the changing relationships that parents have with their children as becoming more attachment-like, particularly when the parents are elderly, widowed and more dependent, both

Figure 9.2 A child's attachment to their parents is most evident when the child is distressed, for whatever reason

Figure 9.3 Renoir 'Dance at Bougival' 1883. Most individuals find a new principal attachment figure in the form of their sexual partner

Figure 9.4 Edward Munch 'Death in the Sick Chamber' 1895. (Detail.) A person's response to the death of a parent usually demonstrates that the attachment has endured

emotionally and materially, on their adult children. Elderly parents may seek real safety and security from their grown-up children, representing a kind of 'crossing-over' or exchange of roles.

This change in the nature of the parent–child relationship is consistent with the view that, in all relationships with attachment properties, contact with the attachment figure may be sought if there is some kind of threat to (i) the self, (ii) the attachment figure, or (iii) the relationship. In all three cases, attachment feelings and behaviours are aroused (Weiss, 1991).

Threat to the self

When children are afraid or unwell, attachment behaviours become more evident, since the need for reassurance, which can normally be taken for granted (at least when the attachment is secure) is heightened. Similarly, elderly parents, especially when widowed and thus deprived of their major life-long source of safety and security (again, assuming a stable, happy marriage), experience an increased need for emotional support.

Threat to the attachment figure

Children are, of course, very distressed by the illness of a parent, just as a husband or wife is by the illness (or suffering of whatever kind or cause) of the partner.

Similarly, even though most individuals are likely to have found a new principal attachment figure in the form of their sexual partner, this does not mean that attachment to the parents no longer exists. Most adults continue a meaningful association with their parents, regardless of the fact that they penetrate fewer aspects of their lives than they did before.

A person's response to the death of a parent usually demonstrates that the attachment has endured, and even after grieving has been resolved, internal models of the lost parent continue to be an influence (Ainsworth, 1989). While parents do not provide the security for their grown-up children which they did when the children were emotionally dependent on them as children, the death of a parent makes the likelihood of one's own death seem greater. While they are still alive, our parents serve as a 'psychological buffer' against death (Moss & Moss, 1983, cited in Hayslip & Panek, 1993): 'As long as a parent is alive, one can still feel protected, cared for, approved of, and even scolded. Stripped of this "protection", one must acknowledge that he or she is now a senior member of the family and that death is a certainty. The orderliness of life and death – that those who are older should die first – is reinforced when a parent dies' (Hayslip & Panek, 1993). Could it also be that with the death of both parents, comes the loss of one's childhood, and perhaps this is grieved for along with the loss of the unique individuals who were one's parents?

Threat to the relationship

When married couples engage in intense quarrelling, involving threats of abandonment and/or the discovery of infidelity, it is the relationship itself that is under threat, independent of the well-being of the partner or the self (Weiss, 1991). In many ways, divorce is as much a death as is the actual death of a spouse (Raphael, 1984); the end of the marital relationship may be grieved for in its own right. If the former spouse dies, there may be intense grief, especially if feelings about the divorce have not been properly resolved (Doka, 1986, cited in Hayslip & Panek, 1993). And if the deceased spouse was also the mother or father of your children, grief may be heightened, since you have lost the mate with whom you produced your offspring and with whom, presumably, you had intended to spend the rest of your life.

According to Ainsworth (1989), a sexual pair bond involves three basic behavioural systems, *reproductive*, *attachment* and *caregiving* (both to the partner and offspring). Although sexual attraction may be the most important component at the start of a relationship, those relationships which depend entirely on the sexual component are likely to be short-lived. As the relationship continues, the caregiving and attachment components are likely to become relatively more important and these will tend to sustain the bond even when sexual interest has waned.

Ainsworth also points out that the caregiving and attachment components may not always be symmetrical and reciprocal; one partner may do most of the giving and the other most of the taking. This resembles the parent–child relationship.

If members of a sexual pair bond are 'meant' to engage in a mutual 'give and take' (unlike the parent–young child pair, in which the parent is all-giving and the child all-taking), then another important difference is to do with the extent to which the attachment figure is seen as wiser and stronger and, therefore, able to be protective at times when the self seems inadequate. In the sexual pair bond, neither partner seems established as wiser and stronger, although each may now and again be seen in this way (Weiss, 1991). According to Hazan and Shaver (1987), romantic love is usually a 'two-way street', with both partners sometimes anxious and security-seeking and at other times the providers of security and care. Weiss (1991) also suggests that patients may often see their therapists or counsellors in this way, once again resembling the child's dependency on its parents. (This, in turn, is very similar to Freud's concept of *transference*; see Chapters 12 and 13.)

A development of the childhood attachment bond?

Despite the differences we have just noted between the attachments of children to their parents and adults to each other, 'the underlying dynamics may be surprisingly similar' (Bartholomew, 1993). Weiss (1991) notes three major respects in which they are similar.

1 As we noted earlier, the loss of an attachment figure, both in childhood and adulthood, produces a grief reaction. Separation protest, as a component of grief in adults, is similar to that of the child in its behavioural expression. The syndrome includes calling and crying, a determined and sometimes frantic search, persisting perceptual recall of the lost figure, restlessness, and eventual despair.

2 It seems that the emotional elements which have become associated with childhood attachment are expressed in adult attachments. In particular, there is evidence that children who lose confidence in their parents as attachment figures (perhaps because of divorce) are likely later on to have difficulties in pair-bonding, because of this distrust of their parents. No such effects are seen in their work relationships.

3 Pair-bonding and bonding (in Ainsworth's terms) to one's own children both appear only after parents have largely faded as attachment figures. This is consistent with the claim that adult attachment represents a later stage of the childhood attachment system.

Again, as we noted above, the child who is securely attached is able, most of the time, to take the attachment figure for granted; this reflects the trust the child has in him or her, *not* indifference. Similarly, as courtship continues between two adults, and the relationship becomes more reliable and stable, less energy need be given over to assuring the continuation of the attachment relationship. Instead, the secure base of the attachment can be taken for granted, freeing up effort and attention for achieving goals in the world outside the self (Weiss, 1991).

For most adults (especially men, in Western culture anyway), the major feature of their lives, other than their attachments and other affectional bonds, is their work. If a secure attachment with the mother(-figure) provides the young child with a safe base from which to explore and investigate unfamiliar surroundings, might work represent the adult equivalent of the child's explorations, and could it be similarly related to the security provided by the attachment figure?

According to Freud, the goal of psychotherapy is to allow the patient to love and to work (*Lieben und Arbeiten*). The themes of love and work are central to some of the most influential theories of psychological well-being, such as those of Erikson (1963), Maslow (1954) and Rogers (1961) (Hazan & Shaver, 1990; see Chapters 6 and 11). They are the key to a successful adult life (Bee, 1994).

There is evidence that adults who are satisfied with their work and their intimate relationships are also satisfied with their lives in general. Furthermore, love may be the more important of the two; Bee (1994) refers to studies which suggest that the single best predictor of overall life satisfaction in adults, of any age, is a person's reported happiness in marriage and other family relationships.

According to Hazan and Shaver (1990), work is the equivalent in the adult of the child's exploration: 'It is the major source of a sense of competence, just as is true of a child's exploration. And like the child's exploration, adult work is best accomplished when the adult has a safe emotional base from which to move outward into the world' (Bee, 1994). We shall return to the connection between work and attachment later.

'Romantic love conceptualized as an attachment process'

This is the title of an article by Hazan and Shaver, published in 1987, in which they reported the findings of a study which has come to be seen as breaking new ground and which has stimulated a growing body of research into adult love relationships from the perspective of attachment theory. As we noted earlier, Bowlby is one of the founders of attachment theory, and although prior to 1987 attachment processes were studied extensively – and almost exclusively – within parent–child relationships, Bowlby himself maintained that 'attachment behaviour is held to characterize human beings from the cradle to the grave' (1977).

Hazan and Shaver's purpose was (i) to explore the possibility that attachment theory offers a valuable perspective on adult romantic love, and (ii) to create a coherent framework for understanding love, loneliness and grief at different points in the life cycle. They argue that attachment theory can help to explain both healthy and unhealthy forms of love, encompassing both positive emotions (caring, intimacy and trust) and negative emotions (fear of intimacy, jealousy and emotional ups and downs). It also deals with separation and loss and helps to explain how loneliness and love are related.

The study was the first attempt to apply the three basic attachment styles, which had been identified by Ainsworth et al. (1978) in their study of twelve- to eighteen-month-old children using the 'strange situation', to adult–adult sexual/romantic relationships. These three styles, which are described in Table 9.1, represent the child's characteristic way of relating to the mother in an unfamiliar setting in which she departs and returns, and in which a stranger is also present; they also describe how the child's play and exploration are affected by her presence or absence.

When describing the three styles, Ainsworth et al. refer to the child's expectations regarding the mother's accessibility and responsiveness. This is similar to Bowlby's claim that infants and young children construct *inner working models* (internal representations or *mental models*, to use Hazan and Shaver's term) of themselves and their major social-interaction partners. These working models become integrated into the personality structure of the individual, thereby providing a prototype for later relationships and representing some of the most important sources of continuity between early and later feelings and behaviours.

Table 9.1 Classification of attachment styles based on the 'strange situation' (Ainsworth et al., 1978)

Classification	Percentage of sample	Description
Securely attached	70	Baby shows signs of missing mother on her departure, seeks proximity on her return, then returns to play. Associated with 'sensitivity to infant signals and communications'.
Anxious–avoidant	15	Baby shows no or few signs of missing the mother and actively ignores or avoids her on reunion. Associated with maternal insensitivity to baby's signals, and specifically with rejection of attachment behaviour.
Anxious-ambivalent	15	Baby is distressed and highly focused on the mother, but cannot be settled by mother on return, often expressing anger and seeking contact in quick succession and generally failing to return to play. Associated with maternal insensitivity and unpredictability of maternal responsiveness.

If what we acquire from our early attachment experiences is a set of fundamental expectations about romantic relationships, we would expect these expectations to have some influence over our initial choice of partner, as well as the course of the relationship; we bring with us, into our relationships, an inner working model which may be as influential as anything to do with the partner him/herself, or with the 'objective' nature of the relationship.

So what did Hazan and Shaver find?

The three attachment styles (based on observational studies of young children) had to be 'translated' in a way which would make them suitable for the study of adult attachments. This was done as shown in Table 9.2, where respondents to a 'Love Quiz' in a local newspaper were asked to indicate which of three descriptions best applied to their feelings about romantic relationships. They were also asked to complete a simple adjective checklist which described their childhood relationships with their parents. The correlation between the attachment style which they chose as best describing their feelings and their recollections of the kind of parenting they received, mirrors remarkably closely the findings of Ainsworth et al. and are shown in Table 9.3.

Table 9.2   Responses to the question 'Which of the following best describes your feelings?' in Hazan and Shaver's (1987) study

Classification	Percentage of respondents	Response
Secure	56	I find it relatively easy to get close to others and am comfortable depending on them and having them depend on me. I don't often worry about being abandoned or about someone getting too close to me.
Anxious– avoidant	23–25	I am somewhat uncomfortable being close to others; I find it difficult to trust them completely, difficult to allow myself to depend on them. I am nervous when anyone gets too close, and often, love partners want me to be more intimate than I feel comfortable being.
Anxious– ambivalent	19–20	I find that others are reluctant to get as close as I would like. I often worry that my partner doesn't really love me or won't want to stay with me. I want to merge completely with another person, and this desire sometimes scares people away.

Table 9.3   Correlation between attachment style and type of parenting of respondents in Hazan and Shaver's (1987) study

Attachment style	Type of parenting
Security attached	Readily available, attentive, responsive
Anxious–avoidant	Unresponsive, rejecting, inattentive
Anxious–ambivalent	Anxious Fussy, out of step with child's needs Only available/responsive *some* of the time

Hazan and Shaver in fact tested two separate samples as part of the same 1987 study. Sample 1 comprised two hundred and five men and four hundred and fifteen women, aged between fourteen and eighty-two (mean age, thirty-six), ninety-one per cent describing themselves as 'primarily heterosexual'. At the time of the survey, forty-two per cent were married, twenty-eight per cent were divorced or widowed, nine per cent were 'living with a lover' and thirty-one per cent were dating. (Some checked more than one category.)

Sample 2 was a non-self-selected sample of one hundred and eight undergraduate students, comprising thirty-eight men and seventy women, with a mean age of eighteen, who completed the questionnaire as a class exercise. They answered additional items which focused more on the 'self' side of the mental model (as opposed to the partner), as well as additional items measuring loneliness.

Hazan and Shaver based their predictions on Ainsworth's original studies, and on later studies involving young children, as summarized by Campos et al. (1983) (sixty-two per cent securely attached, twenty-three per cent anxious–avoidant, and fifteen per cent anxious–ambivalent). They predicted that about sixty per cent of adults would classify themselves as secure, with the other two types being fairly evenly split (but a few more anxious–avoidant). The results went very much as expected: in both samples, fifty-six per cent were secure, twenty-five and twenty-three per cent were anxious–avoidant (Samples 1 and 2 respectively), and for anxious–ambivalent, the figures were nineteen and twenty per cent respectively. When asked to describe the 'most important love relationship you have ever had, why you got involved in it, and why it turned out the way it did . . . It may be a past or a current relationship, but choose only the most important one', both samples produced very similar responses. Those classified as secure described this special relationship as especially happy, friendly and trusting, being able to accept and support their partner despite his or her faults. Their relationships also tended to last longer and, if married, were less likely to end in divorce.

Questions designed to measure the internal working model of self and relationships were answered in line with the prediction only in the case of Sample 1, whose items were more focused on the partner or relationship than on the self.

The secure types expressed belief in lasting love. Even though romantic feelings wax and wane, only sometimes reaching the intensity experienced at the start of the relationship, genuine love is enduring. They also generally find others trustworthy and have confidence in their self as likeable.

The anxious–avoidant types are much more doubtful about the existence or durability of romantic love; the kind of head-over-heels love which is portrayed in fiction doesn't happen in real life and it is rare to find a person you can really fall in love with. They also maintain that they don't need a love partner in order to be happy.

The anxious–ambivalent types fall in love easily and often, but they rarely find what they would call true love. They also express more self-doubts (compared with both the other types), but compared with the avoidants, they do not repress or try to hide their feelings of insecurity.

Finally, the two insecure types, compared with the secure, were found to be the most vulnerable to loneliness, but the anxious–ambivalent (in

Sample 2) obtained the highest scores of all. Hazan and Shaver believe that this reflects the greater defensiveness of the avoidants (so that they only appear to be less lonely etc.), together with the yearning of the anxious–ambivalent types for a love relationship in which they can merge with their partner who shares their intense passion, something which they are extremely unlikely to find.

While noting a number of limitations of their study, both methodological and theoretical, they conclude that the results overall provide encouraging support for an attachment perspective on romantic love. One such note of caution is to do with the continuity between early childhood and adult experience. They say that it would be overly pessimistic – from the point of view of the insecurely attached person, at least – if continuity were the rule rather than the exception. While correlations between parent variables and current attachment style were statistically significant, they were not strong. Also, they were higher for Sample 2 who were much younger, suggesting that continuity decreases as one gets further into adulthood. The average person participates in several important friendships and love relationships which provide opportunities for revising internal working models of self and others.

Support for this more optimistic view comes from a study by Main et al. (1985). Despite an impressive association between adults' attachment history and the attachment styles of their own young children, some parents had freed themselves from the chain of cross-generational continuity; some adults, who reported being insecure in their relationships with their parents, managed to produce children who were securely attached at one and six years of age. They had mentally worked through their unpleasant experiences with their parents and now had mental models of relationships which are more typical of secure types (Hazan and Shaver, 1987).

Adult attachment research since 1987

Hazan and Shaver's findings have been replicated and extended in several studies. According to Bartholomew (1993), their method of operationalizing adult attachment patterns as self-report measures has stimulated a thriving new area of research, such as attachment patterns amongst dating couples, interactive behaviours of couples in the laboratory, the sociocognitive processes associated with attachment patterns, the process of relinquishing parents as attachment figures, attachment patterns and work satisfaction, and attachment styles and religious beliefs and fear of death.

Bartholomew herself has expanded the model of adult attachment patterns provided in the 1987 study by Hazan and Shaver. Based on a series of intensive interviews with young adults about their close relationships (1990, cited in Bartholomew, 1993), she distinguished between two types of *patterns of avoidance* in adults: (i) *fearful avoidant*, whose desire for social contact is inhibited by fears of rejection, and (ii) *dismissive avoidant*, who defensively deny the need or desire for intimate contact. According to Bartholomew, this distinction reflects different *models of the self*: people who fearfully avoid intimacy view themselves as undeserving of the love and support of others, while those who dismiss intimacy possess a positive model of the self that minimizes the subjective awareness of distress and social needs. Only the former (fearful avoidant) corresponds to Hazan and Shaver's avoidant style.

Bartholomew distinguishes between two other styles, this time reflecting different *models of (or orientation towards) others*, namely (i) *preoccupied*, in which people view themselves negatively but possess a positive model of others that motivates them to strive to find self-validation and fulfilment through their intimate relationships, and (ii) *secure*, in which people possess positive models of both themselves and others and enjoy both personal autonomy and satisfying intimate relationships. This produces a four-way classification, as shown in Table 9.4.

To take the secure style to explain what the table means, a positive model of self is defined in terms of low dependence on others for self-esteem and fulfilment, while a positive model of the other is defined as low avoidance of intimacy etc. So, at one extreme, the secure type (positive models of self and others) has the 'best of both worlds', while at the other, the fearful avoidant (negative models of self and others) needs intimacy for self-esteem but cannot achieve it through fear (the 'worst of both worlds', perhaps?).

Table 9.4 Four category model of adult attachment from Bartholomew, K. (1993)

Model of other (Avoidance)	Model of self (Dependence)	
	Positive (Low)	**Negative** (High)
Positive (Low)	**Secure,** comfortable with intimacy and autonomy	**Preoccupied** Preoccupied with relationships
Negative (High)	**Dismissing** Dismissing of intimacy	**Fearful** Fearful of intimacy

According to Collins and Read (1990), when both members of dating couples are asked about their internal models, the securely attached tend to choose other securely attached partners, but the anxiously attached are no more likely to choose one another than one of the other types.

The least happy among young dating couples seem to be (i) any combination involving an anxiously attached woman (perhaps because they tend to be clingy and jealous, thereby producing the unstable, unhappy relationship that she expects) and (ii) any combination involving an avoidant man (again, because his internal model may result in fulfilment of the expectation that relationships have little to offer) (Bee, 1994).

Attachment, exploration and work

As mentioned previously, the child's exploration, using the safe base of the mother, can be seen as having its adult counterpart in work. According to Bowlby, to learn about and become competent at interacting with the physical and social environment, one must explore. But exploration can be tiring and even dangerous, so it is desirable to have a source of protection, a haven of safety, available if needed. According to attachment theory, while both the tendency to form an attachment and the tendency to explore the environment are innate, attachment needs are primary – they must be met before exploration can proceed normally (Hazan and Shaver, 1990).

Adult work activity can be seen as functionally parallel to the young child's exploration: they both represent a major source of actual and perceived competence. Based on these features of attachment theory, as well as on their own previous research, Hazan and Shaver (1990) derived and tested three hypotheses concerning the relationship between attachment style and orientation towards work, using a questionnaire design.

1 In line with Hypothesis 1, secure respondents approach their work with the confidence associated with secure attachments. They enjoy work activity and are relatively free of fears of failure. And, although they value work, they tend to value relationships more and generally do not allow work to interfere with those relationships. They do not, typically, use work to satisfy unmet needs for love, nor do they use work to avoid social interaction.

2 In line with Hypothesis 2, anxious–ambivalent respondents reported that love concerns often interfere with work performance and that they often fear rejection for poor performance. They also reported a tendency to ease up after receiving praise, which may indicate that their main motivation at work is to gain respect and admiration from others. They have the lowest average income of the three groups, even when differences in education are controlled.

3 Consistent with Hypothesis 3, avoidant respondents use work activity to avoid social interaction. They reported that work interferes with having friends and having a social life. While their average income is equal to

that of the secure group, they are less satisfied with their jobs; they are also the least likely to take enjoyable holidays.

Secure attachment was also associated with greater overall well-being. Relative to the two insecure groups, the secure respondents report less loneliness and depression, anxiety or irritability, as well as fewer colds or flu.

As with their original study, Hazan and Shaver are well aware of the limitations of their research, among them the very conceptualization of work as exploration. Although work is probably the major form of exploratory behaviour in adulthood, it is far from being the only form. Also, attachment type (in this and the earlier study) and orientation to work were treated more as traits than as products of unique person–situation interactions (see Chapter 4). There are more objective features of the work environment, such as noise levels, power hierarchies, promotion prospects and so on, which also affect people's attitudes towards work and their satisfaction with it.

However, despite these and other limitations, Hazan and Shaver's findings suggest that one's approach to work is deeply affected by the strengths or deficiencies of one's internal model of attachments and relationships in general (Bee, 1994): 'Scientists often treat love and work as two separate realms, but being deeply social creatures, humans cannot easily separate the two . . . Attachment theory offers a way of explaining why love and work are so closely intertwined' (Hazan & Shaver, 1990).

Attachment, separation and loss

Earlier in the chapter, we drew attention to the belief that, while attachment to the parents is retained throughout our adult lives, it is necessary for us to transfer our major attachments away from our parents to our partner in a sexual pair bond. Only such a major shift in our emotional ties will allow us to achieve psychological adulthood which is necessary if we are to become attachment figures for our children in our turn.

While *detachment* is the essential function of (secure) attachment (Rutter, 1981) – that is, the young child gradually learns to tolerate greater and longer-lasting physical separations from the mother – the most crucial time in our life for achieving the separation from parents is during adolescence. Leaving home is more than just setting up a separate place to live; it also involves a highly significant psychological emancipation process, whereby the young person distances him/herself emotionally from the parents to at least some degree (Hazan and Shaver, 1991, cited in Bee, 1994).

Similarly, if children are eventually to form their own households, their bonds of attachment to the parents must become attenuated and eventually end. Otherwise, independent living would be emotionally troubling: 'The relinquishing of attachment to parents appears to be of central importance among the individuation-achieving processes of late adolescence and early adulthood' (Weiss, 1986, quoted in Bee, 1994).

Some writers take the view that this cutting of the emotional tie to the parents must be total if the adolescent is to achieve emotional independence (see, for example, Blos's 1967 theory of adolescence as a *second individuation process*). However, as we noted earlier, adult grief reactions to the death of our parents are a clear indication that those ties are never severed once and for all. Yet it is clearly difficult trying to make the emotional break while at the same time remaining 'engaged' as a son or daughter, and this may explain why the young person so often appears to be rejecting the parents. Perhaps a feature of maturity is the ability to balance the need for separateness, on the one hand, and the need for attachment, on the other, without having to adopt extreme behavioural or emotional strategies.

Agoraphobia is a common mental disorder, affecting between one and six per cent of the adult population (Liotti, 1991). Such patients seem to have lost the ability to tolerate temporary and explainable separations from attachment figures. They typically tend to avoid staying alone, either in public places or in their own home. In moderately severe cases, they will stay on their own at home only when a trusted family member can be called back easily; in more severe cases, only having a familiar person within immediate reach keeps their anxiety in check. They are usually distressed when they find themselves in daily situations which, while objectively safe, make escape to a familiar place difficult or impossible, such as joining a queue, being in a traffic jam, in the hairdresser's chair, on a motorway and so on.

While any attempt to explain the syndrome in terms of attachment theory would focus on these clinical features, a more subtle feature is that the patient finds it difficult to attribute meaning to any emotions related to the threatened separation from a significant other. In order to properly understand these features, it is necessary to understand (i) the nature of the patient's interpersonal relationships at the time the symptoms first appeared, and (ii) how the patient accounts for his or her symptoms (Liotti, 1991).

As far as the patient's relationships are concerned, it is a widely shared belief among psychotherapists and researchers that the onset of agoraphobia may be related to life events (*psychosocial transitions*; Parkes, 1993) which imply changes or expected changes in the patient's network of affectional bonds. According to Wolpe (1976, cited in Liotti, 1991), for example, the commonest antecedent in his patients of their first fear responses to brief situations of physical loneliness was the presence of unfulfilled fantasies of liberation from an unhappy marriage. These fantasies remained unfulfilled precisely because they evoked such great fear of loneliness. Other interpersonal problems include threats of loss or separation from parents or spouse, marital quarrels, and perceived rejection from a loved one. Liotti (1991) believes that these are not only linked in time to the onset of panic attacks and agoraphobic avoidance behaviour, but are very likely the *cause*.

Regarding patients' accounts for their symptoms, many do not acknowledge the possibility of a link between such (potential) changes in their life and the appearance of their symptoms. They insist that their distress is due to something totally unrelated to their interpersonal life, typically to an impending illness, either physical or mental – that is, a process which is totally alien to their experience of the self. A common feature of every agoraphobic patient is a blindness to the meaning of a certain class of one's own emotions, so that, in a sense, they lose their psychological status and are transformed into the symptoms of a disease (Liotti, 1991).

Clearly, in terms of attachment theory, the agoraphobic patient is reacting in an extreme way to the loss, or threatened loss, of his or her safe base. Although the patient may lack insight into the nature and cause of their symptoms (thereby making a *mis-attribution*; see Chapter 2), the symptoms may nevertheless throw light upon the importance of attachment figures throughout our lives.

Studies of psychosocial transitions that commonly precede the onset of mental illness suggest that the most dangerous life changes are those that (i) require people to undertake a major revision of their assumptive world ('everything that we assume to be true on the basis of our previous experience . . . the internal model of the world that we are constantly matching against incoming sensory data in order to orient ourselves, recognize what is happening, and plan our behaviour accordingly'; Parkes, 1993); (ii) have lasting implications; and (iii) take place over a relatively short period of time, so that there is little time for preparation (Parkes, 1993).

There is no doubt that the loss of an attachment figure, whether through death, divorce, or the natural and necessary process of growing up and having to separate from childhood ties, is a painful process that invalidates assumptions which penetrate many aspects of our life. Adjusting to that loss ('grief work') involves revising our habitual ways of thinking, feeling and acting in order to restore some degree of confidence in our internal world, whether as a widow(er), divorcee, or simply an adult.

Summary

- While the *primary* use of the term 'attachment' is related to other people, a *secondary* use relates to our 'ties' to animals, physical objects etc.
- The common factor in all these attachments may be their importance to our *self-concept*, which would explain why *loss* requires us to adjust, to redefine our self-concept, especially the loss

of the irreplaceable people in our lives.

- An attachment is an *affectional bond*. As with other affectional bonds, there is a desire to remain close to the attachment figure, but a unique feature is that attachment figures provide a *safe/secure base* for approaching the unfamiliar.
- In Ainsworth's 'strange situation', *securely attached* one-year-olds play quite happily in an unfamiliar play room, in the presence of a stranger, provided the mother is present. Once she leaves, the child is distressed and can only be comforted when she returns, after which play is resumed. The mother is *largely ignored*, indicating the security that her presence provides.
- The *insecure/anxious* child largely ignores the mother because of indifference towards her; the child's play and general behaviour are little affected whether she is present or not.
- Adults also take the attachment figure for granted, but even brief separations produce *separation distress*; death of a partner results in deep, persisting grief, with separation protest as a major component.
- One feature of separation protest is a sense of hopelessness and fear.
- Attachments are vital for our emotional security; their loss produces grief.
- According to *attachment theory* (Ainsworth, Bowlby), attachment behaviour occurs throughout life, and early attachment patterns will affect later, adult attachments.
- While attachments are affectional bonds, not all affectional bonds are attachments; children are *attached* to their parents, whereas mothers have *bonds* with their children.
- Affectional bonds between sexual partners (*sexual pair bonds*) have many features in common with children's attachments to parents, and elderly parents, as they become more emotionally and materially dependent, could be said to develop attachments to their (adult) children.
- In all attachments, contact with the attachment figure may be sought if there is threat to *the self, the attachment figure*, or *the relationship*.
- Attachment behaviours become more evident in children who are unwell/afraid, and elderly adults often need greater emotional support.
- The illness of an attachment figure causes distress, and adults will still grieve for the loss of their parents, even though they are no longer emotionally dependent on them.
- Death of one's parents makes our own death seem closer, as well as finally ending our own childhood.
- Divorce is as much a death as the actual death of a spouse, and the end of the marital relationship may be grieved for in its own right, especially if there are children from the marriage.

- A sexual pair bond involves three basic behavioural systems: *reproductive*, *attachment*, and *caregiving*. Unlike in the parent–child pair, there should be mutual 'give and take', with neither partner being predominantly wiser, stronger or more giving than the other.
- Three major ways in which adult–adult attachments are similar to adult–child attachments are: (i) separation protest may be provoked by the loss of an attachment figure, (ii) loss of confidence in parents as attachment figures is likely to affect later pair-bonding (but not work relationships), (iii) pair-bonding and bonding to one's own children both appear only after parents have faded as attachment figures.
- Work represents a major feature in the life of most adults (especially men). Freud saw psychotherapy as trying to help the patient to love and work, themes which are central to theories of psychological well-being, such as Erikson's, Maslow's and Rogers'.
- Work can be seen as the adult equivalent to exploration in the child, the major source of a sense of competence; it is best achieved when the adult (like the child in its exploration) has a safe emotional base.
- Hazan and Shaver applied the three *attachment styles* (*securely attached, anxious–avoidant, anxious–ambivalent*), first identified by Ainsworth et al. in their study of twelve- to eighteen-month-old children, to adults' sexual/romantic relationships.
- These attachment styles are related to the child's expectations regarding the mother's accessibility and responsiveness (Ainsworth). Similarly, children construct *inner working models* (Bowlby) or *mental models* (Hazan & Shaver) of themselves and their major attachment figures, which become integrated into their personality.
- Our inner working models are taken into our subsequent romantic relationships and influence their course.
- In Hazan and Shaver's study of adults, the correlation between (i) the attachment style which they chose as best describing their feelings about their adult relationships and (ii) their recollections of the kind of parenting they received, is remarkably similar to Ainsworth's findings for young children.
- Those classified as *secure* described their most important love relationship as happy, friendly and trusting; their relationships tended to last longer, and, if married, were less likely to end in divorce. They also see genuine love as enduring.
- *Anxious–avoidant* types are much more doubtful about the existence or durability of romantic love and say that they don't need a love partner to be happy.
- *Anxious–ambivalent* types fall in love easily but rarely find 'true love'; they don't try to hide their feelings of insecurity.
- The continuity between current attachment style and the kind of

parenting received as a child may decrease as one progresses into adulthood. Most adults have opportunities for revising their internal working models of themselves and others.

- Bartholomew distinguishes between two *patterns of avoidance*: (i) *fearful avoidant* and (ii) *dismissive avoidant*; this reflects *negative* and *positive* models of the self respectively. Another distinction is between (i) *preoccupied* and (ii) *secure* models of orientation towards others.
- Securely attached individuals tend to choose as partners other securely attached individuals. The least happy and stable combinations involve an anxiously attached woman or an avoidant man.
- Secure respondents approach their work confidently and, although they value and enjoy it, relationships are more important and work is not allowed to interfere with them.
- Anxious–ambivalent respondents often fear rejection for poor work performance and their main motivation for working seems to be to gain the respect of others.
- Avoidant respondents use work to avoid social interaction but complain that that work interferes with having a social life.
- One's approach to work seems to be deeply affected by the strengths/deficiences of one's internal model of attachments.
- We have to transfer our primary attachment from our parents to our sexual partner in order to achieve psychological adulthood. While detachment is achieved in early childhood, the crucial time for achieving emotional separation from parents is during adolescence (e.g. Blos's *second individuation process*).
- In *agoraphobia*, the patient seems to have lost the ability to tolerate temporary and explainable separations from attachment figures. A more subtle symptom is the difficulty in attributing meaning to any emotions related to threatened separations.
- The onset of agoraphobia is commonly linked to *psychosocial transitions*, such as involvement in marital quarrels, and threats of separation by one's spouse.
- The most dangerous (as far as mental illness is concerned) life changes are those that (i) require a major revision of our *assumptive world*, (ii) have lasting implications, and (iii) allow little time for preparation.

Suggestions for further reading

Ainsworth, M.D.S. (1989) Attachments beyond Infancy, *American Psychologist*, 44(4), 709–16.

Hazan, C. & Shaver, P. (1982) Romantic love conceptualized as an attachment process, *Journal of Personality & Social Psychology*, 52(3), 511–24.

Holmes, J. (1993) *John Bowlby and Attachment Theory*, London: Routledge.
Parkes, C.M., Stevenson-Hinde, J. & Marrin, P. (Eds) (1991) *Attachment across the Life Cycle*, London: Routledge.

Psychology and ethics

Ethical questions: do psychologists need to ask them?

Perhaps the most general question that we can ask about ethics is: Why do ethical issues arise at all? Answers to this question might include the following:

1 Human beings and animals have feelings and sensations – they are capable of experiencing pain, fear and so on (that is, they are *sentient*, living things) and so are capable of reacting with pain and fear to certain kinds of aversive (painful) stimulation.

2 In addition, people are *thinking* beings; this means that situations which are not literally, or physically, painful or dangerous may still be experienced as threatening, stressful, offensive, belittling, embarrassing, or may evoke feelings of guilt, self-doubt, inadequacy or incompetence.

3 Any attempt on the part of one person to induce any of the above feelings or sensations in another person (or animal), or the inducement of any of these feelings or sensations in one person (or animal) as a result of the neglect or negligence of another, is usually condemned as immoral or morally unacceptable.

These points may seem perfectly reasonable, and perhaps fairly 'obvious' (at least once they are pointed out), and it may seem fairly clear in what ways they are relevant to psychology. But we should still ask: Why do ethical issues arise for psychologists? Again, answers to this question might include the following:

1 Psychologists study human beings and animals.

2 Psychologists often subject the human beings and animals they study – deliberately or otherwise – to situations and stimulation which induce pain, embarrassment or other unpleasant sensations or feelings.

3 Just as every psychology experiment is primarily a social situation (Orne, 1962; see Chapter 11, on science), so it could be argued that every psychological investigation may be thought of as an ethical situation (Gross, 1992). In other words, whenever one person (the researcher) deliberately creates a situation intended for the investigation of the

behaviour and/or experience of another person (the 'subject' or participant), there is always the possibility that the person being studied will experience one or more of the feelings and sensations identified above. This may be what the researcher is expecting to happen (it may be a crucial feature of the study), or it may genuinely not be anticipated by the researcher, who is as surprised as everyone else by how the participants respond. But while we normally associate 'deliberately created situations' with laboratory studies (whether experimental or not), ethical issues are not confined to such settings. Indeed, naturalistic studies face ethical problems of their own, despite the fact that the researcher is not creating a situation into which other people are brought so that he or she may study their behaviour.

Perhaps the common feature linking the laboratory and naturalistic settings which makes them both 'ethical' situations is the difference in the *power* associated with the roles of researcher and researched. If this is true in the case of humans studying other humans, how much more true is it in the case of humans studying animals! (Again, we shall return to this issue later in the chapter.)

Psychologists as investigators and as practitioners

So far, we have been discussing ethics in relation to the psychologist's role as *scientist* or *investigator* – as someone who wishes to find out more about human behaviour and experience. Sometimes this is done for its own sake (because of its intrinsic interest – *pure research*), sometimes as part of an attempt to solve a practical problem (*applied research*).

While there is no hard-and-fast distinction between these two kinds of research, the distinction between psychologists as scientists/investigators and as *practitioners* is important as far as understanding ethical issues is concerned. Again, while many psychologists are both researchers and practitioners, the difference in these two roles needs to be understood when ethics is being discussed.

The practitioner role refers to the work of clinical, educational and industrial/occupational psychologists, who work in applied, naturalistic settings, such as psychiatric hospitals, schools and commercial organizations respectively.

While all psychologists have responsibilities and obligations towards those they 'work' with, which are common to both the scientist and practitioner roles, there are also important differences in these responsibilities and obligations which are related to the different roles. This is reflected in the various codes of conduct and ethical guidelines which are published by the major professional bodies for psychologists – the British Psychological Society (BPS) and the American Psychological Association (APA).

As shown in Figure 10.1, the *Code of Conduct for Psychologists* (BPS, 1983) applies to both of the main areas of research and practice, while there are additional documents designed for the two areas separately. The *Ethical Principles for Conducting Research with Human Participants* (BPS, 1990, 1993) and the *Guidelines for the Use of Animals in Research* (BPS and Committee of the Experimental Psychological Society, 1985) clearly cover the former, while, for example, the *Guidelines for the Professional Practice of Clinical Psychology* (BPS, 1983) apply to the latter. Clinical psychologists are by far the most numerous single group of psychologists: more than one third of all psychologists classify themselves as clinical and a further ten per cent or so call themselves 'counselling psychologists', the latter tending to work with younger clients in colleges and universities, rather than in psychiatric hospitals (and other mental health facilities) with a much greater age-range of adults.

What clinical and counselling psychologists have in common is responsibility for people with psychological problems – that is, those who are seeking professional help with a whole range of mental disorders. In this respect, they clearly have much in common, both in terms of therapeutic

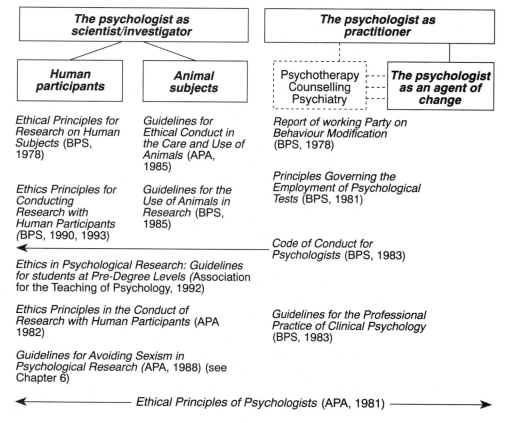

Figure 10.1   Major codes of conduct/ethical guidelines published by the British Psychological Society (BPS) and American Psychological Association (APA) (Adapted from Gross, 1992)

methods and techniques used, and ethically, with psychotherapists. While psychologists are trained largely to use *behaviour therapy*, based on the principles of learning theory, counselling psychologists (and other trained counsellors) mainly use methods based on Rogers' *client-centred therapy*, and psychotherapists (who may have trained initially as psychiatrists, social workers, or even psychologists, but who have all undergone special psychotherapy training, which includes their own psychotherapy) use *psychodynamic* techniques derived from Freud's *psychoanalytic theory* and therapy.

The point here is that, regardless of the particular training the practitioner has received and the particular therapeutic techniques he or she uses, the nature of the relationship between 'helper' and 'helped' is very different, in certain respects, from that between researcher and researched. In particular, the helper is attempting to change something, presumably for the benefit of the helped, while the researcher is 'merely' trying to find out (more) about what the researched is already like. This changes the nature of the respective situations from an ethical point of view.

In the remainder of this chapter, we shall explore some of the major ethical issues and debates which take place in relation to psychologists as both researchers and as practitioners.

Research with human participants

Guidelines such as the *Ethical Principles for Conducting Research with Human Participants* are intended, primarily, to protect the 'rights and dignity' of those who participate in psychological research, and the testing of human participants in research is referred to as a 'privilege', which will be retained only if 'all members of the psychological profession abide by the principles' set out in the document (BPS, 1993). Violation of the principles could also form a basis of disciplinary action, and the Introduction to the *Ethical Principles* points out that 'In recent years, there has been an increase in legal actions by members of the general public against professionals for alleged misconduct. Researchers must recognise the possibility of such legal action if they infringe the rights and dignity of participants in their research' (paragraph 1.4).

As a secondary aim, therefore, the *Ethical Principles* are designed to protect psychologists themselves, but this protection only becomes necessary if the primary aim is not fulfilled.

The document lists nine major principles which are meant to be followed by anyone engaged in psychological research – all professional psychologists, whether members of the BPS or not, research assistants, and all students, from GCSE, through A level and undergraduate, up to postgraduate. These principles concern the following:

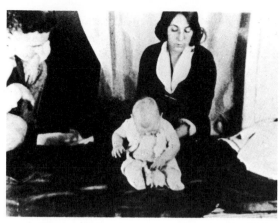

Figure 10.2 A very rare photograph of John Watson and Rosalie Rayner during the conditioning of Little Albert

- Consent
- Deception
- Debriefing
- Withdrawal from the investigation
- Confidentiality
- Protection of participants
- Observational research
- Giving advice
- Colleagues

While these are listed separately, many are overlapping and interrelated and they will not be discussed here in turn, or under exactly these headings.

What are participants being protected from?

We noted at the beginning of the chapter that people are sentient and thinking creatures, which means that they are capable of experiencing a wide range of negative emotions in response to situations that psychologists may create as part of their research. This danger is increased when we consider the difference in the power inherent in the roles of researcher and researched (also noted above).

From a feminist perspective (see Chapter 6), researchers should try to reverse the traditional, orthodox, masculine-dominated approach, whereby the experimenter, who is dominant and has superior status and power, manipulates and controls the experimental situation to which the subordinate subject reacts (see, for example, Paludi, 1992). This difference in status and power creates a social and emotional distance between them; the 'subject' is, in fact, regarded and treated more as 'object', which is what is required from the positivistic, behaviouristic paradigm (Heather, 1976; Unger, 1984).

> To speak of people as 'males' and 'females', to write of 'running subjects in an experiment' and so on is morally troublesome. It denigrates the men and women who give up their time to assist one in one's studies. It displays a contempt for them as people that I find quite unacceptable. I find it deeply disturbing that students are encouraged to adopt this scientific rhetoric.
>
> (Harré, 1993)

By contrast, feminist research requires the researcher to become actively involved in the research process, taking the perspective of the participants: they are not detached investigators but become an integral part of the whole process.

Similarly, Eysenck (1994) argues that the human participant is in a rather vulnerable and exploitable position. He quotes Kelman (1972), who believes that 'most ethical problems arising in social research can be traced to the subject's power deficiency'. As well as possessing knowledge and expertise relating to the experimental situation which is not shared with the participant, the experimenter is on 'home ground' (the laboratory), and the situation is under his or her control.

Deception, consent and informed consent

This 'being in charge' is potentially most detrimental to participants when what they believe is going on in the experimental situation (which may be a study of perceptual judgement, as in Asch's (1951) experiment, or a study of the effects of punishment on learning, as in Milgram's 1963 experiment) is not what is actually going on, as defined by the experimenter (conformity and obedience respectively). Since it is the experimenter who is manipulating the situation, the participant cannot know that he or she is being deceived: this is a feature of the greater power of the experimenter.

The key ethical question here is: Can failure to inform the participant of the true purpose of the experiment ever be justified? Can the end (what the experimenter is hoping to find out) justify the means (the use of deception)? If informed consent involves the participant knowing everything that the experimenter knows about the experiment, and if giving informed consent (together with the right to withdraw from the experiment once it has begun) represents some kind of protection against powerlessness and vulnerability, should we simply condemn all deception and argue that it is always, and by its very nature, unacceptable?

According to Milgram (1992), many regard this as the cornerstone of ethical practice in human experimentation. It is currently estimated that more than half the research published in social psychology journals involves some sort of misinformation or lack of disclosure, and although the 'topic' has received less attention in recent years (compared with the 1960s), the debate still goes on (Krupat & Garonzik, 1994).

Milgram cites Kelman (1974) who identifies two quite different reasons for not fully informing the participant.

1 The experimenter believes that if the participant knew what the experiment was like, he or she might refuse to participate (the *motivational* reason). Milgram believes that 'Misinforming people to gain their participation appears a serious violation of the individual's rights, and cannot routinely constitute an ethical basis for subject recruitement' (Milgram, 1992).

2 More typically, many social psychology experiments cannot be carried out unless the participant is ignorant of the true purpose of the experiment. Milgram calls this the *epistemological* reason and it is the psychologist's equivalent to what the author of a murder mystery does by

not revealing the culprit until the very end: to do so would undermine the psychological effect of the reading experience! But is this sufficient justification? While readers of murder mysteries expect not to find out 'who dunnit' until the very end (indeed this is a major part of the appeal of such literature), people who participate in psychology experiments do not expect to be deceived, and if they did, they presumably would not agree to participate!

But are things as cut and dried as this? What if we found that, despite expecting to be deceived, people still volunteered, or that, not expecting to be deceived, they say that the deception did not particularly bother them? Would this change the ethical 'status' of deception? A number of points need to be made in response to this question.

1 Mannucci (1977, cited by Milgram, 1992) asked one hundred and ninety-two lay people about ethical aspects of psychology experiments. They regarded deception as a relatively minor issue, and were far more concerned about the quality of the experience they would undergo as participants.

2 Most of the actual participants who were deceived in Asch's conformity experiments were very enthusiastic and expressed their admiration for the elegance and significance of the experimental procedure (Milgram, 1992).

3 In defence of his own obedience experiments, Milgram (1974) reports that, as part of the very thorough debriefing of his participants, they all received a comprehensive report when all the experiments were over, detailing the procedure and the results, as well as a follow-up questionnaire concerning their participation. Of the ninety-two per cent who returned the questionnaires (an unusually high response rate), almost eighty-four per cent said they were glad or very glad to have participated, while less than two per cent said they were sorry or very sorry. Eighty per cent said they felt that more experiments of this kind should be carried out and seventy-four per cent said they had learned something of personal importance.

More specifically, the 'technical illusions' (his preferred term for 'deception') are justified for one reason only: they are in the end accepted and endorsed by those who are exposed to them: 'The central moral justification for allowing a procedure of the sort used in my experiment is that it is judged acceptable by those who have taken part in it. Moreover, it was the salience of this fact throughout that constituted the chief moral warrant for the continuation of the experiments.'

He goes on to say that any criticism of the experiment (or any other, for that matter) which does not take account of the tolerant reactions of the participants is hollow. 'Again, the participant, rather than the external critic, must be the ultimate source of judgement' (Milgram, 1974).

4 In a review of several studies focusing on the ethical acceptability of deception experiments, Christensen (1988, cited in Krupat & Garonzik,

1994) reports that, as long as deception is not extreme, participants don't seem to mind. He suggests that the widespread use of mild forms of deception is justified, firstly because apparently no one is harmed, and secondly, because there seem to be few, if any, acceptable alternatives.

5 Krupat and Garonzik (1994) found that, among two hundred and fifty-five university psychology students, those who had had at least one experience of being deceived while participating in some psychological research, compared with those who had not been deceived, were significantly more likely to expect to be deceived again. But the experience of being deceived does not have a significant impact on the students' evaluation of other aspects of participation, such as enjoyment and interest, and consistent with the findings of Christensen and Mannucci, previously deceived participants were not terribly upset at the prospect of being deceived again. Indeed, those who had been deceived at least once, said they would be less upset at being lied to or misled again: 'It almost seems that these people are accepting deception as par for the course and, therefore, not worthy of becoming upset. To the extent that the ethical issue revolves around subjects' negative reactions to deception, our findings are consistent with that of prior research' (Krupat & Garonzik, 1994).

However, there are some very important methodological implications of deception that they discuss (and which are discussed in the chapter on science, Chapter 11).

6 Milgram (1992) acknowledges that the use of 'technical illusons' (a morally neutral term which he prefers to the morally biased or 'loaded' term 'deception') poses ethical dilemmas for the researcher. By definition, the use of such illusions means that participants cannot give their informed consent, and he asks whether they can ever be justified. Clearly, he says, they should never be used unless they are 'indispensable to the conduct of an inquiry', and honesty and openness are the only desirable bases of transactions with people in whatever context.

But does the judgement that they are indispensable justify their use? In other words, while believing that they are crucial may be a necessary reason for using them, is it a sufficient reason? Milgram gives examples of professions in which there exist exemptions from general moral principles, without which the profession could not function. For example, male gynaecologists and obstetricians are allowed to examine the genitals of female strangers, because they are their patients. Similarly, a lawyer may know that the client has committed a murder but is obligated not to tell the authorities based on the principle of 'privileged communication'. This is a very important issue in relation to psychologists as practitioners which is discussed later in the chapter.

In the case of gynaecology and the law, the underlying justification for 'suspending' more generally accepted moral principles ('it is wrong to examine the genitals of strange women' and 'If you know that someone has committed a serious crime, you should tell the police') is that, in the long run, society as a whole will benefit (women need gynaecologists, and people need lawyers whom they can trust implicitly). However, in the case of gynaecology and the law, it is not only 'society in general' that is benefiting, but also the individual patient or client. But in the case of the psychology experiment, the individual participant clearly is not the beneficiary. So how do we resolve this moral dilemma?

The ethical status of psychological research

Any research that psychologists do is carried out within a whole range of constraints – methodological, ethical, financial, social, cultural and political. As the discussion of feminist and cross-cultural psychology shows (see Chapters 6 and 8), the very questions that psychologists ask about human behaviour and experience reflect a whole range of beliefs, values, presuppositions and prejudices which, in turn, reflect the particular cultural, gender and other groups to which they belong. While this raises important questions about the objective nature of psychological inquiry, it also raises very important ethical issues. If sexism, heterosexism, the androcentric/masculinist bias, Eurocentrism and racism are all inherent features of what psychologists do when they study human beings, then it could be argued that traditional, mainstream, Western, academic psychology (as well as the applied areas, such as clinical and educational psychology) is inherently unethical, in that most psychologists, most of the time, are trying to find the answers to questions which themselves stem from all kinds of prejudices. Most of the time, the psychologists will be unaware of these prejudices, but this does not by itself absolve them of the 'crime' ('ignorance of the law is no defence').

Protecting the individual vs benefiting society

The debate about the ethics of psychological research usually focuses on the vulnerability of individual participants and the responsibility of the psychologist towards his or her participants to ensure that they do not suffer in any way from their experience of participating. Wider issues about the 'morality' of the questions which the researcher is trying to answer through the research are much less commonly asked, but these would include the fundamental issue of the values which are, often unconsciously, helping to shape the research questions (as outlined in the previous section).

If the questions themselves are limited and shaped by the values of the individual researcher, they are also limited and shaped by considerations of methodology – what it is possible to do, practically, when investigating human behaviour and experience.

> *Given the clarity with which experiments allow us to test our causal ideas, it may seem strange that anyone would ever use anything other than an experimental design. Unfortunately, the same factor that defines an experiment also limits its use: the manipulation of the independent variable. Researchers can control the information that subjects receive in the laboratory about people they have never met, but they cannot manipulate many of the truly important factors in intimate relationships. We cannot create love in the laboratory. We don't know how to do it . . . For the most part, laboratory experiments are limited to explaining relatively emotionless interactions between strangers. Yet, in the study of relationships, we often want to understand intense encounters between intimates.*

(Brehm, 1992)

Brehm is saying that, in the context of interpersonal attraction, the laboratory experiment, by its nature, is extremely limited in the kinds of questions that it will allow psycholgists to investigate.

Conversely, and just as importantly, there are certain aspects of behaviour and experience that *could* be studied experimentally, but it would be unethical to do so; Brehm gives 'jealousy between partners participating in laboratory research' as an example. Indeed, 'all types of research in this area [intimate relationships] involve important ethical dilemmas. Even if all we do is to ask subjects to fill out questionnaires describing their relationships, we need to think carefully about how this research experience might affect them and their partner' (Brehm, 1992).

So the research that psychologists do is partly constrained by practical (methodological) considerations, and also partly by ethical considerations. What it may be possible to do may be unacceptable, but equally, what may be acceptable may not be possible. As shown in Figure 10.3, the 'what' of research is constrained by both the 'how' and the 'should'.

As already stated, ethical debates (the 'should') are usually confined to protecting the integrity and welfare of the individual participant. This is what the various codes of conduct and ethical principles are designed to try and ensure. But is there a wider ethical issue involved: as important as it surely is to protect individuals, does the 'should' relate to something beyond the particular experimental situation in which particular participants are involved?

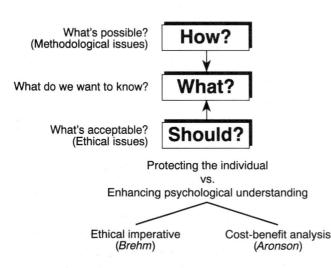

Figure 10.3 Ethical and methodological constraints on the questions that psychologists can try to answer through the research process

The other side of the ethical coin: research that must be done

In our necessary concern with treating subjects well and protecting them from any harmful effects, we must not overlook the other side of the ethical issue: the ethical imperative to gain more understanding of important areas of human behaviour. Intimate relationships can be a source of the grandest, most glorious pleasure we human beings experience; they can also be a source of terrible suffering and appalling destructiveness. It is, I believe, an inherently ethical response to try to learn how the joy might be increased and the misery reduced.

(Brehm, 1992)

Although discussing the study of intimate relationships specifically, Brehm's argument applies to psychology as a whole, perhaps to the whole of social psychology in particular. She is arguing that not only are psychologists obliged to protect the welfare of individual participants, but they are also under obligation to carry out socially meaningful research, research which may improve the quality of people's lives. Social psychologists in particular have a twofold ethical obligation – to individual participants and to society at large (Myers, 1994).

Similarly, Aronson (1992) argues that, in a real sense, social psychologists are under an obligation to use their research skills to advance our knowledge and understanding of human behaviour for the ultimate aim of 'human betterment'. But they face a dilemma when this general ethical responsibility to society comes into conflict with their more specific ethical responsibility to each individual experimental participant.

In talking about the aim of 'human betterment', we are, of course, raising many important questions to do with basic values, but at least it opens out the ethical debate in such a way that values must be addressed and recognized as part of the research process (something that feminist psychologists advocate very strongly; see Chapter 6).

We may now have found a solution to the dilemma whereby the individual participant is not the beneficiary, unlike the gynaecology patient or the lawyer's client: the short-term deception of individual participants (and the distress which this might cause) may be necessary if psychologists are to learn things about human behaviour and experience which can then be used to benefit people in general.

What form might such benefits take? In some of the early, and very famous, studies of bystander intervention, people were deceived as to the 'emergency' that was supposedly taking place. In the Latané and Darley (1968) experiment, steam, which was meant to resemble smoke, poured into the room where the participants were filling out questionnaires, and in a second study (Darley & Latané, 1968), participants believed that another participant, who was supposedly in another part of the building and could only be heard via an intercom system, was having an epileptic fit. Many participants were very distressed by their experience, especially those in the latter experiment. Yet when asked to complete a post-experiment questionnaire (which followed a very careful debriefing), all said that they believed the deception was justified and that they would be willing to participate in similar experiments again. None reported any feelings of anger towards the experimenter.

A later study, by Beaman et al. (1978, cited in Myers, 1994), built on these earlier experiments. They used a lecture to inform some students about how bystanders' refusal to help can influence both one's interpretation of an emergency and one's feelings of responsibility. Two other groups of students heard either a different lecture or no lecture at all. Two weeks later, as part of a different experiment in a different location, the participants found themselves walking (accompanied by an unresponsive confederate) past someone who was slumped over or sprawled under a bike. Of those who had heard the lecture about helping behaviour, fifty per cent stopped to offer help, compared with twenty-five per cent of those who had not heard the lecture.

What this suggests, of course, is that the results of psychological research can be used to make people more aware of the influences that affect our behaviour, making it more likely that we shall act differently armed with that knowledge from how we might otherwise have done. In the case of bystander intervention, this 'consciousness-raising' is beneficial in a very tangible way to the person who is helped; as for the helper, being more sensitive to the needs of others and the feeling of satisfaction from actually having helped another person may be seen as benefits too. (We should note that in the Beaman et al. experiment, the participants were being deceived, both as to the identity of the unresponsive confederate and the apparent 'victim'. But this can be justified in the same way as we have been trying to justify other experiments that use deception.)

How do we decide when to deceive?

If we go along with the preceding argument, then we are rejecting the view that deception can never be justified. But that does not inevitably lead us to the opposite argument, namely that almost any price is worth paying for results which may have profound benefits for humankind (Aronson, 1992). So what is the middle ground?

> *I believe the science of social psychology is important, and I also believe experimental subjects should be protected at all times. When deciding whether a particular experimental procedure is ethical or not, I believe a cost–benefit analysis is appropriate. That is, how much 'good' will derive from doing the experiment and how much 'bad' will happen to the experimental subjects should be considered.*

Put another way, the benefits to society are compared with th[e]
to the subjects, and this ratio is entered into the decision calcul[...]

(Aronson, 19[...])

Unfortunately, this comparison is often very difficult to make, because neither the benefits nor the harm is known or calculable. In addition, our judgement about the ethics of any experiment – the acceptability of the procedure (including any deception involved) – may be (unconsciously) influenced by the results that are obtained. If the results tell us something pleasant or flattering about human nature, the procedure is less likely to be criticized as unethical, whereas the reverse is true if the results tell us 'something we'd rather not know', (Aronson, 1992). This is to confuse the procedure with the outcome, when they need to be assessed independently before being weighed against each other.

There is little doubt that Milgram's experiments told us something about ourselves that 'we'd rather not know'. Aronson agrees with Milgram himself, who is convinced that 'much of the criticism [of his obedience experiments], whether people know it or not, stems from the results of the experiment. If everyone had broken off at slight shock or mild shock, this would be a very reassuring finding and who would protest? (Milgram, 1992).

Consistent with this argument is Aronson's observation that the dilemma faced by social psychologists (regarding their obligations to society and to their individual participants) is greatest when investigating such important areas as conformity, obedience and bystander intervention: in general, the more important the issue, (i) the greater the potential benefit for society, and (ii) the more likely that an individual participant will experience distress and discomfort.

The 'missing middle' from this observation is that, the more important the issue, the more essential it becomes that deception (or 'technical illusion') is used. Why? Because the psychologist wants to know how people are likely to behave were they to find themselves in that situation outside of the laboratory (or, at least, outside of the experimental situation). While this raises a number of crucial methodological questions (such as experimental realism, external validity or mundane realism; see Chapter 11, on science), the key ethical issue hinges on the fact that the use of deception both contributes enormously (and perhaps irreplaceably) to our understanding of human behaviour (helping to satisfy the obligation to society) and at the same time increases significantly the distress of individual participants (detracting from the responsibility to protect individuals). So what is the psychologist to do?

ome suggested solutions to the 'double obligation' lemma

...ing deception only when essential

Having accepted that, under certain circumstances, deception is permissible, most psychologists still advocate the principle that it should not be used unless it is considered to be *essential* to do so (Milgram, 1992; Aronson, 1992). This is consistent with the BPS *Ethical Principles*, according to which 'Intentional deception . . . over the purpose and general nature of the investigation should be avoided whenever possible. Participants should never be deliberately misled without extremely strong scientific or medical justification. Even then there should be strict controls and the disinterested approval of independent advisors' (1990, 1993, paragraph 4.2).

Accurately reflecting human experience

While accepting the above principle, Milgram believes that, if we excluded the experimental creation of stress or conflict, and only allowed studies which produced positive emotions, 'such a stricture would lead to a very lopsided psychology, one that caricatured rather than accurately reflected human experience' (Milgram 1992).

Historically, the most deeply informative experiments in social psychology include those which examine how participants resolve conflicts of one kind or another, such as the Asch studies of conformity (truth vs conformity), the Latané and Darley bystander intervention studies (getting involved in another's troubles vs not getting involved), and Milgram's own obedience experiments (internal conscience vs external authority). If we exclude the study of such core human issues, we would be causing an 'irreparable loss' to any science of human behaviour.

But what about the accusation that Milgram's experiment may produce diminished self-esteem, or sense of self-worth, in those participants who obey the experimenter all the way up to 450 volts?

Milgram's reply is to agree that it is the experimenter's responsibility to make the laboratory session as constructive an experience as possible, and to explain the experiment in a way that allows participants to integrate their performance into their self-concept in an insightful way. But if the experimenter were to hide the truth from the participant, even if this is negative, this would set the experiment completely apart from other life experiences (and, we could add, would simply be dishonest). He also distinguishes between biomedical and psychological interventions, claiming that there is absolutely no evidence that, when an individual makes a choice in a laboratory situation (even difficult ones as in conformity and obedience experiments), he or she suffers any trauma, injury, or lessening of well-being.

Alternatives to informed consent

Two compromise solutions to the problem of not being able to obtain informed consent are (i) *presumptive consent* (of 'reasonable people') and (ii) *prior general consent.*

In the former, the views of a large number of people are obtained about the acceptability of an experimental procedure. These people would not participate in the actual experiment (if it went ahead), but their views could be taken as evidence of how people *in general* would react to participation.

In the latter, prior general consent could be obtained from people who might, subsequently, serve as experimental participants. Before volunteering to join a pool of volunteers to serve in psychological research, people would be explicitly told that sometimes participants are misinformed about the true purpose of the study and sometimes experience emotional stress. Only those agreeing, in the light of this knowledge, would be chosen for a particular study (Milgram 1992). This is a compromise solution because people would be giving their 'informed consent' (i) well in advance of the actual experiment, (ii) only in a very general way, and (iii) without knowing what specific manipulations/deceptions will be used in the particular experiment in which they participate. This seems to fall somewhere between 'mere' consent and full 'informed consent'; perhaps this should be called *semi-* or *partially informed consent.*

Debriefing, the right to withdraw, and using alternative methods

Given the limitations of these compromise solutions (which are only suggestions made by Milgram), the importance of other ethical principles designed to protect the participant assume even greater importance. The experimenter should spend considerable time after the experiment with each participant, carefully explaining its true purpose, the reasons for the deception and so on. He or she should take great pains to ensure that the participants do not feel stupid or gullible for 'falling for' the deception, and that they leave the experimental situation in a frame of mind at least as sound as when they arrived. The researcher should also provide participants with the real option of withdrawing from the experiment – they are not obliged to stay just because they started the experiment, or because of any payment received or promised.

Finally, experimenters should always be alert to alternatives to deception (Aronson, 1992). (This raises, of course, important methodological issues; see Chapter 11, on science.)

The use of animals in psychological research

Why do psychologists study animals?

Because of the very close relationship between the ethical and the practical aspects of animal experimentation, they shall be discussed together here.

1 Experiments which would not be allowed if they involved human participants, or which would be allowed but would be very impractical if involving humans, are allowed (or have been in the past) using animal subjects. This, of course, begs the question as to the ethics of such animal experiments.

2 Even if animals are not subjected to ethically unacceptable procedures, such as severe sensory deprivation (e.g. Riesen, 1947; Blakemore & Cooper, 1970), total social isolation (e.g. Harlow & Zimmerman, 1959), extreme stress (e.g. Brady, 1958; Seligman, 1974), or surgical procedures and eventually 'sacrifice' (e.g. Olds & Milner, 1954), greater *control* can still be exerted over the variables under investigation compared with the equivalent human experiment. For example, the Skinner box is an environment that is totally controlled by the experimenter.

3 There is an underlying *evolutionary continuity* between humans and other species which gives rise to the assumption that differences between humans and other species are merely quantitative (as opposed to qualitative). That is to say, other species may display more simple behaviour and have more primitive nervous systems than humans, but they are not of a different order from humans. In fact, the mammalian brain (which includes rats, cats, dogs, monkeys and humans) is built on similar lines in all these species. Every part of the human brain can also be identified in the rat brain, although evolutionary progress means that the former is more highly developed in terms of size and the number and nature of the interconnections within it. Neurons (or nerve cells) are the same in all species and work in the same way – even neurons in the most primitive invertebrate in the sea operate in the same way. As Green (1994) puts it, 'at the level of its basic units, evolution has been highly conservative' (but see point 6 below). These similarities of biology are, in turn, linked to similarities in behaviour. Again, as Green (1994) points out, rats and monkeys display a whole range of cognitive, affective and motivational behaviour, as do human beings. So, it is argued, studying the more simple cases is a valid and valuable way of finding out about the more complex ones; Skinner's theory of operant conditioning is a good example of this approach. The study of animal behaviour was inspired by Darwin's (1859) theory of evolution, which made it seem quite reasonable to believe that, by studying the more simple species from which we have evolved, we should learn more about ourselves.

Figure 10.4 In a famous study by Brady (1958), electric shocks were administered to pairs of monkeys; one monkey could press a lever to turn off the electricity for both of them. The 'executive' monkey developed ulcers; the passive monkey did not. Such experiments would not be permitted today

Figure 10.5 Darwin was ridiculed by the media of the day for his 'outrageous' ideas of evolution

4   Animals are (mostly) smaller and, therefore, easier to study in the laboratory. They also have much shorter life-spans and gestation periods, making it much easier to study their development – many generations can be studied in a relatively short time.

5   Animal studies can provide useful hypotheses for subsequent testing with human participants; for example, Bowlby's theory of attachment was very much influenced by Lorenz's study of imprinting in geese (see Chapter 9, on attachment). Equally important, animals can be used to test cause-and-effect relationships where the existing human evidence is only correlational, as in smoking and lung cancer. This, of course, raises fundamental ethical questions (see points 1 and 6).

6   Comparisons across the *phylogenetic* (evolutionary) scale are valuable for showing what humans don't have or cannot do – what we have probably evolved away from or out of. Comparison is invaluable in helping us develop a framework for brain analysis based on evolutionary history: an apparently useless or mystical structure in the human nervous system may serve (or have served) a function identified through discovering its current function in another species (Coolican, 1994).

The case for animal experimentation

The main justifications for using animals in experiments are (i) the pursuit of scientific knowledge, and (ii) the advancement of medicine.

To justify the use of animals, especially when the procedures used are likely to be very stressful, the research must be rigorously designed and the potential results must represent a significant contribution to our knowledge of medicine, pharmacology, biopsychology or psychology. This is a safeguard against distressing research being carried out for its own sake or at the whim of the researcher.

Green (1994) points out that many drugs in clinical use (for example, in the treatment of human diseases) have been developed using animals and could not have been developed otherwise, including anaesthetics, anti-cancer drugs, anti-Aids treatments, anti-epilepsy drugs, anti-anxiety and anti-depressant drugs.

> *There are encouraging signs that a treatment for Alzheimer's disease may emerge, which will have depended absolutely on the use of animal testing for its development. If successful it would have a dramatic impact, improving the quality of life for both those with Alzheimer's and those who would otherwise sacrifice their lives in caring for them. Is this potential benefit sufficient to justify the use of animals in psychological research? I would say it is.*

(Green, 1994)

Not everyone would agree with Green, but there are those who would take the 'medical justification' argument even further. For example, Gray (1991) argues that, while most people (both experimenters and animal rights activists) would accept the ethical principle that inflicting pain is wrong, we are sometimes faced with having to choose between different ethical principles; we have to make moral choices, which may mean having to choose between human and animal suffering. Gray believes that *speciesism* (discriminating against and exploiting animals because they belong to a particular – non-human – species; Ryder, 1990) is not only justified, but it is our *duty* to carry out animal research if this may lead to the (long-term) alleviation of human suffering.

Bateson (1986, 1992) proposes a 'decision cube' (similar to Aronson's cost–benefit analysis in human research; see p.210), involving (i) the quality of the research; (ii) the certainty of medical benefit; and (iii) the degree of animal suffering. The last point should only be tolerated if the first two points are high.

The actual question of weighing the likely value of the research against the degree of suffering was addressed by the Institute of Medical Ethics (IME) Working Party (Haworth, 1992). Some of the long-term benefits (and, therefore, justifications) of animal research include (i) improvements in animal husbandry, (ii) contributions to animal welfare on farms and zoos, (iii) wildlife conservation, and (iv) the general challenge to science of increasing our understanding of the 'how and why of animal behaviour'.

How can we assess animal suffering?

Drawing on the IME Working Party's investigations, Bateson has proposed criteria for assessing animal suffering, including: (i) possessing receptors sensitive to noxious or painful stimulation and (ii) having brain structures comparable to the human cerebral cortext (see above). Based on how an animal's nervous system works and its behaviour in the face of noxious stimuli, Bateson (1992) tentatively concludes that insects probably don't experience pain, whereas fish and octopuses probably do. However, the boundaries between the presence and absence of pain are 'fuzzy'.

Safeguards for animals used in research

1 The Scientific Affairs Board of the BPS (1985) published its 'Guidelines for the Use of Animals in Research', offering a checklist of points which researchers should carefully consider when planning experiments with living animals. They have an obligation to

> *avoid, or at least to minimize, discomfort to living animals . . . discuss any future research with their local Home Office Inspector and colleagues who are experts in the topic . . . seek . . . Widespread advice as to whether the likely scientific contribution of the work . . .*

justifies the use of living animals, and whether the scientific point they wish to make may not be made without the use of living animals.

The guidelines draw attention to such issues as caging, social environment, the number of animals to be used, the use of aversive/noxious stimulation, and stressful procedures. They stress that experiments must not be done 'simply because it is possible to do them'.

2 The Animals (Scientific Procedures) Act (1986) requires that premises be licensed, that individuals using animals hold personal licences, and that researchers acquire a project licence specifying the details of the proposed research (including the procedures to be used, any possible benefits of the research, and the anticipated extent of pain and suffering). Also, animals used for experimental purposes must be properly housed to certain controlled standards, with a named laboratory technician and vets responsible for the day-to-day care and welfare of the animals.

3 There has been a decline in the use of animals in psychological research in recent years (Thomas & Blackman, 1991), and the use of animals for psychological research represents a tiny fraction of the use of animals for research in general: 'Banning the use of animals in cosmetics testing would be a greater contribution to animal welfare than would banning their use by psychologists' (Green, 1994).

4 According to the Research Defence Society and the Association for the Study of Animal Behaviour, the number of animals used in experiments is artificially inflated, since the 1986 Act requires that each individual animal is counted as 'an experiment'. It also prevents the use of the same animal in more than one experiment, thus necessitating a larger number of animals than might otherwise be required (Russell, 1992).

5 According to the guidelines, field workers should disturb animals as little as possible, since 'Even simple observation of wild animals can have marked effects on their breeding and survival' (See Rawlins, 1979, in Gross, 1994).

A case study in the ethics of animal research

In 'Teaching Sign Language to a Chimpanzee', Gardner and Gardner (1969) report their famous research with Washoe, estimated to be between eight and fourteen months old when she arrived at their laboratory. When she was five years old, Washoe was sent away with Roger and Deborah Fouts. The Gardners next saw her eleven years later. When they unexpectedly entered the room Washoe was in, she signed their name, then 'Come, Mrs G', led Mrs Gardner to an adjoining room and began to play a game with her which she had not been observed to play since she left the Gardners' home (Singer, 1993).

Observations like this, as well as supporting the argument that non-humans really are capable of using language, also raise important ethical questions – in particular the following, (i) How justifiable is the whole attempt to study language in non-humans, since this involves removing the

Figure 10.6 The teaching of sign language to Washoe raised ethical questions when it was observed that she still remembered the Gardners some eleven years after the experiment had ended

animals from their natural habitat in which they do not spontaneously use language? (ii) What happens to the animals after they have served their purpose as experimental subjects?

Although these kinds of study are not usually the target for attacks against cruel treatment of animals in psychological research, they none the less involve animals, which have not chosen to become involved. But perhaps it is the fact that they are great apes, and not just 'other animals', which makes these ethical questions so fascinating and important.

This relates directly to the *Great Ape Project* (GAP), which is (i) the title of a book (subtitled: *Equality beyond humanity*, edited by P. Singer & P. Cavalieri); (ii) an idea, radical but simple, to extend the 'community of equals' beyond human beings to all great apes (chimpanzees, gorillas, and orang-utans); and (iii) an organization, comprising thirty-four academics and others, set up to work internationally for the immediate inclusion of the great apes within the community of equals. This refers to the moral community within which we accept certain basic moral rights and principles as governing our relationships with each other and which are enforceable at law.

The central tenet of the GAP is that it is ethically indefensible to deny the great apes the basic rights of (i) the right to life, (ii) protection of individual liberty, and (iii) prohibition of torture (collectively, the Declaration of Great Apes; see Gross, 1994).

Psychologists as agents of change

We noted at the beginning of the chapter that there are both important similarities and differences as regards the ethical problems faced by psychologists as scientists and as practitioners. We also noted that there is considerable overlap between clinical psychologists and psychotherapists in terms of the ethical dimensions of their work with people who have some kind of mental disorder.

The major ethical issues which relate to this applied area of psychology (and related professions) include:

- Informed consent
- The influence of the therapist
- Behavioural control
- The abuse of patients by therapists
- Confidentiality and 'privileged communication' (We have already touched on this above.)

Informed consent

Where someone is voluntarily seeking help from a psychologist or psychotherapist (as opposed to the position of an involuntary, sectioned, patient in a psychiatric hospital), it might seem that there would not be an issue regarding informed consent. However, if we think about what this means in relation to participants in research (such as being fully aware of the purpose of the study, and the manipulations and deceptions involved), things begin to look a little less straightforward.

According to Holmes (1994), this is a problem throughout the caring professions. The law in Britain and the USA differs regarding the extent to which doctors are expected to explain in advance every detail of the possible adverse consequences of a procedure or treatment. In the case of psychotherapy, this is especially problematic, for four main reasons.

1 The patient may well be in a vulnerable and emotionally aroused state and, thus, unlikely to be able to make a balanced judgement as to the suitability of the particuar form of therapy on offer and/or his or her compatibility with the therapist.

2 Unlike medical procedures, the range of different forms of psychotherapy that are available tend to be poorly understood by the general public and the media.

3 The lack of any generally agreed standards of training, practice, or regulatory procedures, within psychotherapy as a whole, means that there are no external criteria against which a particular therapy can be assessed.

4 There are special problems of informed consent associated with particular therapies. For example, in psychoanalysis, some degree of 'opacity' is necessary if certain techniques, such as transference, are to be effective. The therapist must remain partially 'obscure' or 'not see-through' if the patient is to be able to transfer onto the therapist unconscious feelings for parents (or other close relatives) which are then discussed and interpreted. When assessing patients for treatment, analysts must strike a balance between providing legitimate information on the one hand, and maintaining their 'professional distance' on the other.

Despite these difficulties, the problems of consent can be overcome. Holmes (1994) believes that recognized standards of training and practice would help. Indeed, most psychotherapy organizations in Britain favour a state-recognized profession of psychotherapy, and are actively trying to achieve this goal through the UK Standing Conference on Psychotherapy. Masson (1992) proposes that there should be a 'psychotherapy ombudsman'.

Most patients probably gravitate towards the therapies and therapists that they feel comfortable with, and word-of-mouth recommendations are very important in private practice. And at least you only pay for each individual session – unlike when buying a used car! (Holmes, 1994).

The influence of the therapist

Psychologists are aware of the subtle coercion that can operate on hospitalized psychiatric patients – even voluntary ones. The in-patient is subjected to strong persuasion to accept the treatment recommendations of professional staff: 'even a "voluntary" and informed decision to take psychotropic medication or to participate in any other therapy regimen is often (maybe usually) less than free' (Davison & Neale, 1994). The issue of the influence of the therapist on the patient has been central to a long-standing debate between traditional (psychodynamic) psychotherapists and behaviour therapists (who, as we saw earlier, are usually clinical psychologists by training).

In the opinion of many psychotherapists, behaviour therapy is unacceptable (even if it works) because it is seen as manipulative and demeaning of human dignity. By contrast, they see their own methods as fostering the autonomous development of the patient's inherent potential, helping the patient to express his or her true self, and so on. Instead of an influencer, they see themselves as a kind of psychological midwife, present during the birth, possessing useful skills, but there primarily to make sure that a natural process goes smoothly (Wachtel, 1977).

This, according to Wachtel, is an exaggeration and misrepresentation of both approaches: for many patients, the 'birth' would probably not happen at all without the therapist's intervention and he or she undoubtedly does influence the patient's behaviour. Conversely, behaviour therapists are at least partly successful because they establish an active, cooperative relationship with the patient who plays a much more active role in the therapy than psychotherapists believe.

Wachtel argues that all therapists, of whatever persuasion, if they are at all effective, influence their patients. Both approaches comprise 'a situation in which one human being (the therapist) tries to act in such a way as to enable another human being to act and feel differently than he has, and this is as true of psychoanalysis as it is of behaviour therapy' (Wachtel, 1977).

The crucial issue is the *nature* of this influence (and not whether or not it occurs), and there are four crucial questions that need to be asked.

1 Is the influence exerted in a direction that is in the patient's interest or in the service of the therapist's needs?
2 Are some good ends (say, reduction in anxiety) being achieved at the expense of others (such as the patient's enhanced vision of the possibilities that life can offer or an increased sense of self-directedness)?
3 Is the patient fully informed about the kind of influence that the therapist wishes to exert and the kind of ends being sought? (This, of course, relates to informed consent.)
4 Is the patient's choice being excessively influenced by a fear of displeasing the therapist, rather than by what he or she would really prefer?

The neutrality of the therapist is a myth. Therapists influence their clients in subtle yet powerful ways.

> *Unlike a technician, a psychiatrist cannot avoid communicating and at times imposing his own values upon his patients. The patient usually has considerable difficulty in finding the way in which he would wish to change his behaviour, but as he talks to the psychiatrist his wants and needs become clearer. In the very process of defining his needs in the presence of a figure who is viewed as wise and authoritarian, the patient is profoundly influenced. He ends up wanting some of the things the psychiatrist thinks he should want.*
>
> (Davison & Neale, 1994)

In the above quotation, we can add 'psychologist' and 'psychotherapist' to 'psychiatrist'.

Behavioural control

While a behavioural technique such as *systematic desensitization* is largely limited to the reduction of anxiety, this can at least be seen as enhancing the patient's freedom, since anxiety is one of the greatest restrictions on freedom. By contrast, methods based on *operant conditioning* can be applied to almost any aspect of a person's life (largely because they are applied to *voluntary*, as opposed to *reflex* or *autonomic*, behaviour).

Those who use operant methods, such as the *token economy*, often describe their work rather exclusively in terms of behavioural control, and they subscribe to Skinner's (1971) view that freedom is only an illusion. (See Chapter 12, on free will and determinism.)

Wachtel (1977) believes that, when used in institutional settings (as with long-term schizophrenic patients in psychiatric hospitals), the token economy is so subject to abuse that its use is highly questionable. It may be justifiable (i) if it works, and (ii) if there is clearly no alternative way of rescuing the patient from an empty and destructive existence. But as a routine part of how society deals with deviant behaviour, this approach raises very serious ethical questions.

One of these relates to the question of power. Just as we noted earlier when discussing the role of the 'subject' in the experiment, the patient is powerless relative to the institutional staff responsible for operating the token economy programme; 'reinforcement is viewed by many – proponents and opponents alike – as somehow having an inexorable controlling effect upon the person's behaviour and rendering him incapable of choice, reducing him to an automaton or duly wound mechanism' (Wachtel, 1977). It is the reinforcing agent's power to physically deprive uncooperative patients of 'privileges' that is the alarming feature of the token economy.

The abuse of patients by therapists

In recent years, there has been a wave of criticism of psychotherapy (especially of the Freudian variety), including its ethical shortcomings. One of its most outspoken critics is an American ex-Freudian psychoanalyst, Jeffrey Masson.

Masson believes that there is an imbalance of power involved in the therapeutic relationship, and individuals who seek therapy need protection from the constant temptation to abuse, misuse, profit from, and bully on the part of the therapist. The therapist has almost absolute emotional power over the patient (Masson, 1992), and in his *Against Therapy: Emotional Tyranny and the Myth of Psychological Healing* (1988), Masson catalogues example after example of patients' abuse – emotional, sexual, financial – at the hands of their therapists.

Naturally enough, Masson's attack has stirred up an enormous controversy. Holmes (1994) agrees with the core of Masson's argument, namely that 'no therapist, however experienced or distinguished, is above the laws of the unconscious, and all should have access to supervision and work within a framework of proper professional practice' (Masson, 1992). But in defence of psychotherapy, Holmes points out that exploitation and abuse are by no means confined to psychotherapy: lawyers, university teachers, priests and doctors are also sometimes guilty. All these professional groups have ethical standards and codes of practice (often far more stringent than the law of the land), with disciplinary bodies that impose severe punishments – usually expulsion from the profession. We should not condemn an entire profession because of the transgressions of a small minority.

Summary

- Ethical issues arise because (i) human beings and animals are *sentient*, living things, and (ii) human beings are *thinking* creatures, capable of experiencing embarrassment, guilt etc.
- Ethical issues arise for psychologists because (i) they study human beings and animals, (ii) they often subject the people or animals they study to painful or embarrassing situations, (iii) every psychological investigation can be thought of as an ethical situation.
- The distinction between *psychologist as scientist/investigator* and *psychologist as practitioner* is important from an ethical point of view.
- The BPS and APA both publish various *codes of conduct* and *ethical guidelines*, some which apply to the two roles (scientist/practitioner) jointly, others which apply to one *or* the other.
- Regardless of the particular training the practitioner has received

(*behaviour therapy/modification*, *client-centred therapy*, *psychodynamic*), the 'helper'–'helped' relationship involves the attempt to change something. The psychologist as researcher is trying to find out what the person being studied is already like.

- Guidelines such as the *Ethical Principles for Conducting Research with Human Participants* are intended, primarily, to protect the 'rights and dignity' of participants. It lists nine major principles to be followed by anyone engaged in psychological research, from GCSE students to professional psychologists; these principles include practice regarding *deception*, *consent/informed consent*, *withdrawal from the investigation*, and *debriefing*.

- Participants need protecting from the possible consequences of the difference in power between the researcher and researched. Feminists argue that this should be reversed, by the researcher becoming actively involved in the research process, as opposed to a detached manipulator of the experimental situation.

- One aspect of the greater power of the experimenter is his or her ability to deceive participants as to the true purpose of the experiment: can deception ever be justified?

- According to Milgram, the *motivational* reason for deceiving participants is quite unacceptable, but the *epistemological* reason is justified.

- If participants themselves are not particularly bothered when they learn that they have been deceived, or they volunteer expecting to be deceived, does deception then become acceptable?

- As far as Milgram is concerned, 'technical illusions' are justified for one reason only: they are in the end accepted/endorsed by those who are exposed to them. But, since their use prevents participants from giving their informed consent, they should only be used if they are absolutely essential.

- In the cases of gynaecology and the law, which are exempt from some generally accepted moral principles, both society as a whole and the individual patient or client benefit. But in the psychology experiment, the individual participant is not the beneficiary.

- To the extent that psychology is inherently sexist, heterosexist, androcentric and in other ways prejudiced, it is inherently unethical.

- The questions that psychologists try to answer through their research are shaped partly by their values, and partly by methodological considerations. The research itself is constrained by what is possible and what is ethically acceptable.

- Ethical debates usually concentrate on the need to protect the integrity and welfare of the individual participant. But psychologists are also obliged to carry out socially meaningful research, for the ultimate aim of 'human betterment'.

- This twofold obligation can present psychologists with a dilemma. If deception (and the related distress) is sometimes justifiable, the psychologists must weigh up the possible benefits to society against the possible costs to the individual participants.

- There is a danger of judging the ethics of an experiment according to the nature of the results, when these should be assessed independently. Milgram's obedience experiments are a good example of this confusion.

- Generally, the more socially significant the issue, the greater the need for deception, and the more likely that an individual participant will experience distress etc.

- Some possible solutions to this dilemma include: (i) the use of deception only if the scientific/medical justification is extremely strong, (ii) the use of *presumptive consent* and *prior general consent*.

- In the case of animal experimentation, ethical and practical issues are very closely tied.

- Some of the reasons for using animals in research include: (i) the greater control over variables; (ii) the *evolutionary continuity* between humans and other species, implying a mere quantitative difference; (iii) the convenience and speed of studying animals' development; (iv) the generation of hypotheses for testing with humans and the testing of cause-and-effect hypotheses from human correlational research.

- The main justifications for using animals are (i) the pursuit of scientific knowledge, and (ii) the advancement of medicine.

- Many drugs used in the treatment of human diseases could not have been developed without animal research, and this may be seen as a sufficient justification for the use of animals.

- According to Gray, not only is speciesism justified, but it is our duty to carry out animal research if this may result in the alleviation of human suffering.

- As with human research, the benefits need to be weighed against the degree of suffering, along with the quality of the research.

- Safeguards for animals used in research include: (i) the BPS and Committee of the Experimental Psychological Society (1985) *Guidelines for the Use of Animals in Research*, which obliges researchers to reduce suffering/discomfort and to justify the use of live animals very carefully; (ii) the Animals (Scientific Procedures) Act, which requires the licensing of premises, individual researchers, and each individual research project.

- According to the *Guidelines*, field workers should disturb animals as little as possible, and the *Great Ape Project* argues that the great apes should be given the basic rights of life, freedom, and protection from torture.

- As agents of change, clinical psychologists (along with

psychotherapists) face the ethical issues of *informed consent, the influence of the therapist, behavioural control, the abuse of patients, confidentiality*, and '*privileged communication*'.

- Psychotherapy faces unique problems regarding putting clients fully 'in the picture' as to possible harmful effects, despite the voluntary nature of the therapeutic relationship. These could be overcome by the setting up of a state-recognized profession of psychotherapy.
- Subtle forms of coercion can operate on hospitalized psychiatric patients (including voluntary ones) to accept particular forms of treatment.
- Many psychotherapists see behaviour therapy as manipulative and demeaning of human dignity, and see their own methods as helping patients to become autonomous, to express their true selves etc.
- This misrepresents and exaggerates both approaches: all therapists influence their patients, and it is the kind of influence involved that is crucial.
- The *token economy*, as a form of behavioural control, is ethically highly dubious, at least as a routine way of dealing with deviant behaviour. One objection is the powerlessness of patients relative to the staff who are operating the programme; another is the patient's reduction to an automaton, who lacks choice.
- Masson condemns psychotherapists for abusing the power that they have over their patients. But exploitation and abuse can be found in all professions and we shouldn't condemn the whole profession for the sins of a small minority.

Suggestions for further reading

Association for the Teaching of Psychology (1992) Ethics, *Psychology Teaching*, New Series (No. 1).

Milgram, S. (1974) *Obedience to Authority* (especially Appendix 1: 'Problems of Ethics in Research'), New York: Harper and Row.

Milgram, S. (1992) *The Individual In A Social World: Essays and Experiments* (2nd edn) (especially Chapters 10, 12 and 15), New York: McGraw-Hill.

Psychology as science

Science as a recurrent theme

Explicitly or implicitly, the nature of science and psychology's status as a science have been discussed throughout the preceding chapters of this book, and will be discussed further in the two that follow.

In Chapter 1, we looked at the ways in which everyone may be thought of as a psychologist, by examining commonsense psychology, and how this is both similar to, and different from, scientific psychology. In the chapter that followed, on attribution, some of the issues raised in Chapter 1 were explored in much greater detail; in particular, the ways in which (according to the theories and research of scientific psychologists) the lay person assigns causes to behaviour and, to that extent, operates as a psychologist (the attribution process).

Identifying the causes of a phenomenon as a way of trying to explain it (as well as a means of predicting and controlling it) is a fundamental part of 'classical' science and relates to *determinism*, which we shall discuss in more detail below and in Chapter 12 ('Free Will and Determinism').

The three aims of explanation/understanding, prediction and control were discussed in Chapter 3 in terms of their appropriateness for a science of psychology. The idiographic and nomothetic approaches refer to two very different views as to what it is about people that is relevant for psychologists to study and the methods that should be adopted to study them, and they correspond to the *social sciences/humanities* and *natural/physical sciences* respectively. We concluded that the distinction is much less clear-cut than it was once thought to be; indeed, the view of natural science current at the time that Windelband originally made the distinction between the *Geisteswissenschaften* ('moral sciences') and the *Naturwissenschaften* ('natural sciences') is now considered by many scientists and philosophers to be outmoded. Ironically, psychologists may still be trying to model their discipline on a view of physics (in particular, and natural science in general) which physicists themselves no longer hold. More of this below.

In Chapter 6 ('Psychology, Women and Feminism'), we saw how feminist psychologists have exposed a major source of bias within psychology, both the research and theorizing making up 'mainstream' academic psychology, and the psychology profession itself. That bias is *androcentrism* or male-centredness, whereby women's behaviour and experience are compared with those of men, who are implicitly taken (by men) as the standard or norm against which women are to be judged.

Whatever the political and ethical objections to that bias may be, there are, from the perspective of classical, orthodox, mainstream scientific psychology, very powerful reasons for 'keeping quiet' about it, namely that science is meant to be *unbiased, objective* and *value-free*. This view of science is called *positivism*, something which feminist psychologists explicitly reject when they advocate a study of human beings in which the researchers 'come clean' about their values.

Positivism was also seen to be 'at work' (in Chapter 7) in the attempts of clinical psychologists and psychiatrists to define, classify, diagnose and treat psychological disorders in an objective, value-free or value-neutral way (comparable to what goes on in general medicine). In other words, definitions of abnormality are influenced by a wide range of (in particular) cultural beliefs, values, assumptions and experiences, but as long as the scientist/practitioner remains unaware of their influence, he or she will perceive the process of defining, diagnosing and so on as being objective. The belief that it is possible at all to be objective about psychological disorders reflects the positivist scientific training of clinical psychologists and psychiatrists.

The fact that the cultural (as well as the class, ethnic and gender) background of the practitioner is usually different from that of the majority of his or her patients introduces a strong *ethnocentric* bias into the area of abnormal behaviour, one which is often even more apparent when Western psychologists travel to other cultures in order to study the behaviour and experience of members of those other cultures (see Chapter 8). While cross-cultural psychology can serve as an important counterbalance to the equation of 'human' with 'member of Western culture', it is even more difficult, both in theory and in practice, for a member of one culture to objectively study a person from another culture than it is when the researcher and the person being investigated share a common culture (although even in the latter situation the differences may be greater than the similarities).

Finally, in Chapter 10 ('Ethics'), reference was made to Orne's (1962) claim that every psychology experiment is a social situation: whatever the particular topic under investigation or the specific hypotheses being tested, there is an interaction between two (or more) people who bring with them to the experimental situation a whole set of expectations, questions and other cognitive processes (both conscious and unconscious) and behaviours, just as they do to other social situations. In other words, what is going on in the minds, and between the minds, of the people involved inevitably affects the outcome, making the experiment something less than a wholly objective situation (unlike the study of chemical reactions in a chemistry laboratory, as some would argue). However, as we shall see below, the classical, positivist view of science (in which objectivity plays such a crucial role) is considered by many to be an oversimplification, indeed a misrepresentation, of what goes on even in the natural sciences.

We also discussed in relation to the ethics of research, the common use of deception, particularly in social psychology experiments. In this chapter, we shall look at some of the *methodological* implications of the use of deception. In the next section, we shall trace some of the historical roots of the classical view of science which has had such an enormous impact on the development of psychology in its present form that is, mainstream, academic ('experimental') psychology.

A brief sketch of the history of science

From the time of Ancient Greece until the Middle Ages, science ('knowledge') was synonymous with philosophy ('love of knowledge'), whose aim was to understand the meaning and purpose of natural phenomena, with 'man' being seen as the most significant. The main focus of study was consciousness, or conscious mental life, which was a reflection of the human soul, psyche or essence. Psychology was the study of the soul and its development, and, as such, was closely linked with religion. Man was the centre of God's creation, the earth the centre of the universe, and everything was seen as having a purpose that was related to man (*orthodox scholasticism*).

This view was challenged during the sixteenth century when Copernicus (1473–1543) challenged the biblical depiction of the earth as the centre of the universe, by claiming that the planets revolve around the sun. By removing the earth from its central place in the universe, it became more difficult to still see man as having his pivotal place in the universe assigned to him by Christian theology.

This revolutionary shift was later confirmed by Kepler's (1571–1630) laws of planetary motion, which led to the new science of astronomy, and Galileo

Figure 11.1 Copernicus was the first to show successfully that the ancient belief that man was at the centre of the universe was false

(1564–1642) finally discredited the old, orthodox world view by showing that the earth does, indeed, revolve around the sun. Man, and the world, were finally displaced as the centre of God's creation.

However, science was still seen as aimed at achieving wisdom and knowledge, until Bacon (1521–1626) challenged this view by claiming that knowledge is power. He advocated that scientific discovery should be used to help man gain mastery over the forces of nature, and that philosophy and science should be kept separate from theology (and not blended with it, as in orthodox scholasticism).

Descartes (1596–1650), the French philosopher who has had an enormous impact on psychology as a science, extended the views of Galileo and Bacon. He divided the universe into two fundamentally different realms, or 'realities': physical matter, which is extended in time and space (*res extensa*) and non-material, non-extended mind (*res cogitans*). This is known as *philosophical dualism*; the opposed view, that only matter exists, is called *materialism*. Both views (and others relating to the mind–body issue) are discussed in detail in Chapter 13.

Figure 11.2 Describing the world objectively became easier with the invention of such instruments as the ruler of Ptolemee for measuring the distance from the ground to the zenith

This distinction between matter and mind allowed scientists to treat matter as inert and completely distinct from themselves, which meant that the world could be described objectively, without reference to the human observer. Objectivity became the ideal of science (and as it was extended to the study of human behaviour and social institutions by Comte in the mid-1800s, it became known as *positivism*; see below).

Descartes believed that the material world comprised objects assembled like a huge machine and operated by mechanical laws that could be explained in terms of the arrangements and movements of its parts. This view of the world is called *mechanism* (machine-ism). Descartes extended this mechanistic view of matter to living organisms, comparing animals to clocks composed of wheels and springs, and later extended it further to the human body, which he saw as a machine, part of a perfect cosmic machine, controlled, at least in principle, by mathematical laws. He also believed that complex wholes may be understood in terms of their constituent parts, and so was one of the first advocates of *reductionism* (see below).

Because the mind is non-material, it cannot be studied in the way that the physical world is studied. Descartes believed that the mind could only be approached by *introspection* – by looking inwards at one's own thoughts and ideas.

Newton (1643–1727) later formulated the mathematical laws and mechanics that were thought to account for all the changes observable in the physical world.

The mechanical model of the universe subsequently guided all scientific activity for the next 200 years. The very existence of God was brought into question, and by the end of the nineteenth century, Nietzsche (1844–1900)

captured the spirit of the age by declaring that 'God is dead', meaning that traditional religious values had been largely negated, replaced by science as the ultimate authority within Western culture (see Figure 11.3).

Science and empiricism

Along with positivism, determinism, mechanism, materialism and reductionism, another fundamental feature of science (and major influence on its development) was *empiricism*. This refers to the ideas of the seventeenth- and eighteenth-century British empiricist philosophers – in particular, Locke, Hume and Berkeley. They believed that the only source of true knowledge about the world is *sensory experience* – what comes to us through our senses or what can be inferred about the relationships between such sensory facts. This belief proved to be one of the central influences on the development of physics and chemistry.

The word 'empirical' is often used synonymously with 'scientific', implying that what scientists do is carry out experiments and observations as the means of collecting data or 'facts' about the world. This, in turn, implies other very important assumptions about the nature of scientific activity and its relationship to the phenomena under investigation.

1 An empirical approach is different from a theoretical one, since the latter does not involve the use of experiment, measurement, and other forms of data collection.

2 It is philosophers, rather than scientists, who use theory and rational argument (as opposed to data collection) to try to establish the truth about the world.

3 The truth about the world (the objective nature of the world – what it is 'really like') can be established through properly controlled experiments and other empirical methods; science can tell us about reality as it is independently of the scientist and of the activity of trying to observe it.

The first point is true and is non-controversial, but the other two are much more the subject of debate among scientists and philosophers of science. Although the use of empirical methods is a defining feature of science and does distinguish it from philosophy, the use of theory is also crucial, which explains why many would reject the view of science as involving the discovery of 'facts' about the world that are uninfluenced by the scientist's theories. These may be to do with what causes the phenomenon under investigation (corresponding perhaps to most people's understanding of what a 'scientific theory' is), but in a broader sense they also include the biases, prejudices, values and assumptions (such as androcentrism, sexism and ethnocentrism) of the individual scientist, as well as the scientific community in general to which he or she belongs. As we have said before, to the extent that such biases influence the scientific process, it cannot be regarded as an objective process. If this is true in the

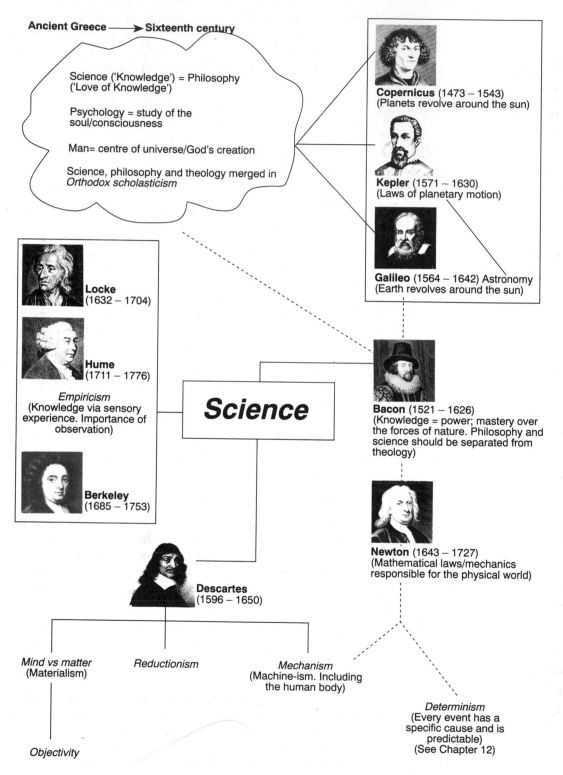

Figure 11.3 Influences on the development of science

cases of physics and chemistry, it is likely to be even more true of psychology, by virtue of the fact that human beings are studying other human beings, rather than aspects of the physical world. We shall discuss later in the chapter examples of the difficulties facing psychologists when they attempt to study people using a model derived from the natural sciences.

The development of psychology as a science: the early days

The secularization of science and philosophy had profound implications for the Western perspective on human beings: 'By the nineteenth century, thinking was essentially analytic, reductionist, objective and positivistic in the sense that it was held that the only valid knowledge is scientific knowledge or positive fact which is objectively verifiable' (Graham, 1986).

The emergence of psychology as a separate discipline (Figure 11.4), distinct from philosophy, clearly reflected this scientific 'mentality' or *Zeitgeist* ('spirit of the time'), but at first the subject matter was what it had traditionally been, namely 'non-material consciousness' (Graham, 1986).

University courses in scientific psychology were taught for the first time in the 1870s, before which time there were no laboratories explicitly devoted to psychological research. According to Fancher (1979), the two professors who set up the first two laboratories deserve much of the credit for the development of academic psychology, namely Wilhelm Wundt (1832–1920) in Germany and William James (1842–1910) in the USA.

The founder of experimental psychology

Wilhelm Wundt, a physiologist by training (having first obtained a medical degree), is generally regarded as the 'founder' of the new science of experimental psychology. As he wrote in the preface to his *Principles of Physiological Psychology* (1874), 'The work I here present to the public is an attempt to mark out a new domain of science' (quoted in Fancher, 1979). In 1879, he converted his 'laboratory' at Leipzig University (in fact, a small, single room used as a demonstration laboratory, in a rather run-down old building) into a 'private institute' of experimental psychology. For the first time, a place had been set aside for the explicit purpose of studying psychology and conducting psychological research. Hence, 1879 is the year which is generally accepted as the 'birthdate' of psychology as a discipline in its own right. At first, the institute was small, but it soon began to attract people from all over the world, who returned to their own countries to establish laboratories, modelled on Wundt's.

Wundt's first book, published in 1858, was concerned with muscular movement. This was followed by *Contributions to the Theory of Sensory*

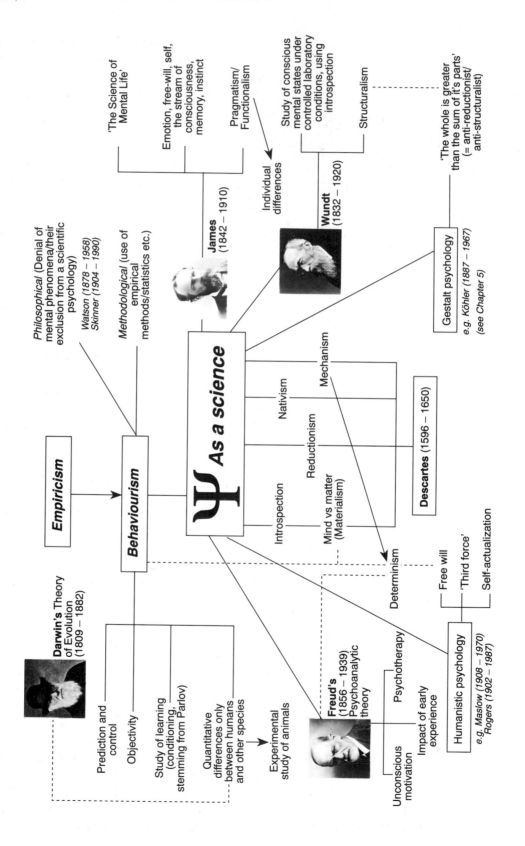

Figure 11.4 Influences on the development of psychology as a science

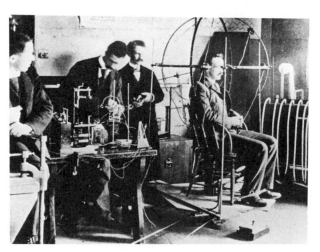

Figure 11.5 In 1879, Wilhelm Wundt founded the first proper laboratory devoted to experimental psychology. Pictured above is a laboratory at Harvard in 1912 which was based on Wundt's original

Perception in 1862. In the preface he outlined the possibility of an experimental psychology, whose aim would be to vary systematically the stimuli and conditions that produce differing mental states. He argued that it should be possible to manipulate and observe the facts of consciousness, just like the facts of physics, chemistry or physiology.

Wundt had worked as assistant to Hermann Helmholtz, the great physiologist who had much to contribute to the psychology of perception, and took over many of his duties when Helmholtz left. Wundt was eventually appointed professor of 'scientific philosophy' at Leipzig in 1875. So Wundt, a medically trained physiologist, was now a professor of philosophy: 'Nothing could better illustrate the lack of distinct boundaries between the various disciplines which combined to bring about the development of psychology' (Fancher, 1979).

In his *Principles of Physiological Psychology*, Wundt elaborated on the experimental psychology which had been only suggested in the preface to his earlier book. He argued that conscious mental states could be scientifically studied through the systematic manipulation of antecedent variables, and analysed by carefully controlled techniques of *introspection*. This represented the first 'call to arms' for the development of a purely psychological laboratory, and this became a concrete reality when his institute was opened in 1879. An indication of the popularity and success of the 'new psychology' was the founding, by Wundt, of the journal *Philosophische Studien* ('*Philosophical Studies*') which, despite its name, was the world's first to be primarily devoted to experimental psychology.

INTROSPECTION

So what did this new, experimental form of psychology look like?

Although Wundt's research interests and methods were broad, including reaction times, perception (the registering of a stimulus in consciousness) and apperception (the conscious 'interpretation' of a stimulus in light of the response associated with it), he is probably best known for his use of introspection as a way of experimentally analysing consciousness.

Introspection was a rigorous and highly disciplined technique for the separation of conscious experience into its most basic elements. Participants were always advanced psychology students who had been carefully trained to introspect properly. Those who found it too difficult were discouraged from pursuing careers in psychology. The aim of introspection was to analyse conscious experience into elementary sensations and feelings.

Sensations referred to the raw sensory content of consciousness, devoid of all 'meaning' or interpretation. All conscious thoughts, ideas, and perceptions were assumed to be combinations of sensations which could be defined on just four dimensions: *mode* (visual, auditory etc.), *quality* (for example, the colours and shapes of the visual sensations), *intensity* and *duration*. Thus, the introspective analysis of the experience of looking at a moving picture would not contain references to the objects in the picture, but the minute description of patches of light, of differing colours, intensities and durations.

Feelings could also be introspectively analysed, in terms of three dimensions. In the classic experiment in which Wundt himself listened to a metronome beating at varying rates, he identified *pleasantness–unpleasantness, tension–relaxation* and *activity–passivity* (inducing a mild excitement or having a slight calming effect).

The attempt to analyse or break down experience into its constituent parts is *reductionism*. Through introspection, Wundt was trying to cut through the learned categories and concepts that define our everyday experience of the world and, thereby, expose the 'building blocks' from which even the earliest childhood experiences are constructed, just as chemical compounds are constructed from hydrogen, oxygen and the other chemical elements.

The most well-known criticism of Wundt's approach to scientific psychology came from Watson, the American founder of *behaviourism*, more of which below. But there were underlying cultural differences between Germany and America which made it difficult for American psychologists to accept Wundt's work wholeheartedly. Wundt, as a representative of the German intellectual tradition that was interested in the mind in general, wanted to discover the universal characteristics of the mind that can account for the universal aspects of human experience.

> *Americans, with their pioneer tradition and historical emphasis on individuality, were more concerned with questions of* individual differences ... *and the usefulness of those differences in the struggle for survival and success in a socially fluid atmosphere. These attitudes made Americans especially receptive to Darwin's ideas about individual variation, evolution by natural selection, and the 'survival of the fittest' when they appeared in the nineteenth century.*
> (Fancher, 1979)

The Principles of Psychology

William James was 'perhaps the greatest writer and teacher psychology has ever had' (Fancher, 1979). He trained to be a doctor, never founded an institute for psychological research, and in fact did relatively little research himself. But he used his laboratory to enrich his classroom presentations, and his classic textbook, *The Principles of Psychology* (1890), was a tremendous popular success, making psychology interesting and personally relevant.

James received no further formal academic training after his medical degree. Having first been appointed to teach anatomy and physiology at Harvard University in 1872, by 1875 he was calling his course 'The Relations between Physiology and Psychology', and it was in connection with this course that he developed his small demonstration laboratory in 1875. In 1878 he dropped anatomy and physiology from his curriculum, and for several years he taught 'pure psychology'.

His view of psychology is summarized in *The Principles of Psychology*, which includes chapters on brain function, habit, the stream of consciousness (see Chapter 13), the self, attention, association, the perception of time, memory, perception, instinct, will (see Chapter 12), and emotion (see Chapter 2).

It is ironic that, in view of the impact that James had on the development of psychology, especially through his *Principles* (which has given us the immortal definition: 'Psychology is the Science of Mental Life'), and how famous it made him as a psychologist, he was very critical both of the book and of what psychology could offer as a science. After its publication, he became increasingly interested in philosophy and thought of himself less and less as a psychologist, although he was (in 1894) the first American to call favourable attention to the recent work of the then still rather obscure neurologist from Vienna, Sigmund Freud (Fancher, 1979).

According to Fancher, James did not put forward a theory so much as a point of view (as much philosophical as psychological) which directly inspired *functionalism*, a movement very popular with American psychologists especially, according to which it is the purpose and utility of behaviour that are important, rather than merely its description. Functionalism, in turn, helped to stimulate interest in *individual differences*, since they determine how well or poorly individuals will adapt to their environments.

The behaviourist revolution: a new subject matter for psychology

In 1909, John B. Watson took over the psychology department at Johns Hopkins University and immediately began trying to cut psychology's ties to philosophy, and to strengthen those with biology.

At first, Watson lived in a kind of 'uneasy alliance' with traditional introspective psychology, which was, for most people, 'real' psychology – that is, the study of human consciousness. He continued to teach courses based on the work of Wundt and James, while conducting his own research on animals, and while becoming increasingly critical of the use of introspection. In particular, he argued that introspective reports were unreliable and difficult to verify: it is impossible to check the accuracy of such reports because they are based on purely private experience, to which the investigator has no possible means of access. Surely this was no way for a scientific psychology to proceed!

The only solution, as Watson saw it, was for psychology to redefine itself, and he gave it a helping hand by publishing, in 1913, an article called 'Psychology as the Behaviourist Views It,' which is often referred to as the 'Behaviourist Manifesto', a charter for a truly scientific psychology.

> *Psychology as the behaviourist views it is a purely objective natural science. Its theoretical goal is the prediction and control of behaviour. Introspection forms no essential part of its methods, nor is the scientific value of its data dependent upon the readiness with which they lend themselves to interpretation in terms of consciousness. The behaviourist, in his efforts to get a unitary scheme of animal response, recognizes no dividing line between man and brute. The behaviour of a man, with all its refinement and complexity, forms only a part of the behaviourist's total scheme of investigation.*
>
> (Watson, 1913)

Three features of this 'behaviourist manifesto' deserve special mention:
1 Psychology must be purely objective, excluding all subjective data or interpretations in terms of conscious experience. Whereas traditional psychology used objective observations of behaviour to supplement introspective data, Watson argued that they should be the *sole* and *exclusive* subject matter: he was redefining psychology as the 'science of behaviour', instead of the traditional 'science of mental life'.
2 Whereas traditional psychology aimed to *describe* and *explain* conscious mental states, Watson's goals were to *predict* and *control* overt behaviour, as they were for the other major behaviourist psychologist, B.F. Skinner (see Chapters 3, 10 and 12).
3 Watson wanted to remove the traditional distinction between human beings and animals. If, as Darwin had shown, humans evolved from more simple species, then it follows that human behaviour is simply a more complex form of the behaviour of other species. (Thus, the difference is merely one of degree – quantitative – rather than one of kind – a qualitative difference; see Chapter 10.) Consequently, rats, cats, dogs and pigeons became the major source of psychological data. Since 'psychological' now meant 'behaviour' rather than 'consciousness', animals that were convenient to study, and whose environments could easily be controlled, could replace people as experimental subjects.

In 1915, Watson was elected president of the American Psychological Association, and his presidential address dealt with his recent 'discovery' of Pavlov's work on conditioned reflexes in dogs. He proposed that the conditioned reflex could become the foundation of a full-scale human psychology 'encompassing everything from habit-formation to emotional disorders. Whereas his behaviourism had been at first little more than a point of view, it promised to become a full-fledged program of research with apparently limitless horizons' (Fancher, 1979).

Although Wundt had been influenced by empiricism through its impact on science as a whole (including physiology), it was behaviourism that was to embody empiricist philosophy within psychology. John Locke, one of the major British empiricist philosophers of the seventeenth century, described the mind at birth as a *tabula rasa* or 'blank slate', on which experience makes its imprint. Despite rejecting the mind as a valid subject matter for a scientific psychology, the extreme environmentalism of Locke's empiricism lent itself very well to the behaviourist emphasis on learning (through the process of conditioning); what the environment shapes simply moves from 'the mind' to observable behaviour (see Chapter 5).

Behaviourism also embodied the positivism of the Cartesian (from Descartes)–Newtonian tradition, in particular the emphasis on the need for scientific rigour and objectivity. Human beings were now being conceptualized and studied as 'natural phenomena', with their subjective experience, consciousness and other characteristics, which had for so long been taken as distinctive human qualities, being removed from the 'universe'. There was no place for these things in the behaviourist world. In the rest of this chapter we shall consider some of the problems that arise when this 'natural science' approach to the study of people is adopted.

What should the subject matter of psychology be?

According to Ornstein (1975), in the process of refining its methods, psychology discarded its essence, namely consciousness, and in

> *trying to imitate the natural sciences and laboratory methods of weighing and counting, dealt with everything except the soul. It tried to understand those aspects of man which can be examined in the laboratory, and claimed that conscience, value judgements, and knowledge of good and evil are metaphysical concepts, outside the problems of psychology; it was often more concerned with insignificant problems which fitted the alleged scientific method than with devising new methods to study the significant problems of man. Psychology thus became a science lacking its main subject matter, the soul.*
>
> (Fromm, 1951, quoted in Graham, 1986)

According to Graham (1986), in the East, psychology is rooted in the tradition of mysticism, with an emphasis on the spiritual, the subjective, and the individual, and its dominant ethos is necessarily *humanistic*. By contrast, as we have seen, Western psychology is rooted in the tradition of science, stressing the material, the objective, and the general, and its predominant ethos (especially since the rise of behaviourism) is *mechanistic* and *impersonal*. Graham regards the fundamental difference between them as one of perspective: mystical *insight* (observing from within) and scientific *outlook* (observing from without). Psychology, both East and

West, has a dual aspect, two perspectives, facing two fundamentally different realities, (i) the inner world of subjective experience and (ii) the outer, public world of overt behaviour. While traditional psychologies of the East fully recognize this double aspect of human existence (an essential dualism), Western psychologists have failed to do so. In order to gain acceptance as a science, it was seen as necessary to 'suppress the human face of psychology, thereby extinguishing its essence, and as Heather (1976) suggests, effectively murdering the man it claims to study' (Graham, 1986).

Since scientific method is implicitly reductionist (from the Latin *reductio*, meaning to 'take away'), psychology,

> [in] *reducing the study of man to those of his aspects which are 'objective facts' – his physical behaviours – and precluding any examination of his experience, takes away from man what is essentially and fundamentally his humanness. Man is thereby reduced to a mere thing or object, from which, Heather (1976) suggests, it is but a small step to accepting the idea that man is a machine, and nothing but a machine.*

(Graham, 1986)

The popular definition of psychology as the study of 'what makes people tick' reflects this mechanistic view of the person, which derives from the nineteenth-century mechanistic view of the universe central to the physical sciences.

Both Freud's psychoanalytic psychology and behaviourism depict people as machine-like, in that they are seen as being controlled by forces over which they have little or no control: these are internal, and mainly unconscious, in the case of Freud, and external 'environmental contingencies of reinforcement' in the case of Skinner. According to both views, the person is pulled, puppet-like, either by internal or external 'strings', with behaviour being largely determined. This, of course, relates to the question of free will, which is discussed in Chapter 12. But it is also very relevant here, where we are trying to define the appropriate subject matter of psychology: only when we have a clear idea about what a person is, can we assess and evaluate psychology's attempts to study people. If we believe that people have personal agency and are responsible for their actions, that they are not mere passive responders to forces beyond their control, either internal or external, but actively influence what they do and what happens to them, then a behaviourist account, such as those of Watson or Skinner, or Freud's psychoanalytic account, simply will not do.

A mechanistic view of people, whether this is meant to be taken literally ('people are machines') or just metaphorically ('people are like machines'), reduces them to something less than human, and this is implied by the

Figure 11.6 Fernand Leger 'Construction Workers' 1951. The term 'subject' reduces a person to something less than human; 'man as a machine'

use of the term 'subject' (see Chapter 10). This, in turn, casts the psychologist in the role of engineer: 'The notion of scientists as engineers, controlling and manipulating a mechanistic universe was . . . Bacon's legacy to the philosophy of science, and it is implicit in scientific method. Therefore . . . psychology, in its adoption of scientific method, reflects Western culture's preoccupation with manipulative technology designed for domination and control' (Graham, 1986).

It was as a reaction against (and a rejection of) such a mechanistic, dehumanizing view of the person, that *humanistic psychology* emerged, mainly in America, during the 1950s. In fact, the term was first coined by John Cohen, a British psychologist, who wrote a book called *Humanistic Psychology* in 1958, aimed at condemning 'ratomorphic robotic psychology' (Graham, 1986).

Abraham Maslow, in particular, gave wide currency to the term in America, calling it a 'third force' (the other two being behaviourism and psychoanalytic theory). However, he did not reject these approaches, but hoped that his approach would act as a unifying force, integrating the other two, thus integrating subjective and objective, the private and public aspects of the person, and providing a complete, holistic psychology.

Maslow insisted that a truly scientific psychology must embrace a humanistic perspective, treating its subject matter as fully human. This meant acknowledging individuals as perceivers and interpreters of themselves and of their world, trying to understand the world from the perspective of the perceiver (that is, using a *phenomenological* approach) rather than trying to study people from the position of a detached observer, recognizing that people help determine their own behaviour, and are not simply slaves to environmental contingencies or to their past, and regarding the self, soul or psyche, personal responsibility and agency, choice and free will as legitimate issues for psychology.

Maslow's humanistic theory is commonly referred to as a 'psychology of being', while that of the other major figure, Carl Rogers, is a 'psychology of becoming'. Although both shared a view of the person as possessing the need for *self-actualization* (realizing one's potential as an individual), a characteristic of human beings which makes them unique among animals, for Maslow this represented an end in itself, while for Rogers it was the *process* of becoming a 'fully functioning person' that was of major interest and importance. This process was described in his *Self Theory* (1961, but originally proposed in 1947), according to which

> *the individual has within him the capacity and tendency, latent if not evident, to move forward to maturity. In a suitable psychological climate this tendency is realized, and becomes actual rather than potential. It is evident in the capacity of the individual to understand those aspects of his life and of himself which are causing pain and dissatisfaction, an understanding which probes beneath his conscious knowledge of himself into those experiences which he has hidden from*

himself because of their threatening nature. It shows itself in the tendency to reorganize his personality and his relationship to life in ways which are regarded as more mature. Whether one calls it a growth tendency, a drive toward self-actualization, or a forward-moving directional tendency, it is the mainspring of life . . . It is the urge which is evident in all organic and human life – to expand, extend, become autonomous, develop, mature.

(Rogers, 1961)

Like Maslow, Rogers stressed the importance of the internal, phenomenological, frame of reference; for Rogers, the proper subject matter of psychology is the individual and the world *as perceived by the individual*. Other psychologists whose ideas were influenced by phenomenology include Kelly (see Chapter 1) and Allport (see Chapter 3).

Just as Maslow hoped to be able to bring behaviourism and Freudian theory together through his humanistic approach, so Rogers never rejected the rigour of empirical methods. (Indeed, he used, and advocated the use of, empirical methods in the assessment of psychotherapy, in particular the Q-sort; see Chapter 3.) But he did maintain that experience must be included in any attempt to understand man and the universe: there can be no scientific knowledge without experiential knowledge.

Similarly, Rollo May (1967) argued that humanistic psychology is not hostile to science, but he urged that psychologists need to recognize the limits of traditional scientific methods and that they should try to find new methods which will more adequately reveal the nature of man.

Although not derived from a humanistic perspective as defined above, new methods for studying people are increasingly being used and developed which represent a significant move away from the traditional, mechanistic, laboratory-based methods which are seen as distorting our understanding of human beings. Some of this *new paradigm research* will be discussed later in the chapter.

Experimenters and subjects are people first

One major criticism of traditional empirical methods, especially the laboratory experiment, has focused on the artificiality of the laboratory situation and the tasks that people are often asked to perform there, in the name of science. The point that is usually made is that the experimental set-up is so far removed from what people are likely to encounter in real-life, everyday situations, that their behaviour inside the laboratory is a very poor indicator of how they will behave outside, in the real world, and since it is the real world that we are interested in, experiments can tell us very little that is of any value. This relates to the *external validity* of experiments.

This criticism seems to assume that what happens in the experiment is somehow valid, within the parameters of the laboratory situation, such that the behaviour that is observed (the dependent variable) is affected by the experimental manipulation (the independent variable) and nothing else. Thus, a well-controlled, properly run experiment has *internal validity*.

This assumption is necessary as part of the objectivity that is claimed for empirical research. The experimenter does not influence the behaviour of the subject (the outcome of the experiment) except to the extent that he or she decides on a hypothesis to be tested, chooses and operationalizes the variables, opts for the design to be used, selects the subjects, runs the procedure, collates and interprets the results, and so on. But isn't this a very significant 'except'? There are two important points involved here.

Observing the world as it is?

The whole situation is the creation of the experimenter and, to this extent, he or she cannot be considered to be objective within that situation. All kinds of biases, preferences, attitudes, beliefs and expectations are reflected in the choices and decisions which go to create the experiment. If 'objectivity' requires that the researcher observe the world as it is, playing no part in what is studied and how it is studied, then clearly objectivity is a non-starter, whether it is in physics, chemistry or psychology.

Is it possible for science to be a 'cool, passionless, absolutely objective exploration of an external reality?' (Gould, 1987). Since all scientists are people, and since science is a human activity, part of human behaviour (at least in Western culture), the answer would seem to be 'No!': 'we scientists are no different from anyone else. We are passionate human beings, enmeshed in a web of personal and social circumstances ... unless scientists understand their hopes and engage in vigorous self-scrutiny, they will not be able to sort unacknowledged preference from nature's weak and imperfect message' (Gould, 1987).

In other words, the world does not reveal itself to us as it is. Scientists have to discover ways of explaining the world which best enable them to predict and control it (at least in the case of the natural sciences), and to do this most efficiently, they must be able to separate their biases and prejudices from the 'accuracy' of those explanations.

The experimental drama

What makes the laboratory experiment such an unnatural and artificial situation is precisely the fact that it is almost totally structured by one 'participant' – the experimenter. (This feature of the experiment is related to the differences in power between the people involved, and the ethical implications of this were discussed in Chapter 10.)

Just as important as the assumption regarding the objectivity of the experimenter, is the assumed 'objectness' of the human 'subject', who is implicitly denied subjectivity, agency and intentionality (Graham, 1986). For the experimental situation to be considered an objective study of human behaviour, the person being studied must be thought of, and treated as, a passive responder to whatever stimuli are presented, and that the only factors that matter (that influence his or her responses) are the variables manipulated by the experimenter, and which are objectively defined. This view of the person really does suggest that 'object' would be a more fitting term than 'subject'; it would be no more offensive and dehumanizing than 'subject' but a lot more descriptively accurate.

But can this view of the actors involved in the experimental drama be justified? Is there anything more that the experimenter is contributing to the situation than what has already gone into the planning and design of the experiment, things to do with his or her being a human being, a social animal? And could perhaps the subject be rather more actively involved, such that he or she is also contributing something to the situation, and ultimately influencing its outcome, contrary to his or her supposed 'object-ness'?

According to Rosenthal,

> *it appears indisputable that the humanness of both the experimenter and the subject interact in numerous ways which are likely to have a profound effect on experimental outcomes. The experimenter's appearance, sex, age, mood, manner, race, social class, dialect and dress are all likely to influence the subject so that instead of the experimenter being an external 'objective' observer, he is, in effect, a participant who actively contributes to the behaviour that he wishes passively and objectively to observe and record.*

(Rosenthal, 1966)

Rosenthal uses the word 'actively' to describe the way that various characteristics of the experimenter (what the experimenter is *like*) may affect the subject's behaviour, but those characteristics are essentially static, unchanging characteristics over which he or she has little control. Such characteristics are, however, correlated with the experimenter's behaviour, and will also influence the subject's perception of, and response to, the experimenter. (This is what is implied by 'actively'.)

For example, Rosenthal (1967, cited in Valentine, 1992) described the pattern of behaviour that female experimenters show towards male participants as 'interested modesty', while that shown by male experimenters towards female participants was described as just plain 'interested'. They took significantly longer to prepare stimulus materials for presentation to female subjects than to males. Sex differences reveal themselves in a wide range of non-verbal behaviours.

Perhaps of even greater significance is the way that the experimenter's expectations can influence the outcome of the experiment, serving as a self-fulfilling prophecy. This is referred to as *experimenter bias*. Such effects have been demonstrated in a wide range of experiments, including reaction time, psychophysics, animal learning, verbal conditioning, personality assessment, person perception, learning, and ability, as well as everyday life situations (Rosenthal & Rubin, cited in Valentine, 1992). What they consistently show is that, if one group of experimenters has one hypothesis about what it·expects to find and another group has the opposite hypothesis, both groups will obtain results in line with their respective hypotheses. These results are not due to the mishandling of data by biased experimenters, but, somehow, the bias of the experimenter creates a changed environment in which participants actually behave differently.

In two separate studies (Rosenthal & Fode, 1960; and Rosenthal & Lawson, 1961, cited in Weisstein, 1993a), experimenters who were told that rats learning mazes had been especially bred for brightness obtained better learning from their rats than did experimenters who believed that their rats had been specially bred for dullness. Both groups of rats had been drawn from the same population. 'The concreteness of the changed conditions produced by expectation is a fact, a reality' (Weisstein, 1993a); exactly how the situation is concretely changed in the case of rats remains unclear.

Valentine (1992) cites a third rat experiment described by Rosenthal and Fode in 1963, which gives identical results to the other two, and she points out that there were certain cases of cheating observed (prodding the rat to encourage it to run the maze). But we cannot be sure, she says, that such effects fully account for the overall results, and Rosenthal was interested in the rather more subtle influences of experimenter expectations.

In the case of people, the way that experimenter bias produces its effects is much more likely to be through a variety of non-verbal behaviours, by which the experimenter's expectations are unwittingly, and unknowingly, conveyed to the subject who, in turn, interprets these signals below the level of consciousness. The most famous demonstration of such bias is the 'Pygmalion' experiment by Rosenthal and Jacobson (published in 1968 in book form as *Pygmalion in the Classroom*).

In a natural classroom situation, teachers were told that a particular group of children would show academic 'promise' during the next academic year. These children showed significantly greater gains in IQ than children for whom such predictions were not made (although this group also showed substantial improvements). The children were, in fact, randomly allocated to the 'academic promise' and the control (no such prediction) conditions. The teachers' expectations of gains in the first group actually produced the predicted improvements – that is, there was a self-fulfilling prophecy. As to the mechanism, it is likely that the children who were expected to excel received more attention, encouragement, praise and so on than those who were not; this in turn, affected their self-concept and motivation in a positive way, reflected in the actual gains in IQ.

This particular study, as well as Rosenthal's work in general, has been criticized in its turn, on a number of methodological and statistical grounds. For example, there is no guarantee that his 'experiments on experiments' are themselves free from the kind of biases which they are trying to expose in others (Valentine, 1992). However, they are still very suggestive of the social dimension of psychological experiments, something which is incompatible with the positivist approach which regards the study of people as objective, neutral, and value-free.

One area of research in which Rosenthal's findings are particularly relevant is sex differences.

> *Since it is beyond doubt that most of us start with notions as to the nature of men and women, the validity of a number of observations of sex differences is questionable, even when these observations have been made under carefully controlled conditions . . . more important, the Rosenthal experiments point quite clearly to the influence of social expectation. In some extremely important ways, people are what you expect them to be or at least they behave as you expect them to behave.*

(Weisstein, 1993a)

(See Chapter 6.)

Turning now to the 'subject's' perspective, a major way of trying to understand what he or she contributes to the experiment is through the concept of *demand characteristics* (Orne, 1962).

Whereas, as we have seen, the mechanistic model stresses what is done to the (passive) participant, Orne is interested in what the human participant *does*, which implies a far more active role. Participants' performance in an experiment could almost be thought of as a form of *problem-solving behaviour* since, at some level, they see it as their task to work out the true purpose of the experiment and to respond in a way which will support the hypothesis being tested. In this context, the *cues* which convey an experimental hypothesis to the participant become significant influences on his or her behaviour, and it is the sum total of those cues that Orne calls the demand characteristics of the experimental situation.

What are these cues? They include 'the rumours or campus scuttlebut [gossip] about the research, the information conveyed during the original situation, the person of the experimenter, and the setting of the laboratory, as well as all explicit and implicit communications during the experiment proper'. Orne goes on to point out that the experimental procedure itself may provide cues. For example, if a task is presented twice, with some intervening task (i.e., a repeated measures design), then even the dullest college student will realize that some change in performance of the first task is expected on the second.

It is very difficult in practice to find truly naive participants who do not believe that they have at least some familiarity with psychology, or who cannot work out the purpose of the experiment from the procedure. The crucial point here is not whether participants are correct in their attempts to 'suss out' what is going on: the fact that such an attempt is being made at all means that participants are not the passive responders implied by the mechanistic model.

This tendency to identify the demand characteristics is related to the tendency to play the role of 'a good experimental participant', wanting to please and cooperate with the experimenter and not to 'upset the experiment'. It is mainly in this sense that Orne sees the experiment as a social situation, in which the participants play different, but complementary, roles; in order for the interaction to proceed relatively smoothly, each participant must have some idea of what the other(s) expect of him or her.

At the same time, the experiment is a rather special type of social situation, with its own rules and norms (some explicit, some implicit). As Moghaddam et al. (1993) point out, when we agree to participate in a laboratory experiment, we are not entering a cultural vacuum; we have a host of ideas and expectations about what an experiment is, the role and nature of psychologists, science and so on. What makes an experiment 'possible' is a set of shared understandings as to the nature of science, and the respective roles of investigator and 'subject'.

If 'experiments' are only meaningful within a particular cultural context, this is another respect in which science cannot claim complete objectivity: science itself is a culture-related phenomenon. Orne points out that, if people are asked to do five push-ups as a favour, they will ask, 'Why?', but if the request comes from an experimenter, they will ask 'Where?' Similarly, he reports an experiment in which people were asked to add sheets of random numbers, then tear the sheets up into at least thirty-two pieces. They showed very few signs of overt hostility or irritation, apparently attaching some meaning to the task, perhaps construing it as an endurance test of some kind. Indeed, they would all have passed with flying colours, because *five-and-a-half hours* later, they were still going strong, and the experimenter had to stop them!

If people are 'problem-solving' when they take part in experiments, they may sometimes work out the experimental hypothesis correctly, which is why an ongoing means of assessing any piece of psychological research is to ask if the results could have occurred because of the demand characteristics involved in the procedure.

While demand characteristics cannot be eliminated, they can be identified and their effect can be studied: what we want to know is, do participants' perceived demand characteristics (all the cues which they believe reveal the hypothesis and, therefore, what their behaviour should be) predict behaviour better than the independent variables do?

Accepting the results of Rosenthal's and Orne's research

> *turns the standard defence of the laboratory method on its head –*
> *that defence being the argument that only by rigorously controlling*
> *variables can effective connections be established, and that control is*
> *almost impossible in natural settings. The counter-argument is that*
> *in 'nature' variables never do interact on a one-to-one basis; there is*
> *always a variety of confounding variables which affect the outcome.*
> *Thus the stripped-down laboratory situation, far from achieving*
> *clarity or simplifying, merely obscures by creating a totally*
> *unrealistic analogue.*

(Westland, 1978, quoted in Graham, 1986)

Deception as an experimental technique: how 'scientific' can it be?

We discussed at length in Chapter 10 the ethical questions raised by the use of deception, especially in social psychology experiments. Here, we are concerned with the scientific or methodological aspects of deception. In the context of demand characteristics, it is sometimes necessary to deceive participants as to the true purpose of the experiment, otherwise the experimenter will be unable to observe behaviour that is relevant to what he or she is trying to find out.

For example, if in his experiments, Milgram had told the teacher-subjects that the learner was not receiving any shocks and that the experiment was to do with obedience, would he have learnt anything useful about obedience? Of course, the whole point of the deception (or 'technical illusion', which he prefers) is that it is accepted 'at face value' – the 'cover story' must be 'swallowed whole' so that it is not suspected of being what it is: a camouflage for the experiment's true purpose. If it isn't accepted, the whole experiment is undermined.

If participants actively search for meaning, they may become suspicious and non-accepting of the information given to them by the experimenter. This is particularly likely to occur where participants are drawn from a large pool of college students, as in America, where the 'typical' participant is a psychology undergraduate who is obliged to take part in a certain number of empirical investigations as a course requirement (see Chapter 8). The use of deception in experiments may well be part of the campus 'scuttlebut' that Orne (1962) speaks about in relation to demand characteristics. Krupat and Garonzik (1994) cite evidence that suggests that once an experiment has been carried out in a given class, dorm, or subject pool, word gets round and many of those who are later recruited are already 'tainted' as reliable sources of data by virtue of their foreknowledge.

If participants have previously taken part in studies where deception was involved (which they know through having been debriefed), they are more likely to be suspicious and to formulate their own hypotheses regarding the experimenter's true interests and purposes. Such suspicion challenges the (internal) validity of the research: although the actual behaviour of suspicious participants may be similar to that of non-suspicious ones, such data are of questionable value, because we cannot know whether the participants are truly acting as if they were in the situation the experimenter is trying to create (for example, whether the teacher-subjects are genuinely distressed because they believe that the learner is being shocked), or if their behaviour is merely a function of their particular set of beliefs about the experiment combined with their motivation to comply with the demand characteristics of the situation as they see it (Krupat & Garonzik, 1994).

Krupat and Garonzik believe that many participants in standard psychological pools already have a low level of trust by the time they set foot in the experimental situation. The common finding that participants do not strongly object to being deceived (see Chapter 10) may help to resolve the ethical debate over deception, but what are the methodological implications of a science in which people *expect to be deceived*, where deception becomes the norm? Expecting to be deceived in some way will bias participants' interpretations of experimental events, and this threatens the validity of any research that is based upon deceptive methods.

But are there any alternatives to deception? According to Krupat and Garonzik (1994), there was a flurry of papers on deception and alternatives to it between 1967 and 1977, with *role play* the main alternative being discussed. However, the weight of opinion turned against role play and no systematic alternative was proposed. Very little discussion or research into deception has taken place since the mid-1980s. Krupat and Garonzik argue that social psychology should break away from its heavy reliance on deception; they are not opposed to it in principle, but they do object to its 'automatic use as a first, if not only, option'. As an alternative, they propose what they call the *honest difference* method, which they used as part of a replication of a social influence (conformity) experiment conducted in 1970 by Willis and Willis, who were interested in the extent to which perceived relative competence at a task (rating a set of pictures and being compared with a partner who also rates the pictures) influences a person's willingness to accept social influence (changing one's ratings after receiving feedback about one's own and one's partner's scores, relative to experts' ratings). In the original experiment, (i) subjects were told the study was about information processing, (ii) the partner was a confederate, (iii) all scores were fictitious, (iv) they were randomly allocated to either an inferior or superior condition.

Krupat and Garonzik devised a parallel honest difference format, in which two real participants are told the true purpose of the study ('This is a study in social influence. We are interested in finding out how much each of you will be influenced by the judgements made by the others'). They then rate a set of photos which have actually been previously rated by experts. Each of their ratings is scored and they are given honest feedback, which is exchanged between the pair. They are told at the start that the purpose of the second lot of ratings is to 'be able to see how much each of you has been influenced by the judgement of the other'.

While the honest difference method can be used only for a limited number of research questions, it presents an approach which may be adaptable to a range of psychological issues as an alternative to false feedback. It is not meant to provide a single, all-encompassing, alternative paradigm, but merely a demonstration of the kind of possibility that may result when 'social psychologists do not accept deception as a standard procedure and put their minds to a serious search for alternatives' (Krupat & Garonzik, 1994).

A shift towards studying people as people

The criticisms of the positivist, mechanistic, behaviourist-dominated scientific psychology that we have considered above (together with others that we have not), began to be drawn together, during the late 1960s, culminating in Harré and Secord's (1972) *The Explanation of Social Behaviour*. This book is widely seen as marking the beginning of a 'new paradigm' in psychology (Harré, 1993). Harré and Secord called their new approach *ethogenics*, partly to indicate the break from experimentation which they were advocating, but also to acknowledge the importance of context and convention in everyday life.

They, in their turn, had been particularly influenced by Garfinkel's (1967) *ethnomethodology* and Goffman's *dramaturgical analysis* of social interaction described in books such as *Stigma* (Goffman, 1963) and *The Presentation of Self in Everyday Life* (Goffman, 1971). Both Garfinkel and Goffman had developed methodologies which were appropriate to the nature of the phenomenon they were studying, namely human beings. For both,

> the central idea of symbolic interactionism, that human life is created in the manipulation of symbols, and not in automated responses to pre-defined situations, animated their research. The root metaphysical idea which Secord and I called the anthropomorphic model, was that people had intentions, plans and projects and the skills to carry out these projects jointly with others, according to the local conventions of propriety.
>
> (Harré, 1993)

New paradigm research (Reason & Rowan, 1981) refers to the attempt to integrate naive enquiry (the kind of ordinary day-to-day thinking that everyone engages in; see Chapter 1) and orthodox research, making it 'objectively subjective'. It openly opposes the positivist, deterministic, reductionist, mechanistic approach (which they call 'quantophrenia'), which typically produces statistically significant but humanly insignificant results. They insist that in the field of human enquiry, it is preferable to be deeply interesting than accurately boring.

They oppose deception and debriefing, manipulation and mystification. But at the same time they advocate that certain aspects of conventional methods and procedures, in particular certain aspects of report-writing, be expanded and developed. For example, the introduction and discussion sections should be written with as much care and attention as is usually given to the main part of the investigation (procedure and results), involving literature searches within sociology, the natural sciences, literature, philosophy, theology and history. They should become part of the research process itself, so that research reports become 'a statement of where the researchers stand, not only theoretically, but politically, ideologically, spiritually and emotionally in as much that they discuss the

many influences which have shaped the thinking and feeling which has led
to the current investigation' (Graham, 1986).

Another new direction taken by new paradigm research is
collaborative/participative research, or *cooperative enquiry*, in which both
the researcher and the participant actively contribute to the planning,
execution and interpretation of the research.

> *The way of cooperative enquiry is for the researcher to interact with
> the subjects so that they do contribute directly both to hypothesis
> making, to formulating the final conclusions, and to what goes on in
> between. This contribution may be strong, in the sense that the
> subject is co-researcher and contributes to creative thinking at all
> stages. Or it may be weak, in the sense that the subject is thoroughly
> informed of the research proposals at all stages and is invited to
> assent or dissent, and if there is dissent, then the researcher and
> subject negotiate until agreement is reached. In the complete form of
> this approach, not only will the subject be fully fledged co-researcher,
> but the researcher will also be co-subject, participating fully in the
> action and experience to be researched.*
>
> (Heron, 1982, quoted in Graham, 1986)

(The continued use of 'subject' seems totally incompatible with the
approach being advocated, with 'participant' being the obvious
replacement; perhaps it's a case of 'old habits die hard'.)

Another major innovation within psychological research is *discourse
analysis* (DA). This brings together a wide variety of perspectives and
influences, from philosophy, linguistics, artificial intelligence, anthropology,
and sociology (as well as various aspects of psychology). One of its central
features is that it sees 'talk' (both conversation between people and written
language) as worthy of study *in its own right* and as a way in which people
(attempt to) achieve their goals. This contrasts sharply with the traditional
view of language as an index of external reality or of a person's inner states.
The prime source of data in DA is conversation, either in natural settings or
in interviews, but the emphasis is very different from that of traditional
social psychological methods. For example, instead of treating what people
say in interviews as acceptable *substitutes* for actual observation of
behaviour, it is the interview data itself that is of interest (the 'subject
matter'; (Lalljee & Widdicombe, 1989).

DA also avoids hypothesis-testing and the use of pre-defined coding
schedules (as is usually the case in observational studies); in this sense, it is
mainly *inductive* (as opposed to hypothetico-deductive) and *data-driven*
(as opposed to theory-driven; Lalljee & Widdicombe, 1989).

One use of DA is in the scrutiny of psychological theories (such as those
of Freud, Skinner, and Piaget) in order to show how they use language to
create a convincing theoretical account of human behaviour. One 'strategy'
is to use metaphors in such a way that they are taken literally, apparently
referring to the 'external reality' of behaviour that the theory is trying to

account for (see Soyland's (1994) *Psychology as Metaphor*).

In everyday life, as well as in putting forward psychological theories, or in politics, we are often trying to get our account of the truth accepted by others as 'fact' or '*the* truth', and this is one sense in which language is seen primarily as a form of social action (rather than primarily a *representation* of reality, including what people really think about the issue being discussed).

According to Edwards and Potter (1992), DA extends beyond a specific method into a fairly radical *rethink* about traditional psychological topics, which they call *discursive psychology*. So, memory and attribution theory are treated as processes of discourse between people: memories are not close or not-so-close attempts at recalling 'the facts', but are motivated constructions by people with a 'stake' in producing an 'account' which may, for example, suit their defence against blame and acountability (Coolican, 1994). We cannot simply take what people say as revealing what they *think*, as if their talk provided a window through which we could peer at their cognitive processes; we must first understand what their talk is trying to do, what it is trying to achieve in a particular social context, at a particular time.

Psychology and postmodernism

These changes in the way that psychologists think about the subject matter of psychology, and the suitable methods for studying people, may be seen in the broader context of cultural changes which, collectively, are referred to as *postmodernism*. While the term has been used for some time in fields such as the arts, architecture, the humanities, and sociology, it is only recently that a 'postmodern psychology' has been discussed, which is partly why there are many interpretations of exactly what this means (a ripe area of study for DA perhaps?). Shotter (1992) summarizes what he believes are the major changes involved, which include:

1 a shift from knowing by 'looking at' (the perspective of the detached, theory-testing onlooker) to knowing by being 'in contact, or in touch with' (the interested, interpretive '*hermeneutical*', procedure-testing participant observer; – this is clearly related to the move towards collaborative research; see above);

2 a shift from a concern with *theories* and *things* towards *practices* (practical, instructive accounts) and *activities/uses*;

3 a shift from what goes on inside the head of individuals towards the (largely social) nature of their surroundings, and what these can (or will) 'allow', 'permit', and 'afford'.

Shotter contrasts the hermeneutical approach with the *empirical* approach, which is the approach of the positivist or 'modern' psychology. In the latter, we *could* say (that is, the facts will 'afford' us saying) that our ways of talking *about* the world depend *on* the world: they are 'rooted' or 'grounded' in its nature. To that extent, our talk is about what we 'find' out there in the world (which clearly relates to the view of science as objective, where scientists study the world *as it is*).

According to the former, however, it is equally true to say that what we take the nature of the world to be depends on our ways of talking about it. Knowledge involves a process of 'making' or construction; instead of seeing the scientist's task as finding or discovering an order that is already there, it should be seen as a process of negotiating, in a back-and-forth fashion, with other people, in order to make 'theories' intelligible and legitimate. Both approaches – the empirical and hermeneutical – are valid and both should be used (Shotter, 1992).

The changing face of science

In his 1983 Presidential Address to the British Psychological Society, Hetherington (cited by Graham, 1986) stressed the need for a paradigm shift in psychology and the development of its own methods. The methods of natural science can at best only provide a partial knowledge of why people behave as they do, and since psychology is part natural science and part interpretive science, it needs to develop methods which are adequate for the study of human beings as organisms, as members of social organizations, and as people with whom we engage in dialogue.

Hetherington cited James's observation that 'the natural science assumptions are provisional and revisable things' – scientific 'facts' are not 'set in stone', but are constantly being changed, not because the world changes but because our theories and explanations change.

As we have seen, new methods of studying people are being developed, and no doubt Hetherington would approve of these developments. However, the great irony about this new paradigm is that what it is replacing (or partially replacing, since most psychologists still subscribe to the positivist methodology) may itself have been out of date for some time. The natural science on which Watson so explicitly and vigorously based psychology (originally in 1913) is in many ways *not* the natural science of the present day (or even of the recent past).

A number of physicists and other scientists, philosophers of science, and other academics, beginning probably with Einstein and his theory of relativity published in 1905, are moving away from the Cartesian–Newtonian view of a clockwork universe, which is completely predictable and determinate, towards a view of the universe as much more uncertain and unpredictable. A major 'ingredient' in this 'new physics' is Heisenberg's *uncertainty principle*, according to which there are limits beyond which there can be no certainty, not because of the lack of precision in our measuring instruments or the extremely small size of the entities being measured – but because of nature itself. More specifically, all attempts to observe sub-atomic particles, such as electrons, *alter* them; at the sub-atomic level, we cannot observe something without changing it, because the universe does not exist independently of the observer who is trying to measure it.

If most psychologists are still trying to model themselves on a physics based on Descartes and Newton, then they are out of date and out of touch, and if they want their science to reveal what people are 'really like', in some absolute, objective, way, they are also out of luck.

Summary

- Mainstream, academic psychology has been very strongly influenced by the classical, *positivist* view of science, according to which science is meant to be *unbiased, objective* and *value-free*. This can also be seen in the practice of psychiatry and clinical psychology.
- Ironically, while psychology has always (and still does) modelled itself on 'classical physics', physics itself no longer adopts a 'classical' view of science.
- Until the Middle Ages, science and philosophy were synonymous, with the main focus of study being consciousness/conscious mental life. Psychology was the study of the soul and was closely linked to Christian theology, which saw man as the centre of the universe (*orthodox scholasticism*).
- This view was challenged in the sixteenth century when Copernicus claimed that the planets revolve around the sun, later confirmed by Kepler's laws of planetary motion and by Galileo.
- Instead of to gain wisdom/knowledge, Bacon advocated that scientific discovery should be used to help man to gain *mastery* over nature; science and theology should also be separated.
- Descartes extended the views of Galileo and Bacon. He divided the universe into *res extensa* (physical matter) and *res cogitans* (non-physical mind). This is *philosophical dualism*.
- Dualism allowed scientists to describe the physical world objectively, without reference to the human observer.
- Descartes also introduced *mechanism* into science and extended this view of matter to living organisms, including the human body. He was also one of the first people to advocate *reductionism*.
- As applied to the study of human behaviour/social institutions, objectivity came to be called *positivism* (Comte).
- *Empiricism* is another fundamental feature of science.
- By the nineteenth century, scientific knowledge was regarded as the only valid knowledge; the emergence of psychology as a separate discipline reflected this scientific 'mentality'.
- At first, the subject matter of scientific psychology was what it had

always been, i.e. non-material consciousness. Wundt and James were the two major pioneers of academic psychology, setting up the first laboratories in 1879 and 1875 respectively.

- Wundt argued that conscious mental states could be analysed into its basic elements (elementary *sensations/feelings*) through carefully controlled *introspection*.
- While Wundt was interested in *universal* aspects of the mind, American psychologists were influenced by Darwin's theory of evolution and James's theory of *functionalism*, which helped to stimulate interest in *individual differences*.
- Watson rejected introspectionism on the grounds that it is based on purely *private* experience, accessible only to the person who is introspecting. To be an objective, natural science, psychology must replace consciousness with *behaviour* as its subject matter.
- Watson saw the difference between human and animal behaviour as one of degree only, so that Pavlov's work on conditioned reflexes in dogs could become the foundation of a full-scale human psychology.
- Behaviourism embodied the extreme environmentalism of Locke's *empiricism*, as well as the *positivist* emphasis on objectivity.
- Traditional psychologies of the East recognize the double aspect of human existence: the inner world of subjective experience and the outer world of overt behaviour. But Western psychologists, by excluding the former, reduce 'man' to a mere thing – an object or machine.
- Humanistic psychology emerged, during the 1950s, as a reaction against the mechanistic, dehumanizing image of the person that was contained in both behaviourism and Freud's psychoanalytic theory.
- Both Maslow and Rogers advocated a *phenomenological* approach, and believed in the fundamental human need for *self-actualization*; however, while for Maslow this was an end in itself, for Rogers it was a *process*.
- Humanistic psychologists don't reject science, but urge that there can be no scientific knowledge without experiential knowledge, and appropriate methods must be found to study people as they are.
- Even if laboratory experiments lack *external validity*, it is still assumed that they have *internal validity*; this assumption is necessary if empirical research is to be considered *objective*.
- But *the world does not reveal itself to us as it is*, and both the experimenter and the 'subject'/'object' might be contributing much more to the outcome of the experiment than is 'permitted' by the positivist account of scientific research.
- The experimenter's physical appearance and behaviour can affect the participant's behaviour, and the experimenter's behaviour will be influenced by the sex of the participant.
- Perhaps even more important is *experimenter bias*, the most famous

demonstration of which is Rosenthal and Jacobson's 'Pygmalion' experiment. This demonstrated how expectations can result in a *self-fulfilling prophecy*.

- Although Rosenthal's 'experiments on experiments' have been criticized, they strongly suggest the social dimension of psychological experiments; this is incompatible with a purely positivist approach.
- *Demand characteristics* refer to the contribution made by the 'subject' to the experiment, in the form of all the *cues* which convey an experimental hypothesis to the subject, who is engaged in *problem-solving behaviour*.
- This is related to the subject's role of 'good experimental subject', which reflects the social nature of the experimental situation.
- There also needs to be a shared understanding of what 'science' is for an experiment to be possible, making science itself a *culture-related* phenomenon.
- The use of deception in experiments may become part of the demand characteristics through the 'word getting round' that this is what goes on in psychology; expecting to be deceived will bias participants' interpretations of experimental events, which threatens the validity of the research.
- An alternative to deception is the *honest difference* method, in which one group of participants is told the *true purpose* of the experiment. Although designed mainly as an alternative to *false feedback*, it demonstrates the possibility – and the need – of alternatives to deception.
- Criticisms of the positivist approach in psychology culminated in Harré and Secord's *ethogenics/anthropomorphic model*, which marked a new paradigm.
- *New paradigm research* attempts to integrate 'everyday psychology' and orthodox research. Reason and Rowan advocate that research reports make clear the researcher's theoretical, political or other values and how these have shaped the current investigation.
- *Collaborative/participative research* or *cooperative enquiry* involves both the researcher and the participant actively contributing to the planning, execution and interpretation of the research.
- *Discourse analysis* is the study of conversation and written language as important in their own right. It has been extended by Edwards and Potter, from a method to a new way of thinking about traditional topics, called *discursive psychology*, which sees language as a form of social action.
- New paradigm research is related to the broader cultural movement of *postmodernism*. One of the major changes within postmodern psychology is a shift towards a *hermeneutical* approach, which

stresses the interpretive, constructivist nature of knowledge. But the *empirical/positivist* approach is not rejected.

- Ironically, the positivist view of science, which the new paradigm is (partially) replacing, may itself have been out of date for some time. Physicists now believe that the world cannot be studied objectively, independently of attempts to measure it.

Suggestions for further reading

Deese, J. (1972) *Psychology as Science and Art*, New York: Harcourt Brace Jovanovich.

Fancher, R. E. (1979) *Pioneers of Psychology*, New York: W. W. Norton & Co.

Graham, H. (1986) *The Human Face of Psychology*, Milton Keynes: Open University Press.

Free will and determinism

Why are psychologists interested?

Historical reasons

The debate about free will and determinism has been a central feature of Western philosphy, at least since Descartes (1596–1650); given psychology's intellectual and historical roots in philosophy, it would be very surprising if psychologists were not interested in the issue.

To understand the causes of thought and behaviour

As we saw in Chapter 11, identifying the causes of some phenomenon, as part of the attempt to explain it, is a fundamental part of 'classical' science. According to the philosophical doctrine of *determinism*,

> *in the case of everything that exists, there are antecedent conditions, known or unknown, given which that thing could not be other than it is . . . More loosely, it says that everything, including every cause, is the effect of some cause or causes; or that everything is not only determinate but causally determined . . . if true, it holds not only for all things that have existed but for all things that do or ever will exist.*

(Taylor, 1963)

'Everything that exists' includes people and their thoughts and behaviour, so a 'strict' determinist believes that thought and behaviour are no different from (other) 'things' or events in the world.

This, of course, begs the question: are thoughts and behaviour the same *kind of thing or event* as chemical reactions in a test tube, a volcanic eruption, or the firing of neurons in the brain? We don't usually ask ourselves if the chemicals 'agreed' to combine in a certain way, or if the volcano just 'felt like' erupting, or if the neurons 'decided' to fire. To do so (assuming we weren't being witty or in some other way not wanting to be taken literally) would involve us in the 'sin' of *anthropomorphizing*, of attributing human abilities and characteristics to non-human things (including animals). No one seriously believes that chemicals can agree, or that volcanos have feelings, or that neurons can make decisions. But we do attribute these abilities to people, they are part of our concept of a person, and this concept forms an essential part of 'everyday' or commonsense psychology (see Chapter 1). For these reasons, psychologists who study the attribution process, for example (see Chapter 2), must take seriously the commonsense view that people make decisions, agree (or not) with each other, and, in a whole host of ways, exercise their *free will*. And having free will depends upon having 'a mind': deciding, agreeing and so on are precisely the kinds of things we do with our minds, they are mental processes or events. However, while it may be necessary to 'have a mind' in order to be able to decide (that is, free will implies having a mind), having a mind does not imply free will; our decisions, agreements and disagreements may be *caused* (determined) even though they seem not to be. These kinds of observations lead us directly into the realm of philosophy, where the arguments become extremely complex, abstract and technical. We shall try to keep to more psychological paths.

To investigate the influence of mental events over behaviour

Even if it is accepted that human thinking and behaviour are different from natural, physical phenomena, and that they are not determined in the same way (or that a different kind of explanation is required), for most of its history as a separate discipline, psychology has operated as if there were no difference. As we saw in Chapter 11, since 1913, when Watson launched the behaviourist 'movement', psychologists have been trying to emulate the natural sciences, and the most obvious form this has taken has been the use of empirical methods, in particular the laboratory experiment. The use of such methods to study people implicitly adopts a view of human behaviour as determined, and is closely related to the positivist and mechanistic nature of experimental research.

Does this mean that all, or most psychologists, are behaviourists? In one important sense, the answer is 'yes'. *Methodological behaviourism* refers to the belief in the importance of empirical methods, especially the experiment, as a way of collecting data about human thought and behaviour which can be quantified and statistically analysed. Most psychologists today would probably describe themselves as behaviourists in this sense. However, most psychologists since the late 1950s would deny that they are behaviourists in the other important sense, namely, *philosophical behaviourism*. In its most extreme form, as represented by Watson, the very existence of mind is denied; thinking, for example, is nothing but a series of vocal or subvocal and verbal responses (that is to say, 'mind' is *reduced* to behaviour). As we saw above, if you reject the mind, you consequently reject free will too: without a mind, there can be no deciding or choosing.

A less extreme view is adopted by Skinner who, despite his firm espousal of environmentalism, does not deny the existence of mental processes. What he does deny is the commonsense explanation of the role of mental events in relation to behaviour, for he sees them as irrelevant in trying to predict and control behaviour; they are mere *epiphenomena*, 'by-products' of behaviour, totally lacking any influence over behaviour. This is one attempt to solve the 'mind–body' (or 'mind–brain') problem, which we shall discuss in detail in Chapter 13. The important point here is that, along with denying the influence of mental events over behaviour, Skinner rejected the notion of free will: while not denying that people *believe* they make choices, he argued that this belief is an illusion. (We shall take a closer look at Skinner's views later in the chapter.)

Philosophical behaviourism involves an explicit rejection or denial of free will, compared with its implicit rejection in the case of methodological behaviourism. Some, perhaps a majority, of the latter might actually express a belief in free will at the same time as believing in the validity of the experimental methods they use to study human behaviour, and this might seem like a contradictory position to adopt. They may, of course, deny that the use of those methods implies a deterministic or mechanistic model of the subject at all, in which case there is no contradiction. Alternatively, they may draw a distinction between (i) 'people as they live their lives on a day-to-day basis' where free will is certainly assumed, and (ii) 'people as subjects in psychological experiments', where the question of free will does not arise or is not relevant. William James drew a similar distinction himself (see below).

These 'solutions' raise more problems and questions in their turn, but the best we can hope for is 'solutions', rather than '*the* solution' (which is true of all major philosophical issues and debates).

To diagnose mental disorders

When psychologists and psychiatrists discuss abnormality, and diagnose and treat mental disorders, they are often making judgements about free will and determinism, either implicitly or explicitly (see Chapter 7).

In a general sense, mental disorders can be seen as the partial or complete breakdown of the control which a person normally has over his or her behaviour, emotions and thinking. For example, *compulsive* behaviour, by definition, is behaviour which the person cannot help but do – he or she is 'compelled' to do it. People are '*attacked*' by panic, *obsessed* by thoughts of germs, become the *victims* of thoughts which are *inserted* into one's mind from outside and are under external influence (one kind of passivity experience and thought disturbance in schizophrenia). In all these examples, things are happening to or being done to the individual (instead of the individual *doing them*), both from the point of view of the individual concerned and that of the psychologist or psychiatrist.

Being judged to have lost the control which we think of as a major feature of normality ('being of sound mind'), either temporarily or permanently, is a legally acceptable defence in cases of criminal offences. Forensic psychiatry is that branch of psychiatry which deals with assessment and treatment of mentally abnormal offenders. There are several clauses within the 1983 Mental Health Act which provide for compulsory detention of prisoners (either while awaiting trial or as part of their sentence) in hospital. Psychiatrists, as expert witnesses, can play an important role in advising the Court about: (i) fitness to plead, (ii) mental state at the time of the offence, and (iii) diminished criminal responsibility (Gelder et al., 1989).

The defence of *diminished responsibility* (for murder) was introduced in England and Wales in 1957 and has largely replaced the plea of 'not guilty by reason of insanity', which was based on the 'McNaughton Rules'. In 1843, Daniel McNaughton shot and killed Edward Drummond, Private Secretary to the then Prime Minister, Sir Robert Peel. He shot Drummond by mistake, intending to shoot Peel. In the Old Bailey trial, the defence of not guilty by reason of insanity was made on the grounds that McNaughton had suffered delusions for many years – his paranoia focused on the Tory Party and he decided to kill Peel. In accordance with the judge's summing up, he was found not guilty on the grounds of insanity. However, he was admitted to Bethlem Hospital and later transferred to the Criminal Lunatic Asylum, Broadmoor, soon after it was opened.

There was a public outcry at the decision, which was debated in the House of Lords, resulting in the McNaughton Rules which, although having no statutory basis, were given the same status by the courts as an actual law. However, they were considered to present far too narrow a concept of insanity (working to the disadvantage of the mentally ill), and the 1957 Homicide Act introduced the plea of diminished responsibility for murder charges. If accepted, there is no trial and a sentence of manslaughter is passed; if not, a trial is held and the jury must decide whether at the material time (the time when the actual crime was committed) the accused was suffering from an abnormality of mind and, if so, whether it was such as to substantially impair his or her responsibility.

In the case of Peter Sutcliffe, the 'Yorkshire Ripper', the jury found him guilty of the murder of thirteen women and the attempted murder of seven others, despite the defence that he heard the voice of God telling him to get rid of prostitutes. He was sentenced to twenty concurrent terms of life imprisonment, which he served initially in an ordinary prison before being sent to Broadmoor Special Hospital.

To discuss moral accountability

Underlying the whole question of legal – and, by the same token, moral – responsibility, is the presupposition that people are, at least some of the time, able to control their behaviour and to choose between different courses of action; otherwise, how could we ever be held responsible for *any* of our actions? We only need expert witnesses (such as psychiatrists) to help juries decide whether or not the accused was suffering from a mental abnormality which, at the time the crime was committed, substantially impaired his or her responsibility, because it is not clear in this particular case. But usually it is; in most everyday situations and interactions, we assume responsibility – our own as well as others' – unless we have reason to doubt it. Imagine having to consult an 'expert' every time we had to blame, criticize, praise, thank, accuse, warn or in any other way perform a social act that implies responsibility on the part of the person concerned.

An influential figure in the free will and determinism debate (as in many other debates crucial to psychology; see Chapters 11 and 13) is Descartes, who made the fundamental distinction between mind and body, the former being non-physical, the latter being physical and essentially a machine; this is the philosophical theory of *dualism*.

The person, according to Descartes, is an agent whose behaviour is governed by no other law than that which the agent himself creates: 'But the will is so free in its nature, that it can never be constrained . . . And the whole action of the soul consists in this, that solely because it desires something, it causes a little gland to which it is closely united to move in a way requisite to produce the effect which relates to this desire' (Descartes, 1649, quoted in Flanagan, 1984). The 'little gland' that Descartes refers to is in fact the pineal gland, situated near the corpus callosum (which joins the two hemispheres of the brain), which is now generally accepted as playing an important role in sleep, but *not* the 'seat of the mind', the meeting point between the mind and the body, as Descartes believed. (See Figure 12.1.)

The mind, via the pineal gland, uses its immaterial (non-physical) powers to move the material body – this is what happens every time we behave in a voluntary way. The mind itself, however, is self-moved. Flanagan (1984) believes that one of the main consequences of dualism, and what most people would regard as its main advantage, is that it makes sense of the intuitive (commonsense) distinction between (i) conscious, purposeful, voluntary actions and (ii) mechanical, unintentional, involuntary actions.

This distinction in turn makes sense of moral discourse:

> *When we speak morally . . . we employ an idiom which assumes certain things about human behaviour. At the most general level, the moral idiom assumes that people are capable of controlling their actions – it assumes that we are*

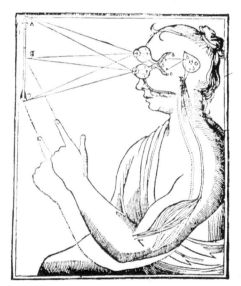

Figure 12.1 The influence of the soul on the machinery of the brain, according to René Descartes, from the 1664 French edition of the *Treatise of Man*. Descartes thought of the pineal gland (the pear-shaped object in the middle of the head) as the point of connection between the soul and the brain. It receives messages from the senses (the eyes in this diagram) by means of waves of vibration through the fluid in the chambers of the brain. In turn, by subtle movements and deflection, conveying the will of the mind, it influences the transmission of signals from the brain to the muscles

*not mere reflex machines . . . it seems silly to have any expectations
about how people ought to act, if everything we do is the result of
some inexorable causal chain which began millenia ago. 'Ought',
after all, seems to imply 'can', therefore, by employing a moral
vocabulary filled with words like 'ought' and 'should', we assume
that humans are capable of rising above the causal pressures
presented by the material world, and, in assuming this we appear to
be operating with some conception of freedom, some notion of free
will.*

(Flanagan, 1984)

Although this may seem to describe the commonsense understanding of
how moral responsibility and free will are related (that is, it is only because
we believe that people have free will that we attribute them with moral
responsibility for their actions), is it necessarily the *only* view that one
could take?

Skinner (1971), consistent with his argument that free will is an illusion,
claims that all the practical sense of doling out rewards and punishments
and speaking in moral terms would be maintained even if we gave up our
shared belief that human nature is free: we would simply be using them to
shape, control and maintain behaviours that we (as a society, as well as
individually) find pleasing. In other words, according to Skinner, the fact
that we do usually attribute responsibility to people (based on the
assumption that they have free will) does not mean that we have to. (A
common argument in support of free will, which could be used against
Skinner, is what is called the 'appeal to experience', which we shall
consider later on in the chapter.)

Perhaps we need to distinguish between a purely *philosophical* position
(one based on logical analysis, the meaning of concepts, and so on) and a
more practical position (based on everyday, intuitive, subjective
experience). As Koestler (1967) says, whatever one's philosophical
convictions, 'in everyday life it is impossible to carry on without the implicit
belief in personal responsibility; and responsibility implies freedom of
choice'.

To understand the theories of major figures in psychology

Most of the major theorists in psychology have addressed the issue of free
will and determinism, including James, Freud, Skinner (as we have already
seen), Fromm, Kelly and Rogers. The issue has also been discussed by those
working in the field of artificial intelligence, such as Johnson-Laird, and
sociobiologists, principally Wilson and Dawkins. This represents perhaps
the single major reason for including a chapter on free will and
determinism in a book on psychology: to appreciate fully the theories of
these major figures we must understand the position they adopt regarding
this fundamentally important feature of human beings.

According to Morea (1990), the 'story' of Adam and Eve losing their innocence in the Garden of Eden when they chose to eat the fruit from the forbidden tree, is a myth suggesting that humans are free. It also suggests how like a god they became in knowing right from wrong and in having a mind. Morea believes that any adequate explanation of human personality must confront these age-old puzzles of free will, morality and mind.

Mind, or consciousness, will be discussed in Chapter 13. In the remainder of this chapter, we shall concentrate on what a number of eminent psychologists, and other scientists, have said about free will and determinism.

Figure 12.2   Adam and Eve were expelled from the Garden of Eden when they chose to eat the forbidden fruit, a choice which, Morea suggests, indicates that humans are free

What do we mean by free will?

Valentine (1992) identifies a number of different definitions or senses in which the term is used.

Having a choice

The commonsense, lay person's, understanding of the term is that the actor could have behaved differently, given the same circumstances; this is what 'having a real choice' means. This is something that we normally 'take on trust'; it is an 'article of faith', because it can never be shown to be true.

Not being coerced or constrained

Behaviour is 'free' if it is uncaused, implying that if behaviour is caused (that is, determined), then it cannot be free. However, 'free' and 'determined' are not opposites: the opposite of 'determined' is 'random' (occurring by pure chance), and, clearly, when we speak of human actions being 'free', we certainly do not mean that they are 'random'. In fact, any such view of behaviour would make it appear even less free than describing it as 'caused'; at least 'cause' implies some kind of pattern or predictability, whereas 'random' implies the very opposite. So what is the true opposite of 'free'? The answer is, 'coerced' or 'constrained'. If someone puts a loaded gun to your head and tells you to undress (otherwise you will be shot), no one – magistrate, priest, or onlooker – could condemn your behaviour, since it is obvious that it is done against your will, you were forced into it, your behaviour was not freely chosen.

The view that all acts are caused, but only those which are not coerced or constrained are free, is called *soft determinism* (first proposed formally by James, 1890; see below).

Voluntary

We noted earlier that the word 'voluntary' is usually meant to convey behaviour over which we have control, whereas 'involuntary' implies the opposite. In one sense, the opposite of voluntary is 'reflex', as in the knee-jerk response to a tap on the patella, or the eye-blink reponse to a puff of air directed at the eye; it is very difficult, if not impossible, to prevent these from happening, however hard you might try. Clearly, when you undress at gunpoint, your behaviour is not involuntary in this sense, but it is involuntary in the sense that you have been forced into it, it is against your will. It could be argued that, if behaviour is neither a reflex response to a specific stimulus (knee-jerk), nor coerced (undressing at gun-point), then it is free (at least in the soft determinism sense).

Valentine (1992) observes that there is both phenomenological and behavioural evidence for the distinction between voluntary and involuntary. As for the former, Penfield (1958) performed what are now classic experiments involving patients undergoing brain surgery, in which their motor cortex was stimulated while they were fully awake, so that they could report their experience. Even though the brain region being stimulated was the same as that which is involved when we move our arms and legs under normal circumstances, these patients reported feeling that their limbs were being moved passively, quite a different experience from initiating the movement themselves. This demonstrates that the *subjective experience* (or phenomenology) of the voluntary movement of one's limbs cannot be reduced to the stimulation of the appropriate region of the brain (otherwise Penfield's patients should not have reported a difference): doing things voluntarily simply *feels* different from the 'same' things 'just happening'. And if this is true for bodily movements, then this adds weight to the claim that having free will is an undeniable part of our subjective experience of ourselves as a person. As Koestler (1967) claims, our sense of our self is most acute (and important and real for us) where moral decisions and feelings of responsibility for one's past actions (the problem of free will) are involved.

One demonstration of people's belief in their free will is *psychological reactance* (Brehm, 1966; Brehm & Brehm, 1981). This refers to a common response to the feeling that our freedom is being threatened, namely the attempt to regain or reassert our freedom, and it is related to the need to be free from the controls and restrictions of others, to determine our own actions, and not be dictated to. A good deal of contrary (resistant) behaviour otherwise known as 'bloody-mindedness', ('Don't tell me what to do'), seems to reflect this process. (Carver & Scheier, 1992).

Similar to this need to feel free from the controls of others is what has been called *intrinsic motivation* or *self-determination* (Deci, 1975, 1980 and Deci & Ryan, 1985, 1987, cited in Carver & Scheier, 1992). The central idea is that people have an intrinsic interest in many things, so that they do not need to be offered extrinsic incentives for doing them. Engaging in such activities is motivated by the desire for competence and self-determination.

So what happens if someone is offered an extrinsic reward for doing something which is already interesting and enjoyable in itself? Research by Lepper et al. (1973), and others, suggests that the activity will lose its intrinsic appeal, so that motivation is reduced (this is called the *paradox of reward*). In attributional terms, the affect of the extrinsic reward is to change people's explanation for their own behaviour, from an *internal* ('I enjoy it') to an *external* ('I'm only doing it for the reward') explanation, and if the reward is withdrawn, they may decide the activity is no longer worth doing (Bem, 1972; Lepper & Greene, 1978; see Chapter 2).

In terms of self-determination, the extrinsic reward is 'turning play into work'; it is 'saying' that you haven't chosen the activity freely; you then conclude that you don't have much interest in it, and, given a free choice, you would rather exercise your will and do something else (Carver & Scheier, 1992). As far as behavioural evidence for the distinction between voluntary and involuntary behaviour is concerned, Valentine (1992) cites a 1964 study by Kimble showing that voluntary eye-blinks can be distinguished from involuntary ones in terms of both form and latency. It is generally agreed that voluntary behaviour is learned, flexible (sensitive to consequences), relatively slow, and may involve verbal processes, while involuntary behaviour is automatic, inflexible and may be interfered with by verbalization (see, for example, Shiffrin & Schneider, 1977).

Intentional behaviour based on models

Johnson-Laird (1983) identifies three main levels in the evolution (*phylogeny*) of automata ('self-operating machines'): (i) the Cartesian, (ii) the Craikian, and (iii) the self-reflective. (We should note here that the word 'automaton' is often used in a derogatory sense to describe people who seem to show no emotion or who are efficient or self-controlled to such a degree that they appear less than human, as if 'programmed' to behave in predetermined, highly predictable ways. This contrasts with the commonsense view of the person as being an emotional being who is less than totally predictable, which seems to imply freedom of choice (see Chapters 4 and 7). This non-technical sense of 'automaton' perhaps relates most closely to the Cartesian level as described by Johnson-Laird.)

The *Cartesian automaton* is an open-loop system, such as that of bacteria and protozoa, whose behaviour is physically mediated by a direct causal link between stimulus and response. It lacks any kind of awareness or symbolism.

The *Craikian automaton* is guided by a representation of the external world, constructing a symbolic model of the world in real time, for example, the flight of insects whose flight is controlled by a perceptual model of certain features of the physical environment. This represents a simple kind of awareness or symbolism.

Self-reflective automata are capable of intentional behaviour, which depends on the 'recursive embedding' (repeating process) of models within models (they have a model of a model of a model and so on). They are self-aware, having at least a partial model of how their operating system works. For example, humans know that they are capable of generating models of future states of affairs and of deciding to bring them about.

Johnson-Laird (1988) believes that freedom consists in the ability to use models of ourselves to select a method of making choices. A detailed summary of his account of how people make decisions, and how this relates to free will, follows.

When you follow a plan, you don't carry out a rigid sequence of actions. Rather, you observe the outcomes of your actions and may, as a result, modify your plan; you may even abandon it. You have the freedom to choose between several options at various points in the execution of your plan (especially if you are using your imagination).
Sometimes you adopt a course of action ('our next move') without conscious thought:

Level 0: 'You just do it'. For example: Carry on reading
Go for a walk

Sometimes, when you are stuck between two equally appealing (or unappealing) alternatives, you might say to yourself, 'This is ridiculous: I'll have to choose one of them' and you may then, as a result of this higher-order reflection, make an arbitrary decision (Level 1, Meta-level). You might even make sure that it is arbitrary by resorting to some external method, such as tossing a coin or throwing a die (as did the hero of Luke Rhinehart's *The Dice Man*). At the meta-level, you think about what to do and make a decision based, say, on a simple preference:

Level 1 (Meta-level): By assessing preferences, you choose from:
Level 0: Carry on reading
Go for a walk

How did you arrive at this Level 1 method of choice? You didn't think consciously about all the different ways you could make a choice and then choose the 'best' method: it simply came to mind as the right way to proceed.

Perhaps most methods of choosing are selected this way. But they need not be; you can confront the issue consciously (Level 2, Meta-meta-level) and reflect on which of the methods of choice you will use. You might try to make a rational choice from amongst them:

Level 2 (Meta-meta-Level): Making a rational assessment, you choose from:
Level 1 (Meta-level): Assessing preferences
Taking your partner's advice ⎫ to choose from:
Tossing a coin ⎭
Level 0: Carry on reading
Go for a walk

Why did you decide to choose rationally from amongst the various methods of choice? Once again, it just came to mind as the right way to proceed. The method of decision at the highest level is always chosen implicitly (not consciously): if it were chosen consciously, there would have to be a still higher level at which that decision was made. In theory, there would be no end to the hierarchy of decisions about decisions about decisions and so on (an infinite regress), but the business of everyday life demands that you do something, rather than get lost in speculation about how to decide what to do. The buck must stop somewhere!

> *We are free, not because we are ignorant of the roots of many of our decisions, which we certainly are, but because our models of ourselves enable us to choose how to choose. Amongst the range of options are even those arbitrary methods that free us from the constraints of an ecological niche or a rational calculation of self-interest . . . one demonstrates freedom (if not imagination) in acting arbitrarily.*
> (Johnson-Laird, 1988)

This example of a hierarchy of decisions about decisions about decisions and so on illustrates the recursive embedding of models which, as was stated above, is necessary for self-reflection or self-awareness. Johnson-Laird believes that it is an open question whether there is more to self-awareness than this embedding of models, as it is whether cognitive scientists will ever be able to construct computer programs that are self-reflective. (Self-awareness is, of course, very closely tied to the concept of *consciousness*, and Johnson-Laird sees the embedding of models as directly relevant to that issue also. See Chapter 13.)

Another cognitive scientist, Garnham (1991), while agreeing with Johnson-Laird that we are unaware of all the factors that influence our decisions, reaches the opposite conclusion: 'They think they are making a free choice, but in an obvious sense they are not . . . It is difficult to see a place for genuinely free will in cognitive science' (Garnham, 1991).

In terms of Johnson-Laird's analysis, it is not at all obvious in what sense we are not making a free choice: we can still 'choose how to choose' without knowing consciously every 'level' involved in the decision-making process.

Deliberate control

Consistent with Johnson-Laird's analysis is the model of processing capacity proposed by Norman and Shallice (1986). In the context of divided attention (an upper limit to the amount of processing that can be performed on incoming information at any one time), they propose three levels of functioning, ranging from (i) *fully automatic processing*, controlled by organized plans (schemata) which occur with very little conscious awareness of the processes involved; through (ii) *partially automatic processing*, which involves *contention scheduling* (a way of resolving conflicts between competing schemata) and which generally involves more conscious awareness than fully automatic processing but which occurs without deliberate direction or conscious control; to (iii) *deliberate control* by a supervisory attentional system, which is involved in decision-making and trouble-shooting and allows flexible responding in novel situations. Deliberate control corresponds to free will.

Driving a car is a sensory-motor skill, performed more or less automatically (if you are an experienced driver, anyway). It does not require deliberate, conscious control – unless some unexpected event throws the performance 'out of gear', such as putting your foot on the brake pedal when there is an obstacle ahead; this is a 'rule of the game'. However, on an icy road, this can be risky; the steering wheel has a different feel, the whole strategy of driving must be changed, 'transposed into a different key' (Koestler, 1967). After doing it a number of times, this too may become a semi-automatic routine,

> *but let a little dog amble across the icy road in front of the driver, and he will have to make a 'top-level decision' whether to slam down the brake, risking the safety of his passengers, or run over the dog. And if, instead of a dog, the jaywalker is a child, he will probably resort to the brake, whatever the outcome. It is at this level, when the pros and cons are equally balanced, that the subjective experience of freedom and moral responsibility arises.*
>
> (Koestler, 1967)

As we move downwards from conscious control, the subjective experience of freedom diminishes. 'Habit is the enemy of freedom . . . Machines cannot become like men, but men can become like machines' (Koestler, 1967). He goes on to say that the second enemy of freedom is very powerful emotions (especially negative ones): 'When they are aroused, the control of decisions is taken over by those primitive levels of the hierarchy which the Victorians called "the Beast in us" and which are in fact correlated to phylogenetically older structures in the nervous system'. It is the arousal of these structures that results in 'diminished responsibility' and 'I couldn't help it' (Koestler, 1967).

To complete Koestler's account of free will, let us return to what we earlier called the 'appeal to experience', one of the commonest (if not one of the philosophically most convincing) arguments in support of the existence of free will.

> *The subjective experience of freedom is as much a given datum as the sensation of colour, or the feeling of pain. It is the feeling of making a not enforced, not inevitable, choice. It seems to be working from inside outward, originating in the core of the personality. Even psychiatrists of the deterministic school agree that the abolition of the experience of having a will of his own leads to collapse of the patient's whole mental structure.*
>
> (Koestler, 1967)

Figure 12.3 The story of Jekyll and Hyde illustrates how the arousal of powerful, primitive emotions can lead to the claim of 'diminished responsibility' and 'I couldn't help it'

The views of William James: soft determinism

As we saw in Chapter 11, William James was one of the pioneers of psychology as a separate, scientific discipline, but he is remembered as much as a philosopher as a psychologist; this perhaps made him especially qualified to express an opinion on the free will and determinism issue.

In his classic *The Principles of Psychology*, James devotes a whole chapter to the 'will', which he related to attention. He described effort, or the sensation of effort, as the primary subjective indication that an act of will has occurred: 'The most essential achievement of the will . . . when it is most "voluntary" is to *attend* to a different object and hold it fast before the mind . . . Effort of attention is thus the essential phenomenon of will' (James, 1890).

But should psychology recognize the existence of free will? Is the feeling of effortful attention strictly a mechanistically determined function of the object of thought, or does subjective consciousness supply certain indeterminate, unpredictable influences of its own, independent of the object? Can a scientific conception of the mind be compatible with our ordinary conception of human nature?

James could find no simple answer to these questions. Belief in determinism seems to fit best with the scientific view of the world, while belief in free will seems to be required by our social, moral, political and legal practices, as well as with our personal, subjective experience.

Given this conflict, James simply distinguished between the two realms – the scientific and the subjective/everyday – claiming that belief in determinism seemed to 'work' best in the former, while belief in free will seemed to work best in the latter. Psychology, as a science, could only progress by assuming determinism, but this does not mean that belief in free will must be abandoned in other contexts: 'Science . . . must constantly be reminded that her purposes are not the only purposes, and the order of uniform causation which she has use for, and is, therefore, right in postulating, may be enveloped in a wider order, on which she has no claims at all' (James, 1890).

In other words, there's 'more to life' than science; scientific explanation is not the only useful kind of explanation. Psychology did not, and could not, provide all the answers.

> *He could entertain the mechanistic ideas and carry them as far as they would go* scientifically, *without allowing their implications to paralyze him* personally. *From his personal point of view it was* useful *to think and behave as if he had free will, just as from a scientist's point of view it was useful to assume that all physiological and psychological phenomena have mechanistic causes. Both views were articles of faith incapable of absolute confirmation or denial. In the absence of any absolute criterion for resolving the free will–determinism issue, utility seemed as good as any other. And since it*

> *was useful to him as an individual to believe in personal freedom,*
> *James would go ahead and do so.*

(Fancher, 1979)

Evaluation of ideas in terms of their practical utility is the central idea in the philosophical theory of *pragmatism*, which James helped to establish.

The other 'solution' to the conflict is what Locke, Hume and others have called *compatibilism* (Flanagan, 1984) and which James called soft determinism, according to which the question of free will depends on the type(s) of cause(s) our behaviour has, not whether it is caused or not caused (see above). According to James, if our actions have, as their proximate, immediate cause, processing by a system such as *conscious mental life* (CLM, which includes consciousness itself, purposefulness, personality and personal continuity – see Chapter 13), then they count as free, rational, voluntary, purposive actions.

As far as *hard determinism* is concerned, CLM is itself caused, so that the immediate causes are only part of the story, only part of the total causal chain which results in the behaviour that we are trying to explain. According to this view, so long as our behaviour is caused at all, there is no sense in which we can be said to act freely. (In some ways, James's soft determinism is similar to the views of Johnson-Laird, for whom it is neither necessary, nor possible, to know consciously all the levels involved in the hierarchy of decision-making, in order to say that the decision was made freely; it is sufficient to say that the decision was made at a level higher than Level 0; see above.)

The views of Sigmund Freud: psychic determinism

Although in most respects their views on human behaviour are diametrically opposed, Freud (1856–1939) and Skinner have one fundamental belief in common, namely, that free will is an illusion. However, in keeping with their theories as a whole, the reasons for holding this belief are very different.

According to James Strachey, one of Freud's translators and the editor of the Standard Edition of Freud's collected works,

> *Freud's discoveries may be grouped under three headings – an*
> *instrument of research, the findings produced by the instrument, and*
> *the theoretical hypotheses inferred from the findings – though the*
> *three groups were of course mutually interrelated. Behind all of*
> *Freud's work, however, we should posit his belief in the universal*
> *validity of the law of determinism . . . Freud extended the belief*
> *[derived from physical phenomena] uncompromisingly to the field of*
> *mental phenomena.*

(Strachey, 1962–77)

According to Sulloway (1979), Freud's entire life's work in science (and he very much saw himself as a scientist) was characterized by an abiding faith in the notion that all vital phenomena, including psychical ones, are rigidly and lawfully determined by the principle of cause and effect. Together with his belief that dreams have meaning and can, therefore, be interpreted, the extreme prominence he gave to the technique of free association in his clinical work was perhaps the most explicit manifestation of this philosophical theory.

Sulloway points out that 'free association' is a misleading translation of the German *freier Einfall*, which conveys much more accurately the intended impression of an uncontrollable 'intrusion' (*Einfall*) by pre-conscious ideas into conscious thinking. In turn, this pre-conscious material reflected *unconscious* ideas, wishes and memories, which was what Freud was really interested in, since here lay the principal cause(s) of his patients' neurotic problems.

It is a great irony that 'free' association should refer to a technique used in psychoanalysis meant to reveal the *unconscious causes* of behaviour. It is the fact that the causes of our thoughts, actions and supposed choices are unconscious (mostly *actively repressed* – made unconscious because of their threatening, disturbing nature), that accounts for the illusion that we are free. The application of his general philosophical belief in causation to mental phenomena is called *psychic determinism*.

Freud's aim was to establish a 'scientific psychology' and he hoped to be able to achieve this by applying to the human mind the same principles of causality as were in his time considered valid in physics, chemistry and, more recently, physiology. If all mental activity is the result of unconscious mental forces that are instinctual, biological or physical in origin, then human psychology could be formulated in terms of the interaction of forces which were, in principle, quantifiable, and psychology would become a natural science like physics (Rycroft, 1966). (Brown, 1961, points out that, strictly speaking, the principle of causality is not a scientific law, but rather a necessary assumption without which no science would be possible.)

According to Brown (1961), Freud's predecessors in psychology thought of behaviour as determined by, for example, rational motives (for example, in the theories of James), instincts (as in McDougall 1908,), or a purely mechanical association of ideas through close occurrence in space or time (which is the basis of *conditioning*, even though 'the mind' is excluded, as we have seen, from the conditioning theories of Watson and Skinner). While all these different theories assume the principle of causation, they distinguish between (i) behaviour for which one or more clear-cut cause were known (or could be readily claimed), and (ii) chance or random events which are the result of many separate and apparently trivial causes, which it would be fruitless or impossible to analyse. It was accepted that most psychological events were of the latter kind, and, therefore, could only be discussed in broad descriptive terms, as opposed to being analysed in detail in any particular case.

Freud took exception to this view. In his early studies of hysterical patients, he showed that the apparently irrational symptoms were in fact meaningful when seen in terms of painful memories that are unconscious; they were not fortuitous or chance happenings, and their causes could be uncovered by (psycho)analysis. This same reasoning was then applied to other seemingly random, irrational events, to 'parapraxes' (the 'psychopathology of everyday life', such as slips of the tongue and pen, and so-called accidents, i.e., 'Freudian slips'), and to dreams.

It is a crucial feature of Freud's theory that there are no accidents in the universe of the mind:

> In his view of the mind, every event, no matter how accidental its appearance, is as it were a knot in intertwined causal threads that are too remote in origin, large in number, and complex in their interaction to be readily sorted out. True: to secure freedom from the grip of causality is among mankind's most cherished, and hence most tenacious, illusory wishes. But Freud sternly warned that psychoanalysis should offer such fantasies no comfort. Freud's theory of the mind is, therefore, strictly and frankly deterministic.
>
> (Gay, 1988)

However, we should make a number of qualifying points here.

Some freedom to change

Freud did not deny that human choices are real and, indeed, one of the aims of therapy is to 'give the patient's ego *freedom* to decide one way or another' (quoted by Gay, 1988). If we become aware of our previously unconscious memories, we are freed of their stranglehold (although there is more to therapeutic success than simply 'remembering'); the whole of psychoanalysis is based on the belief that people *can* change.

However, Freud believed that the extent of change that is possible is very limited, and amongst the modest aims of therapy is to convert 'neurotic misery into everyday unhappiness'. Yet even such a limited degree of freedom is incompatible with hard determinism:

> Since he believes that humans are largely not free he cannot hold that there is any moral dimension, since one can be moral only if one is free. In Freud's account the difference between a Stalin and a Gandhi comes down to a difference in biology (which is ridiculous) or a difference in childhoods (which may be relevant but is not the whole explanation) . . . If we believed Freud, we would empty all our prisons and turn them into mental hospitals. We do not do this because we suspect that there is a moral element in human beings, and that sometimes they are free and responsible for what they do.
>
> (Morea, 1990)

Accidents

Freud did not deny that 'accidents' can and do occur, in the sense of events brought about by intrusions from 'systems' which have nothing to do with the personality of the 'victim'. For example, situations such as being struck by lightning or being aboard a ship that sinks are difficult to attribute to the person him or herself; these are clearly to do with forces beyond the victim's control and are true accidents. But repeated 'accidents', particularly of a similar kind, such as of the woman who has a string of 'tragic' marriages, with husband after husband dying within a short time of their wedding, or the person who is seen as 'accident-prone', point to the 'victim' as somehow, unconsciously, helping to bring the event about; hence, these are not true accidents.

Multiple causes of behaviour

The Freudian concept of psychic determinism does not propose a simple one-to-one correspondence of cause and effect. He used the term *overdetermination* to refer to the observation that much of our behaviour (and our thoughts and feelings) has multiple causes, some conscious, some unconscious. By definition, we only know about the conscious causes and these are what we normally take to be the reasons. However, if the causes also include unconscious factors, then the reasons that we give for our actions can never tell the whole story and, indeed, the unconscious causes may be the more important. According to this view, overdetermination constitutes one aspect of psychic determinism

The semantic argument

According to Rycroft (1966), the principle of psychic determinism remains an assumption, which Freud made out of scientific faith rather than on actual evidence. Rycroft states that nowhere in Freud's writing does he claim to have predicted in advance the outcome of any choice or decision made by a patient. He more than once denied the idea that it is possible in advance to predict whether a person will develop a neurosis, or what kind it will be. Instead, he claimed that all we can do is to determine the cause retrospectively (which is not a very scientific way of going about things, as his critics are fond of pointing out, since predictability is seen as a requirement of a scientific theory); as Rycroft says, this is more reminiscent of an historian than a scientist.

However, Freud successfully claimed that he could show that choices made by patients are not arbitrary and can be understood as revealing and characteristic manifestations of their personality. What he often in fact did was to explain patients' choices, neurotic symptoms, and so on not in terms of causes, but by understanding and giving them meaning. The procedure he engaged in was not the scientific one of identifying causes, but the semantic one of trying to make sense of it:

> *It can indeed be argued that much of Freud's work was really
> semantic and that he made a revolutionary discovery in semantics,
> viz. that neurotic symptoms are meaningful disguised
> communications, but that, owing to his scientific training and
> allegiance, he formulated his findings in the conceptual framework of
> the physical sciences.*

(Rycroft, 1966)

The 'semantic argument' is supported by the title of what many people
consider to be his greatest book, *The Interpretation of Dreams* (as opposed
to 'The *Cause* of Dreams'). He was also well aware that his ideas had been
anticipated by writers and poets, not scientists.

However, there is one type of neurosis that undoubtedly does have a
(fairly specific, identifiable) cause, and that is traumatic neurosis (or *post-
traumatic stress syndrome*), which occurs after a totally unexpected shock;
ironically, this is precisely the neurosis which does not fit the theory (there
are no underlying, unconscious, disguised, causes), and one of its symptoms
(the reliving of the traumatic experience in dreams) is not amenable to
analytic interpretation (Rycroft, 1966).

The views of B.F. Skinner: free will as an illusion

Skinner's *radical behaviourism* probably represents the most outspoken
and extreme expression amongst psychologists of the view that people are
not free, and the most explicit and accessible account of this view is his
Beyond Freedom and Dignity (1971). In it, he argues that *behavioural
freedom is an illusion*.

Radical behaviourists regard their view of behaviour as the most
scientific, because it provides an account in terms of material causes, all of
which, they claim, can be objectively defined and measured. Not only can
mentalistic concepts, such as free will (and other '*explanatory fictions*') not
be defined and measured objectively, there is nothing to which they refer
(which is why they cannot be measured), but nor are they necessary in
order to adequately predict and control behaviour (the two primary aims of
a science of behaviour).

If, as we saw above, there is some reason, however little, for arguing that
Freud was something less than a hard determinist, in the case of Skinner
(1904–90) there is *no* doubt whatsoever – he was as hard as they come!
Just as Freud believed that freedom is an illusion to the extent that we are
unaware of the unconscious causes of our feelings and behaviours, so
Skinner claims that it is only because the causes of human behaviour are
often hidden from us in the environment, that the myth or illusion of free
will survives.

So what is the nature of those causes?

When what we do is dictated by force or punishment, or by the threat of force or punishment (negative reinforcement), it is obvious to everyone that we are not acting freely. For example, when the possibility of prison stops us from committing a crime, there is clearly no choice involved, because we know what the environmental causes of our behaviour are. Similarly, it may sometimes be very obvious what the positive reinforcers are that are shaping our behaviour, such as a bonus for working extra hours.

However, most of the time we are not aware of the environmental causes of our behaviour, so that it looks (and feels) as if we are behaving freely. When we believe that we are acting freely, all this sometimes means is that we are merely free of punishments or negative reinforcements; our behaviour is still determined by the pursuit of things that have been positively reinforced in the past. We believe we are free because, most of the time at least, we do what we 'want'; but doing what we want is simply doing what we have previously been rewarded for doing. When we perceive others as behaving freely, we are simply unaware of their reinforcement histories.

But isn't there a good deal of assuming going on in Skinner's argument? For example, when people act in a law-abiding way, aren't they choosing to do so, and, by the same token, aren't those who take the criminal route also choosing the rewards of their crime over the possibility of punishment? In other words, isn't Skinner simply assuming that it is the threat of imprisonment that determines behaviour, directly, automatically, and without the 'mind' of the actor playing any role whatsoever?

Skinner cannot – and does not – offer any additional evidence to show that his argument ('when someone appears to be making a choice, we have simply failed to identify the real pay-offs') is more valid than the opposing argument ('when someone appears to be making a choice, it is because they are making a choice'). As Morea (1990) says, Skinner's argument seems to be of the 'Heads, I win; tails, you lose' variety: 'Once this is said, and it is the only behaviourist answer to apparently free choices, what seemed like a scientific account begins to look more like faith . . . At least the opposite assertion, of a modest degree of free choice, has the advantage of having common sense and human experience on its side'. Similarly, Skinner suggests that, instead of our behaviour being determined by rewards, it is merely shaped and modified by them, allowing for some active part to be played by the actor.

As we have seen earlier in the chapter, without free will there cannot be any moral – or legal – responsibility: 'Behaviour is called good or bad . . . according to the way in which it is usually reinforced by others' (Skinner, 1971). He more or less equates 'good' and 'bad' with 'beneficial to others' (what is rewarded) and 'harmful to others' (what is punished) respectively, thus removing morality from human behaviour, either inside the individual or 'outside' in society. There is only mutual reinforcement, and if we could arrange the reinforcement appropriately, we could create Utopia. But in Skinner's Utopia (described in his 1948 novel, *Walden Two*), how can the planners plan, since you must be free in the first place to be able to plan?

For Skinner, 'oughts' are not 'moral imperatives', they do not reflect moral but practical guidelines and rules (Morea, 1990).

The views of Carl Rogers: freedom and the fully functioning person

We considered some of the basic beliefs of Rogers (1902–87) in Chapter 11 in relation to psychology and science. As a humanistic, phenomenological psychologist, he stressed the process of self-actualization and the necessity of adopting the perspective of the other person if we are to understand that person: experience (as distinct from overt behaviour) is all-important. In particular, it is crucial to understand our *self-concept*, an 'organized, consistent set of perceptions and beliefs about oneself', including our awareness of 'what we are' and 'what we can do', which influences both our perception of the world and our behaviour. Every experience is evaluated in terms of our self-concept, and most human behaviour can be regarded as an attempt to maintain consistency between our self-image and our actions.

Understanding the self-concept is also central to Rogers' *client-centred therapy*. His experience over many years as a therapist convinced him that real change does occur in therapy; people choose to see themselves and their life situations differently. Therapy, and life, are about free human beings struggling to become more free. Personal experience is important, but it does not imprison us; how we react to our experience is something that we ourselves choose and decide (Morea, 1990).

However, it is also true that we sometimes fail to acknowledge certain experiences, feelings, and behaviours if they conflict with our (conscious) self-image; they are *incongruent* precisely because they are not consistent with our view of ourselves, and they become threatening. So they are denied access to awareness (they remain *unsymbolized*) through actual denial, distortion or blocking.

These defence mechanisms prevent the self from growing and changing and widen the gulf between our self-image and reality (our *true* feelings, our actual behaviour). As the self-image becomes more and more unrealistic, so the incongruent person becomes more and more confused, vulnerable, dissatisfied, and, eventually, seriously maladjusted: defensiveness, lack of congruence, and an unrealistic self-concept may all be seen as a lack of freedom which therapy is designed to restore.

As the concept of self-actualization states, humans are growth-oriented and will naturally progress towards the fulfilment of their innate potential if psychological conditions are favourable. This contrasts sharply with Freud's view of people as essentially 'savage beasts' (in *Civilization and Its Discontents*, 1930), whose aggressive tendencies and unpredictable sexuality can only be controlled by the processes and structures of civilization. Freud was pessimistic about human nature and saw the instinctual drives of the id (especially sexuality and aggression) as pushing individuals towards the selfish satisfaction of primitive needs or the relief of powerful tensions (the *pleasure principle*). As we saw above, this is a very deterministic view. However, Rogers' deep and lasting trust in human nature did not blind him to the reality of evil *behaviour*.

> *In my experience, every person has the capacity for evil behaviour. I, and others, have had murderous and cruel impulses, desires to hurt, feelings of anger and rage, desires to impose our wills on others ... Whether I, or any one, will translate these impulses into behaviour depends, it seems to me, on two elements: social conditioning and voluntary choice ... I believe that, theoretically at least, every evil behaviour is brought about by varying degrees of these elements.*
>
> (Rogers, 1982, quoted in Thorne, 1992)

By making the distinction between 'human nature' and 'behaviour', Rogers is able to retain his optimistic view of human beings, but this did not exclude altogether a deterministic element in his later writings. In *Freedom to Learn for the '80s*, published in 1983, he wrote, 'Yet as we enter this field of psychotherapy with objective research methods, we are, like any other scientist, committed to a complete determinism' (quoted by Morea, 1990). He states that it is becoming clear from science that human beings are complex machines and not free. So how can this be reconciled with his self-actualization, psychological growth, and the freedom to choose?

One proposed solution is in the form of a version of soft determinism: unlike neurotic and incongruent people, whose defensiveness forces them to act in ways they would prefer not to, the healthy, fully functioning person 'not only experiences, but utilizes, the most absolute freedom when he spontaneously, freely and voluntarily chooses and wills that which is absolutely determined' (Rogers, 1983, quoted in Morea, 1990). The fully functioning person chooses to act and be the way he or she has to: it is the most fulfilling.

The views of Erich Fromm: the fear of freedom

Fromm (1900–80) was, like Freud, a psychoanalytic theorist and therapist, but, like many other neo-Freudians, disagreed with Freud on a number of important issues. One of these issues was the influence of social, cultural and historical forces on human behaviour, as well as the crucial nature of the child's relationships, rather than biological forces within the personality, which were so much stressed by Freud.

In *The Fear of Freedom* (1942, published in 1941 in the US as *Escape from Freedom*), Fromm argues that we are both part of nature and apart, separate, from it. Human beings created primitive creeds and religious beliefs to enable them to feel less separated from the world. In Europe, until very recently, the Catholic Church provided a sense of security by mediating between God and humanity, guaranteeing salvation but, in the process, limiting human freedom.

The Reformation and the rise of Protestantism broke the power of the Catholic Church, giving people their freedom, but at what price? 'Separation – both physical and psychological separation from nature, and psychological separation from dogma and authority – makes people free. But separation makes people alone, and potentially insignificant and lonely' (Morea, 1990).

At least while Protestantism flourished, people still had a meaningful place in the universe, but with the rise, in the nineteenth century, of industrialization, capitalism, and science, the universe was turned into a machine, with no room for God, leaving people alone and insecure, their lives meaningless. What do we do? One solution is to escape from freedom by creating and becoming part of authoritarian organizations and totalitarian regimes, such as those in Hitler's Germany and Stalin's Russia.

Figure 12.4 Millions of people lost their identity and 'escaped from freedom' when they submitted to the Nazi regime in Hitler's Germany

People like Hitler and Stalin gave up their freedom by continuously making 'bad' choices; eventually they could only choose what was wrong. By the same token, a fortunate few, because of living lives in which they have made 'good', right choices, opt only for what is right and good. They have arrived at a blessed state in which they are no longer free to choose evil or wrongdoing. At both extremes, as a result of a lifetime of bad or good, an individual will no longer be free; human behaviour is caused/determined at these extremes. For example, after many years of heavy drinking the alcoholic is no longer free to stop, but most of us are not yet alcoholics or compulsive gamblers. It is only at the end of a long chain of acts that such determinism operates. Earlier along the line we are free – and this is where most of us are, so finely balanced between several contradictory inclinations that we are usually still in a position to choose. But freedom is never absolute; it always depends on the available alternatives.

We are all faced with a fundamental decision: either we accept, even welcome, our freedom, or we can choose to escape from it (our 'ultimate' act of freedom?) by surrendering ourselves and our freedom to a person, ideology or organization. In *The Heart of Man* (1964), Fromm talks about 'soft determinism'. His position is closer to this than to the 'hard' variety, but it often seems that he isn't any kind of determinist at all: 'Fromm has to come down on the side of free-choice because, if humans are moral beings, we must be free – to choose good or bad, right or wrong. And Fromm continually stresses our moral nature' (Morea, 1990).

The views of George Kelly: freedom and personal constructs

According to Kelly (1905–66), people are free to the extent that they have *personal constructs* by which to interpret, predict and control the world, but these constructs also restrict freedom, because we can only choose from the constructs we have and, to a very large extent, they determine our behaviour.

> *Constructs are the channels in which one's mental processes run. They are two-way streets along which one may travel to reach conclusions. They make it possible to anticipate the changing tide of events ... constructs are the controls that one places on life – the life within him as well as the life which is external to him. Forming constructs may be considered as binding sets of events into convenient bundles which are handy for the person who has to lug them. Events, when so bound, tend to become predictable, manageable, and controlled.*
>
> (Kelly, 1955)

So, constructs are needed if the world is not to seem totally chaotic and unpredictable. But control is a special case of determinism:

> *A person is to cut a pie. There is an infinite number of ways of going about it, all of which may be relevant to the task. If the pie is frozen, some of the usual ways of cutting the pie may not work – but there is still an infinite number of ways of going about it. But suppose the pie is on the table and there is company present. Certain limiting expectations have been set up about how a meal is to be served. The pie is construed as part of the meal. There are also certain conventions about serving wedge-shaped slices with the point always turned towards the diner. If one accepts all the usual superordinating constructions of the situation, he may, indeed, find his course of behaviour determined and very little latitude left to him. He is not the victim of the pie, but of his notions of etiquette under which the pie-cutting has been subsumed.*
>
> (Kelly, 1955)

In Kelly's terms, once we define what we are doing (construe the situation) as 'serving a meal for guests' (a *superordinate construct*), then everything we do as part of that situation, such as cutting a pie, becomes a *subordinate construct* relative to the superordinate one; the way we construe the pie-cutting is determined by having subordinated the pie-cutting to the superordinate 'serving a meal for guests'. We are free to define natural events as we wish, but if we want to predict them accurately, we need some kind of construction that will serve the purpose; it is the structure that we erect that rules us.

So we are free in some respects, but not others. Freedom and determinism are two sides of the same coin; neither is an absolute but both are relative to something else. Once I see the world in a certain way, what I do inevitably follows (it is determined), but I am free to change my constructs, just as scientists are free to change their theories (see Chapter 1).

Sociobiology: extreme biological determinism

This final section will summarize the critique of sociobiology made by Rose et al. (1984) in *Not in Our Genes*, which is a critique of *biological determinism* in general. Here, we shall concentrate on those aspects which are most relevant to the issue of freedom and determinism.

The central claim of sociobiology is that all aspects of human culture and behaviour, like those of all animals, are coded in the genes and have been moulded by natural selection: 'While sociobiologists sometimes hedge on the issue of direct genetic determination of every detail of social and individual behaviour, the claim for ultimate genetic control ... lies at the heart of a system of explanation that cannot survive otherwise'.

Sociobiology is a reductionist, biological determinist explanation of human existence. Its adherents claim, first, that the details of present and past social arrangements are the inevitable manifestations of the specific action of genes. Second, they argue that the particular genes that lie at the basis of human society have been selected in evolution; therefore, the traits they determine result in higher reproductive fitness of the individuals that carry them (that is, they are more likely to survive to have offspring which will have genes for those traits).

'The academic and popular appeal of sociobiology flows directly from its simple reductionist programme and its claim that human society as we know it is both inevitable and the result of an adaptive process.' What is not always realized is that, if one accepts biological determinism, nothing need be changed, 'for what falls in the realm of necessity falls outside the realm of justice. The issue of justice arises only when there is choice ... To the extent that we are free to make ethical decisions that can be translated into practice, biology is irrelevant; to the extent that we are bound by our biology, ethical judgements are irrelevant'.

Precisely because biological determinism removes guilt and responsibility, it has such wide appeal: it is 'our biology' that is to blame, *not* people, either individually or collectively. Once again, we are faced with one of the recurrent themes of this chapter – namely, moral responsibility and responsibility for criminal acts. Aren't sociobiologists obliged to deny them?

To avoid this dilemma, Wilson and Dawkins propose a free will that enables us to go against the dictates of our genes if we so wish. For example, Wilson (1978, in *On Human Nature*) allows that, despite the genetic instructions that demand male domination, we *can* create a less sexist society (at the cost of some loss of efficiency); he then goes on to speculate on the evolution of culture in *Genes, Mind and Culture* (Lumsden & Wilson, 1981). Similarly, Dawkins (*The Selfish Gene*, 1976) proposes independent evolving cultural units or *memes*.

Rose et al. (1984) object to these attempts to resolve the 'moral responsibility dilemma' on the grounds that they involve a *false dichotomy* between biological and cultural/social. Just as 'nature–nurture' (see Chapter 5) and 'mind–brain' (see Chapter 13) are false dichotomies; 'free will–determinism' is another. What characterizes human development and actions is that they are consequences of an immense array of interacting, intersecting causes. Our actions are not random or independent with respect to the totality of those causes as an interacting system, for we are material beings in a causal world.

> But to the extent that they are free, our actions are independent of any one or even a small subset of those multiple paths of causation: that is the precise meaning of freedom in a causal world. When ... our actions are predominantly constrained by a single cause, like ... the prisoner in his cell ... we are no longer free. For biological determinists we are unfree because our lives are strongly constrained by a relatively small number of internal causes, the genes for specific behaviours or for predisposition to those behaviours. But this misses the essence of the difference between human biology and that of other organisms ... Our biology has made us into creatures who are constantly recreating our own psychic and material environments, and whose individual lives are the outcomes of an extraordinary multiplicity of intersecting causal pathways. Thus, *it is our biology that makes us free.*
>
> (Rose et al., 1984)

Summary

- Free will and determinism have been debated in Western philosophy at least since Descartes.
- *Determinism* is a central feature of classical science; according to strict determinism, human thought and behaviour are causally determined along with everything else in the world.
- It is part of commonsense psychology that people have free will, and to believe that people have free will, we must also believe that they have minds; but our thoughts could be caused.
- The use of experiments to study people implicitly takes the view that human behaviour is determined. But while most psychologists are *methodological behaviourists*, most are not *philosophical behaviourists*, who, like Watson and Skinner, explicitly deny free will.

- Diagnosis and treatment of psychological abnormality often involve judgements about free will; several kinds of mental disorder seem to involve a loss of control of the patient's behaviour, thinking or emotion.
- The 1957 Homicide Act introduced the plea of *diminished responsibility* for murder charges. This implies that most people, most of the time, are responsible for their actions, which, in turn, implies free will.
- According to Descartes' *dualism*, the mind, or will, uses its non-physical powers to move the physical body. It does this by causing the pineal gland to move, but the mind itself is self-moved.
- Dualism makes sense of the commonsense distinction between conscious, purposeful and voluntary actions and mechanical, unintentional and involuntary actions. This distinction, in turn, is consistent with our everyday assumption that moral responsibility and free will are related.
- According to Skinner, the fact that we do usually attribute responsibility to people, doesn't mean that we must.
- Most of the major theorists in psychology have addressed the free will–determinism issue, as any adequate account of human personality must.
- 'Free will' can be defined in different ways 'Free' and 'determined' are not opposites; the opposite of 'determined' is 'random', whereas the opposite of 'free' is 'coerced/constrained'.
- According to *soft determinism*, all acts are caused, but only those which are not coerced/constrained are free.
- Penfield's experiments, in which the motor cortex of patients undergoing brain surgery is stimulated while they are fully awake, provide phenomenological evidence for the distinction between voluntary and involuntary behaviour.
- *Psychological reactance* demonstrates people's belief in their free will, as does the similar *intrinsic motivation/self-determination*.
- According to Johnson-Laird, freedom consists in being able to use models of ourselves to select a method of making choices (*self-reflective automata*). Despite being unaware of the roots of many of our decisions, we are free because our models of ourselves enable us to choose how to choose.
- Norman and Shallice's model of processing capacity identifies three levels of functioning: (i) *fully automatic processing*; (ii) *partially automatic processing*; (iii) *deliberate control*, which corresponds to free will.
- According to Koestler, as we move 'downwards' from conscious control to automatic, habitual behaviour, the subjective experience of freedom diminishes. He uses the 'appeal to experience' as a major argument in support of free will.

- For James, there seemed to be a conflict between scientific belief in determinism, and the commonsense belief in free will. He resolved the conflict by distinguishing between the realms of science and everyday living: what it is useful to believe in one realm may not be in the other.
- James also proposed soft determinism as a second 'solution' to the dilemma: our actions are free if their immediate cause is *conscious mental life*.
- Freud, like Skinner, saw belief in free will as an illusion. He believed very strongly in the validity of the law of determinism, which applied to mental phenomena as much as to physical ones – that is, *psychic determinism*.
- 'Free association' is a misleading translation of the German which conveys an uncontrollable 'intrusion' by pre-conscious ideas into the conscious mind.
- For Freud, there is no such thing as an accident in the universe of the mind. But he did not deny that human choices are real, and psychoanalysis is based on the belief that people can change (although only to a very limited degree).
- Much of Freud's work was concerned with trying to understand and give meaning to neurotic symptoms, dreams etc. (that is, it was *semantic*) rather than with identifying causes.
- Skinner's *radical behaviourism* is probably the most extreme expression amongst psychologists of the view that people are not free. Not only is free will an *explanatory fiction*, but it is not needed in order to adequately predict or control behaviour.
- Skinner argues that most of the time it is not obvious what the environmental causes of our behaviour are, so that we believe we are acting freely, and doing what we 'want' is simply doing what we have previously been reinforced for doing – we cannot help but do it.
- By equating 'good' with 'what is rewarded' and 'bad' with 'what is punished', Skinner seems to have removed morality from human behaviour.
- According to Rogers, people really do change through *client-centred therapy*: they choose to see their selves and their life situations differently.
- Defensiveness, lack of congruence, and an unrealistic self-concept all represent a lack of freedom, which therapy is designed to restore.
- In his later writings, he seems to have switched to a deterministic viewpoint, according to which the fully functioning person chooses to act and be the way they have to.
- For Fromm, the price we pay for our freedom from dogma and authority is isolation and a feeling of being alone, insecurity, and meaninglessness. One way of overcoming these feelings is to create or become part of authoritarian organizations or totalitarian regimes

(the 'escape' from freedom).

- At the extremes of good and bad, at the end of a long chain of acts, people are not free. But most of us are not at these extremes and so are still in a position to choose.

- According to Kelly, people are free in that they have *personal constructs* by which to interpret, predict and control the world, but these constructs also restrict freedom, because we can only choose from the constructs we have, and they largely determine our behaviour. Once we see the world in a certain way, what we do is determined, but we are free to change our constructs. So we are free in certain respects, but not others.

- *Sociobiology* is a reductionist, biological determinist explanation of human existence. By explaining all individual and social behaviour in terms of genes that have been selected in evolution, sociobiologists seem to be denying guilt and responsibility: it is 'our biology' that is to blame, not people, either individually or collectively.

- Wilson and Dawkins, in order to allow for moral and legal responsibility, propose a free will that allows us to defy our genes if we so wish.

- Rose et al. object to these attempts to resolve the 'responsibility dilemma' on the grounds that they involve a *false dichotomy* between biological and cultural/social. What makes humans unique is that our biology has made us into creatures who are constantly re-creating our own psychic and material environments. Our individual lives are the product of an extraordinary multiplicity of intersecting causal pathways: it is our biology that makes us free.

Suggestions for further reading

Flanagan, O. J. (1984) *The Science of the Mind*, Cambridge, Mass.: MIT Press.

Morea, P. (1990) *Personality: An Introduction to the theories of psychology*, Harmondsworth: Penguin.

Rose, S., Lewontin, R. C. & Kamin, L. J. (1984) *Not in Our Genes: Biology, ideology and human nature* (especially Chapters 5, 8 and 9), Harmondsworth: Penguin.

Consciousness and the mind–brain relationship

13

Consciousness and the subject matter of psychology

As we saw in Chapter 11, for the first thirty or so years of its life as a separate discipline, psychology took consciousness (i.e. conscious human experience) as its subject matter, and the process of introspection (observation of one's own mind) was the primary method used to investigate it.

Probably the first formal definition of the new discipline of psychology (certainly the most commonly quoted) is William James's *The Science of Mental Life* (1890), which also probably reflects quite accurately the lay person's idea of what psychology is all about.

In his behaviourist manifesto, John Watson (1913) declared that: 'the time has come when psychology must discard all reference to consciousness . . . Its sole task is the prediction and control of behaviour; and introspection can form no part of its method.' On the strength of this doctrine, the behaviourists proceeded to purge psychology of all 'intangibles and unapproachables'; the terms *consciousness*, *mind*, *imagination*, and all other mentalistic concepts, were declared to be unscientific, treated as dirty words, and banned from the scientific vocabulary. In Watson's own words, the behaviourist must exclude 'from his scientific vocabulary all subjective terms such as sensation, perception, image, desire, purpose, and even thinking and emotion as they were subjectively defined' (Watson, 1928).

According to Koestler (1967), this represented the first ideological purge of such a radical kind in the domain of science, predating the ideological purges in totalitarian politics, 'but inspired by the same single-mindedness of true fanatics'. This was summed up in a

Figure 13.1 René Magritte's painting 'a Reproduction Interdite' 1937 seems to capture the whole idea of psychology being a study of consciousness

classic dictum by Cyril Burt (1962, quoted in Koestler, 1967):

> *Nearly half a century has passed since Watson proclaimed his manifesto. Today, apart from a few minor reservations, the vast majority of psychologists, both in this country and America, still follow his lead. The result, as a cynical onlooker might be tempted to say, is that psychology, having first bargained away its soul and then gone out of its mind, seems now, as it faces an untimely end, to have lost all consciousness.*

Has it regained consciousness since the early 1960s when this was written? There is no doubt that 'mind' has once again become respectable, legitimate subject matter for psychologists, since the 'cognitive revolution' (usually dated from 1956), and that introspection has at the same time become an acceptable means of collecting data (at least in conjunction with other, more objective methods). These developments have coincided with the decline of behaviourism as the dominant force within British and American academic psychology. However, as we shall see later in the chapter, the dominant view of the mind current among cognitive psychologists and other cognitive scientists, is radically different from the one held by the early psychologists such as Wundt and James.

As we also saw in Chapter 11, psychology grew out of philosophy and physiology (among other disciplines), so that it is no surprise that, both in its past and present (and no doubt also in its future), issues of fundamental importance in these disciplines are also of great concern, explicitly or implicitly, for psychology. *Consciousness* represents one of these issues, particularly in the form of the mind–body problem or the problem of mind and brain.

The content of this chapter will be drawn from philosophy, neuroscience, artificial intelligence and biology, as well as psychology itself, since in all these different, but increasingly convergent, disciplines, consciousness and the relationship between mind and brain (or consciousness and brain) represent an increasingly important area of research and debate.

Knowing where to start: does consciousness exist?

Of course, to ask about the relationship between two 'things' presupposes that they both exist; in the case of consciousness and the brain, this actually begs the question. We have already seen that Watson, and the behaviourists who followed him (notably B.F. Skinner), removed terms that refer to 'the mind' from their scientific talk; in fact, they went further than this, and actually denied the existence of internal, subjective phenomena.

Whether or not one agrees with this *philosophical behaviourism*, it represents a (radical) solution to the mind–brain issue, as does the philosophical theory of *mind–brain identity* which, while not actually denying the existence of mental processes, reduces them to states of the brain, effectively explaining them away. But these are only two of a much larger number of theories which attempt to explain the relationship.

Much of the attempt to do this is taken up by trying to describe, define, and generally capture the nature of consciousness, and this often takes place separately from the mind–brain issue. As far as possible, I shall try to keep them apart in the rest of this chapter, but this is no easy task. For example, as Johnson-Laird (1987) states: 'Consciousness lies at the centre of the mind–body problem, because without it there would be no such problem – or, at least if there were, we would be unaware of it'. Similarly: 'The mind–body problem is the problem of explaining how states of consciousness arise in human brains. More specifically . . . it is the problem of explaining how subjective feelings arise in the human brain' (Humphrey, 1992).

It is very difficult in practice, if not also in theory, to begin to describe and define consciousness without trying to relate it to the brain, the 'organ of consciousness'. All psychologists and cognitive scientists, as well as most philosophers, past and present, would accept that without a physical brain, there would be no consciousness (just as without a nervous system of some kind there would be very little in the way of behaviour). That is, a brain is necessary for conscious experience (or a mind), so that 'no brain means no mind'. But we cannot make the logical jump from saying that minds need brains to claiming that minds are brains (although the *mind–brain identity theory* makes exactly this claim).

Why is consciousness a problem?

As soon as we accept that the physical brain is involved in some way in our subjective experience, the philosophical and scientific difficulties start to arise. Why? 'Consciousness is both the most obvious and the most mysterious feature of our minds . . . What in the world can consciousness be? How can physical bodies in the physical world contain such a phenomenon?' (Dennett, 1987).

We saw in Chapter 11 that one of the fundamental principles of 'classical' science is objectivity; the observation and measurement of the world as it is, without reference to the human observer. As applied to the study of human behaviour and social institutions, this ideal is referred to as *positivism*. Is the study of consciousness compatible with such an approach?

Watson clearly didn't think so, but, as we have seen, you have to believe rather fanatically in the 'cause of true science' to take the extreme step that he did, namely to remove consciousness (that is, *subjective experience*) from the universe.

Most people – scientists and non-scientists alike – would take the opposite view to Watson, namely that consciousness is an undeniable, indisputable 'fact' about human beings, and if it won't 'go away', it has to be explained. But how?

As Dennett (1987) points out, science has revealed the secrets of many initially mysterious natural phenomena, such as magnetism, photosynthesis, digestion and reproduction, but consciousness seems utterly unlike these. Particular cases of magnetism and other phenomena are, in principle, equally accessible to any observer with the right apparatus. But any particular case of consciousness seems always to involve a *favoured* or *privileged observer*, whose access to the phenomenon is entirely unlike, and better than, anyone else's, no matter what apparatus they may use.

By its very nature, consciousness is private, while physical objects (and behaviour) are public: we do not have any analogies from our shared concepts of the physical world that are at all adequate for describing our experience of it or our experience of ourselves (Gregory, 1981). In other words, we seem to have a view of the physical world in common with others (whether as a lay person with other lay people, or as a scientist with other scientists), but we cannot use that common view for reaching an equivalent view about what goes on inside our heads: the two 'worlds' are simply too different to enable any comparisons to be drawn between them.

Arguing along similar lines, Humphrey (1992) claims that the problem of consciousness arises from three obvious facts of human life:

1 my pain, for example, is not part of the objective world, the world of physical material, and can hardly count as a physical event;
2 from the fact that there is accompanying brain activity, we could say that my brain-based pain seems to belong nowhere else except in the world of physical material – it is, after all, nothing other than a physical event; and
3 my pain – that is, my experience of pain – depends wholly on the brain activity.

The problem, specifically, is to explain how and why and to what end the dependence of the non-physical mind on the physical brain has come about (Humphrey, 1992).

> *Somehow, we feel, the water of the physical brain is turned into the wine of consciousness, but we draw a total blank on the nature of this conversion. Neural transmissions just seem like the wrong kind of materials with which to bring consciousness into the world . . . The mind–body problem is the problem of understanding how the miracle is wrought.*
>
> (McGinn, 1989, quoted by Humphrey, 1992)

McGinn concludes that the problem is probably insoluble – either because there actually is no solution, or because human intelligence must always be too limited to grasp it.

Underlying the views of Humphrey and McGinn, and indeed the whole mind–brain debate, is the fundamental distinction between the physical and the non-physical. It was the influential French philosopher Descartes who in the 1600s introduced *mind–body dualism* into Western thought, where it has remained ever since. We shall discuss his theory below.

The nature of consciousness

As with so many other terms used in psychology, 'consciousness' (and similar terms) is used in a variety of different ways, which can be less than helpful. Already in this chapter, 'consciousness', 'conscious human experience', 'subjective experience', 'mental life' and 'mind' have all been used interchangeably. 'Awareness', 'self-awareness' and 'self-consciousness' can be added to that list. But there are some crucial differences between them.

'Mind' and 'consciousness'

Clearly, 'mind' is a much broader concept than 'consciousness', since there is always much more 'going on' than we can detect through introspection at any one time. According to Humphrey (1992), consciousness refers to what is felt and what is present to the mind, making it quite limited in scope. Rather than embracing the whole range of higher mental functions (perceptions, images, thoughts, beliefs and so on), consciousness is uniquely the 'having of sensations' ('what is happening to me'), all other mental activities remaining outside of consciousness.

This view of consciousness can be analysed in terms of three features:

1 consciousness (or conscious awareness) as one level in Freud's psychoanalytic theory of personality;
2 consciousness as a form of attention;
3 the 'privileged access' of the observer of his or her own mind not being quite so privileged after all.

Figure 13.2   Dorethea Tanning 'Eine kleine Nacht Musik', 1944. The impossible nature of the imagery depicted in the painting is what gives dreams and other unconscious phenomena their distinctive flavour

CONSCIOUSNESS AS A LEVEL IN PSYCHOANALYTIC THEORY

Freud believed that thoughts, ideas, memories and other psychic material could operate at one of three levels: *conscious*, *pre-conscious* and *unconscious*. These are essentially levels of accessibility.

What we are consciously aware of at any one time (what we can report) represents the mere tip of an iceberg – most of our thoughts and memories are either not accessible at that moment (pre-conscious), or are totally inaccessible (unconscious), at least without the use of special techniques such as free association and dream interpretation (see Chapter 12). The ego (the 'executive', decision-making, rational part of the psyche, governed by the *reality principle*) represents the *conscious* part of the mind, together with some aspects of the superego (the moral part of the psyche and the source of guilt), namely, those moral rules and values that we are able to express in words.

The ego also controls the *pre-conscious*, a kind of 'ante-room', an extension of the conscious, whereby things we are not fully aware of right now can become conscious fairly easily if our attention is directed towards them – for example, when you suddenly realize that you have been in pain for some time.

The *unconscious* (for Freud the most important type of mental material) comprises (i) impulses arising from the id, the biological, inherited part of the psyche (governed by the *pleasure principle*); (ii) all repressed material; (iii) the unconscious part of the ego (the part which is involved in dream work, neurotic symptoms and defence mechanisms); and (iv) part of the superego, such as free-floating or vague feelings of guilt or shame which are difficult to explain in a rational way.

Freud depicted the unconscious as a dynamic force and not a mere 'dustbin' for all those thoughts that are not important enough or too weak to force themselves into awareness. This is best illustrated by the process of *repression*, whereby what is threatening is actively forced out of consciousness by the ego (Thomas, 1985).

While most psychologists would agree that thoughts differ in their degree of accessibility (that is, they can be placed on a continuum of consciousness, with 'fully conscious' at one end and 'completely unconscious' at the other), most would not accept Freud's formulation of the unconscious as based on repression. Indeed, other *psychodynamic* theorists, in particular Carl Jung, disagreed fundamentally with Freud's view. Although he accepted the existence of repression, Jung distinguished between the *personal* and the *collective unconscious*, the former being based on the individual's personal experiences, the latter being inherited and common to all human beings (or at least to all members of a particular cultural or racial group).

CONSCIOUSNESS AS A FORM OF ATTENTION

One way in which experimental psychologists have studied consciousness is through the concept of *attention*. Although consciousness is difficult to describe because it is fundamental to everything we do (Rubin & McNeil, 1983), one way of trying to 'pin it down' is to study what we are paying attention to – that is, what is in the forefront of our consciousness. According to Allport (1980), 'attention is the experimental psychologist's code name for consciousness'.

Focal attention (or focal awareness) is what we are currently paying deliberate attention to and what is in the centre of our awareness (corresponding to Freud's 'conscious'). All those other aspects of our environment, and our own thoughts and feelings which are on the fringes of our awareness, but which could easily become the object of our focal attention, are within our *peripheral attention* (corresponding to Freud's 'pre-conscious').

This distinction between focal and peripheral attention may be seen as overlapping with the model of *processing capacity* (Norman & Shallice, 1986), which is intended to explain divided attention, and which we discussed in relation to free will in Chapter 12.

'PRIVILEGED ACCESS' OF THE OBSERVER

By asking just how important focal attention is, we may begin to see how much our behaviour and our mental processes proceed in quite an automatic fashion, without our having to think consciously about what we are doing, or to plan each part of our performance deliberately.

When we look for examples of 'automatic processing' (as Norman and Shallice call processing that requires no focal attention), we usually think of performance of well-practised psychomotor skills, such as driving, typing, and even walking up or down stairs. But just as valid are cases of cognitive processes, such as perception, which usually involve an immediate (and, most of the time, accurate) awareness of something (an object, person, or other 'stimulus') in our external environment. It is difficult to imagine what it would be like if we were aware of exactly how we perceive – the process by which we come to 'translate' the physical stimulation of our sense organs by the external stimulus into the recognition and identification of a particular object, person, piece of music, or whatever it may be.

Our focal attention or awareness is directed at the identified object (the 'finished product', as it were), not the process of perception itself. Could it be any other way? Trying to discover how we perceive through introspection is unlikely to throw much light, which suggests that all the underlying processing that is involved necessarily takes place outside our conscious awareness; it ensures that we concentrate on what really matters, namely what is going on around us (rather than all the internal processes).

We can take this a step further, and ask, is it actually necessary to be consciously (focally) aware of an object in order to 'perceive' it? See Box 13.1.

Box 13.1 Blindsight

Can we see without really 'seeing'?

According to Humphrey (1986, 1992), there is increasing evidence that the higher animals, including humans, can in fact show the behaviour of perceiving without being consciously aware of what they are doing.

During the 1960s, Humphrey worked with a monkey called Helen. Helen had had her visual cortex removed (as part of a study of brain damage in humans; see Chapter 10, on ethics); however, her lower visual centres were intact. Over a six-month period following the operation, she began to use her eyes again, and over the next seven years, she improved greatly. She was eventually able to move deftly through a room full of obstacles, picking up tiny scraps of chocolate or currants, reaching out to catch a passing fly. Her three-dimensional spatial vision and ability to discriminate between objects (in terms of size and brightness) became almost perfect. However, she did not recover the ability to recognize shapes and colours, and was 'oddly incompetent' in other ways too.

When running around a room, she generally seemed as competent as any normal monkey. But her recovery had cost her great effort and she often seemed bewildered and confused when the least upset (by some unexpected noise, for instance). It was as though she was still uncertain of her own capacity, as though vision now had an entirely different meaning for her – if it had any meaning at all.

At that time, there were no comparable human cases, but what relevant evidence there was suggested that people would *not* recover vision. Then, in 1974, Weiskrantz et al. reported the case of D.B., a young man who had recently undergone surgery to remove a tumour at the back of his brain. The entire primary visual cortex on the right side had been removed, resulting in blindness in the left side of the visual field. So, for example, when he looked straight ahead, he couldn't see (with either eye) anything to the left of his nose. Or could he?

Weiskrantz decided not to accept D.B.'s self-professed blindness at face value. While there was no question that he was genuinely unaware of seeing anything in the blind half of his field, was it possible that his brain was none the less still receiving and processing the visual information? What would happen if he could be persuaded to discount his own conscious opinion? Weiskrantz asked him to forget for a moment that he was blind and to 'guess' at what he might be seeing if he could see. To D.B.'s own amazement, it turned out that he could do it: he could locate an object accurately in his blind field, and he could even guess certain aspects of its shape. Yet all the while he denied any conscious awareness.

Weiskrantz called this phenomenon *blindsight*, 'visual capacity in a field defect in the absence of acknowledged awareness' (Weiskrantz, 1986). Other cases have since been described and unconscious vision appears to be a clinical reality (Humphrey, 1986).

A more specific visual deficit, *prosopagnosia*, involves the inability to recognize the human face as such. Although patients with this deficit have no awareness of faces, some, while denying that they can see their spouse's face, will perform on tests in such a way as to indicate strong discriminative knowledge of that face (Edelman, 1992). What is involved in both this and blindsight is a *loss of explicit*

> *conscious recognition* but the *capacity for implicit behavioural recognition*.
>
> These phenomena raise important questions about the function of consciousness (see below).

Johnson-Laird (1988) makes a similar point when discussing decision-making (see Chapter 12): at whatever point in the hierarchy (of embedded decisions about decisions, and so on) we make a decision, this will always be made implicitly (and not consciously), since if it were chosen consciously, there would have to be a still higher level at which that decision was made (and so on, *ad infinitum*). In other words, there is always more going on cognitively ('in the mind') than is available to consciousness (or, to adapt a popular phrase, 'there is more involved than meets the inner eye'; see below).

According to Ross and Nisbett (1991), countless experiments all point towards the conclusion that the high-level mental activity that is taken to be involved in attitude change and emotion (see Chapter 2), goes on outside of awareness. In a much-cited article, Nisbett and Wilson (1977) argued that such unconscious, high-level processing of information is very prevalent indeed. In fact, they argued that there is no direct access to cognitive processes at all; instead, there is access only to the ideas and inferences that are the outputs resulting from such processes.

Sometimes, we do (or could) accompany our performance (such as solving well-formed problems, which have clear rules for their solution) with a verbal commentary, which seems to track the processes as they occur; hence, our account of how we went about solving the problem may be quite accurate (although even here our introspections are not likely to tell the whole story). But for many problems, especially novel ones involving social judgement (and most everyday, 'real life' problems are 'ill formed'), there is very little conscious representation of underlying cognitive processes: 'People have theories about what effects their judgements and behaviour just as they have theories about all kinds of social processes. These theories, rather than any introspective access to mental processes, seem to be the origin of people's reports about the influences on their judgement and behaviour' (Ross & Nisbett, 1991).

Essentially, Nisbett and Wilson argue that people's belief that they can accurately account for their own behaviour ('commonsense' or intuitive explanations; see Chapter 1) is illusory, because what really guides their behaviour is unavailable to consciousness. If true, this conclusion would seem to have serious implications for our belief in free will, as does Freud's distinction between *our* reasons and *the* reasons, which is very similar to what Nisbett and Ross are saying (although their respective notions of 'unconscious' are very different). (See Chapter 12.)

'Consciousness' and 'self-consciousness'

A distinction is usually made between *consciousness/awareness* and *self-consciousness/self-awareness*.

Edelman (1992) makes a distinction between primary and higher order consciousness which refers to consciousness and self-consciousness respectively. *Primary consciousness* refers to the state of being mentally aware of things in the world, of having mental images in the present; it is not accompanied by any sense of being a person with a past and a future. In other words, to be conscious does not necessarily imply any kind of 'I' who is aware and having mental images, etc., which is why at least some animal species are likely to be conscious, even though they do not possess language. Edelman believes that chimps are almost certainly conscious, and in all likelihood, so are most mammals, and some birds; probably those animals without a cortex (or its equivalent) are not.

Higher order consciousness involves recognition, by a thinking subject, of his or her acts or affections. It embodies a model of the personal, and of the past and future, as well as the present. It shows direct awareness of mental episodes without the involvement of the sense organs or receptors. It is what humans have in addition to primary consciousness: we are conscious of being conscious. In order to acquire this capacity, systems of memory must be related to a conceptual representation of a true self (or social self) acting on an environment and vice versa.

This is rather similar to Johnson-Laird's (1988) description of *self-reflective automata*, which are capable of intentional behaviour, which depends on the 'recursive embedding' of models within models. To be self-aware is to have at least a partial model of how our operating system works; we represent to ourselves how we do things (for example, make decisions), rather than 'just doing them'. As well as providing us with self-reflectiveness (or self-consciousness), having 'models of models' also gives us the freedom to make choices (see Chapter 12).

Equating 'consciousness' with 'self-consciousness'

Not all descriptions/definitions, however, make the distinction between 'consciousness' and 'self-consciousness':

> *By consciousness I mean the inner picture we each have of what it is like to be ourselves – self-awareness: the presence in each of us of a spirit (self, soul . . .) which we call 'I'. It's 'I' who have thoughts and feelings, sensations, memories, desires. It's 'I' who am conscious of my own existence and my continuity in time. 'I' who am, in short, the very essence of a human being.*
>
> (Humphrey, 1986)

This seems to correspond very directly to Edelman's higher order consciousness.

Elsewhere, Humphrey (1992) defines consciousness in a way that seems

Figure 13.3 'To be conscious is essentially to have sensations: that is, to have affect-laden mental representations of something happening here and now to me' (Humphrey, 1992)

to combine primary and higher order consciousness: 'To be conscious is essentially to have sensations: that is, to have affect-laden mental representations of something happening here and now to me.'

The subject of consciousness, 'I', is an embodied self. In the absence of bodily sensations, 'I' would cease: *Sentio, ergo sum* ('I feel, therefore I am' – this is a variant of Descartes' famous *Cogito, ergo sum*, 'I think, therefore I am'; see below). The importance of the body in relation to consciousness and our sense of personal identity is central to the theory of Merleau-Ponty, which is outlined later in the chapter.

Humphrey's equation of 'conscious' with 'self-conscious' corresponds, in turn, with one of the two central features of consciousness identified by Dennett (1987). *From the inside*, our own consciousness seems obvious and pervasive; nothing could be more intimately known to us than those things of which we are, individually, conscious: 'Those things of which I am conscious, and the ways in which I am conscious of them, determine *what it is like to be me*. I know in a way no other could know what it is like to be me'. From the inside, consciousness seems to be an all-or-nothing phenomenon, an 'inner light' which is either on or off. It is true that we are 'more conscious' at certain times than at others; for example, sometimes we are drowsy, inattentive, asleep ('unconscious'), or enjoying abnormally heightened states of consciousness or arousal. But when we are conscious, the fact that we are conscious is not a matter of degree.

For Dennett, this divides the world into two strikingly different kinds of things: those that have consciousness and those that don't. The former are subjects:

> ... *beings to whom things can be one way or another, beings it is like something to be. It is not like anything at all to be a brick or a pocket-calculator or an apple ... and probably like something to be a dog or a dolphin (if only they could tell us!), and maybe even like something to be a spider.*

Similarly, for Humphrey (1993) the 'problem' of consciousness is 'how a man or animal can know what it is like to be itself'.

According to Edelman (1992), consciousness manifests itself in the form of *qualia*, the collection of personal, subjective experiences, feelings and sensations which accompany awareness; they are phenomenal states, 'how things seem to us as human beings.'

As insightful as these observations might seem (although at the same time confirming just how difficult a concept 'consciousness' is to 'pin down'), they appear to raise problems of their own – in particular, the age-old philosophical problem of other minds: it is all very well having access to our own consciousness (if not to our 'mind'), but how do we know that anybody else is conscious? This, in turn, raises the very important and controversial question of whether a machine could have consciousness.

How do we know that anybody else is conscious?

For Dennett, the second central feature of consciousness is how it appears *from the outside*. Other people, and animals, have various observable features which seem relevant to the question of their being conscious: they react discriminatively to events within the scope of their senses, they recognize things, avoid painful stimuli, learn, plan, solve problems, and show intelligence. But doesn't this simply prejudice the issue? In other words, when we describe some behaviour as 'problem-solving', for example, aren't we just assuming that there is consciousness involved, in which case we cannot then use the example of problem-solving as 'evidence' of consciousness? The argument is circular. It does not move us on very far in trying to solve the 'other minds' problem, because, whereas we can directly observe, in our own case, the coincidence (or correlation) between our inner life and our outwardly observable features, as far as others are concerned, we can only assume that the outer and the inner are related.

Although our experience tells us that we must be conscious if we are 'up and about', alive and alert, logic tells us to 'hold on': is there any reason in principle why an animal or even a human being could not be behaviourally alert and yet still be 'unconscious' (that is, unaware of what is going on inside its/his/her mind)? How do we know it/he/she is not some kind of biological robot, that the whole performance isn't some kind of bizarre mechanical charade (Humphrey, 1986)?

As we saw in Chapter 12, for Johnson-Laird (1988), the question of consciousness is very closely tied to the question of free will. He cites the cult science fiction film, *The Invasion of the Body Snatchers* (1956), in which the inhabitants of a small town are transformed, one by one, into perfect replicas that lack free will and are apparently under the control of an alien force. The problem for the film's hero is how to decide who has free will and is a conscious agent, and who is a replica; this problem, according to Johnson-Laird, is an even greater one for cognitive scientists.

There are many clear signs that someone (or some animal) isn't functioning as a conscious agent (for example, a failure to respond to any external stimuli), but the absence of these signs isn't sufficient to establish consciousness. There is no decisive, conclusive observation of behaviour which could establish, with certainty, that an organism is conscious.

Figure 13.4 In the film, *Invasion of the Body-Snatchers*, the hero has to decide who has free will and is a conscious agent, and who is a replica

However, psychiatrists and other 'forensic' experts

recognize cases of diminished responsibility and compulsive behaviour, and lay people are able to distinguish between voluntary and involuntary actions (see Chapter 12).

> *The best tell-tale sign of consciousness is the ability to engage in discourse that explicitly concerns the individual's use of self-reflective judgement. Because the contents of consciousness are identical to the highest level of current reflection, this method allows the investigator to assess the degree of self-reflection that an individual can achieve. People who can tell you that they are choosing a particular course of action because they weighed up the pros and cons of several alternatives and it seemed to be the best, and that they chose this way of choosing as a result of reflection about a number of methods, should be judged to be responsible, conscious agents capable of exercising free will.*
>
> (Johnson-Laird, 1988)

Patients suffering from mental illness, brain damage, and the effects of other traumas, may no longer have access to models of themselves and reflective procedures. Anxiety and stress may also adversely affect the self-reflective capacity of people both in laboratory experiments and in everyday life (see Chapter 7).

Just as we take for granted other people's responsibility for their actions (based on the prior assumption of free will), unless we have good reasons for doubting it, so with consciousness. Unless someone is asleep, heavily sedated, in a coma, or we suspect them of being an alien or some very sophisticated robot, we attribute them with consciousness. Whether or not it is logically possible that we are mistaken, or that we can never be sure that another person is conscious (even if we are certain that they are human), is unimportant as far as our everyday interactions with others are concerned.

Can a machine be conscious? Does having a brain matter?

Many machines 'behave' in ways which, if they were human, would suggest that they had mental states. For example, aeroplanes on autopilot can fly themselves; they respond to external 'sensory' information, make 'decisions' about whether to fly, 'communicate' with other aircraft, and even 'know' when they are 'hungry' for fuel, can 'sense' danger and so on.

But the very fact that the various words in the previous sentence are in speech marks is meant to show that they are not to be taken literally: only in a metaphorical sense do planes make decisions, and that is because they lack consciousness. It is people (and possibly some other animals) who make decisions, communicate and so on, not metal machines. Being *sentient* (living, breathing, made of flesh and blood) seems to be a precondition for primary consciousness, just as primary consciousness is a precondition for higher order consciousness.

But isn't there the danger here of confusing (i) the kinds of things in the world which, currently, as far as we know, and according to the criteria that we use to judge consciousness, *are* conscious (human beings and some animals), and (ii) the kinds of things which might, *in the future, be considered* conscious (due to advances in our ability to construct certain types of machine)? In other words, should we reject the very idea of a conscious machine?

Indeed, supporters of what Searle (e.g. 1980) calls *strong artificial intelligence* (AI) believe that 'the future' is already here. Cognitive scientists, such as Turing, Johnson-Laird, Newell, Simon, Minsky and Boden, believe that people and computers turn out to be merely different manifestations of the same underlying phenomenon, namely automatic formal systems, the essence of which is the manipulation of symbols according to rules (the *computational theory of mind* or CTM). CTM is the underlying theory involved in strong AI, according to which the computer is not merely a tool for formulating and testing hypotheses concerning the human mind, but, if appropriately programmed, *is* a mind, in the sense that it can be literally said to understand and have other cognitive states that is, *it is conscious*.

We shall consider some of Searle's objections to strong AI and CTM later, in relation to the mind–brain issue. But one of his arguments is particularly relevant here.

Mental states and processes are real biological phenomena in the world, as real as digestion, photosynthesis, lactation and so on; they are caused by processes going on in the brain which are entirely internal to the brain. The intrinsically mental features of the universe are just higher-level physical features of the brain. For this reason – and this is the crucial point – Searle argues that, in principle, only a machine (computer, robot) that is made of flesh and blood or *neuroprotein* (a convenient shorthand for the many biochemical substances active in the central nervous system) could be conscious (a view which has been dubbed *carbon/protoplasm chauvinism* by Torrance, 1986).

To Searle it is obvious that metal or silicon cannot support intelligence or consciousness. But to Boden (1993), amongst others, it is not at all obvious. To the extent that we do understand how 'neuroprotein' *as* neuroprotein actually does support intelligence, Boden argues that we focus on the neurochemistry of certain basic *computational functions* embodied in neurons, such as message-passing, facilitation and inhibition. For advocates of strong AI, as well as for psychologists, it is these functions which matter; if the neurophysiologist can tell us which cells and chemical processes are involved, so much the better. But any other chemistry would do, so long as it enabled these functions to be performed.

From an intuitive point of view, it is far from obvious how the neuroprotein ('that grey mushy stuff inside our skulls') could possibly support intelligence, so just because it is not obvious how metal and silicon could, does not mean that they couldn't do so. Also, what is intuitively obvious may (and does) change as scientific knowledge advances (Boden, 1993).

In the same way, Gray (1987) states that we do not know whether non-biological tissue can produce or support conscious states, but it is an open question, to be decided by empirical observation guided by an appropriate theory, and not by purely logical, philosophical debate.

Consciousness and the importance of having a body

But surely part of any such theory will be to do with what we think consciousness is – that is, the nature of consciousness – and we might take a view of its nature which excludes (the possibility of) machine intelligence. According to Eiser (1994), it is in the *content* of experience (rather than in an exclusive analysis of process) that an understanding of human consciousness is to be found.

One of the differences between the way in which the brain processes information (*parallel processing*) and the way in which most computers have been designed to do it (*serial processing*; or, perhaps more accurately, how most computer programs – the software – is designed), is often cited by those who oppose the view that computers could be built to have the kind of consciousness that people naturally have. The counter-argument is that, at least in principle, computers could be programmed to use parallel processing, in which case, where is the objection to the idea of machines being conscious (in the sense of self-reflective)?

In fact, some cognitive scientists would claim that the objection has already been met in practice, in the form of connectionism, the approach to AI which models itself on the interconnection of the neurons in the brain ('neural networks') and which stresses the role of parallel processing ('parallel distributed processing' or PDP; Rumelhart et al., 1986). However, Boden (1993) argues that this alternative to the traditional, formalist AI approach does nothing to show 'that functionalism is mistaken, and that the cognitive science based upon it is doomed to failure'. In other words, she continues to maintain that it is the (fact of the) processes being carried out by the machine that is crucial for defining intelligence – not what the machine is made of or how the processes are carried out.

However, Eiser believes that this emphasis on the processes being carried out is mistaken: 'The error lies in trying to settle the matter by identifying the classes of information-processing operations of which human beings and computers are each capable, whilst ignoring the classes of information with which human and artificial systems actually have to deal'.

If there is something distinctive about human consciousness, where should we look for it?

> *Consciousness is indescribable other than in terms of its contents, that is, the contents of our thoughts. Even if we could build a machine with this full capacity of a human brain [immensely interactive parallelism] we would still be reluctant to attribute to it the* kind *of consciousness, the sense of self, to which we ourselves lay claim . . . To ask what is special about human consciousness, therefore, is not just a question about process. It is also to ask what is special about our experience of the world, the experience we have by virtue of physical presence in the world.*

Any distinction that we try to draw between mind and body (mind–body dualism) is, according to Eiser, objectionable precisely because it divorces mental from physical experience. The most continuous feature of our experience is our own body: personal identity (and that of others) depends on physical identity; we feel our body and we feel the world *through* it, and it provides the anchor and perspective from which we experience other things. This view is very similar to that of the French phenomenologist, Merleau-Ponty (1962, 1968). He distinguishes between 'one's own body' (the *phenomenal* body) and 'the objective body' (the body as *object*).

Experience of our own body is not, essentially, experience of an object. In fact, most of the time, we are not aware of our body as such; it is, as it were, *transparent* to us. But without our body, we couldn't *be*.

We cannot react to the world without treating it as a more or less meaningful system of situations, contexts and relations; this meaningfulness depends not only on the world's physical properties, but also on our own biological, psychological, social and cultural properties. Carrying out goals, plans and intentions necessarily involves our body. We don't 'move' our body like we do other objects: it is as if it moves itself.

Just as sense perception and motor skills function together (as do the different senses), so, for Merleau-Ponty, mind and body, mental and physical, are two aspects of the same thing – namely, a person: the mind is embodied in that it can be identified with one aspect of something which has two aspects, neither of which can be reduced to (explained in terms of) the other (Teichman, 1988).

The body provides us with a continuous patterned stream of input and (simply from the fact that we cannot be in two places at the same time) it imposes constraints on the information received by the brain about the outside world (Eiser, 1994).

This, in turn, relates to 'aboutness' (or *intentionality*). Mental states – beliefs, desires, perceptions, wishes, fears, ideas, as well as intentions – are *about* things and states in the world apart from themselves; they have an external reference, to something outside themselves, and this is (part of) what we mean by saying that the world is *meaningful* to us and that we understand it. According to Searle (1980), intentionality is a fundamental feature of consciousness, and it is the meaninglessness of the symbols which computers manipulate (that is, meaningless for the computer – the meaning has to be applied by a human programmer) that leads to the (inevitable) conclusion that computers (and other machines) do not – and cannot – possess consciousness: 'If both the machine's processing operations *and* the information it processed were indistinguishable from those of a human being, so also would be its mind and consciousness. It is the second of these two conditions, rather than the first, which strikes me as the major stumbling block' (Eiser, 1994). What Eiser seems to be saying, in keeping with the argument of Searle, is that only information that has meaning for the machine that is carrying out the processing of that information can be considered part of the consciousness of that machine, which is why only human 'machines' can be described as possessing consciousness: 'Computer consciousness – in the sense of self-awareness – is merely science fiction' (Eiser, 1994).

What is consciousness for? Taking an evolutionary approach

If Searle is correct, and Boden and the other *functionalists* are mistaken when they claim that our brains just happen to be made from neuroprotein (as opposed to silicon or metal), and that whatever they are made of is irrelevant (or incidental) as far as intelligence is concerned, then a useful path to travel might be the evolutionary one.

According to Humphrey (1986), when we ask what consciousness is doing, what difference it makes to any of our lives, there are three possibilities which might more or less make sense:

1 it might be making all the difference in the world: it might be a necessary precondition of all intelligent and purposive behaviour, both in humans and animals;
2 it might be making no difference whatsoever: it might be a purely accidental feature which happens (at least) sometimes to be present in (some) animals and has no influence on their behaviour; or
3 it might, for those animals which have it, be making the difference between success and failure in some particular compartment of their lives.

Humphrey believes that common sense must back the first argument. Our everyday experience is that consciousness makes all the difference in the world (just as our experience tells us that we have free will): we are either awake, alert and conscious or flat on our backs, inert and unconscious, and when we lose consciousness, we lose touch with the world.

However, what about those cases in which consciousness doesn't seem to be necessary, such as perception (in general, and more specific features such as *subliminal perception*, in which a stimulus affects behaviour despite being presented too quickly or faintly to register in conscious awareness), blindsight, and automatic processing (see above)?

While perception (and other fundamental cognitive and behavioural processes) may not require consciousness, the fact remains that they very often are at least *accompanied by* consciousness, and if (as far as we know) most other species lack it, the implication is that it evolved in human beings for some purpose.

Imagine an animal that lacks the faculty of conscious or self-reflexive 'insight'. It has a brain which receives inputs from conventional sense organs and sends outputs to motor systems, and in between runs a highly sophisticated information-processor and decision-maker. But it has no picture of what this information-processing is doing or how it works: the animal is unconscious.

Now imagine that a new form of sense-organ evolves, an 'inner eye', whose field of view is not the outside world, but the brain itself. Like other sense organs, it provides a picture of its informational field (the brain) which is partial and selective, but, equally, like other sense organs, it has been designed by natural selection to give a useful ('user-friendly') picture, one which will tell the subject as much as he or she needs to know: this animal is conscious (see Figure 13.5).

Suppose our ability to look in upon ourselves and examine our own minds at work is as much a part of human biology as our ability to walk upright or to perceive the outside world. Once upon a time there were animals – our own ancestors presumably – who could not do it. They gave rise to descendants who could. Why should those conscious descendants have been selected in the course of evolution?

(Humphrey, 1986)

If Darwin's theory is correct, the only answer can be that, like every other natural ability and structure, consciousness must have come into being because it conferred some kind of biological advantage on those creatures that possessed it.

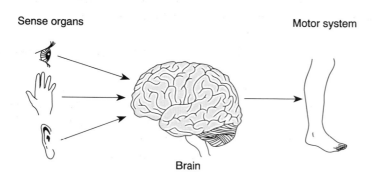

Figure 13.5a How an animal without insight works (From Humphrey, 1987)

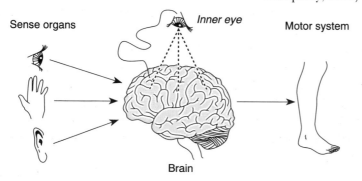

Figure 13.5b How the addition of an 'inner eye' affects the animal (From Humphrey, 1987)

In some particular area of their lives, conscious human beings must have been able to do something which their unconscious forebears couldn't; something which, in competition with the other members of their species, distinctly improved their chances of survival – and so of passing on the underlying genetic trait for consciousness to the next generation.

(Humphrey, 1986)

If consciousness is the answer to anything at all, it must be to a biological challenge which human beings have had to meet: could the challenge lie in the human need to understand, respond to and manipulate the behaviour of other human beings?

In evolutionary terms I suspect that the possession of an 'inner eye' served one purpose before all: to allow our own ancestors to raise social life to a new level. The first use of human consciousness was – and is – to enable each human being to understand what it feels *like to be human and so to make sense of himself and other people* from the inside.

(Humphrey, 1993)

This, of course, is a way of looking at people as *natural psychologists*, which was discussed in Chapter 1.

Humphrey points out that it is no accident that humans are both the most highly social creatures to have evolved and are unique in their ability to use self-knowledge to interpret others.

Blakemore (1988) believes that Humphrey's theory raises two important questions:

1 Why does consciousness use such strange symbolism? For example, the biological value of finding a partner obviously has to do with the nitty-gritty of procreation. But we *feel* we are in *love*, a sensation which tells us nothing about the crude necessity of reproduction: 'consciousness translates biological necessities into feelings of pain and pleasure, need and emotion.'

2 Why does the inner eye see so little? It gives us only a tiny glimpse, and a distorted one at that, of the internal world; as we saw above, when discussing unconscious information processing, much of what our brains do is entirely hidden from the 'spotlight' of consciousness.

At the present time, these questions can find no answers.

Brain research and psychology must try to give an account of the mystery of mind in terms of the structure and organisation of the brain . . . to understand the organ that allows us to understand would be little short of a miracle. The human brain makes us what we are. It makes the mind, which has driven people to escape from the environment that created those people.

(Blakemore, 1988)

Consciousness and communication

Although there may be no answers to these questions, they do raise further important questions and lines of enquiry. For example, Blakemore's reference to the distorted glimpse of the internal world of the mind provided by consciousness is a theme developed by Barlow (1987). He argues that consciousness links the individual to the community within which he or she lives, a link that is crucial to all that is human; it is to a large extent concerned with other people and the content of our consciousness is very much influenced by our past experience with others. This places consciousness in the 'border regions' between the individual and the community.

While fully agreeing with Humphrey's view that the survival value of consciousness derives from its influence on social problems and their solution, Barlow believes that he puts too much faith in the validity of the knowledge gained through introspection about the working of one's own mind: it doesn't give an accurate picture of the causes and motives even of one's own behaviour, let alone others'. Introspection only leads us to *think* we understand others – and it is these limitations that are crucial.

Consistent with Blakemore's first question (concerning the role of symbolism), Barlow maintains that it is hopelessly misleading to try and draw conclusions about the biological survival value of a subjective experience, such as pain or falling in love, by direct introspection. Although this does not mean that we should ignore our introspection altogether, it is important to understand the limitations of consciousness. Given that there are clearly many things which our brain does for us that are not associated with consciousness, we should ask: What is the general characteristic of those brain operations that do accompany consciousness?

The answer, according to Barlow, is that they are concerned with social interactions, especially with the preparation and execution of communications with others. While consciousness of course continues when communication is cut off, 'Whenever one is conscious, even in one's deepest introspections, one is in a sense addressing some other individual . . . Even when the audience cannot be specified . . . it is reasonable to insist on the importance, for all conscious thought, of some internal model of one or more other human minds'.

He refers to a study by Baron-Cohen et al. published in 1985 which showed that autistic children (matched for mental age with a group of normal children and a group with Down's syndrome) failed on a test which required them to understand that another person could hold a false belief because he or she had incomplete information. They failed to demonstrate, therefore, precisely the ability which, according to Humphrey, is facilitated by consciousness – that of understanding the causes of another person's actions and beliefs. This is consistent with a growing body of evidence in support of the claim that autistic children have an impaired '*theory of mind*', which is meant to account for the 'triad' of specific deficits, namely:

Figure 13.6 The self-absorption displayed by this autistic girl prevents her from developing a normal 'theory of mind'

1 an inability to form normal social relationships;
2 a marked difficulty with verbal and non-verbal communication; and
3 no inner world of pretence and imagination. (Leekam, 1993)

Barlow believes that even 'raw consciousness', such as the sensation of redness, has dimensions of communication: we often do want to communicate our experience and colour-blind people often can communicate 'normally' about colour and do not realize they are colour-blind until they are tested. This suggests that language (and, therefore, social experience) has more influence on raw sensations themselves than we normally admit (or realize).

Barlow concludes that consciousness is not simply a property of a brain in isolation – it has to do with communication and interaction *between* brains. This may help to explain the production of an objective, permanently recorded, culture: 'This could be the expression of the mind's desire to communicate and interact, not just with the remembered minds of others, but also with the minds of future generations. If consciousness depends on interaction, it is not surprising that people seek to leave traces for later minds to interact with' (Barlow, 1987).

The relationship between mind and brain

What Blakemore, Humphrey, Searle and other physiologists, biologists, psychologists and philosophers seem to be saying is that consciousness is *real* – it is a property of human beings as much as having a particular kind of body, or walking upright on two legs, or having a particular size and type of brain, are properties of human beings. They also seem agreed that, without the human brain, there would be no consciousness; the two seem to have evolved together. But this does not mean that the physical brain is in some sense 'primary', with consciousness being 'secondary'.

The logical or philosophical difficulty, as we have seen already in this chapter, is trying to understand how two 'things' are related, when one of them is physical (the brain having all the properties or characteristics of all physical objects, such as size, weight, shape, location in space and time), while the other seems to lack all these characteristics, this lack being almost a defining feature of consciousness.

Closely related to this logical and philosophical difficulty is the scientific one of explaining how it is that something non-physical or non-material ('the mind') can influence and produce changes in something physical or material ('the body'). The classic example given by philosophers of the 'problem' of mind and body is the commonplace, everyday, taken-for-granted act of deciding to lift one's arm (an example which is also used in discussing free will): assuming that it is an act of free will, how does my 'deciding' or 'intending' to lift my arm bring about the upward physical movement of my arm (which we call 'lifting my arm')?

The example is 'classic' partly because it involves the idea of causation; how can a non-physical event (my deciding to lift my arm) cause a physical event (the lifting of my arm)? From a strictly materialist, positivistic, scientific perspective (see Chapter 11), this should be impossible. Science, including psychology and neurophysiology, has traditionally rejected any brand of philosophical dualism, which stems from Descartes' belief in the essential difference between the physical and the mental (or non-physical).

However, if consciousness evolved because of its survival value, could it

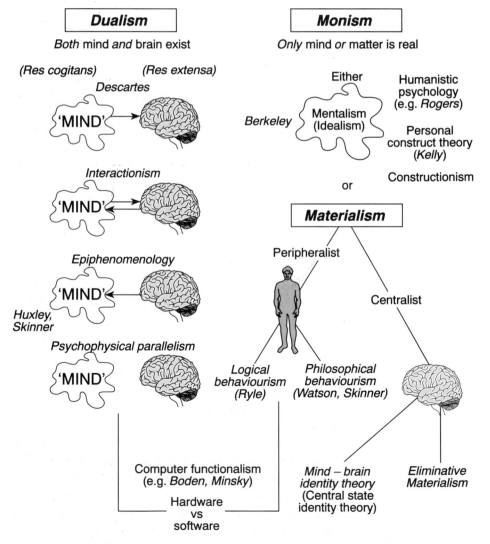

Figure 13.7 An outline of the major theories of the mind-brain relationship

have equipped human beings with such survival value unless it had causal properties (Gregory, 1981) – that is, unless it could actually bring about changes in behaviour?

This seems to be one of the more *psychologically relevant* questions regarding the mind–brain relationship (as opposed to the philosophically relevant and interesting questions). There is no doubt (as with free will) that our experience tells us that our mind affects our behaviour, that consciousness has causal properties. But philosophers and scientific psychologists have not always shared the lay person's commonsense understanding.

An overview of some of the major theories of the mind–brain relationship

Trying to classify the various attempts to 'solve' the mind–body problem is both complex and a matter of some controversy, but it is crucial to have some general picture of the types of theory that have been proposed (see Figure 13.7).

According to Armstrong (1987): 'If we think of mind and body as two opponents in a tug-of-war, then we can distinguish between theories which try to drag body, and matter generally, over into the camp of mind; those which try to drag mind over into the camp of body; and those theories where an equal balance is maintained.'

The 'equal balance' theories are *dualist*, with Descartes' being the most famous, and the most influential: it was his distinction between the physical body and the non-physical mind which really introduced the mind–body problem into philosophy for the first time. As we have seen, this is still very much alive, both in philosophy and cognitive science as a whole, and most alternative theories are an attempt to exorcise the 'ghost in the machine', which is how Ryle (1949), an Oxford philosopher with strong behaviourist leanings, attacked (with deliberate abusiveness) Descartes' belief in the non-physical, non-material mind, with its own separate existence from the body and causal powers to control the body, and hence, behaviour.

Descartes' theory represents a 'pure' form of dualism (or perhaps 'extreme' is more accurate), in the sense that the mind can influence the body (through the operation of the pineal gland in the brain), whereas the body cannot influence the mind. By contrast, *interactionists* believe that body and mind influence each other – the influence works in both directions.

Like Descartes, *epiphenomenologists* believe that the influence is only one way, but unlike him, they maintain that the influence works in the opposite direction, namely the brain influences the mind. An epiphenomenon is an accompanying event, outside the chain of causation, and was first proposed by T.H. Huxley, who claimed that consciousness is 'simply a collateral product, as completely without any power as the steam-whistle which accompanies the work of a locomotive is without influence on its machinery' (quoted in Humphrey, 1986); 'Consciousness, he thought, was simply the noise of the brain's engine at work, huffing and puffing as it went about the business of processing the information which controls behaviour' (Humphrey, 1986).

This is sometimes construed as behaviour affecting mind; Skinner can be seen as an epiphenomenologist in that, in places, he seems to accept the existence of mental phenomena, but denies their influence on behaviour, which is controlled entirely by environmental contingencies of reinforcement. Most of the time, however, he denies their existence altogether. Epiphenomenalism allows the neurophysiologist, in particular, to recognize the independent reality of mental events, while acknowledging the controlling role of the brain in our mental life, and allowing them to give a completely materialist/physicalist account of the brain and the factors which influence it (Armstrong, 1987).

Dualists who believe that there is no interaction between mind and brain, in either direction, are called *parallelists* (or psychophysical parallelists). Any theory that is not dualist is *monist*, implying that there is only one kind of reality (not two, as in dualism): this may be *mentalist* ('trying to drag the body, and matter generally, over into the camp of mind') or *materialist* ('trying to drag mind over into the camp of body').

According to mentalism (or *idealism*), only mental phenomena are real. In 1710 Berkeley, one of the British empiricist philosophers, argued that *'esse'* is *'percipi'* (to be is to be perceived); the universe is occupied only by minds, physical objects existing solely as ideas in someone's mind.

Most psychologists and philosophers do not accept such a view, which seems to be contrary to the commonsense belief in the independent existence of an external reality. However, those who take a phenomenological approach, such as Carl Rogers, according to whom experience (and free will) is of central importance, and Kelly's personal construct theory, according to which the world 'is' how it is defined and interpreted by the individual, may be seen as 'mentalist' in flavour (but they are not denying the existence of the physical world, as such, as Berkeley did; see Chapters 1 and 12). Also, any explanation of behaviour which adopts a constructionist approach (such as many feminist psychologists do when discussing, say, sex differences; see Chapter 6) has a mentalistic dimension.

The vast majority of monists are materialists, who believe that the only kind of reality is physical, a view which, ironically, was inspired by Descartes himself, when he claimed that human and animal bodies are simply machines (or 'physicochemical mechanisms', in today's vocabulary), controlled by precisely the same laws of physics as control the non-organic world.

'Materialism' is often confused with 'mechanism', which sees matter operating according to Newtonian 'billiard-ball' principles (see Chapters 11 and 12). It is best interpreted as the doctrine that the fundamental laws and principles of nature are exhausted by the laws and principles of physics, however 'unmaterialistic' the latter may be (Armstrong, 1987). Armstrong divides materialism into two major forms, *peripheralist* and *centralist*.

The peripheralist version is better known as *logical* or *philosophical behaviourism*, according to which 'the mind' is reduced to behaviour. For example, Watson (the founder of behaviourism) claimed that all thought processes are really no more than the sensations produced by tiny movements of the vocal cords which are too small to produce audible sounds. In fact, he was trying to deny the existence of thought altogether and so reduce it to 'silent speech'.

As for Skinner ('without doubt America's most influential psychologist ever', Flanagan, 1984), all statements about *res cogitans* (the 'mind' of Descartes' dualism), are unscientific gobbledegook, with mentalistic terms being dismissed as 'explanatory fictions' (see Chapter 11). In his early days as a behaviourist (during the 1930s), he advocated a science of psychology that should only talk about overt behaviour: 'I preferred the position of *radical behaviourism*, in which the existence of subjective entities is denied' (Skinner, 1979, quoted in Flanagan, 1984). But from 1945, he began to shift his position somewhat, towards a less radical view, according to which those mental events that do exist are made of the same (physical) stuff and obey the same sorts of laws (those of operant and respondent conditioning) as overt behavioural events. Thoughts, for example, are not the immaterial predecessors of material actions, but are themselves actions: behaviour is both overt (external) and covert (internal), the latter simply being less accessible than the former: 'Skinner seems to have realised that a psychology which simply refused to admit the reality of any subjective, cognitive and affective, phenomena was just too incredible to satisfy the minimal plausibility constraints on an adequate psychology' (Flanagan, 1984). This position gives the behaviourist 'permission' to study existing mental phenomena without worrying about their having any peculiar Cartesian-like, non-physical features. Interestingly, however, Skinner's materialism has never taken him in the direction of trying to reduce psychology to neurophysiology, which is what the centralist form of materialism does (see below).

Ryle's logical behaviourism, which is consistent with Watson's views and the early, radical behaviourism of Skinner, claims that mentalistic terms are simply a *grammatical* alternative to terms which describe behaviour, such that sentences about the mind can be translated into sentences about behaviour, without anything being 'left over'. Sometimes, this will involve reference to *dispositions* to behave; for example, 'John believes it is going to rain' translates into 'John will be disposed to carry an umbrella if he goes out'. According to logical behaviourism, the mind is behaviour plus dispositions to behave (Searle, 1992).

For Ryle, the mind–brain problem is a pseudo-problem resulting from a distinction which is purely grammatical: matter is normally described using nouns or pronouns, while mind is normally described using verbs, adverbs or adjectives. If, for example, we talk about a person's 'intelligence' instead of his or her 'intelligent behaviour', we create the impression that intelligence exists in some equivalent way to the person's body, because we are using a noun when it is more appropriate to use an adjective. These 'category mistakes' have brought about the non-problem of the mind–brain relationship.

Centralist materialism (*mind–brain identity theory* or *central state identity theory*) identifies mental processes with purely physical processes in the central nervous system.

According to Place (1956) and Smart (1959), for example, there is no logical absurdity involved in supposing that there might be separate mental, non-physical phenomena, independent of material reality, it just turns out that, as a matter of fact, mental states are identical with states of the nervous system: 'The sciences of biology and psychology . . . are an application of physics and chemistry to natural history . . . [and] organisms are simply very complicated physico-chemical mechanisms' (Smart, 1959, quoted in Teichman, 1988).

A recent example of this rather extreme form of reductionist materialism is *The Astonishing Hypothesis: The Scientific Search for the Soul* (1994), by Francis Crick (one of the co-discoverers of the structure of DNA; see Chapter 5). *The Astonishing Hypothesis* states that: 'You, your joys and your sorrows, your memories and your ambitions, your sense of personality and free will, are in fact no more than the behaviour of a vast assembly of nerve cells and their associated molecules' (Crick, 1994, quoted in Smith, 1994). His objective is to correlate brain activity and consciousness and, more specifically, to identify which neurons are associated with the mere 'water' of automatism and which with the 'wine' of consciousness. But Smith, in a review of Crick's book, asks if Crick's review of all the evidence for the neurophysiological correlates of visual consciousness in primate (including human) brains, takes us any further towards a solution to the mind–brain problem: 'How is it that consciousness, that "wonder of wonders" [Husserl], is correlated with/emerges from/is the "internal" aspect of all this intricate cerebral activity?' (Smith, 1994).

The problem of mind and brain, according to Smith, is radically different from other cases of contingent identity with which it is usually compared, such as:

1 a cloud is a mass of water droplets or other particles in suspension,
2 heat is mean kinetic energy,
3 a gene is identical with a section of the DNA molecule.

The difference is to do with reductionism, and related to this is the issue of deciding exactly what we mean by identity.

It has generally been assumed that mind–brain identity implies what philosophers call *type identity*. This involves the claim that whenever a mind state of a certain type occurs, a brain state of a certain type occurs, such that we could study the operation of the human system using one or other framework, and the results of our studies could be simply translated from one framework directly into the other. 'Mind talk' would just be an alternative way of describing the same thing as we describe using 'brain talk'. However, the neurophysiological and neuropsychological evidence points instead towards *token identity*; although there can never be a mind state which isn't grounded in a brain state of some kind or other (we cannot have a mind without a brain), a particular kind of mind state is sometimes grounded in one kind of brain state and sometimes in another. We cannot, therefore, substitute a brain state description for mind state descriptions, because these ways of looking at the system are not systematically correlated (Harré et al., 1985).

Broadbent (1981, cited in Harré et al., 1985) has shown that, for reading, we cannot take for granted that the same neurophysiological mechanisms will be used by two different people when they engage in the 'same' activity of reading; there may be many ways that 'the brain' can perform the same task. Although in a certain sense everyone 'reads with their brain', a neurophysiological description of brain function cannot displace, or replace, a psychological description. Token identity means that there must always be a place for an autonomous psychological account of human action and thought (Harré et al., 1985).

Even if a perfectly systematic correlation between mind states and brain states were found, this would not be sufficient on its own to support the attempt to replace a psychological account of behaviour with an account in terms of neurophysiology (*eliminative materialism*), which represents an extreme reductionist form of materialism. Apart from the objections to reductionism itself, such correlational evidence would be equally consistent with psychophysical parallelism which is, of course, a form of dualism.

Steven Rose, an eminent biologist interested in the brain, argues in favour of learning how to translate between mind language and brain language, and against trying to replace the former with the latter: 'the mind is never replaced by the brain. Instead, we have two distinct and legitimate languages, each describing the same unitary phenomena of the material world' (Rose, 1992). He is speaking as a materialist but also as an *anti-reductionist*. While these often go hand in hand, and it is true that most reductionists are also materialists, they do not necessarily go together. Like Rose, Freud was a materialist who believed that no single scientific vocabulary (such as anatomy) could adequately describe – let alone explain – all facets of the material world. He upheld the thesis of the autonomy of psychological explanation (which meant that he completely rejected his original reductionist project): 'psychoanalysis must keep itself free from any hypothesis that is alien to it, whether of an anatomical, chemical or physiological kind and must operate with purely auxiliary ideas' (Freud, 1919, quoted by Flanagan, 1984).

The fact that there are different 'languages' for describing minds and brains (or different *levels of description*) relates to the question of the relevance of knowing, say, what is going on inside my brain when I think/am conscious:

> *The firing of neurons stands to thought in the same relation as my walking across the room (etc.) stands to my getting some coffee. It is absolutely essential in a causal or physical sense, and absolutely superfluous . . . to the logic of the higher-order description. In short, I can accept that it happens, and then happily ignore it.*
>
> (Eiser, 1994)

This explains how it is possible to be a materialist (the brain is necessarily implicated in everything we do and the mind does not represent a different kind of reality) and an anti-reductionist (we can describe and explain my thinking without having to 'bring my brain into it' – two separate levels of description are involved) at the same time.

In other words, from a psychological point of view, it is irrelevant to establish quite how, in physical terms, the brain goes about being a mind. This view is not too dissimilar from that of the *computer functionalists* (such as Boden, Minsky and others) who, as we noted earlier in the chapter, stress the importance of the processes carried out by the brain to the exclusion of what the brain is actually made of ('you don't need brains to be brainy', Boden, quoted by Rose, 1992). They attempt to solve the mind–brain problem by distinguishing between *software* and *hardware*: the mind is to software as the brain is to hardware. Since it is the software/mind (the logical operations involving the manipulation of symbols) that is important, the problem of the relationship between it and the hardware/brain disappears.

However, as Rose (1992) points out, this separation of mind from its actual material base is in some ways a reversion to Cartesian dualism. At the same time, by treating the brain as a sort of black box whose internal biological mechanisms and processes are irrelevant, and insisting that all that matters is matching inputs to outputs, it is also behaviouristic. It, therefore, seems to (re-)create some of the problems it was designed to solve, and to face the same objections as other attempted solutions:

> *The basic thesis of mind–brain identity is taken very much for granted . . . How we should* use *such knowledge . . . however . . . is far less agreed. Even if minds and brains have an identical physical reference, our knowledge of brains as brains is neither similar in kind nor comparable in extensiveness to our knowledge of minds as minds. The task of translating the one kind of knowledge into the other is so difficult – both technically and conceptually – that, for most purposes, it is almost certainly not worth the effort.*

Indeed: 'For much of what it conventionally does, psychology might as well be dualist or Cartesian, and might indeed be better for admitting it' (Eiser, 1994).

Summary

- Psychology began its life as a separate discipline taking consciousness/conscious mental life as its subject matter. This was then rejected by Watson and his behaviourist manifesto.
- 'Mind' has once again become legitimate subject matter and introspection is again an acceptable means of collecting data, coinciding with the decline of behaviourism.
- According to *philosophical behaviourism*, internal, subjective phenomena, including consciousness, do not exist.
- The nature and existence of consciousness is very closely related to the *mind–body problem/the problem of mind and brain*.
- The 'problem of consciousness' arises when we acknowledge that the physical brain is, in some way, involved in our subjective experience. How and why and to what end has the dependence of the non-physical mind on the physical brain come about? Is the study of consciousness compatible with *positivism*?
- One of the unique features of consciousness is that any particular instance seems to involve a *favoured/privileged observer*, who has special access to the phenomenon.
- 'Mind' is a much broader concept than consciousness; there is always much more mental activity than we can detect through introspection at any one time; it is limited to sensations, 'what is happening to me'.
- Freud distinguished between the *conscious*, the *pre-conscious*, and the *unconscious*, which, essentially, are *levels of accessibility* of thoughts/memories, etc.
- Most psychologists accept that thoughts, etc., can be placed on a continuum of consciousness, but most would not accept Freud's theory of the unconscious as a *dynamic* force, whereby what is threatening is actively forced out of consciousness through *repression*.
- Jung distinguished between the *personal* and the *collective unconscious*.
- One way in which experimental psychologists have studied consciousness is through the concept of attention. An important distinction is that between *focal attention* (or focal awareness) and *peripheral attention*.
- It seems to be necessary that much of our behaviour/mental processes takes place outside our focal attention/conscious awareness (using *automatic processing*).
- In the case of perception, for example, we don't want to know about how we do it (the process) but what is going on around us in the external world.

- The phenomenon of *blindsight* suggests that, at least for certain aspects of perception, conscious (focal) awareness may not even be necessary in order to 'perceive', i.e. it is possible to show the behaviour of perceiving without being consciously aware of what we are doing.
- What is involved in blindsight and *prosopagnosia* is a loss of *explicit conscious recognition* but the capacity for *implicit behavioural recognition* increases.
- Nisbett and Wilson argued that we have no direct access to cognitive processes at all: we have access only to the ideas/inferences that are the products/outputs of such processes. This means that our commonsense, 'intuitive' accounts of our own behaviour are *illusory*.
- Edelman distinguished between *primary consciousness* and *higher-order consciousness* (or *self-consciousness*); the latter is similar to Johnson Laird's *self-reflective automata*. Humphrey uses 'consciousness' to mean 'self-consciousness' (or 'primary consciousness').
- One central feature of consciousness is knowing what it is like to be something/someone.
- The difference between *parallel* (brain) and *serial processing* (most traditional computer programs) is an argument used by those opposed to strong AI. But what about *connectionism*?
- For Eiser, the crucial feature of human consciousness is *the contents of our thoughts*, the sense of self, not the kind of information-processing operations that it performs.
- Another objection to strong AI's exclusive emphasis on the processes is that it divorces the mental from the physical: personal identity depends on physical identity. According to Merleau-Ponty, without our body, we couldn't *be*. Mental and physical are both aspects of a person and neither can be reduced to the other.
- Another fundamental feature of consciousness is *intentionality*, which is absent in computers, since the symbols which they manipulate have no meaning for the computer itself.
- Even though perception (and other cognitive processes) may not require consciousness, the fact that consciousness very often accompanies them and that most other species lack it, suggests that it evolved in human beings for some purpose.
- Humphrey describes consciousness as a new form of sense organ, an 'inner eye', which evolved to provide a 'user-friendly' picture of the brain itself. The biological advantage which this conferred on the creatures that possessed it (that is, human beings) was the ability to understand, respond to or manipulate the behaviour of other human beings. People are natural psychologists.
- According to Barlow, the general characteristic of those brain operations which are accompanied by consciousness is that they

are concerned with social interactions, especially with the preparation and execution of communications with others. Culture may represent the mind's desire to interact with the minds of future generations.

- Different theories of the mind–brain relationship are trying to solve two major 'puzzles': (i) how something physical (the brain) can be related to something non-physical (consciousness); (ii) how something non-physical can influence and produce changes in something physical.

- Belief in the non-physical mind, as a reality distinct from the physical brain/body, is called *philosophical dualism*, first proposed by Descartes.

- Positivist, materialist science has traditionally rejected all forms of dualism. But could consciousness have evolved to equip human beings with some kind of survival value unless it had causal properties (which is impossible from a materialist, positivist perspective)?

- *Interactionism* and *epiphenomenology* are both forms of dualism, different from Descartes' version; what they all have in common is the belief that there is some form of interaction between mind and brain, but they differ as to the direction of this influence.

- *Psychophysical parallelists* are dualists who maintain that there is no mind–brain interaction.

- Any theory that is not dualist is *monist*.

- According to *mentalism/idealism*, only mental phenomena are real. *Phenomenological* theories, such as those of Rogers and Kelly, and *constructionist* explanations of behaviour, can be seen as having a mentalist 'flavour'.

- Most monists are *materialists*, who can be divided into *peripheralists* and *centralists*.

- The *peripheralist* version is better known as *logical/philosophical behaviourism*. Skinner's *radical behaviourism* at first obliged him to deny the existence of 'subjective entities' altogether, but he later 'reduced' thoughts to covert/internal behaviour.

- According to Ryle's *logical behaviourism*, the mind–brain problem is a pseudo-problem resulting from a purely *grammatical* confusion.

- *Centralist* materialism (*mind–brain identity theory/central state identity theory*) identifies mental processes with purely physical processes in the central nervous system.

- One of the difficulties with identity theory is that it is generally assumed to imply *type identity*, while the available evidence points instead towards *token identity*: 'Brain talk' can never displace/replace 'mind talk'.

- *Eliminative materialism* represents an extreme reductionist form of materialism. Even type identity would not be a sufficient reason for

rejecting psychological accounts of thought and action in favour of a neurophysiological account.
- It is possible to be *both* a materialist and an anti-reductionist (such as Freud and Rose), because of the independent existence of different *levels of description*.

Suggestions for further reading

Blakemore, C. & Greenfield, S. (Eds) (1987) *Mindwaves*, Oxford: Basil Blackwell.

Eiser, J. R. (1994) *Attitudes, Chaos and the Connectionist Mind*, Oxford: Basil Blackwell.

Humphrey, N. (1992) *A History of the Mind*, London: Vintage.

Searle, J. R. (1992) *The Rediscovery of the Mind*, Cambridge, Mass.: MIT Press.

Baron, R. A. & Byrne, D. (1991) *Social Psychology*, 6th edn, Boston: Allyn & Bacon.

References

Abramson, L. Y. & Martin, D. J. (1981) Depression and the causal inference process. In J. H. Harvey, W. J. Ickes & R. F. Kidd (Eds) *New Directions in Attitude Research*, Vol. 3. Hillsdale, N.J.: Lawrence Erlbaum

Abramson, L. Y., Seligman, M. E. P. & Teasedale, J. D. (1978) Learned helplessness in humans: Critique and reformulation. *Journal of Abnormal Psychology*, 87, 49–74

Ainsworth, M. D. S. (1989) Attachments beyond Infancy. *American Psychologist*, 44(4), 709–16

Ainsworth, M. D. S., Blehar, M. C., Waters, E. & Wall, S. (1978) *Patterns of Attachment: A psychological study of the strange situation*. Hillsdale, N.J.: Lawrence Erlbaum

Allport, D. A. (1980) Attention and performance. In G. Claxton (Ed.) *Cognitive Psychology: New directions*. London: RKP

Allport, G. W. (1937) *Personality: A psychological interpretation*. New York: Holt

Allport, G. W. (1960) *Personality and Social Encounter*. Boston: Beacon Press

Allport, G. W. (1961) *Pattern and Growth in Personality*. New York: Holt Rinehart & Winston

American Psychological Association (1981) *Ethical Principles of Psychologists*. Washington, D.C.: American Psychological Association.

American Psychological Association (1982) *Ethical Principles in the Conduct of Research with Human Participants*. Washington, D.C.: American Psychological Association

American Psychological Association (1985) *Guidelines for Ethical Conduct in the Care and Use of Animals*. Washington, D.C.: American Psychological Association

Anastasi, A. (1958) Heredity, environment, and the question 'How?'. *Psychological Review*, 65, 197–208

Antaki, C. (1984) Core concepts in attribution theory. In J. Nicholson & H. Beloff (Eds) *Psychology Survey 5*. Leicester: British Psychological Society

Argyle, M. (1983) *The Psychology of Interpersonal Behaviour*, 4th edn. Harmondsworth: Penguin

Armstrong, D. M. (1987) Mind–Body Problem: Philosophical theories. In R. L. Gregory (Ed.) *The Oxford Companion to the Mind*. Oxford: Oxford University Press

Aronson, E. (1992) *The Social Animal*, 6th edn. New York: W. H. Freeman & Co.

Asch, S. E. (1951) Effect of group pressure upon the modification and distortion of judgements. In H. Guetzkow (Ed.) *Groups, Leadership and Men*. Pittsburg, Pa.: Carnegie Press.

Asch, S. E. (1952) *Social Psychology*. Englewood Cliffs, N.J.: Prentice-Hall

Association for the Teaching of Psychology (1992) Ethics in psychological research: Guidelines for students at pre-degree levels. *Psychology Teaching*, 4–10, New Series, No. 1

Bailey, C. L. (1979) Mental illness: A logical misrepresentation? *Nursing Times*, May, 761–2.

Bannister, D. & Fransella, F. (1966) A grid test of schizophrenic thought disorder. *British Journal of Social & Clinical Psychology*, 5, 95–102

Bannister, D. & Fransella, F. (1967) *A Grid Test of Schizophrenic Thought Disorder*. Barnstaple: Psychological Test Publications

Bannister, D. & Fransella, F. (1980) *Inquiring Man: The psychology of personal constructs*, 2nd edn. Harmondsworth: Penguin

Barlow, H. (1987) The biological role of consciousness. In C. Blakemore & S. Greenfield (Eds) *Mindwaves*. Oxford: Blackwell.

Barnes, R. D., Ickes, W. J. & Kidd, R. (1979) Effects of perceived intentionality and stability of another's dependency on helping behaviour. *Personality & Social Psychology Bulletin*, 5, 367–72

Baron, R. A. & Byrne, D. (1991) *Social Psychology*, 6th edn. Boston: Allyn & Bacon

Bartholomew, K. (1993) From childhood to adult relationships: Attachment theory and research. In S. Duck (Ed.) *Learning about Relationships*. Newbury Park, Ca.: Sage Publications

Bateson, G., Jackson, D., Haley, J. & Weakland, J. (1956) Toward a theory of schizophrenia. *Behavioural Science*, 1, 251–64

Bateson, P. (1986) When to experiment on animals. *New Scientist*, 109 (1496), 30–2

Bateson, P. (1992) Do animals feel pain? *New Scientist*, 134 (1818), 30–3

Becker, H. S. (1963) *Outsiders: Studies in the sociology of deviance*. New York: Free Press

Bee, H. (1989) *The Developing Child*, 5th edn. New York: Harper & Row

Bee, H. (1994) *Lifespan Development*. New York: HarperCollins

Bem, D. J. (1967) Self-perception: An alternative interpretation of cognitive dissonance phenomena. *Psychological Review*, 74, 183–200

Bem, D. J. (1972) Self-perception theory. In L. Berkowitz (Ed.) *Advances in Experimental Social Psychology*, Vol. 6. New York: Academic Press

Bem, D. J. (1983) Constructing a theory of the triple typology: Some (second) thoughts on nomothetic and idiographic approaches to personality. *Journal of Personality*, 51, 566–77

Bem, D. J. & Allen, A. (1974) On predicting some of the people some of the time: A search for cross-situational consistencies in behaviour. *Psychological Review*, 81, 506–20

Bem, S. L. (1984) Androgyny and gender schema theory: a conceptual and empirical integration. In R. A. Dienstbier (Ed) *Nebraska Symposium* on Motivation. Lincoln, Nebraska: University of Nebraska Press

Bem, S. L. (1993) Is there a place in psychology for a feminist analysis of the social context? *Feminism & Psychology*, 3 (2), 230–4

Bennett, M. (1993) Introduction. In M. Bennett (Ed.) *The Child as Psychologist:*

An introduction to the development of social cognition. Hemel Hempstead, Herts.: Harvester Wheatsheaf

Bentall, R. P. (1993) Personality traits may be alive, they may even be well, but are they really useful? *The Psychologist*, 6 (7), 307

Berger, P. L. & Luckmann, T. (1966) *The Social Construction of Reality*. Harmondsworth: Penguin

Berkowitz, L. (1969) Resistance to improper dependency relationships. *Journal of Experimental Social Psychology*, 5, 283–94

Bernstein, M. D. & Russo, N. F. (1974) The history of psychology revisited: Or, up with our foremothers. *American Psychologist*, 29, 130–4

Berry, J. W. (1969) On cross-cultural comparability. *International Journal of Psychology*, 4, 119–28

Berry, J. W., Poortinga, Y. H., Segall, M. H. & Dasen, P. R. (1992) *Cross-cultural psychology: Research and applications.* New York: Cambridge University Press

Bieber, I. Dain, H. J., Dince, P. R., Drellich, M. G., Grand, H. G., Bundlach, R. H., Dremer, M. W., Rifkin, A. H., Wilbur, C. B. & Bieber, T. B. (1962) *Homosexuality.* New York: Vintage Books

Blakemore, C. (1988) *The Mind Machine.* London: BBC Books

Blakemore, C. & Cooper, G. F. (1970) Development of the brain depends on the visual environment. *Nature*, 228, 477–8

Blos, P. (1967) The second individuation process of adolescence. *Psychoanalytic Study of the Child*, 22, 162–86

Boden, M. (1993) The impact on philosophy. In D. Broadbent (Ed.) *The Simulation of Human Intelligence.* Oxford: Blackwell

Bowers, K. S. (1973) Situationism in psychology: An analysis and critique. *Psychological Review*, 80, 307–36

Bowlby, J. *Child-Care and the Growth of Love.* Harmondsworth: Penguin

Bowlby, J. (1977) The making and breaking of affectional bonds: 1. Aetiology and psychopathology in the light of attachment theory. *British Journal of Psychiatry*, 130, 201–10

Bradbury, T. N. & Fincham, F. D. (1990) Attributions in marriage: Review and critique. *Psychological Bulletin*, 107, 3–33

Brady, J. V. (1958) Ulcers in 'executive monkeys'. *Scientific American*, 199, 95–100

Brehm, J. W. (1966) *A Theory of Psychological Reactance.* New York: Academic Press

Brehm, S. S. (1992) *Intimate Relationships*, 2nd edn. New York: McGraw-Hill

Brehm, S. S. & Brehm, J. W. (1981) *Psychological Reactance: A theory of freedom and control.* New York: Academic Press

Brislin, R. (1993) *Understanding Culture's Influence on Behaviour.* Orlando, Fla.: Harcourt Brace Jovanovich

British Psychological Society (1978) Ethical principles for research with human subjects. *Bulletin of the British Psychological Society*, 31, 48–9

British Psychological Society (1983) *Guidelines for the Professional Practice of Clinical Psychology.* Leicester: British Psychological Society

British Psychological Society (1985) A code of conduct for psychologists. *Bulletin of the British Psychological Society*, 38, 41–3

British Psychological Society (1990) Ethical principles for conducting research with human participants. *The Psychologist*, 3 (6), 269–72

British Psychological Society (1993) Ethical principles for conducting research with human participants (revised). *The Psychologist*, 6 (1), 33–5

British Psychological Society and Committee of the Experimental Psychological Society (1985) *Guidelines for the Use of Animals in Research*. Leicester: British Psychological Society

British Psychological Society Scientific Affairs Board (1985) Guidelines for the use of animals in research. *Bulletin of the British Psychological Society*, 38, 289–91

Bronfenbrenner, U. (1979) *The Ecology of Human Development: Experiments by nature and design*. Cambridge, Mass.: Harvard University Press

Bronfenbrenner, U. (1989) Ecological systems theory. *Annals of Child Development*, 6, 187–249

Brown, J. A. C. (1961) *Freud and the Post-Freudians*. Harmondsworth: Penguin

Burgner, D. & Hewstone, M. (1993) Young children's causal attributions for success and failure: 'Self-enhancing' boys and 'self-derogating' girls. *British Journal of Development Psychology*, 11, 125–9

Burt, C. (1949) The structure of the mind: A review of the results of factor analysis. *British Journal of Educational Psychology*, 19, 110–11, 176–99

Burt, C. (1955) The evidence for the concept of intelligence. *British Journal of Educational Psychology*, 25, 158–77

Butler, J. M. & Haigh, G. V. (1954) Changes in the relation between self-concepts and ideal concepts consequent upon client-centred counselling. In C. R. Rogers & R. F. Dymond (Eds) (1954) *Psychotherapy and Personality Change: Co-ordinated research studies in the client-centred approach*. Chicago: Chicago University Press

Byne, W. (1994) The biological evidence challenged. *Scientific American*, May, 26–31

Campos, J. J., Barrett, K., Lamb, M. E., Goldsmith, H. H. & Stenberg, C. (1983) Socioemotional development. In M. M. Haith & J. J. Campos (Eds) *Handbook of Child Psychology*: Vol 2. Infancy and Psychobiology. New York: Wiley

Cannon, W. B. (1927) The James-Lange theory of emotions: A critical examination and an alternative theory. *American Journal of Psychology*, 39, 106–24

Caplan, P. J. (1991) Delusional dominating personality disorder (DDPD). *Feminism & Psychology*, 1 (1), 171–4

Carver, C. S. & Scheier, M. F. (1992) *Perspectives on Personality*, 2nd edn. Boston: Allyn & Bacon

Cattell, R. B. (1944) Psychological measurement: Normative, ipsative, interactive. *Psychological Review*, 51, 292–303

Cattell, R. B. (1965) *The Scientific Analysis of Behaviour*. Harmondsworth: Penguin

Chomsky, N. (1965) *Aspects of the Theory of Syntax*. Cambridge, Mass.: MIT Press

Chomsky, N. (1968) *Language and Mind*. New York: Harcourt Brace Jovanovich

Clift, S. M. (1984) Should we still teach Freud? *Psychology Teaching*, December, 8–14

Cole, M. (1993) Mind as a cultural achievement: Implications for IQ testing. In M. Gauvin & M. Cole (Eds) *Readings on the Development of Children*. New York: Scientific American Books, W. H. Freeman & Co.

Collins, N. L. & Read, S. J. (1990) Adult attachment, working models, and relationship quality in dating couples. *Journal of Personality & Social Psychology*, 58, 644–63

Coolican, H. (1994) *Research Methods and Statistics in Psychology*, 2nd edn. London: Hodder & Stoughton

Costa, P. T. & McCrae, R. R. (1993) Bullish on personality psychology. *The Psychologist*, 6 (7), 302–3

Crick, F. (1994) *The Astonishing Hypothesis: The scientific search for the soul*. London: Simon & Schuster

Darley, J. M. & Latané, B. (1968) Bystander intervention in emergencies: Diffusion of responsibility. *Journal of Personality & Social Psychology*, 8, 377–83

Darwin, C. R. (1859) *The Origin of Species by Means of Natural Selection*. London: John Murray

Davison, G. C. & Neale, J. M. (1994) *Abnormal Psychology*, 6th edn. New York: John Wiley & Sons

Dawkins, R. (1976) *The Selfish Gene*. Oxford: Oxford University Press

Deary, I. J. & Matthews, G. (1993) Personality traits are alive and well. *The Psychologist*, 6 (7), 299–311

Deese, J. (1972) *Psychology as Science and Art*. New York: Harcourt Brace Jovanovich

Denmark, F., Russo, N. F., Frieze, I. H. & Sechzer, J. A. (1988) Guidelines for Avoiding Sexism in Psychological Research: A report of the ad hoc committee on nonsexist research. *American Psychologist*, 43 (7), 582–5

Dennett, D. C. (1987) Consciousness. In R. L. Gregory (Ed.) The Oxford *Companion to the Mind*. Oxford: Oxford University Press

Doyle, J. A. (1983) *The Male Experience*, Dubuque, Iowa: Wm. C. Brown Co.

Draguns, J. (1980) Psychological disorders of clinical severity. In H. C. Triandis & J. Draguns (Eds) *Handbook of Cross-cultural Psychology*: Vol. 6. Psychopathology. Boston: Allyn & Bacon

Draguns, J. (1990) Applications of cross-cultural psychology in the field of mental health. In R. Brislin (Ed.) *Applied Cross-cultural Psychology*. Newbury Park, CA: Sage

Dunn, J. & Plomin, R. (1990) S*eparate Lives: Why siblings are so different*. New York: Basic Books

Eagly, A. H. (1987) *Sex Differences in Social Behaviour: A social-role interpretation*. Hillsdale, N.J.: Lawrence Erlbaum

Edelman, G. (1992) *Bright Air, Brilliant Fire: On the matter of the mind*. Harmondsworth: Penguin

Edwards, D. & Potter, J. (1992) *Discursive Psychology*. London: Sage

Eiser, J. R. (1994) *Attitudes, Chaos and the Connectionist Mind*. Oxford: Blackwell

Endler, N. S. & Magnusson, D. (1976) Toward an interactional psychology of personality. *Psychological Bulletin*, 83, 956–74

Epstein, S. (1979) The stability of behaviour: On predicting most of the people much of the time. *Journal of Personality & Social Psychology*, 37, 1097–126

Erikson, E. H. (1950) *Childhood and Society*. New York: Norton

Erikson, E. H. (1963) *Childhood and Society*, 2nd edn. New York: Norton

Erikson, E. H. (1968) *Identity: Youth and crisis*. New York: Norton

Ewen, R. E. (1988) *An Introduction to Theories of Personality*, 3rd edn. Hillsdale, N.J.: Lawrence Erlbaum

Eysenck, H. J. (1953) *The Structure of Human Personality*. London: Methuen

Eysenck, H. J. (1965) *Fact and Fiction in Psychology*. Harmondsworth: Penguin

Eysenck, H. J. (1967) *The Biological Basis of Personality*. Springfield, Ill.: C. C. Thomas

Eysenck, H. J. (1970) *Crime and Personality*, revised edn. London: Paladin

Eysenck, M. W. (1994) *Perspectives on Psychology*. Hove: Lawrence Erlbaum

Fairbairn, G. (1987) Responsibility, respect for persons and psychological change. In S. Fairbairn & G. Fairbairn (Eds) *Psychology, Ethics and Change*. London: RKP

Fancher, R. E. (1979) *Pioneers of Psychology: Studies of the great figures who paved the way for the contemporary science of behaviour*. New York: Norton

Fernando, S. (1991) *Mental Health, Race and Culture*. London: Macmillan, in association with MIND Publications

Festinger, L. (1957) *A Theory of Cognitive Dissonance*. New York: Harper & Row

Festinger, L. & Carlsmith, J. M. (1959) Cognitive consequences of forced compliance. *Journal of Abnormal & Social Psychology*, 58, 203–10

Fiske, S. & Taylor, S. (1991) *Social Cognition*, 2nd edn. New York: McGraw-Hill

Flanagan, O. J. (1984) *The Science of the Mind*. Cambridge, Mass.: MIT Press

Fransella, F. (1970) And there was one. In D. Bannister (Ed.) *Perspectives in Personal Construct Theory*. London: Academic Press

Fransella, F. (1972) *Personal Change and Reconstruction: Research on a treatment of stuttering*. London: Academic Press

Fransella, F. (1980) Man-as-scientist. In A. J. Chapman & D. M. Jones (Eds) *Models of Man*. Leicester: British Psychological Society

Freud, S. (1930) *Civilization and Its Discontents*. Pelican Freud Library, Vol. 12. Harmondsworth: Penguin

Fromm, E. (1942) *The Fear of Freedom*. London: RKP

Fromm, E. (1964) *The Heart of Man*. London: RKP

Gahagan, J. (1984) *Social Interaction and Its Management*. London: Methuen.

Gahagan, J. (1991) Understanding other people; understanding self. In J. Radford & E. Govier (Eds) *A Textbook of Psychology*. London: Routledge.

Gardner, R. A. & Gardner, B. T. (1969) Teaching sign language to a chimpanzee. *Science*, 165 (3894), 664–72

Garfinkel, H. (1967) *Studies in Ethnomethodology*. Englewood Cliffs, N.J.: Prentice-Hall

Garnham, A. (1991) *The Mind in Action*. London: Routledge

Gay, P. (1988) *Freud: A life for our time*. London: J. M. Dent & Sons

Gelder, M., Gath, D. & Mayon, R. (1989) *Oxford Textbook of Psychiatry*, 2nd edn. Oxford: Oxford University Press

Gesell, A. (1925) *The Mental Growth of the Preschool Child*. New York: Macmillan

Gilligan, C. (1982) *In a Different Voice: Psychological theory and women's development*. Cambridge, Mass.: Harvard University Press

Gilligan, C. (1993) *Letter to Readers* (Preface). In C. Gilligan (1982) (2nd impression)

Goffman, E. (1963) *Stigma: Notes on the management of spoiled identity*. Englewood Cliffs, N.J.: Prentice-Hall

Goffman, E. (1971) *The Presentation of Self in Everyday Life*. Harmondsworth: Penguin

Gould, S. J. (1981) *The Mismeasure of Man*. New York: Norton

Gould, S. J. (1987) *An Urchin in the Storm*. Harmondsworth: Penguin

Graham, H. (1986) *The Human Face of Psychology: Humanistic psychology in its historical, social and cultural context*. Milton Keynes: Open University Press

Gray, J. (1987) The mind–brain identity as a scientific hypothesis: A second look. In C. Blakemore & S. Greenfield (Eds) *Mindwaves*. Oxford: Blackwell

Gray, J. A. (1991) On the morality of speciesism. *The Psychologist*, 4 (5), 196–8

Green, S. (1994) *Principles of Biopsychology*. Hove: Lawrence Erlbaum

Gregory, R. L. (1981) *Mind in Science*. Harmondsworth: Penguin

Gross, R. (1992) *Psychology: The Science of Mind and Behaviour*, 2nd edn. London: Hodder & Stoughton

Gross, R. (1994) *Key Studies in Psychology*, 2nd edn. London: Hodder & Stoughton

Guilford, J. P. (1959) Three faces of intellect. *American Psychologist*, 14, 469–79

Hampson, S. E. (1988) *The Construction of Personality: An introduction*, 2nd edn. London: Routledge

Haney, C., Banks, C. & Zimbardo, P. (1973) A study of prisoners and guards in a simulated prison. *Naval Research Reviews*, 30 (9), 4–17·

Harlow, H. F. & Zimmerman, R. R. (1959) Affectional responses in the infant monkey. *Science*, 130, 421–32

Harré, R. (1993) Rules, roles and rhetoric. *The Psychologist*, 6 (1), 24–8

Harré, R. & Secord, P. F. (1972) *The Explanation of Social Behaviour*. Oxford: Blackwell

Harré, R., Clarke, D. & De Carlo, N. (1985) *Motives and Mechanisms: An introduction to the psychology of action*. London: Methuen

Harris, P. L. (1989) *Children and Emotion*. Oxford: Blackwell

Hartshorne, H. & May, M. A. (1928) *Studies in the Nature of Character: Vol. 1, Studies in Deceit*. New York: Macmillan

Haworth, G. (1992) The use of non-human animals in psychological research: the current status of the debate. *Psychology Teaching*, 46–54, New Series, No. 1

Hayslip, B. & Panek, P. E. (1993) *Adult Development and Ageing*, 2nd edn. New York: HarperCollins

Hazan, C. & Shaver, P. R. (1987) Romantic love conceptualized as an attachment process. *Journal of Personality & Social Psychology*, 52 (3), 511–24

Hazan, C. & Shaver, P. R. (1990) Love and work: An attachment-theoretical perspective. *Journal of Personality & Social Psychology*, 59 (2), 270–80

Heather, N. (1976) *Radical Perspectives in Psychology*. London: Methuen

Heider, F. (1958) *The Psychology of Interpersonal Relations*. New York: Wiley

Herskovits, M. J. (1948) *Man and His Works: The science of cultural anthropology*. New York: Alfred A. Knopf

Hewstone, M. & Antaki, C. (1988) Attribution theory and social explanation. In M. Hewstone, W. Stroebe, J. P. Codol & G. M. Stephenson (Eds) *Introduction to Social Psychology*. Oxford: Blackwell

Hewstone, M., Stroebe, W., Codol, J. P. & Stephenson (Eds) (1988) *Introduction to Social Psychology*. Oxford: Blackwell

Hilliard, R. B. (1993) Single-case methodology in psychotherapy process and outcome research. *Journal of Consulting & Clinical Psychology*, 61(3), 373–80

Hofstede, G. (1980) *Culture's Consequences: International differences in work-related values*. Beverly Hills, Calif: Sage

Holmes, D. S. (1994) *Abnormal Psychology*, 2nd edn. New York: HarperCollins

Holmes, J. (1992) Response [to Masson's 'The tyranny of psychotherapy']. In W. Dryden & C. Feltham (Eds) *Psychotherapy and Its Discontents*. Buckingham: Open University Press

Holt, R. R. (1967) Individuality and generalization in the psychology of personality. In R. S. Lazarus & E. M. Opton (Eds) *Personality*. Harmondsworth: Penguin

Honderich, T. (1987) Mind, brain, and self-conscious mind. In C. Blakemore & S. Greenfield (Eds) *Mindwaves*. Oxford: Blackwell

Horgan, J. (1993) Eugenics revisited. *Scientific American*, June, 92–100

Humphrey, N. (1986) *The Inner Eye*. London: Faber and Faber

Humphrey, N. (1992) *A History of the Mind*. London: Vintage

Humphrey, N. (1993) Introduction. In N. Humphey, 1986 London: Vintage

Jackson, G. (1992) *Women and Psychology – What Might that Mean?* Paper given at Conference, Association for the Teaching of Psychology July

Jahoda, G. (1978) Cross-cultural perspectives. In H. Tajfel & C. Fraser (Eds) *Introducing Social Psychology*. Harmondsworth: Penguin

James, W. (1884) What is an emotion? *Mind*, 188–205

James, W. (1890) *Principles of Psychology*. New York: Holt

Janis, I. L., Kaye, D. & Kirschner, P. (1965) Facilitating effects of 'eating-while-reading' on responsiveness to persuasive communications. *Journal of Personality & Social Psychology*, 1, 181–6

Jensen, A. R. (1969) How much can we boost IQ and scholastic achievement? *Harvard Educational Review*, 39, 1–123

Johnson-Laird, P. N. (1983) *Mental Models*, Cambridge: Cambridge University Press

Johnson-Laird, P. N. (1987) How could consciousness arise from the computations of the brain? In C. Blakemore & S. Greenfield (Eds) *Mindwaves*. Oxford: Blackwell

Johnson-Laird, P. N. (1988) *The Computer and the Mind*. London: Fontana.

Jones, E. E. & Davis, K. E. (1965) From acts to dispositions: The attribution process in person perception. In L. Berkowitz (Ed.) *Advances in Experimental Social Psychology*, Vol. 2. New York: Academic Press

Jones, E. E. & Nisbett, R. E. (1971) *The Actor and the Observer: Divergent perceptions of the causes of behaviour*. Morristown, N.J.: General Learning Press

Jones, S. (1993) *The Language of the Genes*. London: Flamingo

Kashima, Y. & Triandis, H. C. (1986) The self-serving bias in attributions as a coping strategy: A cross-cultural study. *Journal of Cross-Cultural Psychology*, 17, 83–97

Kelley, H. H. (1967) Attribution theory in social psychology. In D. Levine (Ed.) *Nebraska Symposium on Motivation*, Vol. 15. Lincoln: Nebraska University Press

Kelley, H. H. (1972) Causal schemata and the attribution process. In E. E. Jones, D. E. Kanouse, H. H. Kelley, R. E. Nisbett, S. Valins & B. Weiner (Eds) *Attribution: Perceiving the causes of behaviour*. Morristown, N. J.: General Learning Press

Kelley, H. H. (1973) The processes of causal attribution. *American Psychologist*, 28, 107–28

Kelly, G. (1955) *A Theory of Personality: The psychology of personal constructs*. New York: Norton

Kelly, L. (1988) *Surviving Sexual Violence*. Cambridge: Polity Press

Kirby, R. & Radford, J. (1976) *Individual Differences*. London: Methuen

Kitzinger, C. (1990) Heterosexism in psychology. *The Psychologist*, 3 (9), 391–2

Kline, P. (1993) Comments on 'Personality traits are alive and well'. *The Psychologist*, 6 (7), 304

Kluckhohn, C. & Murray, H. A. (1953) Personality formation: The determinants. In C. Kluckhohn, H. A. Murray & D. M. Schneider (Eds) *Personality in Nature, Society, and Culture*, 2nd edn. New York: Knopf

Koestler, A. (1967) *The Ghost in the Machine*. London: Pan

Kohlberg, L. (1969) Stage and sequence: the cognitive-developmental approach to socialization. In D. A. Goslin (Ed.) *Handbook of Socialization Theory and Research*. Chicago: Rand McNally

Kraepelin, E. (1913) *Psychiatry*, 8th edn. Leipzig: Thieme

Krahé, B. (1992) *Personality and Social Psychology: Towards a synthesis*. London: Sage

Krupat, E. & Garonzik, R. (1994) Subjects' expectations and the search for alternatives to deception in social psychology. *British Journal of Social Psychology*, 33, 211–22

Laing, R. D. (1961) *The Self and Others*. London: Tavistock Publications

Laing, R. D: (1967) *The Politics of Experience and the Bird of Paradise*. Harmondsworth: Penguin

Lalljee, M. & Widdicombe, S. (1989) Discourse analysis. In A. M. Colman & J. G. Beaumont (Eds) *Psychology Survey*, 7. Leicester: British Psychological Society/London: Routledge

Lalljee, M., Watson, M. & White, P. (1982) Explanations, attributions and the social context of unexpected behaviour. *European Journal of Social Psychology*, 12 (1), 17–29

Lamiell, J. T. (1981) Toward an idiothetic psychology of personality. *American Psychologist*, 36, 276–89

Lamiell, J. T. (1982) The case for an idiothetic psychology of personality: A conceptual and empirical foundation. In B. A. Maher & W. B. Maher (Eds) *Progress in Experimental Personality Research*, Vol. 11. New York: Academic Press

Lamiell, J. T. (1987) *The Psychology of Personality: An epistemological inquiry*. New York: Columbia University Press

Latané, B. & Darley, J. M. (1968) Group inhibitions of bystander intervention in emergencies. *Journal of Personality & Social Psychology*, 10, 215–21

Leekam, S. (1993) Children's understanding of mind. In M. Bennett (Ed.) *The Child as Psychologist: An introduction to the development of social cognition*. Hemel Hempstead, Herts.: Harvester Wheatsheaf

Lepper, M. R. & Greene, D. (1978) Overjustification research and beyond: Towards a means–end analysis of intrinsic and extrinsic motivation. In M. R. Lepper & D. Greene (Eds) *The Hidden Costs of Reward*. Hillsdale, N.J.: Lawrence Erlbaum

Lepper, M. R., Greene, D. & Nisbett, R. E. (1973) Undermining children's intrinsic interest with extrinsic reward: A test of the overjustification hypothesis. *Journal of Personality & Social Psychology*, 28, 129–37

Lerner, G. (1979) *The Majority Finds Its Past: Placing women in history*. New York: Oxford University Press

LeVay, S. & Hamer, D. H. (1994) Evidence for a biological influence in male homosexuality. *Scientific American*, May, 20–5

Leyens, J. P. & Codol, J. P. (1988) Social cognition. In M. Hewstone, W. Stroebe, J. P. Codol & G. M. Stephenson (Eds) *Introduction to Social Psychology*. Oxford: Blackwell.

Liotti, G. (1991) Insecure attachment and agoraphobia. In C. M. Parkes,

J. Stevenson-Hinde & P. Marris (Eds) *Attachment across the Life Cycle*. London: Routledge

Littlewood, R. & Lipsedge, M. (1989) *Aliens and Alienists: Ethnic minorities and psychiatry*, 2nd edn. London: Routledge

Lumsden, W. & Wilson, E. O. (1981) *Genes, Mind and Culture*. Cambridge, Mass.: Harvard University Press

Maher, B. A. (1966) *Principles of Psychopathology: An experimental approach*. New York: McGraw-Hill

Main, M., Kaplan, N. & Cassidy, J. (1985) Security in infancy, childhood, and adulthood: A move to the level of representation. In I. Bretherton & E. Waters (Eds) *Growing Points of Attachment Theory and Research* (Monographs of the Society for Research in Child Development, Vol. 50, Serial No. 209). Chicago: University of Chicago Press

Malinowski, B. (1929) *The Sexual Life of Savages*. New York: Harcourt, Brace & World

Markus, H. R. & Kitayama, S. (1991) Culture and the self: Implications for cognition, emotion, and motivation. *Psychological Review*, 98, 224–53

Maslow, A. H. (1954) *Motivation and Personality*. New York: Harper & Row

Maslow, A. H. (1968) *Toward a Psychology of Being*, 2nd edn. New York: Van Nostrand Reinhold

Masson, J. (1988) *Against Therapy: Emotional tyranny and the myth of psychological healing*. New York: Atheneum

Masson, J. (1992) The tyranny of psychotherapy. In W. Dryden & C. Feltham (Eds) *Psychotherapy and Its Discontents*. Buckingham: Open University Press

May, R. (1967) *Psychology and the Human Dilemma*. New York: Van Nostand

McClelland, D. C., Atkinson, J., Clark, R. & Lowell, E. (1953) *The Achievement Motive*. New York: Appleton-Century-Croft

McCrae, R. R. & Costa, P. T. (1989) More reasons to adopt the five-factor model. *American Psychologist*, 44, 451–2

McDougall, W. (1908) *An Introduction to Social Psychology*. London: Methuen

McGurk, H. (1975) *Growing and Changing*. London: Methuen

Merleau-Ponty, M. (1962) *The Phenomenology of Perception*. London: RKP

Merleau-Ponty, M. (1968) *The Visible and the Invisible*. Evanston, Ill.: Northwestern University Press

Milgram, S. (1963) Behavioural study of obedience. *Journal of Abnormal and Social Psychology*, 67, 371–8

Milgram, S. (1974) *Obedience to Authority*. New York: Harper Torchbooks

Milgram, S. (1977) Subject reaction: the neglected factor in the ethics of experimentation. *The Hastings Centre Report*, Oct., 19–23. Reprinted in S. Milgram (1992), *The Individual in a Social World*, 2nd edn. New York: McGraw-Hill

Miller, D. T. & Ross, M. (1975) Self-serving biases in the attribution of causality: fact or fiction? *Psychological Bulletin*, 82, 213–25

Miller, G. A. (1969) Psychology as a means of promoting human welfare. *American Psychologist*, 24, 1063–75

Miller, E. & Morley, S. (1986) *Investigating Abnormal Behaviour*. London: Weidenfeld & Nicolson/Lawrence Erlbaum

Mischel, W. (1968) *Personality and Assessment*. New York: Wiley

Mischel, W. (1977) The interaction of person and situation. In D. Magnusson & N. S. Endler (Eds) *Personality at the Crossroads: Current issues in interactional psychology*. Hillsdale, N. J.: Lawrence Erlbaum

Mischel, W. (1983) Alternatives in the pursuit of the predictability and consistency of persons: Stable data that yield unstable interpretations. *Journal of Personality*, 51, 578–604

Moghaddam, F. M., Taylor, D. M. & Wright, S. C. (1993) *Social Psychology In Cross-Cultural Perspective*. New York: W. H. Freeman & Co.

Morea, P. (1990) *Personality: An introduction to the theories of psychology*. Harmondsworth: Penguin

Murray, H. A. (1938) *Explorations in Personality*. New York: Oxford University Press

Myers, D. (1994) *Exploring Social Psychology*. New York: McGraw-Hill

Nisbett, R. E. & Ross, L. (1980) *Human Inference: Strategies and shortcomings of social judgement*. Englewood Cliffs, N.J.: Prentice-Hall

Nisbett, R. E. & Schachter, S. (1966) Cognitive manipulation of pain. *Journal of Experimental Social Psychology*, 2, 227–36

Nisbett, R. E. & Wilson, T. D. (1977) Telling more than we can know: Verbal reports on mental processes. *Psychological Review*, 84, 231–59

Nisbett, R. E., Caputo, C., Legant, P. & Maracek J. (1973) Behaviour as seen by the actor and as seen by the observer. *Journal of Personality & Social Psychology*, 27(2), 154–64

Norman, D. & Shallice, T. (1986) Attention to action: Willed and automatic control of behaviour. In R. J. Davidson, G. E. Schwartz & D. Shapiro (Eds) *Consciousness and Self-regulation: Advances in research and theory*. New York: Plenum

Oakes, P. J., Haslam, S. A. & Turner, J. C. (1994) *Stereotyping and Social Reality*. Oxford: Blackwell

Olds, J. & Milner, P. (1954) Positive reinforcement produced by electrical stimulation of septal area and other regions of the rat brain. *Journal of Comparative & Physiological Psychology*, 47, 419–27

Orne, M. T. (1962) On the social psychology of the psychological experiment – with particular reference to demand characteristics and their implications. *American Psychologist*, 17 (11), 776–83

Ornstein, R. E. (1975) *The Psychology of Consciousness*. Harmondsworth: Penguin

Paludi, M. A. (1992) *The Psychology of Women*. Dubuque, Iowa: Wm. C. Brown Communications

Parkes, C. M. (1993) Bereavement as a psychosocial transition: Processes of adaptation to change. In M. S. Stroebe, W. Stroebe & R. O. Hansson (Eds) *Handbook of Bereavement: Theory, research and intervention*. New York: Cambridge University Press

Parkinson, B. (1987) Emotion – cognitive approaches. In H. Beloff & A. M. Colman (Eds) *Psychology Survey*, No. 6. Leicester: British Psychological Society

Parlee, M. B. (1991) Happy Birth-day to *Feminism & Psychology*. *Feminism & Psychology*, 1 (1), 39–48

Penfield, W, (1958) *The Excitable Cortex in Conscious Man*. Liverpool: Liverpool University Press

Pervin, L. A. (1985) Personality: Current controversies, issues, and directions. *Annual Review of Psychology*, 36, 83–114

Pettigrew, T. F. (1979) The Ultimate Attribution Error: Extending Allport's cognitive analysis of prejudice. *Personality & Social Psychology Bulletin*, 5 (4), 461–76

Piliavin, I. M., Rodin, J. & Piliavin, J. A. (1969) Good Samaritanism: An underground phenomenon? *Journal of Personality & Social Psychology*, 13 (4), 289–99

Place, U. T. (1956) Is consciousness a brain process? *British Journal of Psychology*, 47, 44–51

Plomin, R. (1994) *Genetics and Experience: The interplay between nature and nurture*. Thousand Oaks, Calif.: Sage

Popper, K. (1959) *The Logic of Scientific Discovery*. London: Hutchinson

Popper, K. (1972) *Objective Knowledge: An evolutionary approach*. Oxford: Oxford University Press

Prince, J. & Hartnett, O. (1993) From 'psychology constructs the female' to 'females construct psychology'. *Feminism & Psychology*, 3 (2), 219–24

Raphael, B. (1984) *The Anatomy of Bereavement*. London: Hutchinson

Reason, P. & Rowan, J. (Eds) (1981) *Human Inquiry: A sourcebook of new paradigm research*. Chichester: Wiley

Riesen, A. H. (1947) The development of visual perception in man and chimpanzee. *Science*, 106, 107–8

Rogers, C. R. (1951) *Client-centred therapy: Its current practice, implications and theory*. Boston: Houghton-Mifflin

Rogers, C. R. & Dymond, R. F. (Eds) (1954) *Psychotherapy and Personality Change: co-ordinated research studies in the client-centred approach*. Chicago: University of Chicago Press

Rogers, C. R. (1961) *On Becoming a Person: A therapist's view of psychotherapy*. Boston: Houghton-Mifflin

Rogoff, B. & Morelli, G. (1989) Perspectives on children's development from cultural psychology. *American Psychologist*, 44, 343–48

Rose, S. (1992) *The Making of Memory: From molecules to mind*. London: Bantam Books

Rose, S., Lewontin, R. C. & Kamin, L. J. (1984) *Not in Our Genes: Biology, ideology and human nature*. Harmondsworth: Penguin

Rosenhan, D. L. & Seligman, M. E. P. (1989) *Abnormal Psychology*, 2nd edn. New York: Norton

Rosenthal, R. (1966) *Experimenter Effects in Behavioural Research*. New York: Appleton-Century-Crofts

Rosenthal, R. & Jacobson, L. (1968) *Pygmalion in the Classroom: Teacher expectation and pupil's intellectual development*. New York: Holt, Rinehart and Winston

Ross, L. (1977) The intuitive psychologist and his shortcomings. In L. Berkowitz (Ed.) *Advances in Experimental Social Psychology*, Vol. 10. New York: Academic Press

Ross, L. & Nisbett, R. E. (1991) *The Person and the Situation: Perspectives of social psychology*. New York: McGraw-Hill

Rubin, Z. & McNeil, E. B. (1983) *The Psychology of Being Human*, 3rd edn. London: Harper & Row

Rumelhart, D. E., Hinton, G. E. & McClelland, J. L. (1986) A general framework for parallel distributed processing. In D. Rumelhart, J. L. McClelland & the PDP Research Group (Eds) *Parallel Distributed Processing: Vol. 1. Foundations*. Cambridge, Mass.: MIT Press

Russell, J. (1992) The use of non-human animals in psychological research: The legal context. *Psychology Teaching*, 39–45, New Series, No. 1

Rutter, M. (1981) *Maternal Deprivation Reassessed*, 2nd edn. Harmondsworth: Penguin

Rutter, M. & Rutter, M. (1992) *Developing Minds: Challenge and continuity across the life span*. Harmondsworth: Penguin

Rycroft, C. (1966) Introduction: Causes and Meaning. In C. Rycroft (Ed.) *Psychoanalysis Observed*. London: Constable.

Ryder, R. (1990) Open reply to Jeffrey Gray. *The Psychologist*, 3, 403

Ryle, G. (1949) *The Concept of Mind*. London: Hutchinson

Sacco, W. P., Dumont, C. P. & Dow, M. G. (1993) Attributional, perceptual, and affective response to depressed and nondepressed marital partners. *Journal of Consulting & Clinical Psychology*, 61 (6), 1076–82

Sarbin, T. R. (1986) The narrative as a root metaphor for psychology. In T. R. Sarbin (Ed.) *Narrative Psychology: The storied nature of human conduct*. New York: Praeger

Scarr, S. (1992) Developmental Theories for the 1990s: Development and individual differences. *Child Development*, 63, 1–19

Schachter, S. (1964) The interaction of cognitive and psychological determinants of emotional state. *Advances in Experimental Social Psychology*, 1, 49–80

Schachter, S. & Singer J. E. (1962) Cognitive, social and physiological determinants of emotional state. *Psychological Review*, 69 (5), 379–99

Schank, R. C. & Abelson, R. P. (1977) *Scripts, Plans, Goals and Understanding*. Hillsdale, N.J.: Lawrence Erlbaum

Scheff, T. J. (1966) *Being Mentally Ill: A sociological theory*. Chicago: Aldine Press

Searle, J. R. (1980) Minds, brains, and programs. *Behavioural and Brain Sciences*, 3, 417–24

Searle, J. R. (1992) *The Rediscovery of the Mind*. Cambridge, Mass.: MIT Press

Segall, M. H., Dasen, P. R., Berry, J. W. & Poortinga, Y. H. (1990) *Human Behaviour in Global Perspective: An introduction to cross-cultural psychology*. New York: Pergamon

Seligman, M. E. P. (1974) Depression and learned helplessness. In R. J. Friedman & M. M. Katz (Eds) *The Psychology of Depression: Contemporary theory and research*. Washington, D.C.: Winston-Wiley

Seligman, M. E. P., Abramson, L. Y., Semmel, A. & Von Beyer, C. (1979) Depressive attributional style. *Journal of Abnormal Psychology*, 88, 242–7

Serpell, R. (1982) Measures of perception, skills, and intelligence: The growth of a new perspective on children in a Third World country. In W. Hartrup (Ed.) *Review of Child Development Research*, Vol. 6. Chicago: University of Chicago Press

Shaver, K. G. (1985) *The Attribution of Blame: Causality, responsibility, and blameworthiness*. New York: Springer-Verlag

Shaver, K. G. (1987) *Principles of Social Psychology*, 3rd edn. Hillsdale, N. J.: Lawrence Erlbaum

Sherif, M., Harvey, O. J., White, B. J., Hood, W. R. & Sherif, C. W. (1961) *Intergroup Conflict and Co-operation: The Robber's Cave experiment*. Norman, Oklahoma: University of Oklahoma Press.

Shiffrin, R. M. & Schneider, W. (1977) Controlled and automatic human information processing: II-perceptual learning, automatic attending and a general theory. *Psychological Review*, 84, 127–90

Shotter, J. (1975) *Images of Man in Psychological Research*. London Methuen

Shotter, J. (1992) 'Getting in Touch': The Meta-Methodology of a Postmodern

Science of Mental Life. In S. Kvale (Ed.) *Psychology and Postmodernism*. London: Sage

Shweder, R. A. (1990) Cultural psychology – what is it? In J. W. Stigler, R. A. Shweder & G. Herdt (Eds) *Cultural Psychology*. New York: Cambridge University Press

Singer, P. (1993) The rights of ape. *BBC Wildlife Magazine*, 11 (6), 28–32

Singer, P. & Cavalieri, P. (Eds) (1993) *The Great Ape Project: Equality beyond humanity*. London: Fourth Estate

Skinner, B. F. (1971) *Beyond Freedom and Dignity*. New York: Knopf

Smart, J. J. C. (1959) Sensations and brain processes. *The Philosophical Review*, 68, 141–56

Smith, P. K. & Cowie, H. (1991) *Understanding Children's Development*, 2nd edn. Oxford: Blackwell

Smith, P. B. & Bond, M. H. (1993) *Social Psychology across Cultures: Analysis and perspectives*. Hemel Hempstead, Herts.: Harvester Wheatsheaf

Smith, C. U. M. (1994) You are a group of neurons. *The Times Higher Educational Supplement*, 27 May, 20–1

Snyder, M. (1987) *Public Appearances/Private Realities. The Psychology of Self-Monitoring*. New York: W. H. Freeman

Snyder, M. & Ickes, W. (1985) Personality and social behaviour. In G. Lindzey & E. Aronson (Eds) *Handbook of Social Psychology*, Vol. 2, 3rd edn. New York: Random House

Soyland, A. J. (1994) *Psychology as Metaphor*. London: Sage

Spearman, C. (1904) General intelligence, objectively determined and measured. *American Journal of Psychology*, 15, 201–93

Spearman, C. (1927) The doctrine of two factors. Reprinted in S. Wiseman (Ed.) (1967) *Intelligence and Ability*. Harmondsworth: Penguin

Spearman, C. (1927) *The Abilities of Man*. London: Macmillan

Stephenson, W. (1953) *The Study of Behaviour: Q-technique and its methodology*. Chicago: Chicago University Press

Stern, W. (1921) *Die differentielle Psychologie in ihren methodologischen Grundlagen*, 3rd edn. Leipzig: Barth

Storms, M. D. (1973) Videotape and the attribution process: reversing actors' and observers' points of view. *Journal of Personality & Social Psychology*, 27 (2), 165–75

Strachey, J. (1962–1977) Sigmund Freud: A sketch of his life and ideas. (This appears in each volume of the Pelican Freud Library; originally written for the *Standard Edition of the Complete Psychological Works of Sigmund Freud*, 1953–74, London: Hogarth Press)

Sulloway, F. J. (1979) *Freud, Biologist of the Mind: Beyond the psychoanalytic legend*. New York: Basic Books

Tavris, C. (1993) The Mismeasure of Woman. *Feminism & Psychology*, 3 (2), 149–68

Taylor, R. (1963) *Metaphysics*. Englewood Cliffs, N. J.: Prentice-Hall

Teichman, J. (1988) *Philosophy and the Mind*. Oxford: Blackwell

Thibaut, J. W. & Kelley, H. H. (1959) *The Social Psychology of Groups*. New York: Wiley.

Thomas, K. (1990) Psychodynamics: The Freudian approach. In I. Roth (Ed.) *Introduction to Psychology*, Vol. 1. Hove, E. Sussex/Milton Keynes: Open University/Lawrence Erlbaum

Thomas, G. V. & Blackman, D. (1991) Are animal experiments on the way out? *The Psychologist*, 4 (5), 208–12

Thomas, R. M. (1985) *Comparing Theories of Child Development*, 2nd edn. Belmont, Calif.: Wadsworth Publishing Co.

Thorne, B. (1992) *Carl Rogers*, London: Sage

Thurstone, L. L. (1938) Primary mental abilities. *Psychometric Monographs*, 1

Torrance, S. (1986) Breaking out of the Chinese room. In M. Yazdani (Ed.) *Artificial Intelligence: Principles and applications*. London: Chapman & Hall

Triandis, H. C. (1972) *The Analysis of Subjective Culture*. New York: Wiley

Triandis, H. C. (1980) Introduction. In H. C. Triandis & W. E. Lambert (Eds) *Handbook of Cross-cultural Psychology*: Vol. 1. Perspectives. Boston: Allyn & Bacon

Triandis, H. C., Kashima, Y., Shimada, E. & Villareal, M. (1986) Acculturation indices as a means of confirming cultural differences. *International Journal of Psychology*, 21, 43–70

Triandis, H. C. (1990) Theoretical concepts that are applicable to the analysis of ethnocentrism. In R. W. Brislin (Ed.) *Applied Cross-Cultural Psychology*. Newbury Park, Calif.: Sage

Turner, J. C. (1991) *Social Influence*. Milton Keynes: Open University Press

Tyerman, A. & Spencer, C. (1983) A critical test of the Sherifs' Robber's Cave experiment: Intergroup competition and cooperation between groups of well-acquainted individuals. *Small Group Behaviour*, 14 (4), 515–31

Unger, R. K. (1979) *Female and Male: Psychological perspectives*. New York: Harper & Row

Unger, R. K. (1984) Sex in psychological paradigms – From behaviour to cognition. *Imagination, Cognition & Personality*, 3, 227–34

Unger, R. K. (1993) The personal is paradoxical: Feminists construct psychology, *Feminism & Psychology*, 3 (2), 211–18

Valentine, E. R. (1992) *Conceptual Issues in Psychology*, 2nd edn. London: Routledge

Valins, S. (1966) Cognitive effects of false heart-rate feedback. *Journal of Personality and Social Psychology*, 4 400–408

Valins, S. & Nisbett, R. E. (1972) *Attribution processes in the development and treatment of emotional disorders*. In E. E. Jones, D. E. Kanouse, H. H. Kelley, R. E. Nisbett, S. Valins & B. Weiner (Eds) Attribution: Perceiving the causes of behaviour. Morristown, N.J.: General Learning Press

Vernon, P. E. (1950) *The Structure of Human Abilities*. London: Methuen

Wachtel, P. (1977) *Psychoanalysis and Behaviour Therapy: Toward an integration*. New York: Basic Books.

Watson, J. B. (1913) Psychology as the behaviourist views it. *Psychological Review*, 20, 158–77

Watson, J. B. (1928) *Behaviourism*. Chicago: University of Chicago Press

Weiner, B. (1972) *Theories of Motivation: From mechanism to cognition*. Chicago: Rand McNally

Weiner, B. (1979) A theory of motivation for some classroom experiences. *Journal of Educational Psychology*, 71, 3–25

Weiner, B. (1985) An attribution theory of achievement motivation and emotion. *Psychological Review*, 92, 548–73

Weiner, B. (1992) *Human Motivation: Metaphors, theories and research*. Newbury Park, Calif.: Sage

Weiskrantz, L. (1986) *Blindsight: A case study and implications*. Oxford: Clarendon Press

Weiskrantz, L., Warrington, M. D., Sanders, M. D. & Marshall, J. (1974) Visual capacity in the hemianopic field following a restricted occipital ablation. *Brain*, 97, 709–28

Weiss, R. S. (1991) The attachment bond in childhood and adulthood. In C. M. Parkes, J. Stevenson-Hinde & P. Marris (Eds) *Attachment across the Life Cycle*. London: Routledge.

Weisstein, N. (1993a) Psychology constructs the female; or, The fantasy life of the male psychologist (with some attention to the fantasies of his friends, the male biologist and the male anthropologist. [This is a revised/expanded version of Kinder, Küche, Kirche as scientific law: psychology constructs the female, 1971] *Feminism & Psychology*, 3 (2), 195–210

Weisstein, N. (1993b) Power, resistance and science: A call for a revitalized feminist psychology. *Feminism & Psychology*, 3 (2), 239–45

Werner, E. E. (1989) Children of the Garden Island. *Scientific American*, April, 106–111

Wilkinson, S. (1989) The impact of feminist research: Issues of legitimacy *Philosophical Psychology*, 2 (3), 261–9

Wilson, E. O. (1978) *On Human Nature*. Cambridge, Mass.: Harvard University Press

Wober, M. (1974) Towards an understanding of the Kiganda concept of intelligence. In J. W. Berry & P. R. Dasen (Eds) *Culture and Cognition*. London: Methuen

World Health Organization (1973) *Report of the International Pilot Study of Schizophrenia*, Vol. 1. Geneva: WHO

World Health Organization (1979) S*chizophrenia: An international follow-up study*. London: Wiley

Yan, W. & Gaier, E. L. (1994) Causal attributions for college success and failure: an Asian-American comparison. *Journal of Cross-Cultural Psychology*, 25 (1), 146–58

Zebrowitz, L. A. (1990) *Social Perception*. Milton Keynes: Open University Press

Zimbardo, P. (1973) On the ethics of intervention in human psychological research with special reference to the 'Stanford Prison Experiment'. *Cognition*, 2 (2, part 1), 243–55

Zimbardo, P. G. (1992) *Psychology and Life*, 13th edn. New York: HarperCollins

Index

Picture credits

The author and publishers would like to thank the following for permission to reproduce material in this book:

Non-Smokers Rights Association (Canada) and ASH for Fig. 2.2; Fig. 2.5 Copyright © 1978 by the American Psychological Association. Adapted by permission; Fig. 2.6 Copyright © 1990 by the APA. Adapted by permission; Lawrence Erlbaum Associates for Fig. 2.5 and Table 9.1; McGraw-Hill for Fig. 2.7; The Portman Group for Fig. 2.11; Methuen for Fig. 3.1; Allyn and Bacon for Fig. 3.6; Figs. 5.2 and 5.4 from J P J Pinel, *Biopsychology* 2/E. Copyright © 1993 by Allyn and Bacon. Reprinted by permission; Penguin for Fig. 4.3; Wadsworth Publishing Co. for Fig. 5.3; National Association for the Education of Young Children (USA) for Fig. 5.7; Fig. 5.10 from 'Evidence for a biological influence in male homosexuality' by Simon LeVay and D Hamer. Copyright © 1994 by Scientific American, Inc. All rights reserved; Fig. 8.2 from G Hofstede *Culture Consequences*, Copyright © 1980 Sage Publications, Inc., reproduced by permission; Fig. 8.4 from *Understanding Culture's Influence on Behaviour* by R Brislin, Copyright © 1993 by Harcourt Brace & Co., reproduced by permission; Tables 9.2 & 9.3 Copyright © 1987 by the APA. Reprinted by permission; Table 9.4 from K Bartholomew 'From Childhood to Adult Relationships: Attachment Theory and Research' in S Duck *Learning about Relationships*, Copyright © 1993 Sage Publications, Inc., reproduced by permission; and Blackwell Publishers for Fig. 13.5.

Figs. 1.1, 6.1, 10.2 and 11.5 Archives for the History of American Psychology, University of Akron; Figs. 1.4, 2.4, 7.5 and 13.4 Ronald Grant Archives; Fig. 1.5 Michael Joseph Publishers; Fig. 2.1 Copyright © Don McCullin; Figs. 2.8, 8.1, 8.3, 9.2 Robert Harding; Figs. 2.10, 9.1 Hulton-Deutsch; Fig. 3.3 Topham Picturepoint; Fig. 3.4 Oxford Scientific Films; Figs. 4.1, 6.3 Kobal Collection; Fig. 4.2 Professor P G Zimbardo; Fig. 4.2 Copyright © Richard Baker 1994; Figs. 4.3, 7.6 and 11.1 (Berkeley) Mary Evans Picture Library; Figs. 5.1, 11.3 (Berkeley), 12.1 and 13.3 Science Photo Library; Fig. 5.5 Reprinted with permission from Streisgutth et al., *Science*, 209 (July 18, 1980) Figure 2, p. 355. Copyright © 1908 American Association for the Advancement of Science; Fig. 5.6 Camera Press; Fig. 5.9 Weimar Archive; Fig. 5.10 Marc Lieberman, courtesy The Salk Institute; Fig. 6.1 Wellesley College (Mary Calkins); Fig. 6.4 Courtesy of Cowan Kemsley Taylor, Art Director: Max Clemens & Copywriter: Alan Moseley; Fig. 7.3, 11.4 (Wundt, James, Freud), Figs. 12.3, 12.4 Range Pictures; Fig. 7.4 Harcourt Brace Jovanovich; Fig. 8.5 Magnum Photos; Fig. 8.6 Free Press Inc.; Figs. 9.3, 12.2 Bridgeman Art Library; Fig. 9.4 photo copyright © Nasjonalgalleriet, Oslo. Copyright © The Munch Museum/The Munch-Ellingsen Group/DACS 1995; Fig. 10.4 Walter Reed Institute of Research; Fig. 10.5 Image Select; Fig. 10.6 Paul Fusco/Magnum Photos; Fig. 11.3 (Bacon, Darwin) Ann Ronan Picture Library; Fig. 11.3 (Galileo, Descartes, Newton Kepler, Locke, Hume, Copernicus) Mansell Collection; Fig. 11.6 Bridgeman Art Library. Copyright © ADAGP/SPADEM, Paris and DACS, London 1995; Fig. 13.1 Museum Boymans-van Beuningen, Rotterdam. Copyright © ADAGP/SPADEM, Paris and DACS, London 1995 Fig. 13.2 Bridgeman Art Library. Copyright © DACS 1995; Fig. 13.7 Bisson/Sygma.